THE BEST OF

Food&Wine

1994 COLLECTION

THE BEST OF
Food&Wine
1994 COLLECTION

American Express
Publishing Corporation
New York

Cover: Asparagus, Shrimp and Penne with
Saffron Sauce (p. 153)

THE BEST OF FOOD & WINE/1994 COLLECTION
Editor/Designer: Kate Slate
Assistant Editor: Martha Crow

AMERICAN EXPRESS PUBLISHING CORPORATION
Editor in Chief/Food & Wine: Mary Simons
Art Director/Food & Wine: Elizabeth Woodson
© 1994 American Express Publishing Corporation

Published by American Express Publishing Corporation
1120 Avenue of the Americas, New York, New York 10036

Manufactured in the United States of America

ISBN 0-916103-22-6

TABLE OF CONTENTS

FOREWORD	7
VINTAGE RATINGS	8
A MODERN WINE PRIMER	10
APPETIZERS & FIRST COURSES	20
SOUPS	42
FISH & SHELLFISH	54
POULTRY	66
MEAT	86
VEGETABLES	100
SALADS	118
PASTA & GRAINS	146
BREADS & BREADSTUFFS	162
CAKES & COOKIES	170
PIES, TARTS & TURNOVERS	192
DESSERTS	204
LOW-CALORIE COOKING	222
SAUCES, PRESERVES & CONDIMENTS	242
INDEX	248
CONTRIBUTORS	259

FOREWORD

By Mary Simons, Editor in Chief

We're pleased to present *The Best of Food & Wine*, our annual collection of treasured recipes. The 1994 edition, which is the eleventh in a series, features a generous and eclectic mix of recipes gathered from some of the finest cooks and chefs in the world.

Inside you'll find a lively blend of homey recipes: 25 of them highlight pastas and grains and 25 offer imaginative ways to prepare everyone's favorite, chicken. There's also a wealth of healthful salads, many of them main courses. Included, too, are signature dishes from well-known chefs and from some of the best restaurants in the United States. For the bakers among you, we have a special treat: nearly 100 ideas for cookies, cakes, pies, tarts and other divine desserts.

You're assured of success with any of these recipes. Each has been tested in *Food & Wine*'s kitchen using home equipment. They are as simple as possible to follow—and foolproof. Be sure to look for the helpful menu plans (highlighted in shaded boxes) and the wine suggestions for adding appropriate flavor to your meals.

A separate wine guide, written by two of our regular contributors, Elin McCoy and John Frederick Walker, is a primer for everything you need to know about varietals, as well as how to buy, taste and store wine.

So for all of us who love to cook and entertain, welcome to *The Best of Food & Wine*. May it make your table a wonderful, happy place to dine with family and friends.

FOOD & WINE'S VINTAGE RATINGS
1982-1992

COMPILED BY ELIN McCOY & JOHN FREDERICK WALKER

	1982	1983	1984	1985	1986
Red Bordeaux	9½ Rich, massive. Start drinking now.	7½ Firm, powerful. Drink now.	5½ Small-scale, firm. Drink up.	8½ Soft, delicious, elegant. Start drinking.	9 Powerful, tannic wines. Try in 2 years.
Sauternes	6½ Variable. Best are big. Start drinking.	9 Rich, classic wines. Start drinking.	5½ Mixed quality. Few good. Drink now.	7½ Soft, full, good. Start drinking.	9 Luscious & rich. Sample now.
Red Burgundy	7 Big, soft wines. Drink now.	8 Variable. Some very good. Start drinking.	6 Variable, thin wines. Drink up.	9 Glorious, rich, round. Drink now.	7 Lean, light wines. Start drinking.
White Burgundy	8 Big, rich wines. Drink up.	7½ Good, rich wines. Drink up.	7 Crisp wines. Some fine. Drink up.	8 Big but soft. Drink up.	8½ Crisp, balanced, classic. Drink now.
Napa/Sonoma Cabernet Sauvignon	7½ Balanced, attractive. Drink up.	7 Good, but not great. Drink up.	8 Big, rich, powerful. Start drinking.	9½ Brilliant, firm & elegant. Start sampling.	8 Deep, rich & powerful. Start sampling.
Napa/Sonoma Chardonnay	7 Variable, light, fading. Drink up.	7 Good but fading year. Drink up.	7½ Good full wines. Fading. Drink up.	8 Good, but fading. Drink up.	9 Excellent. Crisp, leaner style. Drink up.
Barolo & Barbaresco	8½ Big, powerful wines. Start drinking.	7 Lighter vintage. Drink up.	5½ Light, variable. Drink up.	9 Splendid, rich. Start sampling.	7½ Well-balanced & fruity. Start drinking.
Chianti	7½ Attractive, early maturing. Drink up.	7 Attractive, lighter. Drink up.	5 Spotty. Avoid.	9½ Big, rich flavor. Start drinking.	7½ Good quality, firm. Start drinking.
Germany	7 Soft, fruity. Drink up.	9 Excellent year. Marvelous late-harvest wines. Drink now.	6½ Lean & tart. Drink up.	8½ Excellent. Drink up.	6 Light, crisp wines. Drink up.
Vintage Porto	7 Soft, well-balanced. Start drinking.	8 Firm, solid wines. Start sampling.	No vintage declared.	9 Marvelous, deep & fruity. Wait 6 years.	No vintage declared.

The following ratings and comments reflect a variety of opinions, including our own, on the quality and character of various categories of wines from recent vintages. The ratings—0 for the worst, 10 for the best—are averages, and better or worse wine than indicated can be found in each vintage. Assessments of the most current vintages are more predictive and hence less exact than those of older vintages.

Scores are based on a wine's quality at maturity. A lower-rated but mature wine will often be superior to a higher-rated but immature wine. When-to-drink advice is based on how such wines seemed to be developing in mid-1993, and presumes good storage. The earliest date suggested for consumption applies to the lesser wines of the vintage, which will mature faster than the finest examples of the year.

1987	1988	1989	1990	1991	1992
7 Flavorsome, but lightweight. Drink now.	8 Good, medium-weight, balanced. Start sampling.	9 Variable. Some big fleshy wines. Wait.	8½ Promising, big, flavorsome. Wait.	7½ Uneven quality.	7½ Light wines. Average quality.
5½ Light, lean; few good wines.	9 Superlative, rich, concentrated. Start sampling.	8½ Rich & powerful. Start sampling.	8½ Rich, ripe wines.	7 Weak, variable.	5 Patchy quality. Few good wines.
7½ Stylish wines. Start drinking.	9 Concentrated, fruity, classic. Start drinking.	8½ Big fruity wines. Start sampling.	9½ Wonderful; very rich and round.	7½ Average quality. Start drinking.	8 Average to good quality.
7 Light, round, soft. Drink up.	7½ Good; some very fine. Drink up.	8 Big, full, fruity. Start drinking.	8½ Great balance, rich wines. Start sampling.	6½ Light & fruity. Start drinking.	7 Average quality. Some attractive wines.
8½ Dark, firm, balanced. Start sampling.	7½ Mixed vintage; some concentrated. Sample.	7½ Variable quality; start sampling.	8 Good, ripe vintage. Wait.	8½ Promising, concentrated.	8 Average to good quality.
7½ Good & crisp. Drink up.	8½ Good, fruity. Drink now.	7 Uneven quality. Some good. Drink now.	8½ Fruity, balanced. Start drinking.	8½ Delicious, fruity. Start sampling.	7 Average quality. Start sampling.
8 Round, fruity. Start drinking.	8½ Rich, full wines. Wait.	9 Big, powerful, promising wines. Wait.	8½ Ripe & full. Wait.	7½ Average quality.	7 Average quality.
7 Average quality. Drink now.	8½ Ripe, fruity, balanced. Sample now.	7 Fruity, pleasant wines.	8½ Deep & rich but early maturing.	7 Average wines. Start drinking.	6½ Fair to average quality.
7 Mostly lean, some fine. Drink now.	9 Outstanding, full-flavored, fruity. Start drinking.	9 Full, rich & fruity. Start drinking.	9 Excellent; ripe vintage. Start drinking.	7 Good quality. Start drinking.	8 Promising quality.
No vintage declared.	No vintage declared.	No vintage declared.	No vintage declared.	8 Excellent vintage. Wait 10 years.	———

A MODERN WINE PRIMER

By Elin McCoy & John Frederick Walker

Now that wine appears so frequently on American tables, you'd think most wine drinkers would have a better grasp of the essentials of the subject. But (except for those for whom wine is a hobby) many have surprising gaps in their knowledge of the grape. That's rarely a problem—after all, you don't have to be an expert to drink wine—but it's too bad when ignorance interferes with enjoyment. Most wine drinkers can uncork a bottle without a struggle, but far too many don't know how to match a wine with a dish or make a quick selection from a wine list; they may know instinctively how long to chill whites but routinely let leftover wine go to waste—and so on.

Covering these fundamentals is the purpose of this guide. It condenses all the practical knowledge and general savvy a wine lover needs in order to have a commonsense but confident approach to wine. In what follows you'll be able to find answers to just about any question on choosing, storing, serving, or enjoying wine. You'll find out if it matters if you don't let your Bordeaux breathe before serving, how to open

a bottle of Champagne without a wasteful gush, the essentials of storing wines whether you have an underground cellar or a spare kitchen cupboard—and much more.

The emphasis here is on those vital bits of basic knowledge that any modern wine lover should know. This up-to-date advice takes into account the remarkable changes that have transformed today's wine world. For example, new wine-making technology used worldwide now allows fine red wines to reach peak drinkability far sooner than many bottlings did ten years ago, contradicting long-standing guidance on when certain wines are at their best. Then too, as anyone who's shopped in well-stocked wine stores knows, in today's competitive world wine market, the best-value wines may be coming from wine regions unheard of only a decade ago.

Finally, contemporary entertaining with wine is more likely to be casual and sophisticated than elaborately formal—an alfresco lunch rather than a lengthy banquet—influencing the choice of wines to have on hand.

THE TASTE OF WINE

VARIETAL WINES AND THEIR FLAVORS

If you're familiar with the flavors of wines made from certain key grape varieties, you can choose wines similar to those you've enjoyed, pick bottles that will complement various dishes and menus and know what to expect from a wine you haven't yet tried. Catego-

rizing wines this way is by far the easiest—and most useful—way to think about wines and your tasting experiences.

Every wine is made from one or more grape varieties. Wine lovers are far more familiar with wine grape varieties than they were a generation ago, because many labels list the principal grape variety used to make the wine. That's called varietal labeling. In parts of the world where a number of different grape types are grown—such as California, Alsace, and Australia—most wines are labeled this way and wine drinkers rightly regard a

grape name on a bottle as a rough guide to the taste within.

But many wines (especially European ones) don't mention the variety used. Because the grape varieties grown in these districts are often determined by tradition (and sometimes regulation), wines are often labeled only by geographical origin. Consumers soon come to associate varietal characteristics with such bottlings as well, even if no grape type is mentioned on the label.

For example, because red wines made in the Burgundy region of France

are made exclusively with Pinot Noir grapes, such wines share similar taste characteristics with Pinot Noirs made elsewhere.

Although there are hundreds of grape types grown in the vineyards of the world's wine regions, some—the ones below—are more highly regarded than others as sources of outstanding wine. These widely planted grapes are noted for producing wines that have aromas and flavors characteristic of the particular grape used.

Here are the principal classic grape varieties you'll come across and where they're grown, along with their typical taste characteristics.

White Wine Grapes

Chardonnay: The most important dry white wine grape worldwide. Used unblended for the white Burgundies of France; one of the principal grapes of Champagne; bottled under its own name in the U.S., Australia and many other wine countries. Color varies from pale straw to light gold. Aroma is fruity, sometimes suggesting apples or even pineapple; notes of vanilla (derived from aging in oak) are typical, as are buttery flavors. Among the richest and most full-bodied of dry white wines.

Chenin Blanc: Grown extensively in the Loire region of France (where it's used to make Vouvray), California and elsewhere. Typically made into an attractive, light, dry or semidry white with peachy overtones. Usually tart, fruity and simple, occasionally distinguished.

Fumé Blanc: Variant name for Sauvignon Blanc.

Gewürztraminer: An Alsace grape that makes a distinctive, even obvious, wine with strong floral aromas suggesting grapefruit, lychee, cloves, honey and spice. U.S. examples often light and off-dry; Alsace specimens intense and bone-dry with a pleasant bitter note.

Johannisberg Riesling: Variant U.S. name for Riesling.

Moscato/Muscat: Various Muscat grapes make floral, perfumed, grapey semisweet wines around the world.

Pinot Blanc: A minor grape that produces a wine similar to but less flavorful than Chardonnay; high acidity gives it a pleasant bite. Grown in Alsace, California, Italy (as Pinot Bianco) and elsewhere.

Pinot Gris: Yields aromatic, assertive wines with considerable character, especially in Alsace; also grown in Oregon; known as Pinot Grigio in Italy.

Riesling: Classic grape of Germany and Alsace; also grown worldwide (although often with less success). Makes light but striking floral-scented wines unsurpassed for elegance and delicacy. At its best, a pinpoint balance of fruit and acidity makes even semidry examples refreshing. Sweeter late-harvest versions (from extra-ripe grapes) suggest apricots, honey and spice.

Sauvignon Blanc: Often blended with Sémillon in Bordeaux and used on its own in Sancerre (in the Loire valley), California and elsewhere to make medium-bodied, tartly crisp, even citrusy wines with noticeable herbaceous, bell pepper-like nuances. Riper, oak-aged examples hint of melons.

TASTING TERMS

A lot of wine talk may sound like jargon, but the key tasting terms provide a handy way to tag your impressions and help you notice the differences among wines. However, just because a wine has a distinctive scent and flavor doesn't mean it's easy to describe. That's why wines are commonly discussed in terms that associate what's noticeable in the glass with more familiar odors and tastes. But don't be puzzled if you don't find "peaches" in your Chenin Blanc or "bell peppers" in your Cabernet Sauvignon; each taster will have different associations, and it's helpful to come up with your own specific descriptions of flavors when tasting wine. Here are some common terms:

acidity: the presence of fruit acids in wine gives it a refreshing tartness or crispness; a wine that lacks acidity tastes flat.

balanced: a wine with all its taste dimensions in harmony.

body: the sensation of weight in the mouth; some wines seem light and delicate, others seem heavy. Wines higher in alcohol (Port, for example) taste bigger and more powerful than low-alcohol wines (such as German Rieslings).

dry: a wine that lacks noticeable sweetness. Virtually all reds and many whites are dry.

finish: the impression a wine leaves in the mouth after you swallow it; a wine with a short finish fades fast; a wine with a long finish has a lingering flavor.

flavor: many grape varieties have their own characteristic flavors (see "Varietal Wines and Their Flavors," p. 10).

fruit: wine is made from grapes, and depending on the variety, will always have a degree of fruitiness. Young wines (such as Beaujolais Nouveau) are especially fruity.

nose: a fancy word for the smell of a wine, which has both aromas contributed by the specific grapes used to make it and bouquet—other odors contributed by aging (example: the oakiness some Chardonnays show from being aged in barrels, and the pungency some reds can have from long aging in the bottle).

oaky: a vanilla-like nuance in many wines that are aged in oak barrels before bottling.

sweetness: the opposite of dry; the presence of residual fruit sugars in a wine can give it noticeable sweetness, which can vary from just off-dry to semisweet to honeyed.

tannin: the astringent, mouth-puckering quality found in many red wines; like acidity, it gives wine a cleansing bite. Reds high in tannin have a dry, somewhat rasping texture to the palate.

Sémillon: Similar to Sauvignon Blanc, with which it is often blended; attractively round, even waxy in texture, which can give some examples Chardonnay-like weight.

Seyval Blanc: A hybrid variety grown in the Eastern U.S., yielding a clean, assertive crisp white.

Sylvaner: Minor grape of Germany and Alsace producing pleasant, but softer and less distinguished wines than Riesling.

White Riesling: Variant name for Riesling.

Red Wine Grapes

Barbera: An Italian grape made into a notably tart, bright-flavored medium-bodied red in Piedmont that yields similar wines in California and elsewhere. Can be drunk young.

Cabernet Franc: One of several grapes producing similar-flavored wines that are blended to make red Bordeaux; especially St-Emilion. Also grown in the Loire and sometimes bottled on its own in California, it is very fragrant, with a hint of violets, and is lighter and less assertive than Cabernet Sauvignon.

Cabernet Sauvignon: The classic grape of the Médoc in Bordeaux, providing the backbone of the wines of the famous châteaux. Grown successfully worldwide, producing some of the best reds from California, Australia, Chile and other wine regions. Berry-like aromas and flavors (particularly black currant), as well as herbaceous, olive-like or even minty elements, add considerable complexity and depth. Has a tannic character, enhanced by aging in oak barrels, giving most examples astringency and bite when young, hence best aged at least five years before consumption. Balanced specimens can age for ten or more years.

Dolcetto: Italy's answer to Beaujolais—a plummy, delicious, grapey red best enjoyed young.

Gamay: The grape of France's Beaujolais region; used to make grapey, light tart reds particularly enjoyable young; a handful of similar wines are produced in California.

Merlot: Another Bordeaux grape similar in flavor to Cabernet Sauvignon, but less assertive; a major grape in the Bordeaux district of Pomerol. Also grown in Italy to make light reds. Made into a soft, attractively rich Cabernet-like wine in California, which can be enjoyed when young.

Nebbiolo: The grape of Barbaresco and Barolo in Italy's Piedmont; made into big, dry, tannic wines with distinctive aromas—a scent of violets, a hint of tar or licorice. Best when aged for at least five years.

Petite Sirah: A California flavor cousin to Syrah, producing full-bodied, flavorsome reds. Can be drunk when young and fruity or aged for several years.

Pinot Noir: The grape of red Burgundy (and a principal component of Champagne); grown in various regions elsewhere (California, Oregon, Australia) to produce a light to medium-bodied, tart, fragrant wine that can suggest cherries, raspberries or strawberries; some show faintly earthy, mushroom-like nuances. The best have few peers for elegance. Rarely tannic, Pinot Noir can be drunk young; balanced specimens will age well.

Sangiovese: Principal grape of Chianti and other Tuscan reds, made into a medium-bodied, bright-flavored, fragrant, smooth-textured wine. Attractive when young, and ages well for five or more years.

Shiraz: The Australian term for Syrah, the most widely planted red grape down-under; yields solid to superb wines.

Syrah: Grape of the northern Rhône in France, responsible for Hermitage, Côte Rôtie, Cornas, among others; full-flavored, intense wine with deep, fruity scent laced with hints of black pepper and cardamom. Can be drunk when young for its fruit and vigor, but ages well too.

Tempranillo: A major grape of the Rioja and other Spanish wine regions. In Rioja it is blended with other grapes to give the medium-bodied reds of the district their deep color and pointed flavors.

Zinfandel: Of obscure, possibly Italian origin, now California's own grape—and one of its better wines. Top examples are enjoyable in their youth for their exuberant berry-like, peppery-spicy character. Can also gain Cabernet-like nuances with age. (White Zinfandel is a very fruity, often semisweet pink "blush wine" made from the clear juice of these dark-skinned grapes.)

WINE & FOOD

QUICK WINE AND FOOD MATCHUPS

You don't need special expertise to pick a wine that will complement the dish you're serving. Because virtually all wine is intended to be consumed with meals, you can take a mental shortcut: Picture wine as a liquid side dish or condiment to accompany the meal. Once you start thinking of putting wine and food together in terms of attractive combinations of flavors, textures and relative intensity, you've got a strategy for making great matches. You don't have to be a gastronomic genius to think a full-flavored meaty red wine is likely to be just the sort of sauce, so to speak, to have with your pepper steak. In that instance, the wine matches—echoes—the taste of the food. But sometimes a contrast is just as pleasing: If you would naturally add a squeeze of lemon to accent a particular fish dish, it's a good bet that a crisp, tart light white will set off the flavors of that dish. What follows are some broad guidelines.

Aperitif Wines

Many dry or off-dry crisp white wines—simple Chardonnay, Mâcon (white Burgundy), Pinot Grigio or Sauvignon Blanc—stimulate the appetite and pair particularly well with light but flavorful appetizers. Off-dry and semisweet whites, such as Chenin Blanc and Riesling, as well as sparkling wines, accompany salty and smoked foods particularly well—their slight sweetness and/or bubbles counterbalance savory canapés.

Fish

Dry white wines—such as Sauvignon Blanc—often work well because they don't mask the more delicate flavors of fish or seafood—not because of any hard-and-fast rules. In fact, rich fish dishes, such as grilled salmon or halibut in a red wine sauce, can be paired with low-tannin (see "Tasting Terms," p. 11) red wines, such as light Pinot Noir.

Poultry, Pork and Veal

These mild, light meats pair well with a variety of both whites and reds—the choice largely depends on the method of preparation, sauces and spices. A round, fruity California or Australian Chardonnay is good with simpler preparations, and an assertive Alsace Pinot Gris or Gewürztraminer stands up to more flavorful dishes. But Beaujolais, Gamay and other light reds are excellent alternatives with grilled chicken, and medium-bodied reds, such as Pinot Noir, red Burgundy, Chianti and Rioja, are ideal with roast pork or veal stew.

Pasta

Pasta itself contributes relatively little to the flavor of the dish, so matching wines to pasta is primarily a matter of the other ingredients and the sauce. Pasta primavera, with its emphasis on vegetables, is happily underscored by the herbaceous quality of Sauvignon Blanc. A meat-based pasta dish with a zesty tomato sauce, however, would be better matched by a tart, bright-flavored red, such as Barbera or Zinfandel.

Red Meat and Game

The fattiness of beef and lamb calls for wines with enough astringency from the tannins to cut through the flavor and richness, and provide a pleasing contrast. Since whites have little tannin, reds are the obvious choice. Simple cuts of meat—prime ribs, for example—offer a backdrop of subtle flavor that shows off complex, older red wines (aged Bordeaux or Cabernet Sauvignon), while grilled and highly seasoned meats are best with fruity, vigorous young wines (Syrah, Petite Sirah, Barbaresco, Merlot, Cabernet

ORDERING WINE FROM A RESTAURANT WINE LIST

Ordering wine in a restaurant requires the same sort of strategy that choosing wine for a dinner party in your home does—but there are differences. In your home the guests will all have the same menu, but chances are they'll each pick something different in a restaurant. And your wine choices are limited to what's on the list. Here's what to do:

1) Glance through the wine list to get a quick overview of how it's organized, and what's on it. Most lists are organized geographically—country by country, region by region. Like most, you'll probably want to spend less on the wine than the food, so note the price range as you flip through.

2) Narrow the choices the same way you would at home—is everyone having seafood? red meat? If there's quite a range of dishes—one guest is having dover sole, another pork, a third grilled lamb—consider ordering a white to be followed by a red. That way, everyone can start with a glass of white, and those having heartier dishes can then switch to the red.

3) Be adventurous. At some restaurants, suggested wine matches appear on the menu or on a short daily menu, or can be gotten from a knowledgeable member of the staff. Use these opportunities to try unusual and attractive wine combinations.

4) Many restaurants offer a number of wines by the glass, which is a great way to try a couple of different types for a reasonable price—in fact each guest can order something different. But if everyone is going to order the same wine anyway, remember that it is always cheaper by the bottle.

5) The list is confusing and the waiter no help? Safe bets that are usually good values include California Sauvignon Blanc if you're having fish or seafood or a dinner salad, Beaujolais with chicken, pork and veal, and Côtes du Rhône or Merlot with steak or lamb.

Sauvignon, Zinfandel) that won't be overshadowed in flavor by the dish. Pâtés and cold cuts, however, rarely require a more substantial red than a Gamay, and can even be matched with a tart, off-dry white, such as a German Riesling.

Cheese
Contrary to popular belief, cheese and wine are not always the happiest of companions. Only mild, delicate cheeses (such as triple crèmes) pair well with subtle, aged reds. Pungent, strong-flavored cheeses (such as Port Salut and Gorgonzola) are best served with robust, tannic reds (Côtes du Rhône, Syrah or Shiraz, Barolo).

On the other hand, there are some classic combinations: Tangy, fresh goat cheeses go wonderfully with crisp Sauvignon Blancs, and Stilton and Port show each other off beautifully, as the saltiness of the cheese is balanced by the fruity sweetness of the wine. Beaujolais or Gamay is the best single wine to serve with a variety of cheeses, and crisp aromatic whites (such as Gewürztraminer) often work well, too.

Dessert
A delicious sweet wine matched to an equally delicious dessert is a memorable way to end a meal, but it requires planning to make the combination work. Sugary desserts, es-

pecially those prepared with pastry cream, or those with sharp citrus, easily overwhelm a dessert wine such as a Sauternes or late-harvest Riesling, and make it seem stripped of flavor. Choose simple, mild desserts and, to be safe, serve the dessert wine first so that it can be tasted on its own.

Hint: The dessert wine that works best with not-too-sugary chocolate desserts is ruby Port.

Picnic/Casual
For very informal entertaining, choose light, fruity, off-dry whites, rosés, blush wines and simple reds—the kind of wines that don't seem out of place served in a plastic cup. Chenin Blanc, White Zinfandel and Gamay are in fact just the sort of wines that work best with foods like ham, deviled eggs, summer salads, fried chicken, hot dogs and hamburgers—and many spicy Asian dishes, too.

Buffet Wines
When you need wines to match a wide variety of foods all served at once, choose those that are refreshing and straightforward in flavor. Offer both a red and a white to provide alternatives for guests who'll also be making their own food choices. For white wines: Simple Chardonnay (such as Mâcon from Burgundy), Pinot Blanc from Alsace, Bordeaux Blanc and Tuscan whites are all good choices.

For reds: Beaujolais, Chianti, Dolcetto, Chilean Cabernet Sauvignon and's Zinfandel are good.

BUYING WINE

DECODING LABELS: KEY TERMS
Every wine label tells you something about where the wine came from, the producer and sometimes the grape variety or varieties used to make it. But because each wine-producing country (and sometimes each region within a country) has its own labeling regulations, label language can seem confusingly complex. But some of the information that appears on bottles is much more important than the rest. Here's a brief country-by-country overview.

Australian Labels
Varietal labeling helps consumers who know little about Australia's wine regions to find familiar tastes (such as Cabernet Sauvignon) from unfamiliar areas (such as Coonawarra). Unusual blends, such as Cabernet Sauvignon/Shiraz, and Sémillon/Chardonnay are common as well and worth trying.

California and U.S. Labels
Grape names on the label are still the best indicator of what's in the bottle. But regional reputations in the U. S. are beginning to be associated with particular varietals that flourish there—some examples include Cabernet Sauvignon from Napa Valley, Zinfandel from Dry Creek Valley in Sonoma (both in California), Merlot from Washington State and New York's Long Island and Pinot Noir from Oregon. In addition, some very fine Bordeaux-style red blends and white blends are now being produced that don't carry grape names.

French Labels
Regions, not grape names, are the key to French bottlings. The phrase *Appellation Contrôlée*, which appears on the label of all of France's best wines, stems from a comprehensive set of regulations that guarantee the origin and authenticity of the wine so labeled, assuring consumers not only that a wine labeled Bordeaux comes from the region of Bordeaux, but that it will be made in a prescribed manner from particular grape varieties. Because wines in each region can only be made from permitted grape varieties, you don't usually see a grape name on a French label (the major exceptions are wines from the Alsace region, which are labeled varietally). This means you have to become familiar

HOW TO FIND WINE BARGAINS

If you're shopping for nothing more specific than "a nice dry white wine," it's easy to feel bewildered by the seemingly endless choices in a well-stocked wine store. Here's how to avoid the problem.

Focus on the Food and Occasion: If you're shopping for a wine to have with dinner or serve at a party, chances are you've already decided on the menu. That decision narrows the choices dramatically—if you're serving shrimp, there's no point in looking over big, powerful red wines. Before shopping, decide on the kind of wine flavors that would be attractive with your choice of food—would a rich, round Chardonnay be better with the salmon than a sharp, light white? Consider other factors: is the dinner a special occasion? Would your guest particularly enjoy a French wine? In that case, you might find yourself heading directly for the white Burgundy selections.

How to Spot Bargains: Don't shop by price alone—no wine, no matter how cheap, is a bargain if you don't like drinking it. On the other hand, there's no sense in paying more for a famous name or fancy label when you can buy a wine of similar quality for less. By and large, wines from countries and regions that are still building their reputations (such as Washington State and Chile) offer real value. In the California section, look for fine wine producers that offer less expensive basic bottlings (often blends) in addition to their well-known (and pricey) wines.

Among Bordeaux, look for "second wines" from famous châteaux (wines from the same estate not bottled under the famous label) and "petit châteaux" (wines from small, less well-known estates).

And don't forget to look at German wines—many are quite dry, go very well with food (particularly Asian dishes), and are attractively priced.

with the taste and style of these wines area by area. But wine lovers soon learn to associate red Bordeaux with Cabernet Sauvignon and Merlot, and white Bordeaux with Sauvignon Blanc and Sémillon, as well as white Burgundy with Chardonnay and red Burgundy with Pinot Noir, and so on. Consumers need to remember that the *Appellation Contrôlée* system does not guarantee quality: just because a wine is genuine does not mean it will always be a wonderful example of its type.

German Labels
German wine labels can be long-winded, but only look daunting. The labels for the better wines follow a regular pattern: at the top is the region (such as Rheingau); next the township, with the suffix *er* (such as Bernkasteler); on some bottlings, vineyard names and the varietal name (usually Riesling) may appear as well. Some wines, shipped by large firms, keep it simple ("Riesling Dry" is one example).

Because German producers, even those with a small single vineyard, typically divide their production into various quality categories, you need to know these, too. The starting rung of fine German wines is Qualitätswein (abbreviated QbA)—usually a dry or off-dry wine, and good value. The next levels up consist of Qualitätswein mit Prädikat (QmP)—quality wines with a special predicate, as follows: Kabinett (usually off-dry), Spätlese (deeper, usually semi-dry), Auslese (fuller, sweeter), Beerenauslese (very sweet and concentrated), Trockenbeerenauslese (intensely rich and sweet). There are also trocken (dry) and halbtrocken (half-dry) versions of all these categories of ripeness.

Italian Labels
Italy's labeling laws are modeled on the French system, which means they are primarily regional (Tuscany, Piedmont, etc.), not varietal. The highest designation found on Italian labels is *Denominazione di Origine Controllata e Garantita*, which is confined to certain wine types (Barolo, Chianti, Brunello, and a few others) that are not only highly regulated but whose bottlings have been approved by an official tasting panel. These regulations, which can even dictate the length of time a particular wine must stay in barrel, are regarded as overly restrictive by some innovative Italian producers. As a result, some producers whose better wines do not meet the requirements are forced to label them with the simple *vino da tavola* (table wine) designation.

Spanish Labels
Spain's *Denominación de Origen* laws follow those of France and Italy and codify the boundaries of various important wine-producing regions (such as Sherry and Rioja) as well as the grape varieties that can be grown there, as well as the methods of wine production allowed.

WHAT TO KEEP IN THE WINE RACK

If you drink wine regularly, keep some on hand for everyday use as well as entertaining. Even if your wine cellar only consists of a 12-bottle rack in a pantry, you'll always have well-chosen wine available instead of having to make do with a last-minute selection at the wine store. The key is to keep it stocked with a selection of bottlings that suit your consumption patterns.

CHOOSING YOUR OWN HOUSE WINES

The most important wines to have on hand are everyday reds and whites—the kind of wine you open when you want a glass of something while you're preparing dinner or that you serve with a simple family meal. Don't choose something so expensive that you'd hesitate to use it in a recipe that called for half a cup of wine, but make sure it's enjoyable even if modestly priced. Light, crisp dry whites (such as California Sauvignon Blanc and Alsace Pinot Blanc) and medium-bodied reds (such as Rioja from Spain, Zinfandel from California or Chianti from

Italy) are good candidates (see "How to Find Wine Bargains," page 15).

WHERE TO KEEP WINE

Many people keep their wines in a kitchen rack. And that has advantages: The wines are right there when you need some for a recipe; it's easy to notice if you're running low; and, you know exactly what you have on hand. Unfortunately, the storage conditions are all wrong: It's much too hot (especially on top of the refrigerator, a popular spot for wine racks), and there's too much temperature variation, not to mention excessive vibration and strong light, for wines that will be stored more than a week.

For convenient, but suitable kitchen storage, put a wine rack in an unheated closet or pantry nearby, or in a cupboard away from heating pipes or appliances. Store your bottles near the floor where it's coolest. A temperature-controlled under-the-counter unit holding several dozen bottles is the ultimate high-tech solution, but barring that, avoid the kitchen area for long-term storage, particularly of your better bottles. Keep most of your wines in the coolest area of the house, and replenish your kitchen rack from there.

WINE RACKS

Any wine bottle you open with a corkscrew needs to be kept on its side so that the cork remains wet and swollen and maintains a tight seal. A sturdy, flat shelf will suffice, but because bottles on their sides roll around, it's far more convenient to have a rack with individual bottle slots.

Hint: Since wines are best kept out of sight in a quiet dark place anyway, function is more important than decorative value when it comes to choosing a wine rack.

SERVING WINE

OPENING THE BOTTLE

Stoppering wine bottles with a piece of tree bark is a rather primitive thing to do, but it's so much a part of wine tradition, particularly for fine wines, that it's not likely to go out of fashion any time soon—despite the fact that faulty corks account for a tiny but persistant percentage of spoiled wines. Until simpler bottle closures become widespread, a decent corkscrew will remain an essential tool to have on hand.

Corkscrews

Avoid corkscrews whose business end looks like a large screw or auger—these are liable to crumble and tear dry corks. Look for those with a coil (sometimes called a "worm") that looks like a stretched out spring—these are far easier to insert and will hold the cork together. The simplest types require sheer muscle power to use; much better are ones which utilize some form of leverage to help

---

STORAGE REQUIREMENTS

Unless you live in an extreme climate, you may not need a temperature-controlled vault to have a perfectly adequate wine cellar. All you need to be able to keep wines in good condition is a cool, quiet spot that maintains a stable temperature under 70° F (under 65 is better). The temperature can fluctuate lower seasonally (so long as it doesn't drop to freezing), but should not get higher—excessive heat will slowly cook your wines. Although dampness causes labels to deteriorate, it won't hurt the wine. But a bone dry atmosphere will eventually cause premature evaporation, right through the corks (that's why air conditioning your bottles without maintaining about 50% relative humidity is a poor idea). Of course, you can get away with less than ideal conditions if you do not plan to age fine wines for more than a year.

ease out the cork with minimum effort. The classic type is the folding waiter's corkscrew—essentially a specialized jackknife design. The various Screwpull brand designs are particularly easy to use, although bulkier. The twin-prong extractor is a clever gadget that has two flat flexible blades that slide down between the cork and glass, allowing the cork to be twisted out in one piece—a handy tool to have in the kitchen drawer when the cork is crumbly. If you have the space, heavy-duty bar-mounted models are particularly easy to use.

Uncorking Champagne or Sparkling Wine

You don't need a corkscrew, but you do need caution: The contents are under significant pressure, and a flying cork can cause a dent in your ceiling—or injury to a guest. First, uncover the twisted wire loop by tearing the foil covering the cork. Second, place one hand on the cork before untwisting the loop and aim the neck of the bottle away from people (including yourself) at about a 45 degree angle. Third, loosen the wire cage at the bottom with your free hand. Fourth, tighten your grip on the cork and with your free hand twist the bottle off the cork. Try to avoid a loud pop, which usually signals a wasteful gush. Hold the bottle at the same angle for a few seconds to let some of the gas escape.

Hint: To prevent glasses frothing over when serving, pour Champagnes and sparkling wines in two steps —start with a small splash, and then, when that subsides, slowly pour in more until the glass is about two-thirds full.

To Breathe or Not To Breathe

Many connoisseurs believe that opening up red wines sometime prior to serving improves their taste, but this notion actually has little basis in fact, and the vast majority of wine makers and wine professionals ignore it. Although it does soften the taste of a harsh young red or assertive young Port and may make it seem more palatable, aerating a wine ahead of time tends to dissipate its scent, and somewhat flatten its flavor.

Problem Corks

Loose corks are usually discovered after they're pushed too far down in the neck of the bottle to be retrieved by a corkscrew. The solution? Push the cork all the way into the bottle with a chopstick or slim knife. Then—keeping a tool inserted to keep the cork from clogging the neck—invert the bottle and pour the contents carefully into a pitcher. Stubborn or broken corks: If a cork resists removal, don't keep twisting the corkscrew—you'll just dig a large hole in the cork. Instead, remove the corkscrew and reinsert it at

a slight angle, so that you can get a different grip on it, and apply gentle pressure. In the worst case, you might have to remove the cork piece by piece.

Decanting

You decant a wine by pouring it into another container—a carafe or decanter—for serving. You may want to do this simply for convenience in pouring or for appearance, but it's only necessary when serving substantial reds (such as Bordeaux) over ten years old. In that case you pour slowly from an unshaken bottle that's been standing

up for a couple of hours or a day to separate the clear wine from any harmless sediment that may have accumulated in the bottom of the bottle. Place a flashlight (or candle) under the neck of the bottle to help see when to stop pouring.

Recorking and Preserving Leftover Wine

If you expose wine to air for more than a day, it fades in taste and slowly begins to turn to vinegar. To keep leftover wine for serving the next day, recork the bottle promptly after opening, and store it in a cool place (the refrigerator

---

A ONE-CASE WINE CELLAR

The following selection is intended to cover a wide range of dining and entertaining needs and to show how comprehensive a dozen-bottle collection can be. It makes a good starter cellar—but you'll want to make substitutions to suit your budget, cooking interests and favorite wines.

WHITES:
- 1 bottle brut Champagne or California sparkling wine
- 1 bottle California or Washington State Sauvignon Blanc
- 1 bottle Australian or California Chardonnay
- 1 bottle Alsace Pinot Blanc
- 1 bottle German Riesling (QbA or Kabinett)
- 1 bottle late-harvest Riesling or Sauternes

REDS:
- 1 bottle California Cabernet Sauvignon or red Bordeaux
- 1 bottle Chianti or Rioja
- 1 bottle Côtes du Rhône or Petite Sirah
- 1 bottle red Burgundy or Pinot Noir
- 1 bottle Beaujolais or Gamay
- 1 bottle ruby Port

if it's a white wine).

Hint: Make sure the cork is clean so its smell doesn't taint the wine—slice off the top if necessary.

If you want to keep a wine for several days, pouring it into a smaller bottle to minimize the airspace before recorking will help dramatically. Among the various wine preservation systems on the market, the simplest and fastest ones consist of a rubber stopper equipped with a one-way valve that replaces the cork, and a small plastic pump that will create a slight vacuum in a partially empty bottle with a few quick strokes. This method will retard spoilage for several days. Champagne and sparkling wines will stay surprisingly fresh and fizzy for several days in a refrigerator if you use a Champagne stopper, which plugs the bottle securely to keep the gas from escaping.

Although many wine lovers give little thought to serving wine beyond opening and pouring, paying attention to proper serving temperature and suitable glassware ensures that you get the maximum enjoyment from the wines you drink.

Serving Temperatures

Few things have a more dramatic effect on your impression of a wine than the temperature at which you serve it. Different wines do taste better at different temperatures, and it's not hard to see why. Although the smell of a wine is diminished by chilling, whites (and rosés) are enjoyed that way because they're much more refreshing. You serve reds at warmer temperatures because their tannins appear harsh and metallic when chilled. But remember: A red served too warm tastes dull and

soupy. The ideal temperature for a particular wine is the one at which it tastes balanced. Note: The suggested timing for chilling in an ice bucket is based on starting with a room-temperature (70-75° F) wine. Here are some examples:

Light whites, sparkling wines, rosés: about 45° F (or about half an hour in an ice bucket)

Big whites (such as Chardonnay), sweet whites: about 50° F (or about 20 minutes in an ice bucket)

Light reds (Beaujolais, Gamay): about 55° F (or about 10-12 minutes in an ice bucket)

Pinot Noir, red Burgundy: about 60° F (or about 5-8 minutes in an ice bucket)

Big reds (Cabernet Sauvignon, red Bordeaux, Syrah): about 65° (about 2-5 minutes in an ice bucket)

In other words, the heavier the wine, the less chilling it requires to taste its

best. A thermometer isn't necessary—putting your hand on the bottle will tell you if wine is thoroughly chilled, lightly chilled, or just cool. After all, the wine will slowly warm as it sits in the glass anyway.

How to Chill Wine Fast

The fastest way to chill wine is to put it into a deep bucket with half cold water and half ice. This method draws heat from the bottle much more quickly than ice alone does. You can chill a room-temperature white in about 20 minutes, which is equivalent to an hour or more in a refrigerator and is even faster than putting it in the freezer—and there's no danger of forgetting it and having the wine freeze (yes, you can thaw wine, but it doesn't taste as good).

Hint: If the ice bucket is too short to chill the top of the bottle, invert the wine in the bucket for a few minutes before opening.

Pouring Without Dribbles

Pour slowly but steadily. When you finish, tilt the bottle up slightly, and give it a slight twist before raising it away from the glass you just poured. It's always a good idea to have a napkin in the other hand, however, to give the the neck of the bottle a wipe.

Hint: If you drip red wine on a tablecloth, sprinkle white wine or club soda on the stain immediately and launder it as soon as possible.

GLASSWARE

Wineglasses come in a wide variety of shapes, sizes—and prices. Although there are traditional designs for just about every type of wine, most of your entertaining needs can be met with a single all-purpose design: a clear, tulip-shaped 8-ounce bowl on a stem.

Why clear? So you can see and appreciate the color of the wine.

Why tulip-shaped? So that the incurving lip of the bowl will help concentrate the scent of the wine.

Why 8-ounce capacity? Wineglasses are normally filled only halfway to allow you to

sniff and savor the wine without spilling it, so you need a good-size glass.

If your wine budget permits, there are two other glass designs worth having: One is the Champagne flute, a tall, slim glass that shows off sparkling wines much better than an ordinary wineglass. The other is a smaller, more chimney-shaped version of the tulip-shaped wineglass for serving sherry, Port and rich dessert wines, which are normally served in small portions.

Hint: Careful rinsing is a must with wineglasses, because alcohol tends to magnify the off-odors that traces of soap cause.

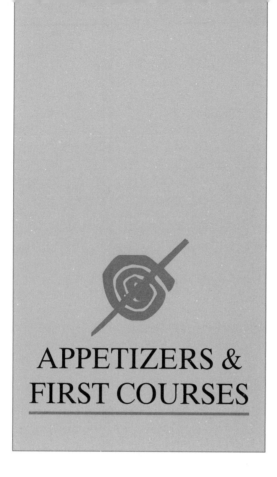

APPETIZERS &
FIRST COURSES

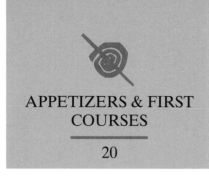

SPICY ORANGE PECANS

These zippy pecans are easy to make. Although you can soak and dry the nuts days in advance, they should be cooked on the day they are to be served. A good trick is to toss the nuts by shaking the pan or stirring with a wooden chopstick instead of a spoon to prevent the sugar from caramelizing on the spoon.

Makes About 4 Cups

1 pound pecan halves (about 4 cups)
Boiling water
1 large or 2 small navel oranges
¼ cup plus 1 teaspoon sugar
1½ teaspoons coarse (kosher) salt
¼ teaspoon freshly ground black or
  white pepper
2 teaspoons hot chili oil*
***Available at Asian markets**

1. In a large bowl, cover the nuts with boiling water. Let stand for 30 minutes. Drain well and roll the nuts in a kitchen towel to absorb excess moisture.

2. Preheat the oven to 300°. Spread the nuts in a single layer on 1 or 2 large baking sheets and bake for 30 minutes. Turn the baking sheet and stir the nuts. Reduce the oven temperature to 250° and bake until the nuts are almost completely dry, with just a touch of moistness at the center, about 20 minutes. Let cool.

3. Using an abrasive scrubber, wash the orange in warm water. Rinse and wipe dry. In a small bowl, combine the sugar, salt and pepper. Finely grate the orange zest into the sugar mixture, then stir to combine.

4. Heat a wok or a large heavy skillet over high heat until hot. Add the chili oil, swirl to coat the pan and reduce the heat to moderate. Add the nuts, tossing to coat with the oil, and cook until very hot, 1 to 2 minutes. Evenly sprinkle 1 teaspoon of the sugar mixture over the nuts and stir with a wooden chopstick to distribute the sugar. Stir-fry until the sugar melts on the nuts. Continue adding the remaining sugar mixture, 1 teaspoon at a time, stir-frying after each addition until the sugar melts and the pecans are glazed. Adjust the heat as necessary to prevent scorching. (The whole process will take 4 to 5 minutes.) Transfer the nuts to a baking sheet to cool. Serve warm or at room temperature.

—*Barbara Tropp*

ROASTED ALMONDS WITH RED CHILE

You can use any pure chile powder—made from ancho chiles or smoky chipotle chiles, for instance—for this recipe.

Makes 2 Cups

1 teaspoon olive oil
2 cups whole blanched almonds
2 teaspoons pure chile powder
1½ teaspoons coarse kosher or sea
  salt

1. Preheat the oven to 300°. Spread the oil over the bottom of a medium baking sheet with sides. Spread the nuts on the baking sheet, rubbing them in the oil to coat. Roast gently for about 30 minutes, turning occasionally, until evenly toasted.

2. Transfer the nuts to a 14-inch square of parchment paper. Season with the chile powder and salt and toss well. Set aside to cool. To transport, bring up the corners of the paper and twist to seal. Serve the nuts directly from the pouch. (*The nuts can be made up to 1 day ahead.*)

—*Deborah Madison*

OLIVES WITH CUMIN

Makes 2 Cups

1 teaspoon cumin seeds
2 cups imported oil- or brine-cured
  black olives, drained
6 fresh thyme sprigs
Three 2-by-½-inch strips of lemon
  zest
1 medium garlic clove, thinly sliced
1½ tablespoons fresh lemon juice
2 teaspoons sweet paprika
¼ teaspoon crushed red pepper
1 tablespoon extra-virgin olive oil
1 tablespoon chopped fresh flat-leaf
  parsley

1. In a small dry skillet, toast the cumin seeds over moderate heat, stirring, until fragrant, 1 to 2 minutes. Transfer the toasted seeds to a mortar and crush slightly with a pestle.

2. In a bowl, toss the olives with the cumin, thyme, lemon zest, garlic, lemon juice, paprika and crushed red pepper. Stir in the oil. Cover and refrigerate overnight, or for up to 3 days. Shortly before serving, stir in the parsley.

—*Deborah Madison*

TAPENADE

Serve this tasty Mediterranean spread on crisp toasts or lightly toasted French bread.

Makes About 2½ Cups

1 pound brine-cured Greek, French or Italian black olives, pitted
One 6½-ounce can of Italian tuna packed in olive oil, undrained
½ cup drained capers
1 small garlic clove, chopped
½ cup extra-virgin olive oil
2 tablespoons brandy

Combine all the ingredients in a food processor and process very briefly just until a coarse spread forms. *(Tapenade can be prepared up to 1 week ahead. Pack it in a container, pour a thin layer of olive oil on top and refrigerate. Bring to room temperature and stir in the excess oil before serving.)*
—Nancy Harmon Jenkins

EGGPLANT DIP WITH COUNTRY BREAD

This cold summer dip is served with warm, crisp garlicky bread.

4 to 6 Servings

2 to 3 medium eggplants (3 pounds), halved lengthwise
¼ cup olive oil
5 scallions, white part only, thinly sliced
1 medium red bell pepper, cut into ⅛-inch dice
½ small jalapeño pepper, seeded and minced, or 1 pinch of cayenne pepper
¼ pound mushrooms, thinly sliced
1 large tomato—peeled, seeded and cut into ⅛-inch dice

⅓ cup (packed) fresh basil leaves, finely chopped
2½ tablespoons finely minced chives, plus more for garnish
2 teaspoons minced garlic
1 small loaf of country bread, cut into small chunks
Salt and freshly ground black pepper

1. Preheat the oven to 350°. Brush the eggplant halves with 1 tablespoon of the olive oil and place them on a baking sheet, cut-sides down. Bake for 45 minutes, or until the skin is wrinkled and the flesh is tender when pierced. Remove from the oven and let cool.

2. Meanwhile, in a medium skillet, heat 1 tablespoon of the olive oil over moderate heat. Add the scallions, bell pepper and jalapeño and cook, stirring occasionally, until softened, about 5 minutes. Scrape the vegetables into a medium bowl and set aside. Add the mushrooms to the skillet and cook until softened and the moisture has evaporated, 5 to 7 minutes. Set aside to cool.

3. Scoop the eggplant flesh onto a work surface, discarding the skins. Add the mushrooms. Finely chop the eggplant and mushrooms and add to the cooked vegetables in the bowl. Stir in the tomato, basil, 2½ tablespoons chives, 1½ teaspoons of the garlic and the remaining 2 tablespoons oil. Cover and refrigerate. *(The dip can be prepared to this point up to 1 day ahead.)*

4. Preheat the oven to 400°. Toss the bread chunks with the remaining ½ teaspoon garlic and toast on a baking sheet for about 10 minutes, turning once, until golden brown.

5. Season the eggplant dip with salt and pepper. Mound it in a bowl and garnish with minced chives. Serve the toast chunks in a basket on the side.
—Daniel Boulud

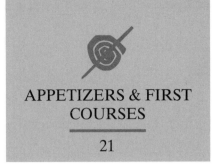

LEMON CHEESE WITH LOVAGE

Lovage has a bright, clean celery-like flavor. If you can't find lovage, use a mixture of chopped parsley and celery leaves instead.

Make this cheese at least one day ahead so that it has time to drain and to absorb the flavors of the herbs.

Makes About 2 Cups

One 15-ounce container of ricotta cheese
4 ounces soft goat cheese, such as Montrachet
½ cup finely chopped fresh lovage leaves plus additional leaves for garnish
3 tablespoons fresh lemon juice
3 tablespoons minced fresh chives or thinly sliced scallion greens
1 medium shallot, finely chopped
2 teaspoons minced garlic
1½ teaspoons finely grated lemon zest
Salt and freshly ground pepper
Seeded crackers, for serving

1. In a food processor, puree the ricotta and goat cheese until smooth, scraping the bowl as necessary. Transfer to a large bowl and stir in the chopped lovage, lemon juice, chives, shallot, garlic and lemon zest. Season with salt and pepper.

2. Line a colander or strainer with a double-layered 12-inch square of dampened cheesecloth. Scrape in the cheese, fold the ends of the cloth over the top

and weigh down with a heavy object, such as a can of tomatoes. Set the colander over a bowl. Refrigerate overnight or for up to 3 days.

3. When ready to serve, pull open the cloth and invert the cheese onto a plate or into a bowl; remove the cloth. Garnish with lovage leaves and serve with crackers.

—*Deborah Madison*

RICOTTA, PROSCIUTTO AND BASIL SPREAD

Leftovers can be used in lasagna, stirred into hot pasta or stuffed into shells.

Makes About 6 Cups

½ cup mild olive oil
½ cup coarsely chopped garlic (one 4-ounce head)
½ pound very thinly sliced prosciutto, cut into ¼-inch squares
2 pounds fresh ricotta cheese (see Note)
1 cup finely chopped fresh basil or flat-leaf parsley
1 tablespoon coarsely ground pepper
Crostini, for serving (at right)

1. In a heavy medium skillet, warm the oil over low heat. Increase the heat to moderate, add the garlic and cook, stirring frequently, until golden, about 6 minutes. Add the prosciutto and stir until it begins to change color, 2 to 3 minutes. Remove from the heat.

2. Put the ricotta in a large bowl. Using a slotted spoon, add the prosciutto and garlic to the bowl. Mix well. Cover and refrigerate for up to 2 days.

3. Before serving, let the spread return to room temperature. Stir in the basil and pepper. Spoon into bowls and serve with Crostini.

NOTE: If fresh ricotta is not available, use 2½ pounds of ricotta from the supermarket and drain it in a fine sieve for a few hours before using.

—*Francine Maroukian*

ARTICHOKE AND GOAT CHEESE SPREAD

Serve this tangy spread with Crostini (recipe follows) or a colorful assortment of sliced fresh vegetables.

Makes About 3¾ Cups

Three 6-ounce jars of marinated artichoke hearts, well drained
1 tablespoon olive oil
½ teaspoon finely grated lemon zest
1 pound mild, soft goat cheese, such as Montrachet
1 tablespoon finely chopped flat-leaf parsley
1½ teaspoons coarsely ground pepper
Fresh lemon juice (optional)

1. In a food processor, pulse the artichoke hearts until coarsely chopped. Transfer to a bowl and toss with the olive oil and lemon zest.

2. Place the goat cheese in the processor and puree until smooth. Gently fold the goat cheese into the artichokes along with the parsley and pepper. Add a squeeze of lemon juice if desired. Cover and refrigerate for up to 2 days. Let return to room temperature before serving.

—*Francine Maroukian*

CROSTINI

You can use any long bread loaves for crostini and you can brush them with a combination of melted butter and oil if you like. For garlicky crostini, rub the toasted slices with a halved garlic clove while they are still warm.

Makes About 120 Crostini

4 baguettes (½ pound each), sliced crosswise ¼ inch thick
1 cup extra-virgin olive oil

Preheat the oven to 350°. Arrange the baguette slices on large baking sheets and brush with the olive oil. Bake for about 15 minutes, until toasted. *(Once cooled, the crostini can be stored overnight in an airtight tin. Recrisp in a 350° oven before serving.)*

—*Francine Maroukian*

BRUSCHETTA ROSSA

Bruschetta, an Italian country dish, was traditionally used to show off the sweetness of a farmer's new olive oil. It was drizzled on garlic-rubbed, grilled peasant bread, which was then sprinkled with coarse salt. The addition of chopped tomatoes and basil was considered heresy by purists, who claimed that nothing should compete with the delicate flavor of the olive oil. But at the height of the tomato season, we are pleased to let the ripe red fruit compete with anything it wants to. The only real trick to creating great *bruschetta* is to be sure you use excellent ingredients.

6 Servings

6 large tomatoes (about 2½ pounds)— peeled, seeded and cut into ½-inch dice
Salt and freshly ground pepper

½ cup (tightly packed) fresh basil
    leaves
8 garlic cloves, halved
1 cup extra-virgin olive oil
Six 1-inch-thick slices of sourdough or
    coarse-grained Italian bread

1. Place the tomatoes in a large bowl and season with salt and pepper. Set aside 6 large basil leaves. Stack the remaining basil leaves. Roll them up and thinly slice them with a sharp knife. Sprinkle over the tomatoes. Add all but 2 pieces of the halved garlic cloves and the olive oil and stir to combine. Set aside to marinate at room temperature for 1 to 2 hours.

2. Grill or toast the slices of bread until well browned. While the toast is hot, rub each slice with the 2 reserved pieces of garlic; the garlic should almost melt into the toast.

3. Pick out the garlic cloves from the tomatoes and discard. Generously spoon the tomato mixture on the toast, making sure to include some olive oil with each spoonful. Garnish each *bruschetta* with one of the reserved basil leaves and serve immediately.

—Michael Romano

CHEESE SWIZZLES

Makes About 60 Swizzles

One 1¼-pound unsliced rectangular
    loaf of day-old sourdough bread
6 tablespoons unsalted butter, melted
½ cup freshly grated Parmesan cheese
    (about 2 ounces)
Paprika, for sprinkling

1. Preheat the oven to 450°. Trim the crust from the bread. Slice the loaf lengthwise ½ inch thick. Cut each slice crosswise into ½-inch strips.

2. On a large baking sheet, toss the

bread strips with the melted butter. Spread the strips in a single layer and bake for 15 to 20 minutes, or until golden brown.

3. Spread the cheese on a large, flat plate. Roll the hot bread strips in the cheese until lightly coated. Sprinkle lightly with the paprika. Serve the warm swizzles in a basket lined with a cloth napkin.

—Lila Jaeger

SMOKED CHICKEN MOUSSE CANAPES

The chicken in this recipe can be replaced with smoked turkey or smoked trout; smoked salmon also works, but the mousse will have a smoother, more delicate texture. Your favorite fresh herb can also be added to the mousse, which can be piped on black bread, cucumber slices or endive spears instead of the toast triangles.

🍷 A fresh, straightforward dry French white would provide an appetizing contrast to these rich, savory canapés. A clean, fruity white Burgundy, such as 1990 Louis Latour Mâcon-Lugny "Les Genièvres," or a flavorful Alsace Pinot Blanc, such as 1990 Hugel "Cuvée les Amours," would be an excellent choice.

Makes 24 Canapés

4 ounces skinless smoked chicken
    breast, coarsely chopped
4 ounces cream cheese, at room
    temperature
½ tablespoon Dijon mustard
1 tablespoon fresh lemon juice
¼ teaspoon freshly ground white pepper
6 slices of thinly sliced white bread,
    crusts removed
1 tablespoon unsalted butter, melted
4 small radishes, thinly sliced
Dill sprigs, for garnish

1. Put the chicken in a food processor and pulse 6 times. Add the cream cheese, mustard, lemon juice and white pepper and process until smooth. *(The mousse can be refrigerated for up to 2 days. Let return to room temperature before using.)*

2. Preheat the oven to 350°. Lightly brush each slice of bread with melted butter and brush any remaining butter on a large baking sheet. Cut each slice of bread into 4 triangles and place them buttered-side up on the baking sheet. Toast for about 15 minutes, until golden and crisp. Let cool.

3. Spoon the mousse into a pastry bag fitted with a large star tip or into a sturdy plastic bag with a corner snipped off. Pipe a heaping teaspoon of the mousse in the center of each toast triangle. Garnish with radish slices and dill and arrange on a platter.

—Carl & Grace Parisi

FONTINA AND TOMATO SQUARES

Makes 40 Hors d'Oeuvres

PASTRY:

2 sticks (½ pound) unsalted butter, at
    room temperature
8 ounces cream cheese, at room
    temperature
1 teaspoon salt
1 teaspoon thyme
2 cups unbleached all-purpose flour

TOPPING:

3 tablespoons Dijon mustard
5 medium tomatoes, thinly sliced

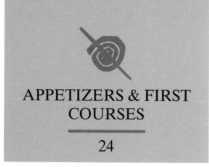

3 cups coarsely grated Italian Fontina cheese (6 ounces)
3 tablespoons finely shredded fresh basil leaves
2 tablespoons olive oil
Coarse (kosher) salt
Freshly ground pepper

1. *Make the pastry:* In a food processor, blend together the butter, cream cheese, salt and thyme. Add the flour and process until the dough comes together. Pat the dough into a rectangle, wrap in wax paper and refrigerate for 1 hour.

2. Preheat the oven to 375°. On a lightly floured work surface, roll out the dough ¼ inch thick. Cut it into an 18-by-14-inch rectangle and carefully fit it into a 16-by-12-inch sheet pan, pressing the dough up the sides. Bake the pastry for 20 to 25 minutes, until golden brown and cooked through. (If the pastry bubbles up at any point during baking, poke the bubbles down with the tip of a paring knife.) Remove from the oven and let cool slightly. Leave the oven on.

3. Brush the mustard over the cooled pastry. Arrange the sliced tomatoes in a single layer on the pastry. Sprinkle with the grated Fontina and shredded basil and drizzle the olive oil over all. Season with coarse salt and pepper and bake for about 20 minutes, until the cheese is bubbling. Cut the pastry into 40 squares. Serve warm or at room temperature.

—Mary Novak

PECORINO AND FRESH MINT CANAPES

La Palazzetta restaurant, outside of Todi, serves this unusual antipasto.

4 Servings

¼ cup freshly grated Pecorino cheese
1½ tablespoons extra-virgin olive oil
1 tablespoon heavy cream
8 fresh mint leaves, chopped, plus 12 small leaves for garnish
Salt and freshly ground pepper
Twelve 2-inch cubes of peasant bread

Put the cheese in a small bowl. Slowly pour in the oil, stirring with a fork. Stir in the cream. Mix in the chopped mint and season with salt and pepper. Spread the cheese on the bread, top each cube with a mint leaf and serve.

—La Palazzetta

WATERCRESS AND CREAM CHEESE SWIRLS

Makes About 36 Tea Sandwiches

8 ounces cream cheese
2 tablespoons minced fresh chives
¼ teaspoon salt
⅛ teaspoon freshly ground white pepper
One 1-pound unsliced rectangular loaf of white bread
One bunch of watercress, stems removed and leaves chopped

1. In a large bowl, using an electric mixer, beat the cream cheese, chives, salt and pepper until spreadable.

2. Trim the crust from the bread. Slice the loaf lengthwise ½ inch thick. Flatten the slices with a rolling pin until about ¼ inch thick.

3. Spread each slice with 2 heaping tablespoons of the cream cheese mix-

ture. Top with 1 heaping tablespoon of the watercress. Gently roll the bread into a cylinder beginning at a short end. Roll each cylinder tightly in plastic wrap and refrigerate until firm, at least 30 minutes or up to 4 hours.

4. Slice the rolls crosswise ½ inch thick and arrange the sandwiches on a platter to show off the swirls.

—Lila Jaeger

CRUNCHY CHICKEN SALAD SANDWICHES

Makes 26 Tea Sandwiches

1 cup finely chopped cooked chicken (about 6 ounces)
¼ cup finely chopped dry-roasted unsalted peanuts or almonds
About 3 tablespoons mayonnaise
About 3 tablespoons nonfat yogurt
2 tablespoons finely chopped celery
Salt and freshly ground pepper
One 1-pound loaf of whole wheat or multigrain bread, very thinly sliced
About 13 seedless red or green grapes, halved lengthwise

1. In a large bowl, mix the chicken, nuts, mayonnaise, yogurt and celery to form a paste. Add more mayonnaise or yogurt if necessary. Season with salt and pepper.

2. Using a 2-inch round cookie cutter, cut the bread into 26 rounds. Spread with the chicken mixture and garnish with a grape half.

—Lila Jaeger

ROAST BEEF AND GOAT CHEESE TRIANGLES

Makes 24 Tea Sandwiches

*12 thin 3-inch-square slices of
  pumpernickel bread*
2 tablespoons mayonnaise
1 tablespoon horseradish
*6 thin slices of rare roast beef (about ¾
  pound), halved*
4 ounces mild goat cheese, softened
Freshly ground pepper
Parsley sprigs, for garnish

Trim the crusts from the bread. Spread each slice with ½ teaspoon of the mayonnaise and ¼ teaspoon of the horseradish. Top with a half slice of roast beef; trim the meat to the size of the bread. Spread 2 teaspoons of the goat cheese over the meat and season with pepper. Halve each open-faced sandwich diagonally and garnish with a sprig of parsley.

—*Lila Jaeger*

CALIFORNIA TEA SANDWICHES

The ginger-lime butter for these deceptively simple and refreshing canapés is best made at least a day ahead to allow the flavors to blend.

Makes 48 Sandwiches

6 tablespoons unsalted butter, softened
1½ tablespoons minced fresh ginger
*¾ teaspoon finely grated lime zest plus
  very fine strips of zest, for garnish
  (optional)*
1½ teaspoons fresh lime juice
¼ teaspoon salt
*12 slices firm-textured white bread,
  crusts removed*
*1 large European seedless cucumber,
  very thinly sliced*

*Radish sprouts or other thin sprouts,
  for garnish*

1. In a small bowl, beat the butter with the ginger, ¾ teaspoon grated lime zest, lime juice and salt. *(The butter can be refrigerated for up to 4 days or frozen for up to 1 month. Let soften to room temperature before using.)*

2. Using a butter knife, spread each slice of bread with a rounded teaspoon of the ginger-lime butter. Cut each slice into 4 squares. Cut the cucumber slices in half and arrange 3 halves on each bread square. Garnish with the radish sprouts and strips of lime zest.

—*Carl & Grace Parisi*

HERBED SHALLOTS IN PHYLLO

Makes 12 Hors d'Oeuvres

2 tablespoons olive oil
36 medium shallots, peeled
Salt and freshly ground pepper
*¼ cup finely chopped mixed fresh herbs,
  such as parsley, thyme, marjoram
  and oregano*
6 sheets of phyllo dough
*3 tablespoons melted unsalted butter,
  for brushing*

1. In a large heavy skillet, heat the oil. Add the shallots and cook over moderately high heat, stirring, for 2 minutes. Season with ½ teaspoon each of salt and pepper. Cover and cook over low heat, stirring occasionally, until fork-tender and golden brown, 20 to 30 minutes. Set aside 2 teaspoons of the fresh herbs; add the remaining herbs to the shallots and toss well. Remove from the heat.

2. Preheat the oven to 400°. Lay out 1 sheet of phyllo dough on a work surface. Keep the remaining phyllo cov-

ered with a damp towel. Brush the phyllo sheet lightly with some of the melted butter. Lay another sheet of phyllo on top of the first and brush with more butter. Repeat with a third phyllo sheet. Using a large sharp knife, cut the layered sheets of phyllo into six 5-inch squares. Place 3 shallots in the center of each phyllo square, draw up the corners and pinch together into a bundle, leaving the top open slightly. Repeat with the remaining phyllo, butter and shallots to make a total of 12 bundles.

3. Place the bundles on a large ungreased baking sheet and bake for about 12 minutes, or until golden brown all over. Sprinkle the remaining 2 teaspoons fresh herbs into the openings of the shallot bundles. Serve warm.

—*Jamie Davies*

PHYLLO PURSES WITH BLACK BEANS AND PEPPER-JACK CHEESE

Creamy black beans, cumin and jalapeño-spiked cheese give these hors d'oeuvres a southwestern flavor.

Makes 48 Purses

6 tablespoons unsalted butter
1 large garlic clove, halved
*One 15-ounce can black beans, drained
  and rinsed*
5 scallions, coarsely chopped
*¾ cup (loosely packed) fresh coriander,
  (cilantro) coarsely chopped*
*¾ cup shredded jalapeño Monterey
  Jack cheese (3 ounces)*

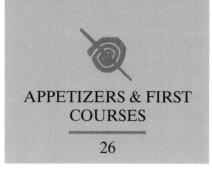
¼ *teaspoon cumin*
Salt
12 sheets of phyllo dough

1. Preheat the oven to 400°. Lightly butter 2 large baking sheets. Melt the butter in a small saucepan. Add the garlic and cook over moderately low heat until sizzling, about 3 minutes. Discard the garlic. Let the butter cool.

2. Preheat the oven to 400°. In a bowl, coarsely mash the beans. Mix in the scallions, coriander, cheese and cumin. Season with salt.

3. Cut the sheets of phyllo dough in half to form twenty-four 8½-by-12-inch sheets. Place 1 sheet on a work surface. Keep the remaining sheets covered with a damp towel. Lightly brush the phyllo with the melted butter. Place a second sheet on top, butter lightly and repeat with a third sheet. Using a sharp knife, cut the stacked phyllo sheets into six 4-inch squares.

4. Place 1 rounded teaspoon of the black bean filling in the center of each square. Bring the 4 corners and the edges of each square together in the center. Pinch around the filling and flare the tops. Place the purses on 1 of the prepared baking sheets. Repeat to form the remaining purses.

5. Bake 1 sheet at a time for 8 to 10 minutes, or until the phyllo is crisp and golden and the filling is heated through. Transfer to a serving platter and serve warm. *(The purses can be baked up to 2 days ahead and refrigerated or they can be frozen for up to 3 weeks. Rewarm them in a 375° oven.)*

—*Carl & Grace Parisi*

SHEER SHRIMP DUMPLINGS WITH CORIANDER-MINT DIPPING SAUCE

The wrappers used for these delicate dumplings are called *gyoza* skins. They are the Japanese version of wonton skins but are made without eggs and rolled much thinner. They are available at Japanese and other Asian markets.

4 to 6 Servings

DUMPLINGS:

1 pound medium shrimp—shelled, deveined and halved crosswise
1 scallion, thinly sliced crosswise
1 tablespoon coarsely chopped fresh coriander (cilantro)
½ tablespoon coarsely chopped fresh spearmint
2 teaspoons soy sauce
Salt
2 tablespoons heavy cream
56 gyoza skins
1 egg, beaten with 2 tablespoons water

DIPPING SAUCE:

6 large garlic cloves, thinly sliced
1 tablespoon vegetable oil
1 tablespoon sugar
2 teaspoons soy sauce
2 tablespoons fresh lime juice
½ cup chopped fresh coriander (cilantro)
¼ cup chopped fresh spearmint
1 to 2 minced Thai, or bird, chiles
¼ teaspoon salt

1. *Make the dumplings:* In a food processor, combine the shrimp, scallion, coriander, mint, soy sauce and ⅛ teaspoon salt. Process briefly just to blend but do not puree; there should be some chunks of shrimp along with some paste. Put the mixture in a bowl and fold in the cream.

2. Working with 4 *gyoza* skins at a time, put a rounded teaspoon of the shrimp filling off center in each wrapper. With a finger, spread some of the beaten egg halfway around the edge of each *gyoza* skin and fold it over the filling to form a half-moon; press to seal the dumpling. Continue until you have made all the dumplings. Once formed, keep the dumplings covered with a lightly dampened cloth.

3. *Make the dipping sauce:* In a small skillet, cover the sliced garlic with ¼ cup of water and simmer over low heat until the water has evaporated, about 5 minutes. Add the oil, sugar and soy sauce and increase the heat to moderate. Cook, stirring, until the sugar caramelizes and has reduced to a bubbling syrup, about 2 minutes. Scrape the contents of the pan into a food processor. Add the lime juice, coriander, mint, chiles, salt and ¼ cup of water and process to a coarse puree. Pour into a bowl.

4. Bring a large saucepan of salted water to a boil over high heat. Add all the dumplings at once and boil until the skins are transparent and the shrimp filling is pink, about 3 minutes.

5. Gently drain the dumplings in a colander, shaking it just enough to remove excess water. Pour the dumplings out onto a large platter and serve immediately with the dipping sauce.

—*Marcia Kiesel*

RICE PAPER ROLLS WITH SHRIMP AND VEGETABLES

♟ The Asian flavors in these rolls suggest an off-dry fruity white, such as a West Coast Gewürztraminer. Look for 1991 Clos du Bois "Early Harvest" from California or 1991 Columbia Crest from Washington State.

Makes 24 Pieces

1 tablespoon sesame seeds
2 tablespoons low-sodium soy sauce
2 teaspoons Dijon mustard
2 teaspoons honey
¼ teaspoon sesame oil
*Dash of Oriental chili oil or pinch of
    cayenne pepper (optional)*
*4 ounces jicama, peeled and cut into 24
    thin 2-inch-long matchsticks*
2 teaspoons fresh lime juice
*Six 8- or 9-inch round rice paper
    wrappers**
*12 peeled cooked medium shrimp,
    halved lengthwise*
*1 Hass avocado, peeled and cut into 12
    thin slices*
*1 small bunch of fresh coriander
    (cilantro) or mint or a combination,
    leaves only*
*1 small head of Boston or Bibb lettuce
    (about ½ pound), leaves shredded
    into ¼-inch-wide strips*
*Available at Asian markets

1. Preheat the oven to 350°. Toast the sesame seeds on a small baking sheet for 5 to 7 minutes, until golden.

2. In a small bowl, combine the soy sauce, mustard, honey, sesame oil and chili oil, if using. In a medium bowl, toss the jicama with the lime juice.

3. On a work surface, brush both sides of 1 rice paper wrapper with water until pliable and just beginning to turn white and opaque. Place 4 shrimp halves in a row across the lower third of the wrapper, leaving a 1-inch border on the bottom. Brush the shrimp generously with the soy-honey sauce and sprinkle with a little of the toasted sesame seeds. Top with 2 of the avocado slices, 4 jicama sticks, about 6 coriander leaves and about ¼ cup of the shredded lettuce.

4. Starting from the bottom, roll up the wrapper, folding in the sides after a complete turn; tuck with your fingers while rolling to make a tight cylinder. Repeat with the remaining rice paper wrappers and fillings, reserving some of the soy-honey sauce and sesame seeds. *(The rolls can be prepared up to 1 hour ahead; leave a little space between them. Cover with plastic wrap and set aside.)*

5. To serve, cut each roll in half crosswise and then in half again and arrange on a serving platter, cut sides up. Lightly brush with the remaining soy-honey sauce and sprinkle with the reserved sesame seeds.

—Carl & Grace Parisi

POTATO NESTS WITH CREME FRAICHE AND CAVIAR

Domestic golden whitefish roe is an economical alternative to more expensive imported caviar.

♟ Serve with Champagne, such as a nonvintage Pol Roger, or a top California sparkling wine, such as 1988 Piper-Sonoma Blanc de Noirs.

Makes About 24 Nests

*3 baking potatoes (about 1½ pounds),
    unpeeled*

Salt
1 tablespoon vegetable oil
½ tablespoon unsalted butter, melted
*½ cup crème fraîche or sour cream, at
    room temperature*
1 to 2 ounces sevruga or osetra caviar

1. In a medium saucepan, cover the potatoes with cold salted water. Simmer until barely cooked through, about 20 minutes. Do not overcook or undercook the potatoes; if not just cooked through, the centers will discolor. Drain the potatoes, let cool and refrigerate until chilled.

2. Preheat the oven to 425°. Peel the potatoes and coarsely grate them on a box grater. Add ½ teaspoon of salt and gently toss.

3. Combine the oil and melted butter and generously grease two 12-cup mini-muffin tins (½ inch deep). Place a heaping tablespoon of grated potatoes into each cup and press against the bottoms and sides. Bake the nests for about 30 minutes, or until nicely browned. *(The nests can be baked up to 4 hours ahead. Let stand at room temperature on a plate lined with paper towels; recrisp in a 375° oven.)*

4. To serve, transfer the warm nests to a warm platter. Spoon 1 teaspoon of crème fraîche into each nest and top with about ¼ teaspoon of caviar.

—Carl & Grace Parisi

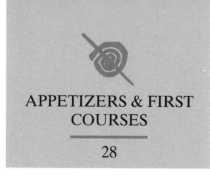

ASPARAGUS CHEESE PUFFS

❦ The distinctive taste of asparagus, enriched with Gruyère and Parmesan in the choux pastry, needs a light, fruity dry white with a bit of acidity, such as 1991 Torres Viña Sol from Spain or 1991 Robert Mondavi Woodbridge Sauvignon Blanc from California.

Makes About 48 Puffs

½ cup milk
¼ cup water
3 tablespoons unsalted butter
¾ teaspoon salt
¼ teaspoon cayenne pepper
¼ teaspoon ground coriander
¾ cup all-purpose flour
3 large eggs
4 ounces asparagus
½ cup coarsely grated Gruyère cheese
    (2 ounces)
¼ cup freshly grated Parmesan cheese

1. In a heavy medium saucepan, bring the milk, water, butter, salt, cayenne and coriander to a boil. Reduce the heat to moderately low and add the flour all at once. Using a wooden spoon, beat the mixture until it pulls away from the bottom and sides of the pan, about 1 minute. Let cool for 4 minutes.

2. Transfer the warm dough to a food processor and pulse 5 to 6 times to break it up. Add the eggs, 1 at a time, and process, scraping down the sides, until just combined and the dough is smooth and shiny. Let cool slightly.

3. Preheat the oven to 400°. Lightly butter 2 baking sheets, line them with parchment paper and butter the paper.

4. In a medium saucepan of boiling salted water, blanch the asparagus until just tender, 1 to 2 minutes. Drain and rinse under cold running water; drain again thoroughly and pat dry. Coarsely chop the asparagus.

5. Mix the asparagus, Gruyère and Parmesan into the dough. Spoon rounded teaspoons of the dough onto the prepared baking sheets 1 inch apart. Smooth the tops of each puff with a lightly moistened pastry brush.

6. Bake the puffs, 1 sheet at a time, in the middle of the oven for about 25 minutes, or until deep golden brown. Transfer to a platter and serve immediately. *(The puffs can be made up to 1 month ahead and frozen. Rewarm them in a 350° oven.)*

—*Carl & Grace Parisi*

ASPARAGUS WITH TARRAGON LEMON SAUCE

This easy dish is good fare for a party. Served on individual plates, it also makes a nice first course or accompaniment to the main dish.

12 to 16 Servings

2 pounds medium asparagus, peeled
½ cup mayonnaise
½ cup sour cream or plain yogurt
1 tablespoon minced fresh tarragon or
    ½ teaspoon dried
2 teaspoons fresh lemon juice
1 teaspoon finely grated lemon zest
½ teaspoon Dijon mustard
Salt and freshly ground pepper

1. Bring a large skillet of salted water to a boil. Add the asparagus and return to a boil over high heat. Lower the heat to maintain a steady simmer and cook until tender, 3 to 5 minutes. Drain, cool under cold running water and drain again thoroughly.

2. In a medium bowl, whisk together the mayonnaise, sour cream, tarragon, lemon juice, lemon zest and mustard. Season with salt and pepper and transfer to a small serving bowl. *(The recipe can be prepared to this point up to 3 hours ahead. Cover and refrigerate the sauce and set aside the asparagus at room temperature.)*

3. Arrange the asparagus on a large platter and serve the lemon sauce alongside for dipping.

—*Jeannette Ferrary & Louise Fiszer*

BOMBAY CHICKEN WINGS

Roasted rather than deep-fried, Bombay wings are easier to make and less fattening than Buffalo wings. Be sure to start them a day ahead to allow time for marinating. Serve them hot with cold, crisp cucumber sticks and a bowl of cumin- and cayenne-spiked yogurt.

6 Servings

1½ teaspoons cumin seeds
5½ pounds chicken wings (about 30)
1½ tablespoons minced fresh ginger
2 teaspoons minced garlic
1 tablespoon ground coriander
1¼ teaspoons cayenne pepper
¼ teaspoon plus ⅛ teaspoon paprika
Coarse (kosher) salt
Freshly ground black pepper
1 cup plain low-fat yogurt
⅓ cup plus 1 teaspoon fresh lemon
    juice
About ¼ cup peanut or corn oil, for
    basting
2 tablespoons unsalted butter

1. In a small dry skillet, toast the cumin seeds over moderate heat until fragrant, about 1 minute. Transfer the seeds to a spice grinder or mortar and grind them.

2. Cut off the wing tips from the chicken wings and discard them (or reserve for stock). Using a thin skewer, deeply pierce the wings all over.

3. In a large bowl, combine the ginger, garlic, coriander, ground cumin, 1 teaspoon of the cayenne, ¼ teaspoon of the paprika, 1½ teaspoons coarse salt and ½ teaspoon black pepper. Stir in the yogurt and ⅓ cup of the lemon juice. Add the chicken wings to the bowl and stir to coat evenly. Cover and refrigerate for 24 hours, turning the wings occasionally. Let the wings stand at room temperature for 1 hour before proceeding.

4. Preheat the oven to 450°. Lightly oil a large wire rack and set it over a large roasting pan. Remove the wings from the marinade and place them on the rack without touching. Reserve the marinade.

5. Using a pastry brush, dab the wings lightly with the peanut oil and roast them for 15 minutes. Turn them over, baste with the reserved marinade and dab lightly with more oil. Roast for about 20 minutes longer, or until cooked through. Transfer the wings to a warmed serving platter.

6. In a small nonreactive saucepan, melt the butter with the remaining ¼ teaspoon cayenne and ⅛ teaspoon paprika. Stir in the remaining 1 teaspoon lemon juice and a pinch of coarse salt and cook over moderately high heat until hot. Brush the spicy butter over the roasted chicken wings and serve.

—Leslie Newman

PROSCIUTTO AND PAPAYA WITH LIME-TEQUILA SPLASH

This twist on the traditional prosciutto and melon combo benefits from the unexpected tingle of tequila. Try ripe cantaloupe, honeydew or fresh figs in place of the papaya.

Makes 24 Hors d'Oeuvres

12 thin slices of prosciutto (about 6 ounces), trimmed of fat
1 large papaya—peeled, seeded and cut into 24 bite-size chunks
1½ tablespoons fresh lime juice
1 teaspoon tequila
1 teaspoon grated lime zest
Mint leaves, for garnish (optional)

Cut each slice of prosciutto in half lengthwise and wrap the slices around the papaya chunks. Arrange on a serving platter. *(The hors d'oeuvres can be prepared to this point up to 1 hour ahead. Cover with plastic wrap.)* In a small bowl, combine the lime juice and tequila and sprinkle over the prosciutto. Garnish with the lime zest and mint leaves if using.

—Carl & Grace Parisi

ASPARAGUS, GOAT CHEESE AND PROSCIUTTO STRUDEL

This delicious dish is appropriate for brunch or lunch.

8 First-Course Servings

⅔ cup whole-milk ricotta cheese (about 6 ounces)
1 pound medium asparagus, peeled
4 ounces mild goat cheese, such as Montrachet
1 large egg yolk

3 tablespoons minced fresh chives
Salt and freshly ground pepper
8 sheets of phyllo dough
4 tablespoons melted unsalted butter, for brushing
4 thin slices of prosciutto (about 2 ounces)

1. Set a strainer over a large bowl and line it with a double layer of dampened cheesecloth. Spoon the ricotta cheese into the strainer and let it drain for 4 hours.

2. Bring a large skillet of salted water to a boil. Add the asparagus and cook until just tender, 2 to 3 minutes. Drain well, pat dry with paper towels and let cool.

3. In a medium bowl, combine the drained ricotta, goat cheese, egg yolk and chives and mix with a spoon until smooth. Season with ½ teaspoon each of salt and pepper.

4. Preheat the oven to 400°. Lay 1 sheet of phyllo on a work surface, short end toward you. Keep the remaining phyllo covered with a damp towel. Brush the phyllo sheet lightly with some of the melted butter. Lay another sheet on top and brush with more melted butter. Repeat with 2 more phyllo sheets. Lay 2 prosciutto slices, overlapping slightly, horizontally across the lower quarter of the phyllo; leave a 1½-inch margin on both sides and the bottom edge. Spread half of the goat cheese mixture evenly over the prosciutto. Arrange half the asparagus stalks crosswise on top of the cheese, trimming the ends if necessary. Fold in the sides and bottom edge of the phyllo over the filling,

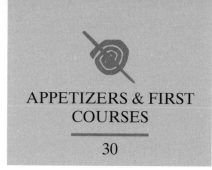

then roll up the strudel from the short end. Place it seam-side down on an ungreased baking sheet. Repeat with the remaining ingredients to make a second strudel. Brush the strudels with more melted butter and cut several ½-inch vents in the top of each.

5. Bake the strudels for about 25 minutes, or until golden brown all over and heated through. Using 1 or 2 metal spatulas, transfer the strudels to a wire rack and let cool for 10 minutes. Using a serrated knife, cut each strudel into four slices and serve warm.

—*Jeannette Ferrary & Louise Fiszer*

SPICY GRILLED RADICCHIO WITH BOCCONCINI

Look for *bocconcini* (miniature mozzarella balls) that are packed in water. They will be moist and fresh tasting.

4 Servings

Four 4-ounce heads of radicchio
Four 1-ounce miniature mozzarella balls (bocconcini), drained
4 small anchovy fillets, coarsely chopped
Salt and freshly ground black pepper
Crushed red pepper
2 teaspoons chopped flat-leaf parsley
Extra-virgin olive oil, for drizzling
Lemon wedges, for serving

1. In a medium saucepan of boiling salted water, blanch the heads of radicchio until wilted, 2 to 3 minutes. Transfer to a colander with a slotted spoon.

Gently press out as much water as possible. Drain well on paper towels.

2. Light a grill or preheat the broiler. Gently open the leaves of each head of radicchio and place a ball of mozzarella in the center. Top with some of the anchovy and season with salt, black pepper and a pinch of crushed red pepper. Sprinkle with parsley and a few drops of olive oil. Carefully enclose the cheese in the leaves. Secure each bundle with 2 toothpicks.

3. Lightly brush the radicchio with olive oil. Grill over moderate heat or broil, turning once, for about 6 minutes, or until the radicchio is golden brown. Remove the toothpicks and serve with lemon wedges.

—*Viana La Place*

ROASTED VEGETABLE AND GOAT CHEESE TERRINE

Lusty Provençal flavors characterize this beautiful, easy-to-serve first course, which can be made up to two days in advance. The slowly roasted plum tomatoes are a wonderfully moist alternative to commercial sun-dried tomatoes, and together with the goat cheese they provide a pleasantly acid note to balance the mild bitterness of the eggplant and zucchini. (It takes six hours to oven-dry the tomatoes for this recipe, so plan accordingly.)

Makes One 9-by-5-by-3-Inch Terrine

12 large plum tomatoes
½ teaspoon coarse (kosher) salt
3 medium eggplants (2 pounds), peeled and sliced lengthwise ⅛ inch thick
½ cup olive oil
Table salt and freshly ground pepper

3 medium zucchini (1½ pounds), sliced lengthwise ⅛ inch thick
3 medium yellow squash (1½ pounds), sliced lengthwise ⅛ inch thick
¾ pound fresh goat cheese
2 eggs, beaten
2 ounces prosciutto, minced (optional)
1 teaspoon chopped fresh rosemary
1 teaspoon chopped fresh sage
1 teaspoon chopped fresh thyme

1. Preheat the oven to 200°. Using a small sharp knife, core the tomatoes and halve them lengthwise. Arrange them on a baking sheet cut-sides up in a single layer and sprinkle with the coarse salt. Bake for 6 hours. Let cool, then refrigerate overnight.

2. Preheat the oven to 400°. Lay the eggplant slices on 2 baking sheets. Brush lightly with some of the olive oil and season with salt and pepper. Roast in the oven for about 10 minutes, until just soft. Transfer the eggplant to a platter and let cool. Repeat the process with the zucchini and yellow squash.

3. In a medium bowl, combine the goat cheese, eggs, prosciutto, rosemary, sage and thyme. Season with salt and pepper.

4. To assemble the terrine, completely line the bottom and sides of a 9-by-5-by-3-inch glass or ceramic terrine (1½ quarts) with slices of roasted eggplant, layering them lengthwise and overlapping them slightly as necessary; a 2- to 3-inch piece of eggplant should extend beyond the rim of the terrine all around. Next, make a lengthwise layer of one-third of the zucchini and one-third of the yellow squash on the bottom of the terrine. Using a spatula, evenly spread half of the goat cheese mixture over the squash. Arrange 12 roasted tomato halves on the cheese. Repeat with another third of the zucchini and yellow squash followed by the rest of the goat cheese and tomatoes. Cover with the remaining zucchini and yellow squash and any leftover eggplant. Fold in the overhanging eggplant to seal the terrine.

5. Preheat the oven to 325°. Cover the terrine with wax paper and place it in a larger baking dish half-filled with hot water. Bake the terrine for 45 minutes. Remove from the water bath and let cool to room temperature. Gently weight the terrine with a piece of cardboard or wood wrapped in foil topped with canned goods. Refrigerate overnight. This rids the terrine of excess moisture and allows it to set.

6. To serve, remove the weights and peel off the wax paper. Unmold the terrine by inverting it onto a cutting board and carefully tapping one end until the terrine drops out. Cut in ¾-inch slices, wiping the knife between cuts. Serve at room temperature. *(Any leftover terrine can be wrapped in plastic and refrigerated for up to 2 days.)*

—*Michael Romano*

FRENCH ONION TART

Makes One 11-Inch Tart

CRUST:
6 tablespoons unsalted butter, softened
1½ cups all-purpose flour
1 large egg yolk
3 tablespoons milk
¼ teaspoon salt

FILLING:
3½ tablespoons unsalted butter
2½ pounds onions, finely chopped
3 large eggs
1 cup heavy cream
1¼ teaspoons salt
1 teaspoon freshly ground pepper

1. Make the crust: In a medium bowl, combine the butter and flour until the mixture resembles coarse meal. In a small bowl, stir the egg yolk, milk and salt with a fork. Stir the egg mixture into the flour, then work the dough with your fingertips until it comes together. Pat the dough into a 6-inch disk; wrap and refrigerate until firm, at least 1 hour.

2. On a lightly floured surface, roll the dough into a 14-inch round. Place the dough in an 11-by-1-inch fluted tart pan with a removable bottom, fitting it in without stretching. Trim the overhang to ½ inch and fold it in, pressing to form a lip ¼ inch above the pan rim. Prick the dough all over with a fork. Freeze the shell for 10 minutes, or until firm.

3. Preheat the oven to 350°. Place the tart pan on a cookie sheet. Line the pastry with foil and fill with pie weights or dried beans. Bake for 20 minutes. Remove the foil and weights and bake for 20 minutes longer, or until the pastry is golden.

4. Make the filling: Melt the butter in a large skillet. Add the onions and cook over moderate heat, stirring, until soft but not brown, about 15 minutes. Let cool.

5. In a large bowl, beat the eggs. Stir in the onions, cream, salt and pepper. Ladle the filling into the tart shell and bake for 40 minutes, or until just set. Let the tart cool on a rack for about 20 minutes. Unmold and serve warm.

—*Les Alisiers, Lapoutroie, France*

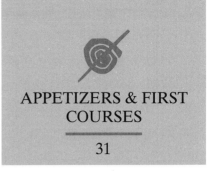

CREAMED OYSTERS AND MUSHROOMS

This first course is handsome served in scallop shells, but shallow ramekins would work nicely too.

8 Servings

4 tablespoons unsalted butter
1 cup fresh bread crumbs, toasted
1 pound mushrooms, coarsely chopped
Salt and freshly ground white pepper
3 tablespoons finely chopped shallots
2 tablespoons water
1 tablespoon plus 1 teaspoon all-purpose flour
1 cup heavy cream
1 pint shucked oysters, liquor reserved
1½ tablespoons medium-dry Spanish sherry or Madeira
¼ teaspoon mace
2 tablespoons chopped parsley, for garnish

1. In a large skillet, melt 1 tablespoon of the butter over moderately high heat. Add the bread crumbs and stir until crisp and browned, about 5 minutes. Transfer to a small bowl.

2. Add another tablespoon of the butter to the skillet. Add the mushrooms and cook, stirring occasionally until they release their juices, 2 to 3 minutes. Season with salt and white pepper and sauté until just cooked through but not browned, about 4 minutes longer. Transfer to a bowl. Reserve the skillet.

3. In a medium saucepan, melt the remaining 2 tablespoons butter over moderate heat. Add the shallots and water and cook until soft but not

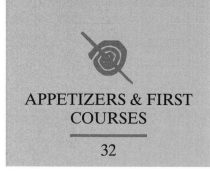

browned. Add the flour and stir for 1 minute. Gradually stir in the cream and simmer until the sauce thickens, about 1 minute. Thin with some of the oyster liquor if needed. *(The recipe can be prepared to this point up to 4 hours ahead. Rewarm the sauce before proceeding.)*

4. Preheat the oven to 350°. Drain the oysters and snip them in half or thirds with sharp scissors. Add them to the skillet and cook over moderate heat until they just begin to curl, about 1 minute.

5. Stir the mushrooms, oysters and sherry into the cream sauce. Season with salt, white pepper and the mace and cook over moderate heat until warmed through; do not boil. Spoon the creamed oysters into scallop shells and sprinkle with the toasted bread crumbs. Place the scallop shells on a baking sheet and bake for about 7 minutes, until piping hot. Garnish with the parsley and serve immediately.

—*Camille Glenn*

SAUTEED SOFT-SHELL CRABS WITH HAZELNUTS

Soft-shell crabs are a harbinger of summer, and their availability "comes and goes with the phases of the moon," according to Inn at Little Washington's chef Patrick O'Connell, whose menus resonate with the rhythms of the seasons. He recommends serving the dish with asparagus and morels.

♥ To balance the delicate flavor of the crab and the spice, you want a clean white with good depth and acidity, such as Chablis Grand Cru Moutonne, Domaine Long-Depaquit 1986. A Sauvignon Blanc or a dry Riesling from Oregon or Alsace would also go well.

4 First-Course Servings

¼ cup mayonnaise
2 tablespoons fresh lemon juice
1 tablespoon Dijon mustard
½ tablespoon dry mustard
Salt and freshly ground pepper
1 stick (4 ounces) plus 2 tablespoons unsalted butter
⅓ cup hazelnuts
1 cup small, thin green beans
2 teaspoons olive oil
1 teaspoon white wine vinegar
Flour, for dredging
4 medium soft-shell crabs
1 large tomato—peeled, seeded and diced
1 tablespoon fresh lime juice
Lime segments
2 tablespoons fresh coriander (cilantro) leaves
1 tablespoon snipped chives

1. In a small bowl, mix the mayonnaise, lemon juice, Dijon mustard and dry mustard into a smooth sauce. Season with salt and pepper and set aside.

2. In a small saucepan, melt the stick of butter over low heat. Remove from the heat and let the milk solids settle to the bottom of the pan, then skim the foam off the top. Pour the clear yellow liquid (clarified butter) through a strainer into a small bowl and set aside.

3. In a small saucepan, cook the remaining 2 tablespoons butter over moderate heat until it turns a nut brown, about 3 minutes. Pour into a small dish and set aside.

4. Preheat the oven to 400°. Spread the hazelnuts on a baking sheet and toast in the middle of the oven for about 8 minutes, until fragrant. Transfer the hot nuts to a kitchen towel and rub them together vigorously to remove most of the skins. Coarsely chop the hazelnuts and set aside. Leave the oven on.

5. In a medium saucepan of boiling salted water, blanch the green beans until just tender, about 3 minutes. Drain and refresh in cold water. Drain well and pat dry.

6. In a small bowl, whisk the oil and vinegar. Season with salt and pepper. Set aside.

7. Place the flour on a large plate and season with salt and pepper. In a large ovenproof skillet, heat the clarified butter until almost smoking. Dredge the crabs in the seasoned flour, then shake off any excess. Place the crabs upside down in the skillet and cook until well browned, about 3 minutes. Turn the crabs over, drain the liquid from the skillet and add the tomato, reserved browned butter and hazelnuts.

8. Place the skillet in the oven and bake the crabs for 2 minutes. Drizzle with the lime juice.

9. To serve, dress the green beans with the reserved vinaigrette and arrange them on 4 plates; top with the crabs. Spoon the tomato and hazelnuts from the skillet over the crabs and garnish with the lime segments and coriander leaves. Using a spoon, drizzle the mustard-mayonnaise sauce around the crabs and sprinkle the chives on the sauce.

—*Patrick O'Connell*

Sheer Shrimp Dumplings with Coriander-Mint Dipping Sauce (p. 26).

Above, Roasted Vegetable and Goat Cheese Terrine (p. 30).
At right, Turkey-Paprika Soup with Spaetzle (p. 50).

SCALLOPS WITH ZUCCHINI AND THYME

4 First-Course Servings

2 small zucchini (about 6 inches long)
1 tablespoon olive oil
Salt and freshly ground pepper
20 sea scallops (1 pound), patted dry
1½ tablespoons all-purpose flour
9 tablespoons unsalted butter, 7
*   tablespoons cold and cut into small*
*   pieces*
3 shallots, finely chopped
1 cup Riesling
1 cup heavy cream
1 fresh thyme sprig
2 ripe medium tomatoes at room
*   temperature—peeled, seeded and cut*
*   into small dice*
1 tablespoon plus 1 teaspoon chopped
*   fresh chervil, for garnish*

1. Using a vegetable peeler, strip each zucchini lengthwise at 4 intervals, leaving 4 strips of green skin and 4 strips of white flesh. Cut the zucchini crosswise into ¼-inch rounds.

2. Heat the oil in a large nonreactive skillet. Add the zucchini in a single layer and cook over moderately high heat until golden brown on both sides, about 3 minutes. Transfer to a heatproof plate, sprinkle with salt and keep warm in a low oven. Wipe out the skillet.

3. Place the scallops in a bowl and season with ⅛ teaspoon each of salt and pepper. Sprinkle the scallops with the flour and toss lightly to coat.

4. Melt the 2 tablespoons of unchilled butter in the skillet. Add the scallops in a single layer and cook over moderately high heat just until firm and golden, 2 to 3 minutes per side. Spread the scallops on a heatproof plate and keep warm in the oven.

5. Add the shallots to the skillet and cook over moderate heat, stirring, until softened. Pour in the Riesling and bring to a boil over moderately high heat, stirring to deglaze the pan. Stir in the cream and thyme and boil until reduced by half, about 4 minutes. Remove from the heat and whisk in the 7 tablespoons chilled butter until incorporated. Remove the thyme sprig and stir in the tomatoes.

6. While the sauce reduces, arrange overlapping zucchini slices in a semicircle on 4 small warmed plates. Spoon the butter sauce on the plates and set 5 scallops in the center of each. Garnish with the chervil and serve.

—Auberge de l'Ill, Illhaeusern, France

SHRIMP IN KATAIFI WITH PURPLE RELISH

Michel Richard, the French chef and owner of Citrus in Los Angeles, embraces California whimsy in the emphasis on color and presentation of his dishes and the light and airy decor of his restaurant.

This appetizer is surprisingly simple to make. *Kataifi,* shredded dough, is available in the freezer section of Greek and Middle Eastern groceries.
♉ A California Chardonnay with lots of tropical fruit tastes, such as 1988 Au Bon Climat from Santa Barbara County, is a good match for this dish.

4 First-Course Servings

⅓ cup mayonnaise
2 tablespoons fresh lemon juice
1 tablespoon red wine vinegar
1½ teaspoons soy sauce
2 thin coins of peeled fresh ginger

2 tablespoons olive oil
3 cups thinly sliced red cabbage
Salt and freshly ground pepper
1 quart vegetable oil, for frying
½ cup all-purpose flour
12 large tiger shrimp or prawns (1
*   pound), shelled and deveined*
2 eggs
⅓ of a 1-pound box of kataifi

1. In a food processor, combine the mayonnaise, lemon juice, vinegar, soy sauce and ginger. Process in long pulses until smooth. With the machine on, gradually drizzle in the olive oil. Add the cabbage and pulse, scraping down the sides as necessary, until coarsely chopped. Season to taste with salt and pepper. Transfer the relish to a bowl, cover and refrigerate. *(The relish can be prepared up to 1 day ahead. Remove it from the refrigerator 30 minutes before serving.)*

2. In a large saucepan, heat the vegetable oil over moderately high heat to 350°. Meanwhile, in a medium bowl, toss the flour with ½ teaspoon each of salt and pepper. Add the shrimp and toss to coat, shaking off the excess. Set aside.

3. In a medium bowl, beat the eggs with a fork. Pull the *kataifi* apart into strands and place in a bowl.

4. Dip each shrimp in the beaten eggs, then coat well with the *kataifi,* pressing it on gently with your hands.

5. Fry 3 shrimp at a time in the hot oil, turning several times, until golden and cooked through, about 3 minutes.

Bombay Chicken Wings (p. 28).

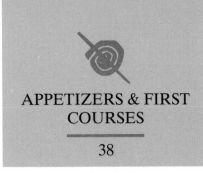
Drain on paper towels and sprinkle lightly with salt.

6. Place the relish on 4 plates with 3 shrimp on top. Serve hot.

—Michel Richard

CORN WAFFLES WITH SMOKED SALMON AND OSETRA CAVIAR

Chef Guenter Seeger is in charge of the kitchen at The Dining Room restaurant in Atlanta, which is often compared to a private club. His corn waffles are a crunchy variation on the traditional blinis served with smoked salmon and caviar. Enjoy this dish as a starter or on its own as a special lunch.

❦ A fresh, fruity 1989 or 1990 Pinot Blanc from Alsace, such as those made by Domaine Weinbach or Gustave Lorentz, will balance the strong flavors of salmon and caviar.

6 First-Course Servings

1 cup milk
3½ tablespoons unsalted butter
¾ cup fine cornmeal
1 teaspoon fresh lemon juice
6 tablespoons crème fraîche or sour cream
4 eggs, beaten
¼ cup heavy cream
Salt and freshly ground pepper
6 large slices of smoked salmon (about ½ pound)
4 ounces osetra caviar
Dill sprigs, for garnish

1. In a medium saucepan, bring ⅔ cup of the milk and the butter to a boil over moderate heat. Add the cornmeal and cook, stirring, until it begins to come away from the sides of the pan, about 1 minute. Remove from the heat and let cool slightly, about 5 minutes.

2. Meanwhile, in a small bowl, stir the lemon juice into the crème fraîche; set aside.

3. Beat the eggs, heavy cream and the remaining ⅓ cup milk into the cooled cornmeal. Season with salt and pepper.

4. Preheat a waffle iron. Spoon about ⅓ cup of the batter in the center of the iron to make 1 waffle and cook until crisp. Repeat with the remaining batter to make 6 waffles. Place each waffle on a plate and top with 1 slice of smoked salmon, 1 tablespoon of the reserved crème fraîche mixture and a heaping tablespoon of caviar. Garnish with a dill sprig and serve.

—Guenter Seeger

SEARED SALMON WITH SWEET CORN, SHIITAKES AND SPINACH

This is the most popular salmon dish served at New York's Union Square Cafe. The colors of the vegetables sing out late summer. This recipe serves three as a main course.

6 First-Course Servings

1½ sticks (12 tablespoons) unsalted butter
1 cup thinly sliced red onion
3 garlic cloves—2 thinly sliced, 1 left whole
¼ pound shiitake mushrooms—stems removed and reserved, caps quartered
1 medium tomato, coarsely chopped
1 teaspoon whole black peppercorns
1 bay leaf
⅓ cup balsamic vinegar
Salt and freshly ground pepper
3 tablespoons olive oil
1 pound spinach, stemmed
2 cups fresh corn kernels, sliced from the cob
1 pound center-cut salmon fillet, sliced crosswise into 6 strips
3 tablespoons finely chopped chives

1. Cut 6 tablespoons of the butter in ½-inch cubes and refrigerate. In a medium nonreactive saucepan, melt 2 tablespoons of the remaining butter over moderately low heat. Add the red onion, sliced garlic, shiitake stems, tomato, black peppercorns and bay leaf and cook until the vegetables are soft but not brown, about 12 minutes. Add the balsamic vinegar and ⅓ cup of water and cook over moderately high heat, stirring occasionally, until just a syrupy liquid remains, about 4 minutes.

2. Reduce the heat to very low and add the cold cubed butter, 2 to 3 pieces at a time, whisking it in thoroughly between additions. When all the butter has been added, season the sauce with salt and pepper. Pass the sauce through a very fine strainer; discard the solids. Keep the sauce warm over a double-boiler.

3. Spear the whole garlic clove securely with a dinner fork. In a large skillet, heat 2 tablespoons of the olive oil over high heat until just beginning to smoke. Add the spinach and immediately begin stirring with the fork and garlic clove. When the spinach is wilted, season with salt and pepper and drain in a colander. Discard the garlic clove.

4. Wipe the skillet clean and add 3 tablespoons of the butter. Add the shiitake caps and cook over moderate heat, stirring, until softened, about 3 minutes. Stir in the corn kernels and cook until completely heated through, about 3 minutes. Season with salt and pepper. Transfer to a bowl and keep warm.

5. In the same skillet, heat the remaining 1 tablespoon each of butter and olive oil over high heat. Season the salmon fillets with salt and pepper. Sear them in the hot pan, turning once, until browned but barely cooked through, about 3 minutes per side.

6. Mound the spinach in the center of each plate and surround with the corn and shiitakes. Place a salmon fillet on top of the spinach on each plate and spoon the balsamic vinegar sauce on the fish. Garnish with a sprinkling of chives and serve at once.

—*Michael Romano*

ROASTED QUAIL WITH MARINATED TOMATOES, EGGPLANT AND TOMATILLO SAUCE

Chef Mark Cox of Tony's in Houston emphasizes regional Texas foods with Neapolitan undertones. The marinade enhances the birds' flavor and gives them an attractive glazed finish. Green tomatoes may be substituted for the tomatillos.

🍷 A dry, crisp Italian white, such as 1990 Pinot Grigio Santa Margherita, has an essence that pairs well with the tangy tomatillo sauce.

4 First-Course Servings

¼ cup plus 1 tablespoon balsamic vinegar
2 tablespoons honey
4 sage leaves, torn in pieces
4 partially boned quail, butterflied
2 tablespoons plus 1 teaspoon extra-virgin olive oil
1 tablespoon minced garlic
1 cup diced eggplant (½-inch pieces)
3 plum tomatoes—peeled, seeded and finely diced
½ teaspoon fresh lemon juice
Salt and freshly ground white pepper
10 tomatillos, cored
2 teaspoons minced onion
1½ tablespoons chicken stock or canned broth
1 teaspoon minced serrano chile
Pinch of sugar
1 tablespoon minced fresh coriander (cilantro)

1. In a large nonreactive dish, mix ¼ cup of the balsamic vinegar and the honey. Place the sage leaves on the breast meat of the quail and add the quail to the marinade. Coat the birds completely with the marinade. Let marinate for 1 hour.

2. In a medium skillet, heat 1½ tablespoons of the olive oil over low heat. Add the garlic and cook, stirring, for 1 minute. Add the eggplant and cook, stirring, until tender and golden brown, about 5 minutes. Transfer the eggplant and garlic to a nonreactive bowl and let cool to room temperature. Fold in the tomatoes, lemon juice and remaining 1 tablespoon balsamic vinegar. Season with salt and white pepper to taste; set aside.

3. In a medium saucepan of boiling salted water, blanch the tomatillos for 3 minutes to soften. Drain well and puree in a food processor. Set aside.

4. In a medium nonreactive saucepan, heat the remaining 2½ teaspoons olive oil over moderate heat. Stir in the onion and cook until softened, about 4 minutes. Stir in the chicken stock, serrano and sugar. Stir in the tomatillo puree and bring to a boil. Season with the coriander and salt and white pepper to taste.

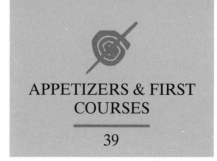

5. Preheat the broiler. Season the marinated quail with salt and white pepper and place skin-side up on a broiling pan. Broil, rotating the pan, for about 3 minutes; the breast meat should remain pink. Spoon the tomato and eggplant mixture in the center of each warmed plate and place a quail on top. Spoon the tomatillo sauce around.

—*Mark Cox*

SPICY SQUID SALAD

You can make a meal out of the pleasantly chewy squid as long as there is plenty of crusty bread to dip in the dressing. Make the salad as hot as you like, but don't let the red pepper overwhelm it.

🍷 Serve with a chilled, crisp white, such as Pinot Grigio or Orvieto.

6 First-Course Servings

⅔ cup extra-virgin olive oil
⅓ cup fresh lemon juice, or more to taste
4 plump garlic cloves, minced (1½ tablespoons)
¾ teaspoon crushed red pepper, or more to taste
4 tender inner celery ribs with leaves, minced (1¼ cups)
20 drained pimiento-stuffed green olives, quartered crosswise
2 pounds very fresh squid
2 tablespoons sea salt

1. In a medium bowl, stir together the oil, lemon juice, garlic and crushed red pepper. Stir in the celery and olives and set the dressing aside.

2. Rinse and drain the squid thoroughly. Slice off the tentacles just above the eyes. Squeeze out and discard the hard little beak just inside the tentacles at the point where they join the head. Pull out the innards and the cuttlebone, or quill, from the body and discard. Do not worry about removing the skin, which is edible. Slice the squid bodies crosswise in ¼-inch rings. Cut the tentacles in half lengthwise. Rinse the squid again and drain thoroughly.

3. In a large saucepan, bring 3 quarts of water to a rolling boil. Add the sea salt. Add the squid rings and tentacles and cook just until they turn opaque, not more than 1 minute, or they will toughen. (I usually begin testing the squid about 30 seconds after it hits the water.) Drain but do not rinse. Transfer the hot squid to the dressing and toss to coat. Cover and refrigerate for at least 3 hours or overnight. Season to taste with sea salt.

—*Patricia Wells*

CRISP PAN-FRIED SWEETBREADS WITH BALSAMIC VINEGAR SAUCE

Sweetbreads have long been a staple at New York's Four Seasons restaurant. The food served in the dramatic Grill Room and the plush, romantic Pool Room now comes from a kitchen presided over by the Swiss-born chef Christian Albin. Balsamic vinegar is his addition to a Four Seasons classic, and he likes to serve the dish with fried polenta and fresh asparagus.

🍷 A steely, crisp 1990 Pinot Blanc from Chalone Vineyard in Monterey County pairs well with this sharp, unctuous dish.

4 First-Course Servings

1 pound sweetbreads
Ice water
Salt and freshly ground pepper
¼ cup heavy cream
⅓ cup all-purpose flour
2 tablespoons unsalted butter
¼ cup balsamic vinegar
¼ cup chicken stock
1 tablespoon chopped shallots
1 teaspoon Dijon mustard
¼ cup olive oil
1 tablespoon chopped parsley

1. Bring a medium saucepan of salted water to a boil. Add the sweetbreads and blanch for 30 seconds. Transfer the sweetbreads to a bowl of ice water to cool, then remove and pat dry. Peel off the thick outer membrane and any fat. Slice the sweetbreads on the diagonal about ½ inch thick.

2. Season the sweetbreads lightly with salt and pepper and dip the slices in the cream. Dredge the sweetbreads in the flour, shaking off the excess.

3. In a medium nonreactive skillet, melt the butter over moderately high heat. Add the sweetbreads and panfry until crisp, brown and just cooked through, about 3 minutes per side. Transfer the sweetbreads to 4 plates and keep warm.

4. Add the vinegar, stock and shallots to the skillet and bring to a boil, scraping the bottom of the pan. Add the mustard and whisk in the olive oil. Season the sauce with salt and pepper. Spoon the sauce over the sweetbreads and garnish with the parsley.

—*Christian Albin*

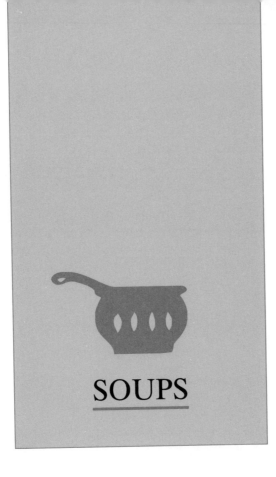

SOUPS

TOMATO AND RED PEPPER SOUP

10 Servings

Three 28-ounce cans Italian peeled
   tomatoes, drained
10 red bell peppers (about 4 pounds),
   cut into 2-inch pieces
10 garlic cloves, peeled and halved
1 bottle (750 ml) dry white wine,
   preferably Sauvignon Blanc
3 cups chicken stock or canned broth
½ cup coarsely chopped flat-leaf
   parsley and/or fresh basil
½ teaspoon thyme
1 to 2 tablespoons sugar (optional)
1 cup heavy cream
Salt and freshly ground black pepper
¼ cup crumbled goat cheese
5 sun-dried tomato halves packed in
   oil, drained and diced
5 fresh basil leaves, shredded

1. In a large enameled cast-iron
casserole, combine the tomatoes, bell
peppers, garlic, wine, stock, parsley and
thyme. Bring to a boil over high heat.
Cover and simmer over moderately low
heat, stirring occasionally, until the peppers are tender, about 45 minutes.

2. Working in batches, puree the
soup in a blender. Pass the puree
through a food mill or a coarse strainer.

3. Return the soup to the casserole
and add some sugar if the soup is too
tart. Stir in the cream. Bring just to a
simmer over moderate heat and season
with salt and pepper.

4. To serve, ladle the soup into cups
or bowls. Garnish with the crumbled
goat cheese, sun-dried tomatoes and
shredded basil and serve hot.

—*Mary Novak*

GAZPACHO SEVILLANO

Unlike its many chunky relatives, this
gazpacho is smooth and creamy.

8 Servings

2-inch piece of stale French bread,
   crusts removed, diced
3½ pounds tomatoes, peeled and
   chopped
1 garlic clove, chopped
1 green bell pepper, chopped
1 European seedless cucumber (12
   ounces)—peeled, seeded and
   chopped
½ small red onion, chopped
1 cup extra-virgin olive oil
2 tablespoons sherry vinegar
Salt
Sugar (optional)
Finely diced cucumber, green bell
   pepper, onion and hard-cooked egg,
   for serving

1. In a small bowl, pour 1 cup of
cold water over the diced bread and set
aside for about 10 minutes. When the
bread is thoroughly soaked, gently
squeeze out the excess water.

2. In a blender, working in batches,
puree the bread, tomatoes, garlic, bell
pepper, cucumber, red onion, oil and
vinegar until the soup is light and
smooth. Season with salt and a little
sugar if the tomatoes are acidic. Just
before serving, garnish with the diced
cucumber, bell pepper, onion and egg.

—*Nancy Harmon Jenkins*

BREAD-AND-TOMATO SOUP

The Tuscan country cooking of restau-
rateur and chef Francesco Ricchi is
based on old family recipes. This thick
almost porridge-like soup, *pappa al po-
modoro* in Italian, is a traditional
favorite in Florentine homes and trat-
torias. It may be served warm or hot; it
can also be reheated the next day.

♟ A complex white wine with good
fruit, body and a bit of acidity, such as
1989 Colutta Nojar, or a young, light,
fruity red, such as 1990 Colutta Schiop-
pettino, will complement and not overpower this flavorful soup. Another
good option would be a 1988 Chianti
Classico.

6 to 8 Servings

1 pound very ripe fresh plum tomatoes,
   peeled and finely chopped, juices
   reserved
One 16-ounce can Italian peeled
   tomatoes, chopped, juices reserved
1 pound stale, white or dark Tuscan or
   other peasant bread, cut into small
   dice
4 cups Chicken Stock (p. 44) or canned
   low-sodium broth
5 garlic cloves
1 medium leek, white and tender green
   only, finely chopped
1 medium onion, finely chopped
Pinch of crushed red pepper
½ cup extra-virgin olive oil, plus
   more for serving
Salt and freshly ground black pepper
6 to 8 fresh basil leaves

1. In a large heavy nonreactive
saucepan or flameproof casserole, stir
together the fresh and canned tomatoes, bread, stock, garlic, leek, onion,
red pepper and the ½ cup of oil. Cover
and simmer over very low heat, stirring occasionally, for 1 hour. Remove

from the heat and set aside, covered, for 1 hour.

2. Remove and discard the garlic cloves. Stir well to break up all the bread. Ladle the soup into serving bowls, sprinkle a little oil on top, season with salt and black pepper and garnish with the basil.

—*Francesco Ricchi*

JAMAICAN GOLDEN SPLIT PEA SOUP

Alicia Campbell makes this soup from her native Jamaica; she is the talented assistant of my friend Cecily Brownstone, the former food editor of the Associated Press.

Makes About 3 Quarts

1 pound yellow split peas, rinsed
3 quarts Light Chicken or Turkey
  Broth (recipe follows)
2 large celery ribs, with or without
  leaves, thinly sliced
2 medium carrots, thinly sliced
1 large onion, chopped
1 large turnip, quartered and thinly
  sliced
1 large parsnip, peeled and thinly
  sliced
1 large scallion, white portion only,
  thinly sliced
2 large fresh thyme sprigs
¼ teaspoon ground allspice, plus more
  to taste
2 teaspoons salt
Freshly ground pepper

1. In a large saucepan, bring the split peas and broth to a boil over moderate heat. Cover and boil gently until the peas are tender, about 45 minutes.

2. Add all the remaining ingredients to the saucepan, cover and boil gently until the vegetables are very tender, about 45 minutes longer.

3. Pick out and discard the thyme sprigs. Puree the soup in batches in a food mill, food processor or blender. Season with additional allspice, salt and pepper and serve hot. *(The soup can be refrigerated for up to 5 days or frozen for several weeks.)*

—*Lydie Marshall*

LIGHT CHICKEN OR TURKEY BROTH

Buy chicken backs or necks, or turkey wings, whichever is the least expensive. Ask the butcher to cut the parts in several pieces; this gives more flavor to the broth than keeping the bones in large pieces.

Makes About 3 Quarts

3 pounds chicken backs and necks or
  turkey wings, cut into small pieces
1 pound carrots, sliced ¼ inch thick
1 large celery rib with a few leaves,
  sliced ¼ inch thick
1 large onion, halved lengthwise and
  stuck with 2 whole cloves
Several flat-leaf parsley sprigs
1 fresh thyme sprig
1 small leek, slit and washed well

1. Place the chicken parts in a large stockpot and add 5 quarts of water. Bring to a boil over high heat, skimming as necessary.

2. Add all the remaining ingredients and return to a boil. Reduce the heat and simmer until the broth is reduced to 3 quarts, about 4 hours.

3. Strain the broth, pressing on the vegetables to extract the juices. Let cool, then refrigerate. Degrease the broth before using. *(The broth can be refrigerated for up to 3 days or frozen for up to 1 month.)*

—*Lydie Marshall*

SOUPS

43

ASPARAGUS, LEEK AND NEW POTATO CHOWDER

This soup is moderately thick and delicately flavored.

6 Servings

3 tablespoons unsalted butter
2 leeks, white parts only, halved
  lengthwise and thinly sliced
  crosswise
1 pound unpeeled red potatoes, cut into
  ⅓-inch dice
6 cups chicken stock or canned
  low-sodium broth
Salt
1 teaspoon finely chopped fresh
  tarragon or ½ teaspoon dried
2 pounds medium asparagus, peeled
  and cut into ½-inch pieces
½ cup heavy cream
Freshly ground pepper
¼ cup finely chopped flat-leaf parsley

1. Melt the butter in a large saucepan. Add the leeks and cook over moderate heat, stirring occasionally, until softened, about 7 minutes. Stir in the potatoes, chicken stock, 1 teaspoon of salt and the tarragon. Bring to a boil, then cover and cook at a steady simmer until the potatoes are just tender, about 15 minutes.

2. Stir in the asparagus and cook uncovered until the vegetables are soft, about 10 minutes longer.

3. Using a slotted spoon, transfer 2 cups of the cooked vegetables to a food processor. Add the cream and puree until smooth. Stir the pureed mixture back into the saucepan and season with ½ teaspoon of pepper. *(The chowder can be refrigerated for up to 1 day.)*

4. Reheat the chowder gently. Spoon into soup bowls and garnish each serving with parsley.

—Jeannette Ferrary & Louise Fiszer

CREAM OF GARLIC SOUP

Ted Fondulas found "places with good food, service and wine in the middle of nowhere" while traveling through Europe and wanted to re-create that experience in Vermont. He does that and better at his 10-year-old restaurant, Hemingway's, set in a restored 1860 house at the foot of Killington Mountain in Vermont.

❦ The flavor components of the soup are reminiscent of smoky, garlicky Alsatian charcuterie and work well with a wine from that area. Try a gently floral, fruity 1990 Trimbach Pinot Blanc, a rich, smoky Gewürztraminer, like 1988 or 1989 Domaine Zind-Humbrecht, or a big, rich but graceful Gewürztraminer, such as 1989 or 1990 Hugel.

4 Servings

2 quarts Chicken Stock (recipe follows)
1 pound boiling potatoes, peeled and
*   cut into eighths*
½ pound smoked ham, cut into
*   1-inch pieces*
10 garlic cloves

1 leek, white part only, coarsely
*   chopped*
½ cup heavy cream
Salt and freshly ground white pepper
Minced flat-leaf parsley, for garnish

1. In a large saucepan, bring the stock to a boil and cook until reduced to 6 cups, about 15 minutes.

2. Add the potatoes, ham, garlic and leek and cook, stirring frequently, for 10 minutes. Return to a boil, then reduce the heat to low and simmer, stirring occasionally, until the potatoes and leek are very tender and the flavors blended, about 2 hours.

3. In a food processor, puree the soup in batches until smooth. Strain the soup back into the saucepan through a coarse sieve. Add the heavy cream and cook over moderate heat, stirring frequently, until heated through. Season with salt and white pepper to taste. Ladle the soup into bowls, garnish with parsley and serve.

—Ted Fondulas

CHICKEN STOCK

Makes About 2 Quarts

7 pounds chicken backs and wings
2 medium onions, quartered
3 celery ribs, halved lengthwise

1. In a stockpot, combine the chicken parts, onions and celery and 3 quarts of cold water. Bring to a boil over high heat. Reduce the heat to moderately low, cover partially and simmer for 2 hours.

2. Strain the broth through a colander set over a large bowl, pressing with a wooden spoon to extract all the juices; discard the solids. Refrigerate the stock for up to 3 days. Skim off the fat before using. *(The stock can be frozen for up to 1 month.)*

—F&W

MILANESE VEGETABLE SOUP

There are probably as many versions of minestrone as there are Italian cooks. This recipe, sampled at the Antica Trattoria della Pesa in Milan, includes the region's famed arborio rice.

8 to 10 Servings

1 cup dried white beans, such as navy
*   beans, rinsed and picked over*
Boiling water
4 tablespoons unsalted butter
2 ounces pancetta, minced (½ cup)
2 medium onions, minced
4 medium carrots, cut into ⅓-inch dice
2 large celery ribs, with leaves, cut into
*   ⅓-inch dice*
½ pound green beans, cut in ½-inch
*   lengths*
½ pound cabbage, cored and
*   shredded*
2 medium boiling potatoes, cut into
*   ⅓-inch dice*
One 16-ounce can imported crushed
*   plum tomatoes with their juice*
Sea salt
Freshly ground pepper
¾ cup arborio rice
Freshly grated Parmesan cheese

1. Place the beans in a large bowl and cover with boiling water. Set aside to soak for 1 hour. Drain the beans, discarding the water. Set aside.

2. In a heavy 6-quart nonreactive stockpot, melt the butter over low heat.

Add the pancetta and onions and stir to coat with the fat. Cook until the onions are soft and translucent, 3 to 4 minutes. Stir in the carrots, celery and white beans and cook for 5 minutes.

3. Stir in the green beans, cabbage, potatoes, tomatoes and 8 cups of water. Season with sea salt and pepper. Cover and simmer until the white beans are soft, about 1½ hours. (Cooking time will vary according to the freshness of the beans.)

4. Add the rice and simmer, covered, just until the rice is tender but still slightly firm to the bite, about 20 minutes more.

5. To serve, ladle the piping hot soup into warm shallow bowls and pass the cheese separately. (*The soup can be refrigerated and reheated over a period of several days. It will thicken, so add water each time you reheat it.*)

—*Patricia Wells*

ARTICHOKE AND POTATO STEW WITH MINT

Serve the stew with garlic-rubbed grilled bread for sopping up the juices.

4 Servings

4 medium artichokes
½ of a lemon
3 medium boiling potatoes (about ¾ pound)
¼ cup extra-virgin olive oil, plus more for drizzling
3 large garlic cloves—2 finely chopped, 1 halved
3 tablespoons chopped flat-leaf parsley
¼ cup chopped fresh mint
Salt and freshly ground pepper
4 thick slices of country bread
Freshly grated Pecorino Romano cheese (optional)

1. Snap back and pull off all the tough outer leaves of the artichokes. Cut off the tops of the remaining leaves, leaving about 1 inch of tender, pale yellow leaves. Using a small sharp knife, peel off the tough, dark green areas around the base of the hearts and the stems. Rub the lemon half over the cut portions of the artichokes to prevent discoloration. Cut the stems into 1-inch-long pieces. Quarter each artichoke lengthwise and cut away the hairy chokes. Then cut each quarter in half lengthwise.

2. Peel the potatoes. Cut each one in eighths and rinse in cold water.

3. In a medium nonreactive saucepan just large enough to hold the vegetables, warm the ¼ cup oil over moderately low heat. Add the chopped garlic and cook until fragrant, 2 to 3 minutes. Add the artichokes, potatoes, parsley and mint and season with salt and pepper. Cook, stirring, until heated through, 2 to 3 minutes. Add 1 cup of water, cover and cook over moderate heat, stirring occasionally, until the vegetables are tender, about 20 minutes.

4. Just before serving, grill or toast the bread. Rub with the halved garlic clove and drizzle lightly with olive oil.

5. Ladle the vegetables and their juices into shallow soup bowls. Grind pepper over the top and sprinkle with a few drops of olive oil. If desired, dust lightly with cheese. Serve the garlic toast alongside.

—*Viana La Place*

NEW ENGLAND CHEDDAR CHEESE SOUP

🍷 A lightly herbaceous 1991 California Sauvignon Blanc, such as Buena Vista or Silverado, is crisp enough to serve as an aperitif and would contrast well with the flavors of the soup.

8 Servings

1 tablespoon unsalted butter
2 medium onions, coarsely chopped
2 Idaho potatoes (1 pound), peeled and cut into 1-inch cubes
1½ tablespoons minced garlic
6 cups chicken stock or canned low-sodium broth
½ teaspoon dry mustard
2 cups heavy cream
2 cups grated sharp or smoked Cheddar cheese (7 ounces)
¼ teaspoon hot pepper sauce
2 dashes of Worcestershire sauce
½ teaspoon salt
½ teaspoon freshly ground pepper
3 tablespoons chopped fresh chives

1. In a medium saucepan, melt the butter over moderate heat. Add the onions, potatoes and garlic and cook, stirring occasionally, until the onions are translucent, about 10 minutes; do not let them brown. Add the chicken stock and bring to a boil over high heat. Reduce the heat to moderate and simmer until the potatoes are tender, about 12 minutes.

2. Working in batches, puree the soup in a food processor or blender until smooth.

3. In a large saucepan, whisk the dry mustard into the cream and bring to a

boil over high heat. Reduce the heat to moderate and simmer for 3 minutes. Stir in the pureed soup and simmer, stirring occasionally, for 4 minutes. *(The recipe can be prepared to this point up to 2 days ahead; cover and refrigerate. Reheat before proceeding.)*

4. Stir in the grated cheese and stir until just melted. Season with the hot sauce, Worcestershire sauce, salt and pepper. Sprinkle with the chives and serve at once.

—Larry Forgione

THREE MUSHROOM SOUP

For this soup, use whatever varieties of dried mushrooms you can find.

❦ A California Blanc de Noir, such as NV Domaine Chandon or 1987 S. Anderson, would provide an attractive contrast to the soup.

8 Servings

½ cup dried porcini mushrooms (¾ ounce)
1 cup dried morels (⅔ ounce)
2 tablespoons unsalted butter
1 medium onion, chopped
1 pound white mushrooms, chopped
6 cups Rich Chicken Stock (recipe follows)
Salt and freshly ground pepper
½ cup sour cream or yogurt, or a combination
¼ cup chopped fresh chives or slivered scallions

1. In a medium bowl, soak the porcini and morels in 1½ cups of hot wa-ter for 30 minutes. Strain the soaking liquid, leaving the grit behind, and reserve. If the mushrooms feel at all sandy, clean them under running water with a soft brush. Coarsely chop the mushrooms.

2. In a large heavy saucepan, melt the butter. Add the onion and cook over moderately low heat until translucent, about 5 minutes. Add the white mushrooms and cook, stirring, until they release their liquid, about 2 minutes. Stir in the dried mushrooms and increase the heat to moderately high. Cook for 1 minute.

3. Stir in the Rich Chicken Stock and the reserved mushroom soaking liquid. Simmer gently for 20 minutes, then season with salt and pepper. Pour into warm soup bowls. Garnish each serving with 1 tablespoon of the sour cream and a sprinkling of chives.

—Evan Jones

RICH CHICKEN STOCK

Makes 1½ Quarts

7 pounds chicken backs and wings
2 onions, quartered
3 celery ribs, halved lengthwise

1. In a stockpot, bring 3 quarts of water to a boil. Add the chicken parts and boil for 1 minute. Drain and rinse the chicken under cold water. Return the chicken to the pot. Add the onions, celery and 3 quarts of cold water. Cover and bring to a boil over high heat. Reduce the heat to moderately low, cover partially and simmer for 4 hours.

2. Strain the stock, then boil it down to 6 cups. Let cool, then cover and refrigerate for up to 3 days. Skim off the fat before using. *(The stock can be frozen for up to 1 month.)*

—F&W

PROVENCALE SEAFOOD SOUP

You can substitute skinned striped bass fillets for the orange roughy.

❦ The briny Mediterranean flavors in this soup are a classic match with a chilled, dry, assertive Bandol Rosé, such as 1991 Domaine Tempier or 1991 Domaines Ott; alternatively, consider a crisp, lean Sauvignon Blanc, such as 1991 Murphy-Goode "Reserve Fumé."

6 to 8 Servings

1 medium red bell pepper
1 medium yellow bell pepper
⅓ cup olive oil
1 bunch of leeks, white and tender green only, thinly sliced crosswise (2 cups)
1 fennel bulb (12 ounces), finely sliced and feathery fronds chopped
1 medium onion, finely chopped
1 tablespoon fresh thyme or 2 teaspoons dried
1 teaspoon turmeric
½ teaspoon crushed red pepper
1½ cups dry white wine
Four 8-ounce bottles clam juice
1 pound plum tomatoes—peeled, seeded and cut into ¼-inch dice —or 1½ cups canned Italian peeled tomatoes, drained and chopped
2 pounds mussels, scrubbed and debearded
½ pound medium shrimp, shelled and deveined
1 pound orange roughy fillets, cut into 1-inch cubes

½ pound sea scallops
½ cup shredded fresh basil (about 20
    leaves)
Salt and freshly ground black pepper

1. Roast the bell peppers directly over a gas flame, turning frequently, until blackened all over. Place them in a paper bag and let steam for 10 minutes. Under running water, remove the blackened skins, cores, seeds and ribs. Slice the peppers ⅛ inch thick.

2. In a large enameled cast-iron casserole, heat the olive oil. Add the leeks, fennel and onion, cover and cook over moderate heat for 10 minutes. Add the thyme, turmeric and crushed red pepper. Cook, stirring occasionally, until fragrant, about 5 minutes.

3. Add the wine to the casserole and boil over high heat until almost evaporated, 5 to 7 minutes. Add the clam juice and boil until reduced by half, about 12 minutes.

4. Stir in half the tomatoes, all of the mussels and the shrimp. Cover and cook for 3 minutes. Add the orange roughy and scallops and cook, covered, until the seafood is just cooked through, 3 to 4 more minutes.

5. Stir in the remaining tomatoes, the bell peppers and basil and cook until heated through, 3 to 5 minutes. Season with salt and black pepper. Garnish the soup with a sprinkling of the chopped fennel fronds.

—Ann Chantal Altman

LOBSTER AND COCONUT MILK SOUP WITH GINGER, LEMON GRASS AND A GARDEN OF VEGETABLES

This recipe is Fleur de Lys's first deviation from its traditional French menu. Hubert Keller, chef and co-owner of this San Francisco restaurant, spent three years in Brazil, where he got his inspiration for combining lobster and coconut milk in this soup. As a vegetarian alternative, he likes the broth without lobster. It can be made two days ahead.

❢ To complement the lobster and broth, try a spicy, rich, aromatic Gewürztraminer from Alsace, such as 1989 Trimbach or Zind-Humbrecht, or a powerful, fruity, full-bodied California Chardonnay, such as 1988 Sonoma-Cutrer Les Pierres.

4 to 6 Servings

5 cups unsweetened coconut milk*
1 cup dry white wine
¼ cup plus 2 tablespoons fresh lemon
    juice
4 stalks of fresh lemon grass,* tops
    trimmed and bulb crushed
½ pound fresh ginger, peeled and
    minced
1 celery rib, coarsely chopped
¼ cup minced fresh coriander (cilantro)
1 tablespoon minced garlic
Salt and freshly ground pepper
One 1½-pound live lobster
1 tablespoon olive oil
1 medium onion, halved lengthwise and
    thinly sliced
1 medium carrot, thinly sliced
1 small leek, white and tender green
    only, halved lengthwise and thinly
    sliced crosswise
10 medium shiitake mushrooms, caps
    only, minced
3 ounces thin French green beans, cut

into 1-inch pieces
¼ cup coarsely chopped fresh basil
2 tablespoons finely chopped chives
1 large tomato—peeled, seeded and cut
    into ⅓-inch dice
*Available at Asian markets

1. In a large nonreactive casserole, combine the coconut milk, wine, lemon juice, lemon grass, ginger, celery, coriander, garlic and ½ teaspoon each of salt and pepper. Bring to a boil over moderately high heat. Add the lobster, cover and cook for 10 minutes. Remove from the heat. Transfer the lobster to a platter and let cool. Strain the cooking liquid and reserve.

2. Twist off the lobster tail. Using shears, cut along the underside of the tail shell; separate the shell and remove the meat. Twist off the claws and crack them. Remove the meat. Cut the lobster meat into ½-inch pieces. Set aside.

3. In a large saucepan, heat the olive oil over moderately high heat. Add the onion, carrot, leek and shiitakes and cook, stirring, for 2 minutes. Add the reserved coconut broth and the green beans and bring to a boil. Reduce the heat to moderately low and simmer gently until the vegetables are tender, about 5 minutes. (The soup can be prepared to this point up to 1 day ahead. Let cool, then cover and refrigerate overnight. Wrap the lobster meat and refrigerate separately. Rewarm the soup over moderate heat before continuing.)

4. Stir in the lobster meat, basil, chives and tomato and bring the soup to a boil over moderately high heat. Season with salt and pepper to taste and serve immediately.

—*Hubert Keller*

CORN SOUP WITH ROASTED PEPPERS AND CRAB

6 to 8 Servings

2 large red bell peppers
2 large green bell peppers
2 teaspoons cumin seeds
6 tablespoons unsalted butter
1 large red onion, finely diced
3 garlic cloves, minced
1 to 2 serrano chiles or jalapeño
*   peppers, seeded and finely chopped*
¼ cup all-purpose flour
5 cups chicken stock or canned
*   low-sodium broth*
Three 10-ounce packages frozen corn,
*   thawed, or 6 cups fresh kernels*
1 pound lump crabmeat, picked over
3 tablespoons fresh lime juice
3 tablespoons chopped fresh coriander
*   (cilantro)*
Salt and freshly ground black pepper

1. Roast the bell peppers directly over a gas flame, turning frequently, until blackened all over. Place them in a paper bag and let steam for 10 minutes. Under running water, remove the blackened skins, cores, seeds and ribs. Cut the peppers into ¼-inch dice.

2. In a small skillet, toast the cumin seeds over high heat, shaking the pan, until fragrant, about 50 seconds; let cool. Grind the seeds in a spice mill or finely chop them with a knife.

3. In a large saucepan, melt the butter. Add the onion and cook over moderately high heat, stirring occasionally, until translucent, about 5 minutes. Add the garlic, serrano chiles and cumin seeds and cook, stirring, until fragrant, about 3 minutes. Stir in the flour and cook for 1 more minute. Slowly whisk in the chicken stock and bring to a simmer. Add the corn and roasted peppers and simmer over high heat for 6 minutes. Reduce the heat to low and simmer for 5 minutes longer.

4. Just before serving, add the crabmeat, lime juice and coriander and cook just until heated through. Season with salt and black pepper.

—*Ann Chantal Altman*

SPICY TOMATO-MUSSEL SOUP

This soup comes from La Capannina di Sante, a simple family fish restaurant in Florence, where the chef and owner, Sante Collesano, serves the mussels in their shells. Use the freshest, smallest mussels you can possibly find.

♟ Any young, crisp, chilled white wine would be fine here. Try a Tuscan white—Bianco di Toscana—from Antinori, Brolio or Castello di Volpaia.

4 Servings

½ cup plus 1 tablespoon extra-virgin
*   olive oil*
12 plump garlic cloves, peeled
¾ teaspoon crushed red pepper
One 28-ounce can imported Italian
*   peeled tomatoes or crushed tomatoes*
*   in tomato puree*

Sea salt
1 small onion, minced
1 cup dry white wine, such as
*   Chardonnay*
A handful of flat-leaf parsley stems,
*   tied in a bundle with string, plus ¼*
*   cup coarsely chopped parsley*
4 pounds small mussels, scrubbed and
*   debearded*
Freshly ground black pepper
8 thick slices of country bread, toasted
*   and rubbed with fresh garlic, for*
*   serving*

1. In a heavy, medium, nonreactive saucepan, combine 6 tablespoons of the oil, the garlic and crushed red pepper. Cook over moderate heat until the garlic becomes fragrant and the pepper begins to color the oil, 2 to 3 minutes. If using whole canned tomatoes, place a food mill over the saucepan and puree the tomatoes directly into it. Crushed tomatoes can be added directly from the can. Cover and simmer just until the sauce begins to thicken, 10 to 12 minutes. Season with sea salt.

2. In a large flameproof casserole, combine the remaining 3 tablespoons oil with the onion, wine and parsley stems and bring to a boil over high heat. Boil for 2 minutes. Stir in the mussels and sprinkle generously with black pepper. Cover and cook just until the mussels open, about 5 minutes. Remove the mussels as they open; do not overcook. Discard any mussels that do not open.

3. Place 2 slices of toasted garlic bread at an angle at the edge of 4 warm shallow soup bowls. With a slotted spoon, transfer the mussels to the bowls. Line a fine sieve with moistened cheesecloth and place the sieve over the saucepan of tomato sauce. Strain the mussel-cooking liquid through the cheesecloth, stopping when you reach the grit at the bottom. Simmer for 1 to

2 minutes to blend the flavors. Taste for seasoning. Spoon the sauce over the mussels, and sprinkle each serving with 1 tablespoon of the chopped parsley. Serve immediately.

—*Patricia Wells*

TUSCAN CHICKEN AND ARTICHOKE SOUP

This soup should be served with a densely textured peasant bread so that you can mop up the last drops.

6 Servings

1 ounce dried porcini mushrooms
4 large artichokes (about 9 ounces each)
¼ cup plus 2 tablespoons fresh lemon juice
2 tablespoons tomato paste
2½ cups chicken stock or canned low-sodium broth
4 skinless, boneless chicken breast halves
¼ cup plus 2 tablespoons good-quality olive oil
1 medium red onion, minced
3 garlic cloves, minced
½ cup finely chopped flat-leaf parsley
Freshly ground pepper
1 tablespoon plus 1 teaspoon all-purpose flour
½ cup dry white wine
Salt

1. Cover the dried mushrooms with 1 cup of very hot water. Let stand until softened, about 20 minutes.

2. Using a sharp knife, cut off the artichoke stems and peel off the dark outer leaves near the base. Cut off the crowns to within 2 inches of the base and trim off the dark skin from the artichoke bottoms. Scrape out the hairy chokes with a spoon and cut each artichoke into quarters. Cut each quarter into ⅛-inch-thick slices and add to a bowl of water mixed with 3 tablespoons of the lemon juice.

3. Remove the porcini mushrooms from the soaking liquid and finely chop them. Carefully pour the soaking liquid into a bowl, stopping when you reach the grit at the bottom. Stir in the tomato paste until dissolved.

4. In a medium skillet, bring the stock to a boil. Add the chicken, cover and simmer over low heat for 8 minutes. Remove from the heat and let stand covered.

5. In a large nonreactive saucepan, heat the oil. Add the mushrooms, onion, garlic and 6 tablespoons of the parsley and cook over moderately high heat, stirring, until the vegetables are soft and aromatic, about 5 minutes.

6. Drain the artichokes and pat dry. Add them to the saucepan and season with pepper. Cook, stirring occasionally, for 5 minutes.

7. Remove the chicken breasts from the stock. Cut them into thin strips, about ⅛ by 1½ inches long. Add the stock and mushroom liquid to the saucepan and bring to a simmer. Stir the flour into the white wine to make a slurry and stir it into the saucepan. Simmer for 10 minutes. *(The soup can be prepared to this point up to 3 days ahead. Refrigerate the chicken separately. Reheat the soup before proceeding.)* Add the chicken to the soup, season with salt and pepper and cook until heated through. Stir in the remaining 2 tablespoons chopped parsley and 1 to 3 tablespoons of lemon juice (to taste) and serve hot.

—*Ann Chantal Altman*

CHINESE CHICKEN SOUP WITH RICE

4 to 6 Servings

2 quarts chicken stock or canned low-sodium broth
4 cups water
1 large bone-in chicken breast half, with skin (12 ounces)
¾ cup medium-grain Asian rice, such as Nishiki
1 medium leek, white and tender green only, cut into 2-by-¼-inch strips
1 nickel-size slice of fresh ginger, peeled and bruised
Salt and freshly ground white pepper
2 tablespoons thinly sliced scallion greens
Oriental sesame oil and chili oil, for serving

1. In an enameled cast-iron casserole, bring the chicken stock and water to a rolling boil over high heat. Add the chicken breast and return to a boil. Immediately cover the pan, reduce the heat to maintain a strong simmer and cook for 6 minutes. Remove from the heat and let the chicken steep for 15 minutes. Do not lift the lid during the cooking or steeping process. Transfer the chicken breast to a large bowl of ice water and let stand, completely submerged, for 16 minutes.

2. Strain the cooking liquid into a large saucepan and skim off any fat. Boil over high heat until reduced to 9 cups, about 45 minutes. Let cool completely, then cover and refrigerate.

3. Pat the chicken dry. Discard the skin and bones and trim the membranes and tendons. Tear the chicken into 2-inch shreds following the grain. *(The recipe can be prepared to this point up to 2 days ahead. Refrigerate the stock and chicken separately.)*

4. Place the rice in a large bowl and cover with cold water. Stir with your fingers until the water is milky, then drain the rice. Repeat this process several times until the water is clear.

5. In a large saucepan, combine the drained rice with the leek, ginger and chicken stock and bring to a boil. Simmer over moderate heat for 2 minutes. Stir well, cover and simmer gently over low heat, stirring occasionally, until the rice has almost melted in the broth and the soup is thick like porridge, about 1 hour. Discard the ginger.

6. Add the shredded chicken to the soup and stir gently until heated through. Season with salt and white pepper and serve in warmed bowls, garnished with a sprinkling of scallion greens. Serve the sesame oil and chili oil alongside.

—*Leslie Newman*

TURKEY-PAPRIKA SOUP WITH SPAETZLE

Spaetzle are little dumplings made from flour-and-egg dough. In this recipe the spaetzle dough is more like a loose batter and cooks very quickly.

6 Servings

1½ tablespoons unsalted butter
1 medium onion, chopped
½ pound shiitake mushrooms, stemmed, caps quartered
2½ teaspoons sweet Hungarian paprika
2½ teaspoons hot Hungarian paprika
1 teaspoon tomato paste
1½ cups plus 1½ tablespoons all-purpose flour
2 quarts Turkey Stock (recipe follows)
2 medium carrots, cut into ½-inch pieces
2 cups cubed leftover turkey
1¼ teaspoons salt
2 small eggs, beaten
¾ cup sour cream, at room temperature
Freshly ground black pepper
1 tablespoon chopped flat-leaf parsley

1. In a large heavy flameproof casserole, melt the butter over low heat. Add the onion and cook, stirring, until golden, about 5 minutes. Add the mushroom caps and cook until wilted, about 3 minutes. Stir in the sweet and hot paprika and cook until fragrant, about 2 minutes. Add the tomato paste and cook, stirring, for 1 minute. Stir in the 1½ tablespoons of flour. Increase the heat to high and gradually whisk in the stock, 2 cups at a time. Bring the soup to a boil, whisking constantly, then reduce the heat to low and simmer for 20 minutes, whisking frequently.

2. Meanwhile, in a small saucepan of boiling water, cook the carrots over moderately high heat until tender, about 8 minutes. Stir the carrots and their cooking liquid into the soup. Add the turkey meat to the soup and let simmer.

3. Bring a large saucepan of water to a boil. Meanwhile, make the spaetzle batter. In a medium bowl, combine the remaining 1½ cups flour with the salt. With a wooden spoon, beat in the eggs and 1½ cups of water until a smooth batter forms; it should be rather loose.

4. When the water boils, use a perforated spoon (the larger the holes the better) to scoop up the batter. Hold the spoon over the boiling water and tap it against the pan so the spaetzle can fall through the holes into the water in strands. The spaetzle are done as soon as they rise to the surface. Use another slotted spoon or a skimmer to transfer them to a colander to drain. Repeat with the remaining batter.

5. Stir the spaetzle into the soup. Stir the sour cream to loosen it, then slowly whisk it into the soup. Do not let the soup boil once the sour cream has been added; the sour cream may curdle. Remove the soup from the heat. Season to taste with salt and black pepper. Ladle the soup into bowls and garnish with the chopped parsley. Serve hot.

—*Marcia Kiesel*

TURKEY STOCK

Makes 4 Quarts

Leftover turkey carcass, bones, skin and
    meat
2 medium onions, chopped
1 carrot, chopped
Green tops of 3 leeks
2 bay leaves

1. Place all the ingredients in a large
stockpot and add 6 quarts of water.
Bring to a boil over high heat. Reduce
the heat to low and simmer for 2½
hours, occasionally skimming the surface with a ladle.

2. Strain the stock and let cool. Refrigerate for up to 5 days. Skim the fat
from the surface before using.

—F&W

OXTAIL AND LENTIL SOUP

🍷 A lively, light red, such as Italy's Dolcetto d'Alba, would work well with this
soup; the fruitiness of the wine balances
the heat of the sauce. Look for 1990
Aldo Conterno Bussia Soprana or 1990
Ceretto Rossana.

6 to 8 Servings

6 pounds of oxtails, cut into 2-inch
    pieces
½ cup olive oil
½ cup balsamic vinegar
2 bay leaves
2 teaspoons salt
1 tablespoon freshly ground pepper
4 large carrots, coarsely chopped
2 large Spanish onions—1 coarsely
    chopped and 1 finely diced
2 cups lentils (13½ ounces), rinsed
    and picked over

12 large garlic cloves, peeled
2 teaspoons dried thyme
2 cups drained canned Italian peeled
    tomatoes, chopped
¼ cup finely chopped flat-leaf parsley
Hot pepper sauce (optional)

1. In a large nonreactive bowl, toss
the oxtails with 2 tablespoons of the
olive oil, the vinegar, bay leaves, salt
and 2 teaspoons of the pepper. Marinate for 1 hour, tossing occasionally.

2. In a large enameled cast-iron
casserole, heat 2 tablespoons of the
olive oil. Drain the oxtails, reserving
the marinade. Add them to the casserole and cook over moderately high
heat, turning, until browned on all
sides, about 10 minutes. Add the carrots, coarsely chopped onion, marinade
and enough water to cover the oxtails
by 1 inch. Bring to a boil, skimming the
surface. Cover and simmer over low
heat until the meat is very tender,
about 2 hours.

3. Strain the oxtails, reserving the
cooking liquid. Discard the vegetables
and bay leaves. Remove the meat from
the bones, discarding any cartilage and
fat, and cut it into ½-inch pieces. Skim
the fat from the surface of the cooking liquid; there should be about 2
quarts. If necessary, add enough water to measure 2 quarts.

4. In a large saucepan, sauté the
finely diced onion in the remaining ¼
cup olive oil over moderately high heat
until translucent, about 5 minutes. Stir
in the lentils, garlic, thyme, remaining
1 teaspoon pepper and the cooking liquid and bring to a simmer. Reduce the
heat to moderate, cover and cook until the lentils are very soft, about 1 hour.

5. Transfer all of the garlic to a food
processor or blender. Add half of the
soup and puree it with the garlic. Return the puree to the pan and stir in the
tomatoes, parsley and oxtail meat. Simmer until heated through, about 3 minutes. Season with salt and hot pepper
sauce, if using, and serve hot. (The soup
can be prepared up to 3 days ahead and
refrigerated. Reheat before serving.)
—Ann Chantal Altman

MUSHROOM SOUP WITH CABBAGE ROLLS

For these little veal-stuffed rolls, use
Savoy cabbage—the loosely packed
leaves are easy to separate.

🍷 The tastes in this soup would be set
off nicely by a fruity young Pinot Noir
served slightly cool. A 1990 California
bottling, such as Sanford or Acacia St.
Clair Vineyard, is a particularly good
choice.

6 to 8 Servings

¼ cup long-grain rice, preferably
    basmati
1 head of Savoy cabbage (1½ pounds)
1¼ pounds boneless lean veal shoulder,
    trimmed and cut into 1-inch pieces
1 small onion, coarsely chopped
2 tablespoons chopped flat-leaf parsley
2 large eggs, beaten
2 teaspoons tomato paste
½ teaspoon ground allspice
½ teaspoon salt
¼ teaspoon freshly ground pepper
⅓ cup dried currants

7 cups chicken stock or canned
    low-sodium broth
2 bay leaves
10 ounces mushrooms, thinly sliced
¼ cup all-purpose flour
3 tablespoons unsalted butter, softened
1 cup heavy cream
¼ cup finely chopped fresh dill
2 tablespoons finely chopped fresh
    chives

1. In a small saucepan, cover the rice with ⅓ cup of water and bring to a boil over high heat. Reduce the heat to low, cover and cook for 8 minutes. Remove from the heat and let rest, covered, for 5 minutes. Uncover and fluff the rice.

2. Meanwhile, bring a large saucepan of salted water to a boil over high heat. Separate 20 large leaves from the head of cabbage. Add 5 of the leaves to the saucepan, cover and blanch for 3 minutes. Remove the leaves and drain. Repeat with the remaining leaves. Cut each leaf in half lengthwise, discarding the central rib.

3. Working in 2 batches, pulse the veal in a food processor until it is roughly ground. Transfer to a large bowl. Add the onion and parsley to the processor and pulse for 5 seconds. Add the eggs, tomato paste, allspice, salt and pepper and process for 5 seconds. Mix the onion puree, cooked rice and currants into the ground veal.

4. Place about 1 tablespoon of the stuffing on the inner side of a cabbage leaf. Tuck the sides over the filling, trimming the leaf if it is very long. Starting at the wide end, roll up the leaf like a cigar; the roll should be about 2

inches long. Repeat with the remaining stuffing and cabbage leaves.

5. In a large enameled cast-iron casserole, arrange the rolls snugly seam down in a single layer; a few may rest on top. Add 3 cups of the chicken stock and the bay leaves and bring to a simmer. Cover and simmer over low heat for 45 minutes. Transfer the rolls to a platter and keep warm.

6. Discard the bay leaves. Add the remaining 4 cups chicken stock and the sliced mushrooms to the casserole and simmer over moderate heat for 5 minutes. In a small bowl, combine the flour and butter to form a paste and gradually whisk it into the liquid. Cook, whisking, for 5 minutes. Stir in the heavy cream and heat through. Add the dill and chives and season with salt and pepper.

7. To serve, place 6 or 7 cabbage rolls in each bowl and ladle the hot soup on top.

—*Ann Chantal Altman*

WHITE BEAN, FENNEL AND SAUSAGE SOUP

🍷 With the following soup, which is chock-full of vegetables, macaroni and sausage, try a Dolcetto. The wildly delicious 1991 Dolcetto d'Alba from Cordero di Montezemolo in Italy's Piedmont region, for example, works like a charm. Or try a Beaujolais, such as the 1991 Sylvain Fessy Beaujolais-Villages.

8 Servings

2 teaspoons extra-virgin olive oil
1 pound sweet Italian sausage, casings
    removed
2 medium fennel bulbs (about 1
    pound), coarsely chopped
2 medium onions, sliced
3 garlic cloves, minced

½ cup coarsely chopped flat-leaf
    parsley or fresh basil, firmly
    packed
6 cups chicken stock or canned
    low-sodium broth
One 28-ounce can Italian peeled
    tomatoes and their juice
2 cups cooked white beans, such as
    cannellini or Great Northern, rinsed
    if canned
1 cup cooked elbow macaroni
Salt and freshly ground pepper
Sixteen ⅓-inch-thick slices of French
    or Italian bread, well toasted and
    rubbed with garlic
Parmigiano-Reggiano cheese
Chopped feathery fennel fronds, for
    garnish

1. In a large nonreactive saucepan, heat the oil. Crumble in the sausage and cook over high heat until well browned, about 5 minutes. Drain off all the fat. Lower the heat to moderate and add the fennel, onions, garlic and parsley. Cook until the vegetables are just crisp-tender, 10 to 15 minutes.

2. Add the chicken stock and the tomatoes with their juice. Break up the tomatoes with a spoon and bring to a boil over high heat. Lower the heat and simmer until all the vegetables are tender, about 30 minutes.

3. When ready to serve, stir in the beans and macaroni and heat through. Season with salt and pepper. Spoon the soup into wide, shallow soup bowls. Place 2 pieces of toast in the center of each bowl. Grate Parmigiano-Reggiano over the toasts and sprinkle the fennel fronds on top.

—*David Rosengarten*

FISH & SHELLFISH

BLACK BASS WITH PORT WINE

New York's Le Bernardin is renowned for its seafood prepared under the supervision of a brother and sister team, Gilbert and Maguy Le Coze. Executive Chef Eric Ripert uses Asian spices as an exciting accent for black bass. The fish must be cooked at the last minute to keep the coating crunchy. At the restaurant, this is served on a bed of wild mushrooms.

❦ Because of the port in the sauce, a red Burgundy—such as 1988 Chassagne-Montrachet or Volnay—or a red Bordeaux, such as 1985 St-Emilion Château l'Angélus, is suggested. If you prefer a white, a 1989 Mercurey from the Côte Chalonnaise has the required full body, character and acidity.

4 Servings

1 cup ruby port
½ cup sherry vinegar
1 stick (8 tablespoons) unsalted butter, softened
Salt and freshly ground pepper
¼ cup vegetable oil
Four 6-ounce skinless striped bass fillets
¼ cup Chinese five-spice powder
1 tablespoon peanut oil
1½ pounds mushrooms, such as cèpes, shiitakes or portobellos, caps only, sliced ¼ inch thick
2 large shaliots, finely chopped
1 tablespoon minced fresh parsley
1 tablespoon chopped fresh thyme

1. In a heavy, medium, nonreactive saucepan, boil the port over moderately high heat until thick and syrupy, about 10 minutes; there should be just enough liquid to thinly coat the bottom of the pan. Stir in the vinegar and boil until syrupy, about 5 minutes. Remove from the heat and whisk in the butter. Season to taste with salt and pepper. Cover to keep warm.

2. In a large skillet, heat the vegetable oil over moderately high heat. Season the fish fillets lightly with salt and pepper. Coat each fillet on both sides with the Chinese five-spice powder. Sauté the fillets in the hot pan, turning once, until crusty on the outside and opaque throughout. Transfer the fillets to a platter and keep warm.

3. In a large skillet, heat the peanut oil over moderately high heat. Add the mushrooms and cook, stirring frequently, until softened and browned. Add the shallots, parsley and thyme and cook until the shallots are translucent, 3 to 4 minutes. Season with salt and pepper.

4. To serve, arrange the mushrooms in the center of 4 plates and place the bass on top. Spoon the sauce over the fish.

—*Eric Ripert*

JULIA CHILD'S FISH EN CROUTE

On reminiscing about the enticing aromas and impressive look of the first fish en croûte she and Simone Beck made in the South of France, Julia Child says: "I shall add it again to my repertoire, even though this sumptuous style of cooking has largely disappeared due to present trends toward minimalist cuisine and fear-of-fun-with-food.

"The sauce for the fish is up to you. It could be plain melted butter with lemon wedges passed separately, lemon-butter sauce, white butter sauce or a light hollandaise—your usual recipe with a beaten egg white or two folded in at the end.

"One solemn warning: Be sure your fish is the right size for your baking equipment, your oven and your serving platter. I like to construct the fish on a lightly buttered baking sheet that will fit into a jelly-roll pan lined with a couple of folded strips of overhanging heavy-duty foil. Then I can grab the foil strips and lift the fish on its baking sheet out of the jelly-roll pan and slide it onto my handsome wooden carving board."

6 Servings

3½- to 4-pound whole striped bass, salmon or trout, or 2½ to 3 pounds of skinless salmon fillets
Salt and freshly ground white pepper
Fresh fennel, dill or tarragon plus a few sprigs of parsley
Food Processor Brioche Dough (recipe follows), chilled

SHOWSTOPPING FISH DINNER

Serves 6

Olives with Cumin (p. 20)
❦ *Champagne*

Wild Mushroom Consommé

Julia Child's Fish en Croûte (at right)
Asparagus with Tarragon Lemon Sauce (p. 28)
❦ *Sauvignon Blanc*

Buttercrunch Lettuce and Belgian Endive Salad

Chocolate Custards (p. 211) with Crème Chantilly
Café Filtre   Cognac

Unsalted butter, softened
Egg wash: 1 egg beaten with 1 teaspoon
*   water and a pinch of salt*

1. Preheat the oven to 450°. Season the fish with salt and white pepper. Stuff the cavity of the whole fish with the herb sprigs (or, if using fillets, strew them with chopped herbs). Place the fish on a lightly buttered baking sheet and place the fish and baking sheet in a jelly-roll pan.

2. Roll the chilled brioche dough into a thin rectangle. Drape it over the fish, cut off the excess and tuck the rest under the fish all around. (If desired, use the dough scraps to fashion fins, eyes, eyebrows and a mouth. Use the large end of a metal pastry tip to make "scales.") Glaze the crust with the egg wash.

3. Bake the fish until the crust starts to color nicely, about 20 minutes. Drape a sheet of foil loosely over the dough to prevent it from browning too much. Turn the oven down to 425° and bake for another 20 minutes, or until the fish's exuded juices just begin to perfume the air.

—*Julia Child*

FOOD PROCESSOR BRIOCHE DOUGH

Makes Enough for a 4-Pound Whole Fish or 2½ to 3 Pounds Fillets

1 package active dry yeast
¼ cup lukewarm water (about 105°)
½ teaspoon sugar
4 large eggs, lightly beaten
3½ cups all-purpose flour
1½ teaspoons salt
1 stick (4 ounces) cold unsalted butter,
*   cut into 12 pieces*
¼ cup lukewarm milk

1. In a quart measure, whisk the yeast with the water and sugar and let dissolve for several minutes, until it begins to foam. Whisk in the eggs.

2. Meanwhile, measure the flour into the bowl of a food processor. Add the salt and chilled butter. Process for 5 seconds, then in spurts, until the butter is completely broken up in the flour.

3. Watching carefully and with the machine on, gradually start pouring in the yeast-egg mixture and then the milk; stop pouring as soon as the dough starts balling up on the blade. (If the dough becomes too soft, it will clog the machine; if so, process in more flour by teaspoonfuls.) Process the dough for 30 seconds longer.

4. Transfer the dough to a lightly floured work surface and let rest for 2 minutes to allow the flour particles to absorb the liquids. Knead the dough vigorously by hand for a minute or two, until it is perfectly smooth. It should be soft and silky.

5. Turn the dough into an ungreased bowl, cover with plastic wrap and let rise until almost doubled in volume, about 1 hour.

6. Turn the dough out onto the work surface and pat and push it into a 16-inch oval. Fold the dough in thirds like a business letter, pressing down, and repeat the process. This redistributes the yeast for a strong second rise. Return the dough to the bowl. Cover and let rise again, until almost tripled in volume, about 2½ hours.

7. Punch the dough down to deflate it. Cover with plastic wrap, a plate and a 5-pound weight of some sort. Refrigerate the dough, punching it down every 30 minutes or so, until it is well chilled; the congealed butter will hold it down. *(The dough can be kept covered airtight in the refrigerator for 2 to 3 days.)*

—*Julia Child*

SAUTEED MONKFISH AND PORTOBELLO MUSHROOMS ON A BED OF MESCLUN

Mesclun is a mixture of young salad greens. You can make your own mesclun salad with watercress, baby Boston lettuce leaves, arugula, frisée and radicchio. The greens can be washed and spun dry early in the day, then wrapped in kitchen towels and stored in the refrigerator.

4 Servings

¼ cup plus 2 tablespoons olive oil
½ pound portobello mushrooms, caps
*   only, cut into ½-inch wedges*
1 medium garlic clove, minced
1 tablespoon chopped flat-leaf parsley
1 tablespoon plain low-fat yogurt
1 tablespoon red wine vinegar
½ teaspoon dried thyme, crumbled
Salt and freshly ground black pepper
1 teaspoon whole black peppercorns,
*   coarsely cracked*
1 pound monkfish fillets, dark portions
*   trimmed off*
2 tablespoons minced shallots
½ cup dry white wine
4 tablespoons cold unsalted butter, cut
*   into pieces*
8 cups mesclun, torn into bite-size
*   pieces if large*

1. In a large nonstick skillet, heat 1 tablespoon of the oil over moderately high heat. Add the mushrooms, garlic and parsley and cook, stirring occasionally, until the mushrooms begin to brown, about 2 minutes. Reduce the heat, cover and cook until tender,

about 5 minutes longer. Scrape the contents of the skillet into a bowl.

2. In a small bowl, whisk the yogurt, vinegar, thyme and ¼ teaspoon salt. Gradually whisk in 3 tablespoons of the oil and season with salt and freshly ground pepper.

3. Place the cracked peppercorns and ¼ teaspoon of salt on a plate. Roll the monkfish fillets in the mixture. *(The recipe can be prepared to this point up to 3 hours ahead. Refrigerate the dressing and fish.)*

4. In the large skillet, heat the remaining 2 tablespoons oil over moderately high heat. When the skillet is very hot, place the monkfish in the pan and cook, turning as necessary, until well browned on all sides, about 4 minutes. Reduce the heat to moderately low, cover and cook the fish until opaque throughout, about 5 minutes longer. Transfer to a cutting board.

5. Add the shallots and wine to the pan and boil over moderately high heat for 3 minutes. Add the juices exuded from the fish and cook until the liquid is reduced to 2 tablespoons, about 1 minute more. Remove from the heat and whisk in the butter.

6. Quickly toss the greens in a large bowl with ¼ cup of the yogurt dressing. Arrange the salad greens on 4 plates. Toss the mushrooms with the remaining dressing.

7. Slice the fish crosswise into 12 medallions. Arrange 3 medallions in the center of each salad and sprinkle the mushrooms around the fish. Spoon the warm butter sauce over the fish and serve at once.

—Lydie Marshall

BROILED SALMON WITH MUSTARD CREAM SAUCE

4 Servings

¾ cup chicken stock or canned low-sodium broth
½ cup heavy cream
2 tablespoons Dijon mustard
Salt and freshly ground pepper
Four 6-ounce salmon fillets

1. Preheat the broiler. In a small saucepan, bring the stock and heavy cream to a boil over moderately high heat. Reduce the heat to moderate and simmer until reduced by half, about 5 minutes. Whisk in the mustard and salt and pepper and bring just to a simmer. Cover and keep warm.

2. Sprinkle the salmon on both sides with salt and pepper. Broil until just cooked through, about 4 minutes per side. Transfer the fillets to warmed plates, spoon the sauce on the fish and serve.

—Stephanie Lyness

SNAZZY SALMON DINNER

Serves 4

Poached Salmon Fillets with Two Vinaigrettes (at right)

Orzo with Green and Black Olives (p. 146)

❦ Sauvignon Blanc

Tossed Salad with Herb Vinaigrette

Vanilla Ice Cream and Lemon Sorbet with Blueberries

—Bob Chambers

POACHED SALMON FILLETS WITH TWO VINAIGRETTES

If desired, serve the fish with a tossed green salad dressed with some of the herb vinaigrette (set aside about 3 tablespoons of it).

❦ Salmon goes well with a wide variety of whites and reds, but a crisp, herbaceous Sauvignon Blanc would best tolerate the added tartness of the vinaigrettes used here.

4 Servings

½ pound small beets, with ½ inch of the stems attached
Salt
3 tablespoons balsamic vinegar
1 tablespoon fresh lemon juice
2 teaspoons Dijon mustard
1 teaspoon anchovy paste
Freshly ground pepper
½ cup plus 2 tablespoons olive oil
¼ cup safflower oil
2 tablespoons finely chopped mixed fresh herbs, such as tarragon, thyme, summer savory and dill
1 small onion, cut into ¼-inch dice
One 8-ounce bottle clam juice
Four 6-ounce skinless center-cut salmon fillets

1. Place the beets in a small saucepan and add enough water to cover by ½ inch. Salt the water and bring to a boil over moderate heat. Simmer until the beets are tender, about 20 minutes. Rinse under cold running water and drain thoroughly. Peel the beets and transfer to a food processor.

2. Meanwhile, in a medium bowl, whisk together the balsamic vinegar, lemon juice, mustard, anchovy paste, 1 teaspoon pepper and ½ teaspoon salt. Slowly whisk in ½ cup of the olive oil and the safflower oil.

3. Add half of the vinaigrette to the beets in the food processor and pulse until the beets are finely chopped. Stir the chopped fresh herbs into the remaining vinaigrette in the bowl.

4. Heat the remaining 2 tablespoons oil in a large high-sided nonreactive skillet. Add the onion and cook over high heat until lightly browned, about 2 minutes. Add the clam juice, 1 cup of water and ½ teaspoon pepper and bring to a boil. Set the salmon fillets in the pan without touching and bring the liquid back to a boil. Cover the pan, remove from the heat and let stand for 4 minutes. Carefully turn the fillets over and let stand uncovered for 2 minutes longer. Using a slotted spoon, transfer the fillets to a large plate and let cool slightly.

5. To serve, spoon the beet vinaigrette onto 4 plates. Set the salmon fillets on top. Spoon the herb vinaigrette over the fish (setting aside 3 tablespoons of it to use on an accompanying salad, if desired) and serve.

—Bob Chambers

CORNMEAL-TOASTED RED SNAPPER

Have your fishmonger skin the fillets to save time. In place of the snapper, you can substitute any white-fleshed fish, such as sole, haddock, cod or catfish. The thinner the fillets, the faster they'll cook. Serve the fish with your favorite tartar sauce.

♟ Choose a light Chardonnay with fruity, floral characteristics. Top choices include 1990 Simi or 1991 White Oak.

4 Servings

⅓ cup yellow cornmeal
3 tablespoons unbleached flour
¾ teaspoon salt
¾ teaspoon freshly ground pepper

Four 6-ounce skinless red snapper fillets, about ½ to ¾ inch thick
3 tablespoons olive oil
Lime wedges, for garnish

1. On a plate, mix together the cornmeal, flour, salt and pepper. Rinse 1 snapper fillet with cold water, shake off any excess and dip both sides in the cornmeal mixture to coat. Shake off any excess and transfer the fillet to a clean plate. Repeat with the remaining fillets.

2. In a large heavy skillet, preferably cast iron, heat the oil over moderately high heat until hot, 3 to 4 minutes. Place the fish fillets in the skillet and cook, turning once, until the coating is golden brown and the flesh is opaque throughout, 6 to 7 minutes. (Reduce the heat if the fish browns too quickly.)

3. Transfer the fillets to paper towels to drain. Serve with the lime.

—Susan Shapiro Jaslove

BRAISED SNAPPER WITH SAKE AND SOY SAUCE

If mirin is unavailable, substitute the same amount of dry sherry and increase the sugar to one teaspoon.

♟ Because the savory sauce with its accents of soy and ginger would overpower a dry white (the usual pairing for snapper), choose instead a fruity-tart off-dry Riesling, such as the 1990 Deinhard Riesling Dry from Germany, or a refreshing California Gewürztraminer, such as the 1992 Alexander Valley Vineyards, to balance the salt and spice. Sake, heated in a water bath before serving, is certainly a thematically consistent option.

4 Servings

Four 6-ounce red snapper fillets with skin

⅔ cup sake
¼ cup mirin
¼ cup soy sauce
1½ tablespoons slivered fresh ginger
⅛ teaspoon sugar
1 scallion, green part only, thinly sliced on the diagonal

1. Make 3 shallow slashes through the skin of the snapper fillets to keep them from curling.

2. In a large skillet, combine the sake, mirin, soy sauce, ginger and sugar and bring to a simmer over high heat. Add the fish, skin-side up, in a single layer. Cover and simmer over moderate heat until just cooked through, about 4 minutes. Transfer the snapper to large plates, spoon a little sauce over each fillet and sprinkle with the scallion greens.

—Stephanie Lyness

TUNA, SWORDFISH OR STURGEON ALABARDERO

The menus from around the world that decorate Ambria in Chicago are, according to the chef and owner Gabino Sotelino, his tribute to the many chefs who have inspired him. This recipe is Catalonian, and Sotelino offers it as a special only when he gets exquisitely fresh fish.

♟ The mild fish and flavorful sauce call for a delicate but fruity white, such as 1990 Albariño Martin Codax from Rías Baixas in Spain, or a Riesling from Alsace, such as 1990 Schlossberg Domaine Weinbach or 1988 Herrenweg Turckheim Zind-Humbrecht.

FISH & SHELLFISH

58

6 Servings

SAUCE

1 yellow bell pepper
½ cup plus 2 teaspoons olive oil
1 shallot, finely chopped
½ cup fish stock or water
¼ cup semisweet white wine, such as dry Riesling
4 small yellow tomatoes (¾ pound), chopped
1 tablespoon sherry vinegar
2 teaspoons chopped fresh tarragon
Salt and freshly ground black pepper

1 medium eggplant, peeled and cut into ¼-inch dice
¼ cup plus 2 tablespoons olive oil
2 garlic cloves, finely chopped
2 shallots, finely chopped
1 medium zucchini, cut into ¼-inch dice
2 large red tomatoes—peeled, seeded and cut into ¼-inch dice
1 small lemon
1 lime
Six 6-ounce center-cut fillets of tuna, swordfish or sturgeon
1 tablespoon chopped fresh chives
6 oil-cured black olives, pitted and cut in small dice

1. *Make the sauce:* Roast the yellow bell pepper directly over a gas flame or under the broiler as close to the heat as possible, turning often, until charred all over. Put the pepper in a paper bag to steam for a few minutes. Peel the pepper and discard the core and seeds. Coarsely chop the pepper.

2. In a small nonreactive saucepan, heat the 2 teaspoons olive oil over low heat. Add the shallot and cook until softened, about 2 minutes. Add the fish stock, wine, yellow tomatoes and the roasted yellow pepper. Increase the heat to high and boil until the liquid has reduced by half, about 10 minutes.

3. Pour the mixture into a coarse strainer set over a blender. Using a rubber spatula, press to extract all the tomato pulp, leaving behind the skins and the shallot. Add the vinegar and blend to a puree. With the machine on, pour in the remaining ½ cup olive oil to emulsify the sauce. Pour the sauce into a clean nonreactive saucepan. Add the tarragon and season with salt and black pepper to taste. Cover to keep warm.

4. Put the diced eggplant in a colander, sprinkle with ¼ teaspoon salt and toss well. Weight the eggplant down with a plate and set the colander on a plate or in the sink. Let the eggplant drain for 20 minutes.

5. In a large nonreactive skillet, heat 2 tablespoons of the olive oil over low heat. Add the garlic and shallots and cook for 2 minutes. Increase the heat to high and stir in the diced eggplant and the zucchini. Cook, stirring frequently, until the vegetables are tender, about 5 minutes. Add the diced red tomatoes and season with salt and black pepper to taste. Remove from the heat and cover to keep warm.

6. Using a sharp knife, peel the lemon and lime. Cut in between the membranes to release the sections. Cut the sections in small dice.

7. In a large skillet, heat 2 tablespoons of the olive oil over high heat until very hot. Season 3 pieces of fish on both sides with salt and pepper and put in the skillet. Cook the fish, turning once, until well browned, about 2 minutes per side. Transfer the fish to a plate and repeat with the remaining 2 tablespoons olive oil and 3 pieces of fish.

8. *To serve:* Thickly slice each piece of fish on the diagonal. Arrange the slices in a half-moon pattern on each dinner plate. Spoon the vegetables around the fish. Spoon the yellow tomato sauce around the vegetables. Sprinkle the chives over all and garnish the vegetables with the diced lemon, lime and black olives. Serve hot.

—*Gabino Sotelino*

A NEW TAKE ON TUNA

Serves 4

Seared Fresh Tuna Niçoise (at right) with Mustard-Anchovy Vinaigrette (p. 242)

Italian Bread

Garlic Butter

♟ Bandol Rosé

Fresh Blueberry Tart (p. 199)
—*Susan Shapiro Jaslove*

SEARED FRESH TUNA NICOISE

The process of searing (browning quickly over high heat) seals in juices and develops color and flavor. For this recipe, buy tuna that is dark red, such as yellowfin.

4 Servings

1½ pounds small red potatoes, cut into ¾-inch pieces
2 tablespoons olive oil
1 pound green beans, trimmed and cut into 1-inch pieces
Four 5-ounce fresh tuna steaks (about ½ inch thick)
1 teaspoon freshly ground pepper
½ teaspoon salt
Mustard-Anchovy Vinaigrette (p. 242)
2 medium tomatoes, cut into ½-inch dice
¼ cup Niçoise olives, for garnish

1. In a large saucepan, cover the potatoes with salted water and bring to a boil over high heat. Boil until tender, about 10 minutes. Drain and reserve in a medium bowl.

2. Heat a large cast-iron skillet over moderately high heat until hot but not smoking. Add 1 tablespoon of the oil, then the green beans; watch out for spattering. Stir-fry until lightly browned and crisp-tender, about 5 minutes. Remove the skillet from the heat and transfer the beans to a bowl.

3. Season both sides of the tuna steaks with the pepper and salt. Return the skillet to moderately high heat and add the remaining 1 tablespoon oil. Add the tuna steaks and cook, turning once, until browned on the outside and medium-rare on the inside, about 2 minutes per side. Transfer the tuna to warm plates.

4. Toss 3 tablespoons of the Mustard-Anchovy Vinaigrette with the potatoes. Stir 1 tablespoon of the dressing into the tomatoes and 1 tablespoon into the green beans. Drizzle the rest over the tuna.

5. Neatly distribute the vegetables around the fish and garnish with the olives. Serve immediately.
—*Susan Shapiro Jaslove*

MARINATED FILET MIGNON OF TUNA

Flavorful, unfussy food is the mainstay of Manhattan's Union Square Cafe. The owner Danny Meyer came up with this signature recipe as an alternative to the classic fillet of beef. Look for the reddest tuna you can find and have it cut into steaks that are at least three inches thick and wide. Don't overmarinate the fish, or it will be cooked before it gets to the grill. For an alternative to the greens, try braised baby bok choy.

🍷 Either a 1991 Sauvignon Blanc from Steltzner Vineyards in Napa or a 1990 Bordeaux Blanc Château Clos Floridene will do well. If you want a red, try 1989 Côtes du Rhône, Château de Fonsalette. Each has the necessary smoky flavor with a little bit of sweetness to go with the ginger on the tuna.

4 Servings

2 cups teriyaki sauce
½ cup dry sherry
Juice of 2 lemons
2 medium scallions, coarsely chopped
¼ cup finely chopped fresh ginger
2 garlic cloves, minced
2 tablespoons freshly ground black pepper
½ teaspoon cayenne pepper

Four 10-ounce yellowfin tuna steaks, each 3 inches thick
4 baby eggplants or zucchini, halved lengthwise and each half sliced lengthwise 4 to 5 times in a fan
¼ cup plus 2 tablespoons olive oil
1 pound mixed greens—such as spinach, kale, Swiss chard and dandelion—cleaned and stemmed
Salt
¼ cup Japanese pickled ginger

1. In a medium bowl, whisk the teriyaki sauce, sherry, lemon juice, scallions, ginger, garlic, black pepper and cayenne.

2. Place the tuna steaks in a large, shallow, nonreactive dish. Pour three-quarters of the marinade on top and turn the tuna to coat. Refrigerate for 2 to 3 hours, turning occasionally. Place the eggplant fans in another shallow dish and pour the remaining marinade on top; turn to coat completely. Let marinate at room temperature for 1 hour.

3. In a large skillet, heat ¼ cup of the olive oil over high heat, then toss in the greens and cook, stirring constantly, until wilted, about 2 minutes. Add ½ cup of water and cook the greens just until tender, but not overdone or discolored, about 1 minute longer. Drain well, season with salt and black pepper to taste, cover and keep warm.

4. Preheat the broiler. Drain the tuna steaks and the eggplants. In a large skillet, heat the remaining 2 tablespoons olive oil over high heat until smoking. Add the tuna steaks and cook, turning with a spatula, until nicely

charred on all 6 sides and the centers are barely warm, about 2 minutes per side.

5. Meanwhile, arrange the eggplant fans on a large baking sheet and broil, rotating the pan, until browned evenly all over, about 4 minutes.

6. To serve, place each tuna steak on a small bed of the cooked greens. Garnish each plate with a fanned eggplant and top each steak with 1 tablespoon of the pickled ginger.

—*Danny Meyer*

GRILLED LIME-GLAZED SEAFOOD KEBABS

8 Servings

1 pound large shrimp in their shells
1 pound sea scallops
1 pound swordfish, cut into 2-inch
*   chunks*
¼ cup fresh lime juice
1 teaspoon sugar
⅔ cup extra-virgin olive oil
Freshly ground pepper

1. Using kitchen shears, snip down the back of each shrimp shell and remove the veins. Place the shrimp, scallops and swordfish in a large bowl.

2. In a small bowl, mix the lime juice and sugar with a fork until the sugar dissolves. Beat in the olive oil until blended.

3. Pour the marinade over the seafood and stir to make sure every piece is well coated. Season with pepper, cover the bowl and refrigerate for 2 to 6 hours.

4. Light a grill with a rack set 4 to 5 inches above the coals. The fire is ready when you have a good thick bed of glowing coals.

5. Skewer the seafood horizontally through the middle. Use only one type of seafood on each skewer as they all tend to cook at different rates. Set the skewers on the grill and brush the seafood with some of the marinade. Grill for about 3 minutes per side, turning once and brushing once more with the marinade, until the seafood is just cooked through; the shrimp should be pink, with papery shells, the scallops firm and white and the swordfish just beginning to flake. Serve immediately.

—*Nancy Harmon Jenkins*

GARLIC-CLAM PIZZA WITH THYME

This is an adaptation of the famous clam pie served at Pepe's in New Haven, Connecticut. The sharp bite of fresh thyme suits this pizza beautifully. ❦ This crusty, rustic dish needs nothing more than a crisp, lively lean white to play off against the garlic, clam and pepper flavors. A straightforward Spanish white, such as 1991 Marqués de Riscal Rueda or 1991 Torres Viña Sol, would be an excellent choice.

Makes 4 Individual Pizzas

¾ cup plus 2 tablespoons very warm
*   water (about 115°)*
2 teaspoons active dry yeast
2 cups unbleached all-purpose flour
½ cup fine cornmeal, plus more for
*   sprinkling*
Salt
3 dozen littleneck clams, scrubbed

⅓ cup olive oil
6 garlic cloves, minced
¼ cup freshly grated Parmesan cheese
1 tablespoon plus 1 teaspoon chopped
*   fresh thyme*
Freshly ground black pepper
Crushed red pepper (optional)

1. Pour the warm water into a small bowl. Sprinkle the yeast on top and let it dissolve for a few minutes.

2. In a large bowl, blend the flour with the ½ cup cornmeal and ½ teaspoon of salt. Pour in the yeast mixture and mix with a wooden spoon until a soft, slightly sticky dough forms. Turn the dough out onto a lightly floured surface and knead briefly until smooth. Put the dough in a large, lightly oiled bowl, cover and set aside to rise until doubled in bulk, about 1 hour.

3. Preheat the oven to 500° and place a pizza stone, if using, on the bottom of the oven.

4. Shuck the clams over a bowl in the sink, allowing the clams and their

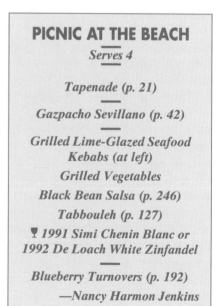

PICNIC AT THE BEACH

Serves 4

Tapenade (p. 21)

Gazpacho Sevillano (p. 42)

Grilled Lime-Glazed Seafood
Kebabs (at left)

Grilled Vegetables

Black Bean Salsa (p. 246)

Tabbouleh (p. 127)

❦ *1991 Simi Chenin Blanc or*
1992 De Loach White Zinfandel

Blueberry Turnovers (p. 192)

—*Nancy Harmon Jenkins*

liquor to fall into the bowl. When all the clams have been shucked, swish each clam around in the liquor to rinse off any sand and shell bits. Coarsely chop any clams that are not very small and put them all in a clean bowl.

5. Let the clam liquor sit for about 5 minutes so that the sand and grit settle to the bottom. Pour the clear liquor into a cup, leaving the grit behind. Measure out ¼ cup of the liquor and stir it into the shucked clams along with the olive oil and garlic.

6. Generously sprinkle cornmeal over a large flat cookie sheet. Punch down the dough and transfer it to a lightly floured work surface. Cut the dough into quarters and flatten each piece into a smooth disk. Using a rolling pin, roll 1 disk into a 9-inch round. Lift the dough with your hands and let it fall over loosely closed fists. Start stretching it by gently pulling in a circular motion until the dough is about 12 inches in diameter and very thin. Lay the dough on the prepared cookie sheet.

7. Spoon one-fourth of the clam mixture evenly over the dough to within ½ inch of the rim. Sprinkle the pizza with 1 tablespoon of the Parmesan cheese and a little salt. Shake the pan to see if the pizza is sticking; if it is, carefully lift the dough where the trouble spot is and throw some cornmeal underneath. With a quick jerk, slide the pizza off the sheet and onto the hot stone; if you are not using a stone, simply set the cookie sheet on the bottom rack of the oven.

8. Bake the pizza for about 5 minutes, until crusty brown on the bottom. Remove from the oven, season with 1 teaspoon of the thyme, black pepper and crushed red pepper if you like. Cut and eat at once. Assemble and bake the remaining pizzas.

—Marcia Kiesel

LOBSTER WITH FAVA BEAN PUREE AND BLACK TRUMPET MUSHROOMS

4 Servings

2 tablespoons red wine vinegar
4 live 1-pound lobsters
1 tablespoon olive oil
1 pound chicken backs and/or wings, cut into pieces
2 fresh rosemary sprigs
3 garlic cloves, crushed
1 large shallot, sliced
¼ cup dry vermouth
2 plum tomatoes, cut into cubes
3 cups chicken stock or canned low-sodium broth, heated
3 pounds fresh fava beans, shelled
4 tablespoons unsalted butter
1 small onion, coarsely chopped
Salt and freshly ground pepper
¼ pound fresh black trumpet mushrooms—trimmed, rinsed and patted dry

1. In a nonreactive stockpot, combine 1 gallon of water and the vinegar. Bring to a boil over high heat. Plunge in the lobsters, head first, cover the pot and return to a boil. Boil for 4 minutes, then remove the lobsters and set aside to cool. Discard the cooking water.

2. Preheat the oven to 425°. Detach the lobster tails from the bodies. Twist off the claws and crack them. Remove the meat and set aside in a bowl. Using shears, cut along the underside of the tail shells. Separate the shells to release the meat and add to the bowl. Split the lobster bodies lengthwise and pull out and discard the cottony membranes. Set aside all the shells.

3. In a shallow nonreactive roasting pan, heat the olive oil. Add the chicken parts and roast in the oven for 10 minutes. Add the reserved lobster shells, 1 sprig of rosemary, the garlic and shallot and roast for 20 minutes, stirring occasionally.

4. Add the vermouth and tomatoes and roast for 10 minutes longer. Stir in the hot chicken stock and simmer in the oven for 30 minutes.

5. Strain the liquid into a small nonreactive saucepan; discard the solids. Cook the liquid over moderately high heat until reduced to ½ cup, about 10 minutes. Set the lobster glaze aside.

6. In a large saucepan, bring 4 cups of water to a boil over high heat. Add the fava beans and blanch for 1 minute. Drain the beans in a colander and refresh under cold running water. Using your fingers, peel the beans and discard the tough skins.

7. In the same pan, melt 1½ teaspoons of the butter over moderate heat. Add the onion and the remaining rosemary sprig and cook, stirring occasionally, until softened, about 5 minutes. Add the fava beans and ½ cup water and cook until the beans are tender, 8 to 10 minutes. Discard the rosemary sprig.

8. Scrape the fava beans into a food processor. Add 2 tablespoons of the butter and puree until smooth. Season with salt and pepper to taste. *(The recipe can be made to this point up to 1 day ahead. Cover the lobster meat, lobster glaze and the fava bean puree separately and refrigerate. Return to room temperature before proceeding.)*

9. In a medium skillet, melt 1½ teaspoons of the butter over high heat. Add the mushrooms and cook, tossing, for 2 minutes. Add a pinch of salt and pepper. Remove from the heat; cover to keep warm.

10. To serve, rewarm the lobster glaze over moderate heat in a medium skillet. Stir in the remaining 1 tablespoon butter and season with pepper to taste. Reduce the heat to very low, add the lobster meat and toss gently with a wooden spoon to warm through, 2 to 3 minutes. Reheat the fava bean puree in a double boiler over simmering water.

11. Spoon the puree into the center of 4 warmed deep plates. Arrange the lobster over the puree and strain about 1½ tablespoons of the glaze over each serving. Garnish with the mushrooms and serve at once.

—*Daniel Boulud*

LOBSTER FRICASSEE WITH ARTICHOKES

"Unlike a lot of vegetables, artichoke goes well with the sweetness of lobster," explains the chef Theo Schoennegger, whose food is inspired by the kitchens of Italian nobility.

♟ The lobster and mild butter sauce call for an oaky and fruity Chardonnay. A good Italian choice is 1989 Terre Rosse dei Colli Bolognesi di Monte San Pietro made by the Vallania family.

4 Servings

4 large artichokes
1 stick (4 ounces) plus 2½ tablespoons cold unsalted butter, cut into tablespoons
2 ounces pancetta, minced
1 large onion, halved lengthwise and thinly sliced
2 medium carrots, thinly sliced
2 parsley sprigs plus 1 tablespoon minced parsley
2 tablespoons fresh lemon juice
2 boiled lobsters (1½ pounds each), meat removed and cut into 1-inch chunks (about 1½ cups of meat weighing approximately ½ pound)
1 tablespoon chopped fresh tarragon
Salt and freshly ground pepper

1. Trim the stems of the artichokes. In a large steamer basket, steam the artichokes until tender, about 20 minutes. Let cool.

2. In a large saucepan, heat 2½ tablespoons of the butter over moderately high heat. Add the pancetta and cook until the fat begins to melt, about 2 minutes. Reduce the heat to moderately low and cook, stirring, until the pancetta is browned, about 7 minutes longer.

3. Add the onion, carrots and parsley sprigs and cook, stirring occasionally, until the onion is soft, about 10 minutes.

4. Meanwhile, remove the leaves from the artichokes and reserve for another use. Scoop out the hairy chokes. Cut the bottoms in 1-inch wedges and add to the onion and carrot mixture with 1 cup of water. Bring to a simmer over moderate heat and cook until the carrots are tender, about 10 minutes longer.

5. Strain and reserve the vegetables and liquid separately. Discard the parsley sprigs. Set the liquid aside for 10 minutes, then skim off as much fat as possible from the surface. Pour the liquid into a medium nonreactive saucepan and add the lemon juice. Boil over moderately high heat until it has reduced to ¼ cup, about 5 minutes. Reduce the heat to low and whisk in the remaining stick of butter, 1 tablespoon at a time, until it is thoroughly incorporated and the sauce is creamy.

6. Add the reserved vegetables, the lobster meat, minced parsley and the tarragon. Season to taste with salt and pepper. Warm just until heated through. Serve immediately.

—*Theo Schoennegger*

SEARED SCALLOPS WITH CITRUS-GINGER VINAIGRETTE

8 Servings

2 cups vegetable oil, for frying
2 large leeks, white and tender green, cut into ⅛-by-2-inch strips
1 shallot, minced
½ tablespoon minced fresh ginger
½ teaspoon finely grated lime zest
1 tablespoon fresh lime juice
1 tablespoon Champagne vinegar
1 tablespoon soy sauce
¼ cup peanut oil
Salt and freshly ground pepper
About ¼ cup olive oil
1½ pounds sea scallops, halved horizontally
3 large Belgian endives, separated into 40 spears
8 cups assorted lettuces—such as red leaf, arugula, radicchio, Boston and frisée—torn into bite-size pieces

1. In a medium skillet, heat the vegetable oil to 325°. Add half the leeks to the oil and fry, stirring occasionally, until golden, 3 to 4 minutes. Using a slotted spoon, transfer the leeks to paper towels to drain. Repeat with the remaining leeks. *(The leeks can be fried up to 6 hours ahead and kept at room temperature.)*

2. In a small bowl, combine the shallot, ginger and lime zest. Whisk in the lime juice, vinegar and soy sauce. Gradually whisk in the peanut oil and season with salt and pepper.

3. In a large skillet, heat 1 tablespoon of the olive oil until smoking. Season the scallops with salt and pepper and, working in batches, add them to the skillet in a single layer without crowding. Cook the scallops over high heat until nicely browned on the bottom and just cooked through, 1 to 2 minutes; do not turn them over. Transfer the scallops to a large plate, cover loosely with foil and keep warm. Repeat with the remaining scallop halves and olive oil.

4. In a large bowl, toss the endive spears with about 1½ tablespoons of the vinaigrette. Arrange 5 endive spears on each plate. Add the lettuces to the bowl and toss with the remaining vinaigrette. Divide the lettuces among the plates, arrange the scallops on top and garnish each serving with a little of the fried leeks. Serve immediately.

—Annie Roberts

SCALLOPS WITH PESTO CREAM SAUCE

If you can manage two skillets at once, this easy recipe will be even quicker. You can substitute bay scallops for the sea scallops, but don't halve them in Step 2. Also, reduce the cooking time.

2 Servings

¼ cup Basic Pesto (p. 246)
2 plum tomatoes—peeled, seeded and chopped
¼ cup heavy cream
1½ tablespoons fresh lemon juice
A few drops of hot pepper sauce
1 teaspoon anise-flavored liqueur
Salt and freshly ground pepper
¾ pound sea scallops, tough outer membrane removed
1 teaspoon extra-virgin olive oil

1. In a small bowl, combine the pesto, tomatoes, cream, lemon juice, hot sauce, anise liqueur and ¼ teaspoon each of salt and pepper. Stir well to blend. Set aside at room temperature for 1 hour.

2. Halve the scallops horizontally and pat dry with paper towels. Rub a large heavy skillet with ½ teaspoon of the oil; heat until very hot but not smoking. Add half the scallops in 1 layer without crowding. Cook over high heat until lightly browned, 20 to

30 seconds per side. Transfer the scallops to a dish and cover with foil to keep warm. Repeat with the remaining oil and scallops.

3. Season the scallops with ¼ teaspoon each salt and pepper. Arrange the scallops on 4 plates. Spoon 2 tablespoons of the pesto on each portion and serve.

—Carol Cutler

SHRIMP IN HOT AND SOUR BROTH

This may look like a soup, but it's not. In Thailand, *tom yum gung* is always made extremely hot and eaten with rice. We call for unshelled shrimp in this recipe, as is traditional; the shrimp look prettier, and the shells give the broth extra depth and flavor. If you would rather serve the shrimp shelled, lift them out of the broth after cooking, peel them and return them to the broth before stirring in the lime juice and fish sauce. As you savor this dish, either eat your way around the lemon grass, lime leaves and chiles or pick them out as you come to them.

To turn this dish into a meal, serve it with Plain Jasmine Rice (p. 158), a mild dish like Fried Tofu with Holy Basil (p. 116) and a plate of sliced cucumbers and tomatoes.

2 Servings

3 cups chicken stock or canned broth
2 stalks lemon grass

*5 fresh kaffir lime leaves or 8 dried
    leaves soaked in ¼ cup warm water
    for 20 minutes*
*4 to 6 bird chiles—stemmed, halved
    lengthwise and seeded*
*¼ pound oyster mushrooms, coarsely
    chopped*
*½ pound tiger shrimp or regular
    shrimp in their shells (see
    headnote)*
3 tablespoons fresh lime juice
2 tablespoons fish sauce

1. In a medium saucepan, bring the stock to a boil over moderately high heat. Meanwhile, trim off and discard the grassy upper stalks of the lemon grass and the hard root stumps. Peel off and discard the tough outer layer. Flatten the stalks with the flat side of a knife or cleaver, then cut the stalks into 1½-inch pieces.

2. When the stock is boiling, add the lemon grass, lime leaves and chiles. Simmer for 4 minutes, then add the mushrooms. Bring to a vigorous boil and add the shrimp. Cook until the shrimp have completely changed color, about 2 minutes, then remove from the heat. Stir in the lime juice and fish sauce. Serve in bowls.

—*Jeffrey Alford & Naomi Duguid*

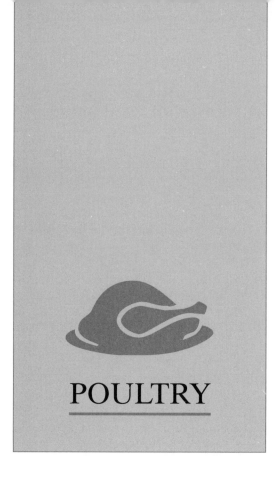

POULTRY

SAUTEED CHICKEN BREASTS WITH MUSTARD SAUCE

4 Servings

4 skinless, boneless chicken breast
  halves (about 4 ounces each)
Salt and freshly ground pepper
1 tablespoon olive oil
¾ cup dry white wine
1 tablespoon fresh lemon juice
2 teaspoons Dijon mustard
2 tablespoons unsalted butter, cut into
  small pieces

1. Pound each chicken breast half between sheets of wax paper until flattened to about ¼ inch. Season with salt and pepper.

2. In a large, heavy, nonreactive skillet, heat ½ tablespoon of the oil. Add 2 of the breast halves and sauté over moderately high heat until golden brown and just cooked through, about 1½ minutes per side. Transfer to a platter and keep warm. Sauté the remaining chicken in the remaining ½ tablespoon oil.

3. Add the wine and lemon juice to the skillet and cook over high heat, scraping up any browned bits, until the wine is reduced by half, about 2 minutes. Whisk in the mustard. Remove the pan from the heat and whisk in the butter, a few pieces at a time. Add any accumulated juices from the chicken to the sauce and season with salt and pepper. Spoon the sauce over the chicken and serve hot.

—Susan Shapiro Jaslove

POACHED CHICKEN BREASTS WITH HERB AND SHALLOT VINAIGRETTE

You can serve the chicken alongside or on top of Summer Vegetable Salad (p. 121); the flavors complement one another. The chicken also makes a great sandwich served in a roll.

8 Servings

½ of a small onion, thinly sliced
Six 1½-by-½-inch strips of lemon zest
10 whole black peppercorns
6 fresh thyme sprigs
5 parsley sprigs
3 fresh marjoram sprigs
2 bay leaves
½ teaspoon salt
8 small skinless, boneless chicken
  breast halves (about 5 ounces each)
½ cup Herb and Shallot Vinaigrette
  (p. 242)

1. In a large, straight-sided nonreactive skillet, bring 2 quarts of water and the onion, lemon zest, peppercorns, thyme, parsley, marjoram, bay leaves and salt to a simmer. Add the chicken and simmer gently, turning once or twice, until the breasts are opaque but still give a little when pressed, about 15 minutes.

2. Using tongs, transfer the chicken to a shallow glass dish with sides and baste with the Herb and Shallot Vinaigrette. Let cool.

3. Slice each chicken breast crosswise on the bias and serve with the remaining vinaigrette.

—Deborah Madison

SAUTEED CHICKEN BREASTS WITH FRESH SAGE

In this simple chicken dish from Trattoria Antico Fattore in Florence, a marinade of lemon juice, oil and sage infuses the chicken with flavor.
❦ We drank the trattoria's house wine, Ruffino Chianti, Riserva Ducale, a good local choice from Tuscany.

4 Servings

4 skinless, boneless chicken breast
  halves (6 ounces each)
3 tablespoons fresh lemon juice
¼ cup plus 1 tablespoon extra-virgin
  olive oil
28 fresh whole sage leaves
3 tablespoons unsalted butter
Sea salt
Freshly ground pepper
2 whole lemons, halved, for serving

1. Place the chicken breasts in an 8-inch-square glass baking dish. Add the lemon juice, 3 tablespoons of the oil and the sage leaves. Turn the chicken to coat evenly, cover and set aside at room temperature for 30 minutes.

2. Remove the chicken from the marinade and pat dry. Strain the marinade into a small bowl; reserve the sage leaves separately.

3. In a large nonreactive skillet, melt the butter in the remaining 2 tablespoons oil over moderately high heat until hot and bubbly. Place the chicken breasts, smooth-side down, in the pan and cook until nicely browned on the bottom, about 5 minutes. Turn the breasts and season them with sea salt and pepper. Tuck the reserved sage leaves around the chicken and cook until the chicken is browned on the bottom and just white throughout, about 5 minutes longer.

4. Remove the skillet from the heat.

Transfer the chicken to a cutting board and season to taste with sea salt and pepper. Slice the chicken breasts on the diagonal ½ inch thick and arrange on a warm platter. Place the sage leaves over the chicken. Cover loosely with foil.

5. Pour off the grease, then heat the skillet over moderately high heat until hot. Pour in the reserved marinade and stir with a wooden spoon, scraping up the brown bits from the bottom of the

pan. The sauce will boil almost immediately. As soon as it becomes a brown glaze (in less than 1 minute), pour the sauce over the chicken and garnish with the lemon halves.

—Patricia Wells

POULET BASQUAISE

4 Servings

One 3½- to 4-pound chicken
¼ cup extra-virgin olive oil
1 large red onion (1 pound), thinly sliced crosswise
2 large green bell peppers, cut into ½-inch strips
8 garlic cloves, chopped
1 small hot pepper, such as jalapeño, seeded and chopped (about 2 teaspoons)
1½ pounds plum tomatoes—halved, seeded and cut into ¾-inch pieces
¾ teaspoon salt
4 very thin slices of prosciutto (about 2 ounces)
2 tablespoons finely chopped flat-leaf parsley

1. With a sharp knife, remove the legs from the chicken and pull off the skin. Cut each leg in 2 pieces, separating the drumsticks from the thighs. Set aside on a plate. Cut the 2 wings from the chicken at the shoulder joints; cut each wing into 3 pieces at the joints. Pull the skin off the chicken breast and back. Using the breastbone as your guide, cut the breast halves from the carcass. Set the breasts aside with the thighs and drumsticks, the 4 meatier wing pieces and the heart and gizzard if you have them. (Reserve the carcass and wing tips for making stock; save the liver for another use.)

2. In a large nonreactive skillet, heat the oil over moderately high heat until

POULTRY

67

hot but not smoking. Add the 4 wing pieces, the heart and the gizzard and cook, turning occasionally, until golden brown, about 2 minutes. Add the 4 leg pieces and cook until golden, about 2 minutes per side.

3. Stir in the onion and bell peppers. Reduce the heat to moderate and cook, stirring occasionally, until the vegetables are wilted, about 8 minutes. Stir in the garlic and hot pepper and then the tomatoes. Reduce the heat to moderately low, cover and cook until the tomatoes are soft but still hold their shape, about 10 minutes.

4. Add the 2 breast halves to the pan, nestling them in the cooking liquid. Sprinkle the salt on top, cover and simmer until the chicken is cooked through, about 10 minutes.

5. To serve, arrange the chicken pieces, heart and gizzard on a warmed platter or plates. Drape the prosciutto slices over the chicken. Spoon the vegetables and pan juices all around. Sprinkle on the parsley and serve.

—Jacques Pépin

FAMILY-STYLE CHICKEN FRICASSEE

This is an old-fashioned feast updated for the Nineties. Rather than using the traditional method of cooking an elderly hen in water, this version calls for simmering a young bird in stock and wine for maximum flavor. The fricassee is finished with only three tablespoons of cream and no egg yolks (instead of the usual one-half to one cup of heavy cream and two to four egg

SANTA FE OPERA MENU
Serves 8

Overnight Squash and Red Onion Pickles (p. 246)
Roasted Almonds with Red Chile (p. 20)
Olives with Cumin (p. 20)
Lemon Cheese with Lovage (p. 21)
🍷 *1990 Trimbach Pinot Gris from Alsace or Tio Pepe Fino Sherry*
———
Poached Chicken Breasts with Herb and Shallot Vinaigrette (at left)
Swiss Chard Omelet (p. 114)
Summer Vegetable Salad (p. 121)
Sourdough Bread
🍷 *1990 Jadot Moulin-à-Vent Beaujolais*
———
Polenta Cookies (p. 184)
Pine Nut-Brown Sugar Shortbread (p. 184)
Fresh Fruit
Coffee
—Deborah Madison

yolks). And instead of a skimpy garnish, we include all the vegetables needed for a fine family dinner.

❦ For a wine whose taste would echo the tarragon and parsley flavors in the sauce, try a Chardonnay, such as 1991 Rodney Strong from California or 1991 Black Opal from Australia.

4 to 6 Servings

5 medium carrots, cut into 2-by-¼-inch sticks
3 large celery ribs, peeled and cut into 2-by-¼-inch sticks
2 small leeks, white and tender green only, cut into 2-by-¼-inch strips
¾ teaspoon crumbled tarragon
Coarse (kosher) salt
One 4-pound frying chicken, cut into 8 pieces
Freshly ground black pepper
1 tablespoon vegetable oil
3 cups chicken stock or canned low-sodium chicken broth
1 cup dry white wine
1 small bay leaf
⅛ teaspoon crumbled thyme
3 tablespoons unsalted butter
6 tablespoons all-purpose flour
3 tablespoons heavy cream
1½ teaspoons fresh lemon juice
Pinch of cayenne pepper
Pinch of ground mace
1½ tablespoons finely chopped flat-leaf parsley
Steamed rice, for serving

1. In a large enameled cast-iron casserole, toss the carrots, celery and leeks with ¼ teaspoon of the tarragon and ⅛ teaspoon coarse salt.

2. Cut off the wing tips from the chicken and discard (or reserve for stock). Sprinkle the chicken lightly with coarse salt and black pepper.

3. Heat the oil in a large heavy skillet. Add the chicken thighs and legs and cook over moderate heat, turning once, just until lightly golden, 3 to 5 minutes per side. Place the dark meat pieces on top of the vegetables in the casserole, skin-side down. Repeat with the breasts and wings, arranging the chicken in a single layer in the casserole; set the unwashed skillet aside.

4. Pour the stock and wine over the chicken. Add the bay leaf and thyme and bring to a boil over moderately high heat. Reduce the heat to moderately low, set the lid slightly askew and simmer until the chicken is cooked through and the vegetables are tender, about 25 minutes.

5. Transfer the chicken and vegetables to a large bowl and set aside to cool. Discard the bay leaf. Strain the cooking liquid into a medium saucepan and skim off the fat; you should have about 4 cups.

6. Melt the butter in the unwashed skillet. Whisk in the flour and stir over moderate heat for 3 minutes. Off the heat, gradually whisk in the hot cooking liquid. Simmer, stirring, until the sauce is thickened and smooth, about 6 minutes. Stir in the cream, lemon juice, cayenne, mace and the remaining ½ teaspoon tarragon. Simmer, stirring, to blend the flavors, about 2 minutes. Season well with coarse salt and black pepper. Return the chicken and vegetables to the casserole and pour the sauce on top. *(The fricassee can be prepared to this point and refrigerated up to 1 day ahead. Let return to room temperature before proceeding.)*

7. Cover the casserole and rewarm the fricassee over moderately low heat for 10 to 15 minutes. Sprinkle with the parsley and serve on warmed plates, accompanied with steamed rice.

—*Leslie Newman*

BROILED GINGER-HOISIN CHICKEN THIGHS

If you prefer, you can grill the thighs. This dish goes well with plain boiled rice.

4 Servings

½ cup coarsely chopped fresh ginger (about 3 ounces)
1 tablespoon coarsely chopped garlic
½ cup hoisin sauce
2 tablespoons soy sauce
2 tablespoons sugar
8 large boneless chicken thighs

1. In a food processor, puree all the ingredients, except the chicken thighs, with ¼ cup of water until smooth. Transfer the puree to a large bowl.

2. Using a small sharp knife, score the underside of each thigh in 3 or 4 places. Add the thighs to the puree in the bowl and rub all over. Cover tightly and refrigerate for at least 6 hours or overnight.

3. Preheat the broiler. Place the thighs skin-side up in a single layer in a roasting pan. Broil, rotating the pan as necessary to cook evenly, until the skin is crisp and brown, 7 to 8 minutes. Turn the thighs over and broil, rotating the pan, until just cooked through, 3 to 4 minutes longer.

—*David Rosengarten*

Grilled Lime-Glazed Seafood Kebabs (p. 60) and a mug of Gazpacho Sevillano (p. 42).

Above, Lobster Fricassee with Artichokes (p. 62). At left (clockwise from top), Appalachian Dressing (p. 83), Roast Goose with Plum Glaze (p. 82) and Crisp Root-Vegetable Cakes (p. 115).

FRIED CHICKEN WITH PEPPERY PAN GRAVY

This is real southern chicken—soaked in milk, fried in a cast-iron skillet and drained on a paper bag. Crisp on the outside, juicy on the inside and served with hot gravy and Buttermilk Spoonbread (p. 164), fried chicken doesn't get any better than this.

❧ Because fried chicken calls for a white wine with good acidity for contrast and the gravy is best balanced by a hint of fruity sweetness, the choice is narrowed to off-dry whites. Try a Chenin Blanc, such as 1990 Hogue Cellars from Washington State or 1991 Preston from California, or a Galestro from Italy, such as 1991 Antinori.

4 Servings

FRIED CHICKEN:
One 3½-pound frying chicken, cut into 8 pieces
1 small lemon, halved
Coarse (kosher) salt
Freshly ground black pepper
3 cups milk
1 cup all-purpose flour
⅛ teaspoon cayenne pepper
1½ pounds solid vegetable shortening (about 3 cups)

PAN GRAVY:
2 tablespoons all-purpose flour
2 cups cold milk
Freshly ground black pepper
⅛ teaspoon cayenne pepper
1¼ teaspoons Worcestershire sauce
1 tablespoon fresh lemon juice
Coarse (kosher) salt

Little Devils (p. 76).

1. *Prepare the fried chicken:* Rub the chicken with the cut lemon and season lightly with coarse salt and black pepper. Put the chicken in a bowl and add the milk; the chicken should be barely submerged. Cover and refrigerate for at least 4 hours or overnight. Let stand at room temperature for 1 to 2 hours before proceeding.

2. In a large sturdy brown paper bag, combine the flour with 1½ teaspoons coarse salt, 2 teaspoons black pepper and the cayenne. Remove 2 pieces of chicken from the milk, letting the excess milk drip off. Add the chicken to the bag and shake vigorously until well coated, then transfer to a wire rack. Repeat with the remaining chicken pieces.

3. Heat the shortening in a 12-inch cast-iron skillet until very hot but not smoking. Using tongs, add the thigh and leg pieces to the skillet, skin-side down. Add the breast and wing pieces, leaving a little space between the pieces, cover and cook over moderate heat for 15 minutes. Turn the pieces over and fry uncovered until the chicken is cooked through and nicely browned on both sides, about 15 minutes. Transfer the white meat pieces to a brown paper bag, followed by the dark meat pieces and let drain while you make the gravy.

4. *Make the pan gravy:* Pour off all but 2 tablespoons of the hot fat from the skillet, leaving behind any browned bits. Sprinkle in the flour and stir rapidly over low heat, scraping up any browned bits, until the flour is lightly browned, about 2 minutes. Raise the heat to moderate and gradually whisk in the milk. Season with ½ teaspoon black pepper and the cayenne and bring to a gentle boil. Stir in the Worcestershire sauce and simmer over moderately low heat until slightly thickened, about 1 minute.

Stir in the lemon juice, remove from the heat and season the gravy with coarse salt. Pour into a warmed gravy boat. Transfer the chicken to a heated platter and serve with the gravy.

—*Leslie Newman*

CHICKEN WITH RAISINS AND BLACK PEPPER

Despite Le Lion d'Or's primarily classic French menu, this Washington restaurant's international clientele of ambassadors and dignitaries often request this homey dish—*poulet au poivre et raisins.* Chef/owner Jean-Pierre Goyenvalle says he prepares the chicken almost like a pepper steak, and he serves it with spinach and fresh fettuccine tossed with butter or olive oil and parsley.

❧ To work with the sweetness of the peppery sauce you want a wine with lots of rich, ripe fruit and a spicy bouquet, such as 1987 Silver Oak Cabernet Sauvignon, Alexander Valley. Another interesting choice would be a red Burgundy, 1985 Aloxe-Corton Les Chaillots, Louis Latour.

2 Servings

One 2½-pound chicken
1 medium onion, cut into eighths
1 medium carrot, coarsely chopped
1 large celery rib, coarsely chopped
1 teaspoon tomato paste
1 bay leaf
¼ teaspoon thyme
4 whole black peppercorns
¼ cup raisins

¼ cup Cognac
1 tablespoon cracked black
    peppercorns
½ teaspoon salt
3 tablespoons unsalted butter
1 tablespoon olive oil

1. Preheat the oven to 400°. Using a sharp knife, cut the legs off the chicken in one piece (thigh and drumstick intact). Holding the end of one of the thigh bones, scrape down and around the bone to free the meat. Remove the thigh bone at the knee joint, leaving the drumstick and boned thigh intact. Repeat with the other chicken leg. Set aside. Reserve the thigh bones.

2. Slice down 1 side of the breast bone and remove the breast meat by sliding the knife as close to the bones as possible. Remove the boneless breast half with the wing attached. Then cut off the first two sections of the wing, leaving the drumette attached to the breast. Repeat with the other breast half. Cut the rib cage in half.

3. Place the wing tip sections, thigh bones, rib cage, gizzard, neck and the carcass in a medium roasting pan. Add the onion, carrot and celery and roast in the oven for 50 minutes, stirring once, until well browned.

4. Transfer the contents of the roasting pan to a large saucepan. Add 4 cups of water to the roasting pan, place over 2 burners on high heat and, using a wooden spatula, scrape the bottom to release the browned bits. Pour the liquid into the saucepan with the bones and vegetables. Stir in the tomato paste, bay leaf, thyme and whole peppercorns and bring to a gentle boil.

Cook over moderately low heat, skimming the surface occasionally, until the liquid has reduced by half, about 1 hour.

5. Strain the stock into a small saucepan; discard the solids. Skim any fat from the surface of the stock with a small ladle. Boil the stock over high heat until syrupy and reduced to ⅓ cup, about 20 minutes. Set aside. *(The recipe can be prepared to this point 1 day ahead. Cover the chicken parts and the reduced stock separately and refrigerate overnight.)*

6. Meanwhile, place the raisins in a small saucepan, cover with water and boil for 1 minute. Drain off the water and add the Cognac. Set aside to macerate for 1 hour.

7. Preheat the oven to 350°. Season the chicken with the cracked black pepper and salt. In a large ovenproof skillet, melt 1 tablespoon of the butter in the olive oil over moderately high heat. Add the chicken to the pan, skin-side down, and cook, turning once, until well browned all over, about 10 minutes per side. Transfer the chicken to a plate and pour off the fat; wipe out the skillet.

8. Return the chicken to the pan and bake in the oven for 25 to 30 minutes, until the juices run clear when a thigh is deeply pierced. Transfer the chicken to a plate and keep warm.

9. Pour off any fat from the skillet. Pour in the raisins and Cognac and ignite carefully over low heat. When the flame dies down, add the reduced chicken stock and bring to a boil. Reduce the heat to low and stir in the remaining 2 tablespoons butter until melted. Season the sauce with salt and pepper to taste. Add the chicken to the pan and turn to coat. Serve 1 leg and 1 breast per person, with the sauce and raisins spooned on top.

—*Jean-Pierre Goyenvalle*

RED CHICKEN CURRY

Preparing a Thai curry used to be difficult and time-consuming. Now, with good curry paste and coconut milk readily available, it is simple and quick. ♟ Slightly sweet whites aren't the only wines that can make a successful match with spicy Asian dishes. Fruity red wines with direct flavors, such as 1987 Lindemans Shiraz from Australia or 1989 Guigal Côtes du Rhône, can offer attractive taste affinities with moderately hot curries.

4 to 6 Servings

2 tablespoons vegetable oil
2 tablespoons red curry paste
3 cups coconut milk (two 13-ounce
    cans)
1 pound skinless, boneless chicken
    breasts, trimmed of fat and sliced
    crosswise ¼ inch thick
5 to 6 fresh kaffir lime leaves
½ cup fresh basil leaves, chopped
2 long fresh red chiles—stemmed,
    seeded if you wish and thinly sliced
    lengthwise
Plain Jasmine Rice (p. 158) and sliced
    cucumbers, for serving

1. Set a heavy medium saucepan over moderately high heat. Add the oil and when it is hot, add the curry paste. Stir for 1½ minutes; the paste will stick slightly to the bottom of the pan. Add the coconut milk and bring to a boil over high heat.

2. Add the chicken and lime leaves and cook, stirring, until the chicken changes color and firms up, about 4 minutes. Reduce the heat to low and simmer for 4 minutes. Stir in the basil. Transfer to a serving dish and garnish with the strips of red chile. Pass the rice and cucumbers separately.

—*Jeffrey Alford & Naomi Duguid*

CHICKEN AND THREE-MUSHROOM CASSEROLE

Plan to marinate the chicken early in the day or the night before cooking.

8 Servings

12 skinless, boneless chicken breast halves (about 4 ounces each)
1 tablespoon chopped fresh thyme or 1½ teaspoons dried
1 tablespoon chopped fresh rosemary or 1½ teaspoons dried
Freshly ground pepper
⅓ cup plus 1 tablespoon extra-virgin olive oil
½ ounce dried porcini mushrooms (about ½ cup)
1 pound fresh shiitake mushrooms, stems discarded
1¼ pounds white mushrooms, sliced
4 cups chicken stock or canned low-sodium broth
Salt
1 cup dry white wine
3 medium shallots, minced
1 tablespoon tomato paste
1½ tablespoons all-purpose flour
1 teaspoon fresh lemon juice

1. Place the chicken breasts in a bowl. Rub them with half of the thyme, half of the rosemary and a generous grinding of pepper. Drizzle ⅓ cup of the oil over the chicken, cover and refrigerate for at least 6 hours or overnight.

2. In a small bowl, cover the porcini with 1½ cups of hot water. Let soak for 30 minutes. Drain, reserving the soaking liquid. Coarsely chop the mushrooms and set aside. Strain the soaking liquid through a strainer lined with cheesecloth and set aside. Reserve 24 of the shiitake mushroom caps and slice the remaining shiitakes. Set aside.

3. Heat a heavy, medium, nonreactive skillet over high heat. Add 1 teaspoon of the oil, then add the sliced white mushrooms and cook without stirring until golden brown on one side, about 5 minutes. Stir, reduce the heat to moderately high and cook for another 5 minutes until well browned and dry. Transfer to a large bowl.

4. Reduce the heat to moderate and add the remaining 2 teaspoons oil to the skillet. Add the shiitake mushroom caps and slices and cook, stirring, for 5 minutes. Add 1 cup of the chicken stock, 1 cup of water and the chopped porcini. Cover partially and cook, stirring, until the mushrooms are tender, about 20 minutes. Uncover, bring to a boil over moderately high heat and boil until the cooking liquid has evaporated. Transfer the shiitakes and porcini to the bowl of white mushrooms and season with salt and pepper to taste.

5. Add ½ cup of the chicken stock to the skillet and bring to a boil, scraping to dislodge any browned bits. Add this liquid to the porcini soaking liquid.

6. Wipe the skillet clean and dry and heat over moderately high heat. Pat the chicken breasts dry and season with salt and pepper. Add 4 chicken breast halves to the skillet and cook, turning once, until lightly browned, about 2 minutes on each side. Reduce the heat to moderate and cook until the chicken is opaque, about 2 minutes; transfer to a platter. Repeat with the remaining chicken in 2 batches.

7. Add the wine and shallots to the skillet and bring to a boil over moderately high heat. Boil until the wine is reduced to a glaze, about 5 minutes. Remove from the heat and stir in the porcini liquid, tomato paste and the remaining 2½ cups chicken broth, thyme and rosemary.

8. In a small bowl, combine the flour and enough water to make a thin, smooth paste (about 1½ tablespoons) and stir into the skillet. Add any accumulated chicken juices and bring to a boil, stirring, over moderately high heat. Reduce the sauce to about 2⅔ cups, 10 to 12 minutes. Season with salt and pepper to taste and add the lemon juice. Set aside.

9. Set aside the shiitake mushroom caps and spread the remaining mushrooms in a 16-by-10-by-2½-inch baking dish. Arrange the chicken on top and pour the sauce over the chicken. Garnish with the reserved mushroom caps. Cover with foil. *(The casserole can be prepared to this point up to 1 day ahead and refrigerated. Bring to room temperature before proceeding.)*

10. Preheat the oven to 375°. Bake

POTLUCK FOR EIGHT

Serves 8

Spicy Orange Pecans (p. 20)

Chicken and Three-Mushroom Casserole (above)

Roasted Onions with Red Peppers and Garlic Croutons (p. 106)

Baked Tomatoes with Crunchy Crumbs (p. 114)

Mashed Potatoes with Goat Cheese

Tossed Salad with Radish Sprouts and Parsley (p. 119)

Italian Breadsticks (p. 164)

Chocolate Apricot Torte (p. 180)

Pear and Custard Tart (p. 198)

the chicken, covered, until steaming hot, 20 to 30 minutes.

—*Diana Sturgis*

LITTLE DEVILS

The baby chickens known as poussins have become increasingly available in butcher shops and large supermarkets across the country; if you can't find them, substitute small fresh Cornish hens. A tangy mustard coating and crisp crumb crust make either bird devilishly good.

❦ The pleasing bite of the mustard and seasoned bread crumb topping point to a light fruity red as a flavorful, but not overwhelming, choice. A 1991 or 1992 Beaujolais-Villages, such as Georges Duboeuf, or a light Pinot Noir, such as 1991 Bridgeview from Oregon, would be excellent.

4 Servings

½ cup olive oil
2 tablespoons fresh lemon juice
½ teaspoon coarsely chopped fresh thyme or a pinch of dried
1 large garlic clove, smashed, plus 1 teaspoon minced garlic
4 poussins (about 1 pound each)
1⅛ teaspoons dry mustard
3½ tablespoons Dijon mustard
1½ teaspoons Worcestershire sauce
¼ teaspoon hot pepper sauce
1⅓ cups fresh bread crumbs
2 tablespoons finely chopped shallots
3 tablespoons finely chopped flat-leaf parsley
Coarse (kosher) salt
⅛ teaspoon cayenne pepper

Freshly ground black pepper
Lemon wedges, for serving

1. In a 9-by-13-inch glass baking dish, whisk together the olive oil, lemon juice, thyme and smashed garlic. Set aside.

2. Using kitchen shears, cut each poussin along both sides of the backbone from tail to neck; discard the backbones (or reserve for stock). Lay the birds out on a work surface, breasts up. With the heel of your hand, press down on the breast bones to crack them and flatten the birds. Tuck the wing tips behind the shoulders. Place the poussins in the marinade, turning to coat. Cover and let stand at room temperature for 1 hour, turning once.

3. Preheat the broiler. In a small bowl, stir together 1 teaspoon of the dry mustard with ½ teaspoon water to form a paste. Stir in the Dijon mustard, Worcestershire sauce and hot pepper sauce. In a medium bowl, combine the bread crumbs, shallots, minced garlic and parsley. Add 1 teaspoon coarse salt, the cayenne and the remaining ⅛ teaspoon dry mustard.

4. Remove the poussins from the marinade and season lightly with coarse salt and black pepper; reserve the marinade. Place the birds breast up on a rimmed baking sheet. Broil for 10 minutes, or until the skin is nicely browned. Turn, brush with a little of the marinade and broil for 10 minutes longer. Remove the birds from the broiler and lower the oven temperature to 425°.

5. Turn the birds over and spread the mustard mixture evenly over the skin with a rubber spatula. Sprinkle the seasoned crumbs on the poussins, patting lightly to help them adhere. Bake the poussins in the middle of the oven for about 18 minutes, or until the

crumbs are crisp and the juices run clear when a thigh is pierced with a knife. Serve hot with lemon wedges.

—*Leslie Newman*

ROCK CORNISH HENS WITH ROSEMARY AND GARLIC

4 Servings

4 large garlic cloves, minced
2 tablespoons olive oil
1 tablespoon finely minced fresh rosemary or 1½ teaspoons dried
½ teaspoon salt
Freshly ground pepper
Four 1¼- to 1½-pound Rock Cornish hens
Rosemary sprigs, for garnish

1. Preheat the oven to 400°. In a small saucepan, heat the garlic and oil over very low heat for about 5 minutes; do not let the garlic brown.

2. In a small bowl, stir together the rosemary, salt and several grindings of pepper.

3. Using a large sharp knife or poul-

GAME HENS FOR DINNER
Serves 4

Rock Cornish Hens with Rosemary and Garlic (above)

Cheesy Polenta

Sautéed Zucchini and Cherry Tomatoes

❦ *1986 Rioja CUNE "Contino" Reserve*

Baked Pears with Ginger (p. 220)

—*Stephanie Lyness*

try shears, remove the backbone from each hen by cutting down either side of the bone. Lay the hens skin-side up and flatten with the heel of the hand to crack the breast bones.

4. Work your fingers underneath the skin on the breasts and legs of the hens to loosen it. Spoon one-quarter of the rosemary mixture underneath the skin of each, spreading it over the entire breast and the thighs. Place the hens on a rack in a roasting pan, season with more salt and pepper and brush with the garlic oil.

5. Roast the birds for 35 to 40 minutes, basting once or twice, until the juices run clear when the legs are pierced with a fork or skewer. Place 1 hen on each dinner plate and garnish with a rosemary sprig.

—*Stephanie Lyness*

ROASTED ROCK CORNISH HENS

6 Servings

¼ *cup plus 2 tablespoons fresh lemon juice*
¼ *cup plus 2 tablespoons olive oil*
3 garlic cloves, peeled and minced
2½ teaspoons minced fresh thyme or ¾ teaspoon dried
Twelve 1-inch sprigs of fresh rosemary or 1½ teaspoons dried rosemary
1 bay leaf
¼ *teaspoon crushed red pepper (optional)*
Salt and freshly ground black pepper
Six 1¼- to 1½-pound Rock Cornish hens
3 tablespoons unsalted butter, melted
Watercress, for garnish

1. In a glass or ceramic bowl, combine the lemon juice, olive oil, garlic, thyme, rosemary, bay leaf, crushed red

pepper, if using, and ¾ teaspoon each of salt and black pepper.

2. With a large sharp knife or poultry shears, remove the backbone from each hen by cutting down either side of the bone. Halve the hens and place in a large nonreactive bowl.

3. Pour the marinade over the birds and turn to coat. Cover and refrigerate for 2 hours. Remove the hens from the refrigerator about 30 minutes before cooking.

4. Preheat the oven to 500°. Remove the hens from the marinade and pat dry. Arrange, skin-side up, in a single layer in 1 or 2 roasting pans. Brush the hens with some of the melted butter and season with salt and black pepper. Roast for 20 to 25 minutes, brushing with more of the butter, until the juices run clear when a thigh is pierced. Transfer the hens to a platter and garnish with watercress. Serve warm or at room temperature.

—*Jamie Davies*

ROAST THANKSGIVING TURKEY WITH WILD RICE STUFFING

❢ Although the mildness of turkey makes it easily compatible with wine, the trimmings and side dishes typical of Thanksgiving add sweet and salty notes best balanced by a straightforward, lively, fruity red. Beaujolais Nouveau would carry out the harvest theme, but a more substantial example, such as 1991 Sylvain Fessy Beaujolais-Villages "Cuvée Pierre Soitel," would be even better. A West Coast Pinot Noir, such as 1988 Alpine from Oregon's Willamette Valley or 1990 Gundlach-Bundschu from Sonoma, would be an appealing alternative.

8 Servings

2½ cups wild rice (14 ounces)
3 cups Rich Chicken Stock (p. 46) diluted with 3 cups of water
1½ cups drained sliced water chestnuts
1 bunch of watercress, leaves and tender stems only, coarsely chopped
4 large scallions, white and tender green, coarsely chopped
¾ *cup whole blanched almonds (4 ounces)*
½ *pound country ham or prosciutto, finely chopped*
Salt and freshly ground pepper
One 16- to 18-pound turkey, neck and giblets reserved
1 onion, halved
1 celery rib, cut into 2-inch pieces
3 tablespoons unsalted butter, softened
3 tablespoons all-purpose flour

1. Rinse the wild rice in several changes of cold water and drain. Put the rice in a medium saucepan, add 5 cups of the diluted chicken stock and bring to a boil over moderately high heat. Cover, reduce the heat to low and cook slowly, stirring occasionally, until the rice is tender and the stock has been absorbed. The cooking time can vary from 35 to 60 minutes. If the rice is not done and the stock has boiled away, add another cup of stock; if the rice is done but stock remains, uncover and boil over high heat until evaporated. *(The rice can be cooked up to 1 day ahead. Let cool, then cover and refrigerate.)*

2. In a large bowl, toss the cooked rice with the water chestnuts, watercress, scallions, almonds and ham. Sea-

son with pepper and, if needed, salt. Let the stuffing cool thoroughly.

3. In a medium saucepan, cover the turkey neck, heart and gizzard (reserve the liver for Step 5) with 4 cups of water. Add the onion, celery and a pinch of salt and bring to a boil over high heat. Reduce the heat to low and simmer for 1½ hours, skimming occasionally. Strain the broth and set aside; you should have about 3 cups. Reserve the turkey gizzard and heart.

4. Meanwhile, preheat the oven to 325°. Spoon the stuffing into the chest and neck cavities of the turkey. Fold the neck skin over the stuffing and secure with skewers. Truss the bird with twine. Season the turkey liberally with salt and pepper and rub the butter all over. Wrap any leftover stuffing in a foil packet.

5. Place the turkey, breast down, on a foil-lined rack in a roasting pan and roast for 2 hours. Turn the turkey breast-side up and roast for about 2 hours longer, basting often with the pan juices. Ten minutes before the roasting time is up, add the turkey liver to the pan. The bird is done when an instant-read thermometer inserted in the inner thigh registers 170°.

6. Transfer the turkey to a warm platter, reserving the liver. Let the bird rest for about 30 minutes before carving. Heat the extra stuffing in the oven for about 25 minutes.

7. Meanwhile, make the gravy. Pour all the juices in the roasting pan into a large measuring cup. Spoon about 3 tablespoons of fat from the juices into the roasting pan and set it over two burners. Stir the flour into the pan and cook

over moderate heat for 1 minute, scraping up the browned bits. Whisk in 1 cup of the reserved turkey broth until smooth. Whisk in the remaining broth and simmer until thickened. Degrease the remaining juices in the measuring cup and stir them into the gravy.

8. Finely chop the reserved gizzard, heart and liver and stir them into the gravy. Season with salt and pepper. Pour into a warmed gravy boat and serve alongside the carved turkey.

—*Evan Jones*

SAGE-ROASTED ROLLED TURKEY

Start this recipe at least one day before serving so that you can make the turkey stock (Step 2) and refrigerate it overnight.

12 Servings

One 15-pound turkey
4 medium carrots, coarsely chopped
2 large onions, coarsely chopped
1 bunch of celery, coarsely chopped
4 sprigs of fresh thyme
1 large sheet of caul fat*
2 tablespoons unsalted butter
3 medium shallots, minced
1 teaspoon finely chopped fresh sage or
½ teaspoon dried rubbed sage
1 teaspoon coarse (kosher) salt
½ teaspoon freshly ground pepper
2 heads of garlic (about 4½ ounces),
separated into unpeeled cloves
2 sprigs of fresh rosemary
¼ cup apple cider or unsweetened apple
juice
¼ cup all-purpose flour
Table salt
*Available from the butcher

1. Rinse the turkey in cold water and pat dry with paper towels. Using a thin sharp knife, cut down the length of

the breast bone on each side, keeping the knife as close to the bone as possible, to remove the breast halves. Pull off and discard the skin. Remove the legs in 1 piece, then cut them into drumsticks and thighs. Bone the thighs, keeping the meat in 1 piece. Pull off and discard the skin; reserve the meat and bones.

2. Using a large heavy knife, cut the carcass into large pieces, or break it apart with your hands. In a large stockpot, combine the carcass, thigh bones, wings, neck and drumsticks. Add half of the carrots, onions, celery, 2 thyme sprigs and 5 quarts of water. Bring to a boil over high heat. Reduce the heat to moderate and boil gently, skimming occasionally with a slotted spoon, for about 3½ hours. Strain the stock into a large glass measure; you should have about 1 quart. If necessary, boil

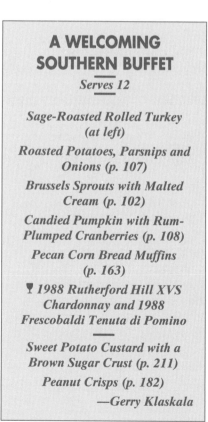

A WELCOMING SOUTHERN BUFFET

Serves 12

Sage-Roasted Rolled Turkey
(at left)
Roasted Potatoes, Parsnips and
Onions (p. 107)
Brussels Sprouts with Malted
Cream (p. 102)
Candied Pumpkin with Rum-
Plumped Cranberries (p. 108)
Pecan Corn Bread Muffins
(p. 163)
♟ 1988 Rutherford Hill XVS
Chardonnay and 1988
Frescobaldi Tenuta di Pomino

Sweet Potato Custard with a
Brown Sugar Crust (p. 211)
Peanut Crisps (p. 182)
—*Gerry Klaskala*

again in the pot to reduce the liquid. Cool, cover and refrigerate overnight. Skim the fat from the surface of the stock before using.

3. Place the caul fat in a large bowl of cool water; let sit until it softens and loosens into a sheet, about 10 minutes.

4. In a medium skillet, melt the butter over moderate heat. Add the shallots and cook, stirring occasionally, until softened, about 5 minutes. Stir in the sage and cook for 1 minute. Remove from the heat.

5. Cover a work surface with a piece of plastic wrap larger than the size of the caul fat. Gently lay the caul fat on the plastic in as even a layer as possible. Sprinkle the shallot mixture on top. Season the turkey breasts and thighs with the coarse salt and pepper. Place the breasts skinned-side down on the caul fat with the narrow ends side by side and touching so that the turkey breasts form a long rectangle. Lay the thighs next to each other in the center of the breast meat. Using the plastic wrap to guide you, roll up the turkey in the caul fat from the long side, wrapping the fat around twice. Discard the plastic wrap. (*The turkey can be prepared to this point up to 1 day ahead. Cover the turkey roll well with plastic wrap or foil and refrigerate. Return to room temperature before proceeding.*)

6. Preheat the oven to 350°. In a roasting pan slightly larger than the turkey roll, toss the garlic cloves, rosemary sprigs and the remaining carrots, onion, celery and thyme. Set the turkey roll on top of the vegetables and roast for 1 hour and 10 minutes, or until an instant-read thermometer inserted in the center of the turkey roll reads 150°.

7. Using 2 large metal spatulas, carefully transfer the turkey roll to a carv-ing board with grooves; cover loosely with foil and let rest for at least 30 minutes before slicing.

8. Place the roasting pan over moderately high heat and cook the vegetables, stirring occasionally, until lightly caramelized, about 3 minutes. Stir in the apple cider, then the flour and continue to cook until pasty, 2 to 3 minutes longer. Gradually stir in the reserved turkey stock. Bring to a boil and cook, stirring often, until thickened, about 25 minutes. Strain the gravy into a medium saucepan and stir in any juices that have accumulated on the carving board. Season with table salt and pepper and keep warm.

9. Slice the turkey roll crosswise and transfer to a platter. Pour the gravy into a sauceboat and serve alongside the turkey.

—Gerry Klaskala

TURKEY AND SWEET POTATO HASH

Serve this hash piping hot with eggs and sautéed spinach (or Swiss chard) with balsamic vinegar.

4 Servings

1 large sweet potato (about ¾ pound), unpeeled, halved crosswise
2 large baking potatoes (about 1 pound), unpeeled
6 tablespoons corn oil
4 cups diced or torn cooked turkey (about 1 pound)
4 tablespoons unsalted butter
2 medium onions, finely chopped
1½ teaspoons minced fresh thyme or ½ teaspoon dried
¾ teaspoon salt
½ teaspoon freshly ground pepper

1. Place the sweet potato halves and the baking potatoes in a large saucepan with salted water to cover by 1 inch. Bring to a boil over moderately high heat. Reduce the heat to moderate and boil gently until tender, 35 to 40 minutes. Drain and let cool. Peel the potatoes and cut them in ⅓-inch dice, keeping the two types separate.

2. Heat a large heavy skillet, preferably cast iron, over moderately high heat until hot, about 5 minutes. Add 2 tablespoons of the corn oil and swirl to coat the pan. Add the diced baking potatoes in a single layer and fry until crisp on the bottom, at least 2 minutes. Turn the potatoes with a metal spatula and fry until golden brown all over, about 3 minutes longer. Transfer to a large bowl. Add 3 more tablespoons of the oil to the skillet and fry the diced sweet potato in the same fashion. Add to the other potatoes.

3. Add the remaining 1 tablespoon oil to the skillet. Add the turkey and cook, stirring occasionally, until well browned and crusty, about 4 minutes. Transfer to the bowl with the potatoes.

4. Reduce the heat to moderately low and melt the butter in the skillet. Add the onions and thyme and cook, stirring frequently, until the onions are soft and translucent, about 8 minutes. Add to the turkey and potatoes and toss to combine. Sprinkle with the salt and pepper and toss again. (*The hash can be prepared up to 3 hours ahead and set aside at room temperature.*) Reheat the hash over moderate heat, stirring until warmed through.

—Tracey Seaman

TURKEY BURGERS WITH HERBED LEMON MAYONNAISE

These tasty patties make good use of leftover roast turkey.

4 Servings

7 to 8 thick slices of bacon (½ pound)
3 cups finely chopped cooked turkey
3 large celery ribs, minced
1 medium onion, minced
½ cup bread crumbs made from
*   day-old Italian bread*
¼ cup plus 1 tablespoon minced
*   flat-leaf parsley*
½ teaspoon salt
½ teaspoon freshly ground pepper
2 eggs, lightly beaten
¾ cup mayonnaise
1 tablespoon fresh lemon juice
1 tablespoon minced fresh tarragon
2 tablespoons minced fresh chives or
*   scallion greens*
1 tablespoon unsalted butter
1 tablespoon vegetable oil

1. In a large heavy skillet, fry the bacon over moderately high heat, turning occasionally, until browned and crisp, 8 to 10 minutes. Drain on paper towels. Discard the fat from the pan; set the pan aside. Chop the bacon.

2. In a large bowl, mix the turkey, celery, onion, bread crumbs, bacon, ¼ cup of the parsley and the salt and pepper. Stir in the eggs. Divide the mixture into 8 portions. Shape each portion into a 3-by-½-inch disk and place on a baking sheet. Refrigerate for 20 minutes.

3. Meanwhile, in a small bowl, stir together the mayonnaise, lemon juice, tarragon, chives and the remaining 1 tablespoon parsley. *(The recipe can be prepared to this point several hours ahead. Cover and refrigerate the herbed mayonnaise.)*

4. In the skillet used to fry the bacon, melt ½ tablespoon of the butter in ½ tablespoon of the oil over moderately high heat. When the fat is very hot, add 4 of the burgers to the pan. Reduce the heat to moderate and cook until browned on the bottom, about 5 minutes. Turn carefully and cook until browned on the second side, about 4 minutes longer. Keep warm in a low oven and repeat with the remaining butter, oil and burgers. Serve at once, with the herbed lemon mayonnaise on the side.

—*Diana Sturgis*

TURKEY SCHNITZEL

Turkey cutlets are an economical and readily available alternative to veal for an easy dinner. In this recipe, the cutlets are coated with egg whites and mustard and breaded to keep them moist; they are then pan-fried.

4 Servings

2 egg whites
2 tablespoons Dijon mustard
1½ teaspoons salt
1 cup dry bread crumbs
½ teaspoon freshly ground pepper
1 pound thinly sliced (about ¼ inch
*   thick) turkey cutlets*
6 tablespoons olive oil
4 lemon wedges, for serving

1. In a medium bowl, beat the egg whites with 1 teaspoon of water. Mix in the mustard and ½ teaspoon of the salt. On a plate, mix the bread crumbs with the remaining 1 teaspoon salt and the pepper.

2. Dip each turkey cutlet in the egg-white mixture, then coat both sides with the bread crumbs. Place them on a large platter and refrigerate for about 30 minutes.

3. In a large skillet, heat 3 tablespoons of the oil over high heat until very hot. Add half of the cutlets and cook, turning once, until golden brown and cooked through, 1 to 2 minutes per side. Transfer to paper towels to drain. Wipe out the skillet and cook the remaining cutlets in the remaining 3 tablespoons oil. Serve with lemon wedges.

—*Susan Shapiro Jaslove*

TURKEY COTTAGE PIE

In this version of a classic dish, rutabaga, the peppery yellow turnip, is added to the traditional mashed potato topping.

6 to 8 Servings

1 small rutabaga (about 1¼ pounds),
*   peeled and cut into ½-inch dice*
3 baking potatoes (1½ pounds), peeled
*   and quartered*
4 tablespoons unsalted butter
1 teaspoon salt
½ teaspoon freshly ground pepper
¾ pound mushrooms, halved or
*   quartered if large*
4 small carrots, very thinly sliced
*   crosswise*
3 large leeks, white and tender green,
*   thinly sliced crosswise*

3 cups Turkey Stock (p. 51) or canned low-sodium chicken broth
1 cup frozen peas
1 tablespoon fresh thyme, minced, or 1 teaspoon dried
1 bay leaf
3 tablespoons all-purpose flour
3 cups diced cooked turkey (½-inch pieces)

1. In a large saucepan, cover the rutabaga with 3 inches of cold water and bring to a boil over high heat. Cover and reduce the heat to maintain a simmer for 25 minutes.

2. Add the potatoes, return to a boil and cook until the vegetables are tender, about 20 minutes.

3. Drain the potatoes and rutabaga well and place in a bowl. Add 2 tablespoons of the butter and the salt and pepper; toss well. Pass the vegetables through a ricer or a food mill or mash them until smooth. (Do not use a food processor or the consistency will be gluey.) Set aside.

4. Heat a large heavy skillet over moderately high heat and swirl in 1

tablespoon of the butter. Spread the mushrooms in the pan and cook without turning until well browned on one side, 4 to 5 minutes. Stir and cook for 1 minute longer. Transfer the mushrooms to a bowl.

5. In the same skillet, melt the remaining 1 tablespoon butter over moderate heat. Spread the carrots in the pan in a single layer and cover with the leeks. Cook for 5 minutes. Stir once and cook until the carrots are tender and the leeks are wilted but not browned, about 2 minutes longer.

6. Stir in the Turkey Stock, peas, thyme, bay leaf and the mushrooms. Bring to a boil over high heat, then reduce the heat to moderate and simmer, covered, for 10 minutes.

7. In a small bowl, mix the flour with ½ cup of water until smooth. Stir it into the skillet and cook over moderately low heat until bubbly, about 1 minute. Discard the bay leaf. Mix in the turkey and season with salt and pepper. Remove from the heat. Add a few more tablespoons of water if the sauce is too thick. *(The recipe can be prepared to this point up to 1 day ahead. Cover and refrigerate the potato-rutabaga puree and the turkey mixture separately. Let return to room temperature before proceeding.)*

8. Preheat the oven to 400°. Spread the turkey mixture in a large, shallow baking dish, about 9 by 13 inches. Stir the potato-rutabaga puree and, beginning around the edge of the dish, spoon it evenly over the turkey mixture. Spread it smoothly, then score the surface decoratively with a fork. Bake the pie for about 25 minutes, until bubbling around the edges. Serve piping hot.

—*Diana Sturgis*

SIMPLE AND SAVORY WEEKDAY DINNER

Serves 4

Turkey Schnitzel (at left)
Oven-Toasted Potato Chips (p. 107)
Broccoli, Orange and Roasted Pepper Salad (p. 120)
🍷 *1991 St. Francis or 1990 Arrowood California Chardonnay*

Cranberry-Apple Pie
—*Susan Shapiro Jaslove*

TURKEY SANDWICHES ON CORN BREAD WITH CURRY-APPLE MAYONNAISE

This corn bread was developed for firmness, so don't worry about overmixing the batter. Its round shape will yield some square sandwiches and some triangular ones.

Makes 8 Sandwiches

½ cup cornmeal
1 cup all-purpose flour
2 teaspoons baking powder
2 teaspoons sugar
½ teaspoon salt
2 eggs, beaten
⅔ cup milk
1 tablespoon vegetable oil
2 teaspoons curry powder
¾ cup mayonnaise
1 large tart apple, such as Winesap or Greening, peeled and finely diced (1 cup)
2 teaspoons fresh lemon juice
Sliced cooked turkey for 8 sandwiches
½ cup cranberry sauce, preferably with whole berries

1. Preheat the oven to 450°. Place a 10-inch cast-iron skillet over moderate heat. Meanwhile, sift the cornmeal, flour, baking powder, sugar and salt into a large bowl. With a wooden spoon, stir in the eggs and milk.

2. Add the vegetable oil to the hot skillet, tilting the pan to distribute the oil around the sides. Scrape the corn bread batter into the skillet and spread evenly. Place the pan in the middle of the oven and bake for about 10 min-

utes, until the corn bread feels firm and springy when pressed. Turn the corn bread out on a rack to cool.

3. In a small skillet, toast the curry powder over moderate heat, stirring constantly, until very fragrant, about 1 minute. Scrape the curry powder into a medium bowl to cool. Mix in the mayonnaise, diced apple and lemon juice. Season with salt to taste.

4. To make the sandwiches, cut the whole corn bread in 3 strips of equal width. Cut the center piece into 3 squares. Cut one side strip into 2 triangles and 1 square; cut the last strip into 2 triangles. Slice each piece in half horizontally. For each sandwich, spread 1 to 2 tablespoons of the curry-apple mayonnaise on the bottom half of the corn bread and pile the turkey on top. Spread 1 tablespoon of the cranberry sauce over the turkey and cover with the other corn bread half. Stack the sandwiches on a platter and serve immediately.

—*Marcia Kiesel*

CHINESE LACQUERED DUCK WITH COFFEE MANDARIN GLAZE

The Grill Room's chef Kevin Graham describes the menu at this elegant, contemporary New Orleans restaurant as "international eclectic." This recipe is a customer favorite. For a more intense orange flavor, substitute orange liqueur for the coffee liqueur.

❦ A slightly mature Burgundy, such as Louis Jadot's 1983 Beaune Clos des Couchereaux, has the characteristics to pair with the sweetness of the glaze and the saltiness of the meat. Another good match for the strong, meaty flavor of the duckling is an earthy Rhône wine, like 1989 Hermitage from J.L. Chave.

4 Servings

Two 5-pound ducks
4 cups coarse (kosher) salt
2 cups honey
¼ cup sugar
2 tablespoons unsalted butter
½ cup fresh orange juice
½ cup strong black coffee
¼ cup coffee liqueur
1 teaspoon arrowroot

1. Rub the ducks thoroughly with the salt. Place the ducks on a rack set over a shallow pan and refrigerate uncovered for 24 hours.

2. Rinse the ducks well under cold running water to remove the salt. Cut off any excess fat and discard.

3. Preheat the oven to 450°. In a stockpot, bring 1 gallon of water to a boil over high heat. Stir in the honey. Immerse 1 of the ducks in the boiling honey-water for 4 minutes. Carefully remove the duck from the water and drain well. Repeat with the second duck. Set the ducks on a wire rack in a roasting pan.

4. Roast the ducks for 30 minutes. Reduce the oven temperature to 300° and roast for about 1 hour longer, until the duck skin resembles black lacquer.

5. Meanwhile, in a heavy, medium, nonreactive saucepan, cook the sugar over moderate heat, stirring, until it becomes a light brown caramel. Immediately stir in the butter. When it has melted, stir in the orange juice, coffee and coffee liqueur. Simmer until the sugar dissolves completely, then stir in the arrowroot and simmer until thickened, about 3 minutes. Remove from the heat and keep warm.

6. To carve the ducks, remove the breasts and legs from the carcasses, leaving the skin intact. Slice the leg meat off the bone and place on warm plates. Slice the breasts crosswise and fan the slices on the plates. Drizzle with the sauce and serve immediately.

—*Kevin Graham*

ROAST GOOSE WITH PLUM GLAZE

This recipe is delicious served with Appalachian Dressing (recipe follows).

❦ The roast goose and gravy would be nicely underscored by a young fruity California Cabernet Sauvignon, whose tannins would check the fattiness of the meat. Look for a 1987 example, such as Conn Creek or Clos du Val.

8 Servings

¾ cup plum ketchup or chutney*
½ cup fresh orange juice
1 tablespoon coarsely ground pepper
One 15- to 16-pound goose, neck
**   reserved**
Salt
4 medium onions, sliced
4 medium carrots, sliced
4 garlic cloves, sliced
6 cups chicken stock or canned
**   low-sodium broth**
¼ cup cornstarch
¼ cup port
***Available at specialty food shops**

1. Preheat the oven to 375°. In a small bowl, combine the plum ketchup, orange juice and pepper.

2. Thoroughly rinse the goose inside and out and pat it dry. Brush the cavity with 2 tablespoons of the plum ketchup mixture. Truss the goose with kitchen twine, folding the wings under and tying the legs together to close the cavity.

3. Set the goose breast-side up on a rack in a large roasting pan and season with salt. Roast for 30 minutes.

4. Remove the goose from the oven and prick the skin all over with a fork. Loosely cover the goose with foil and roast for 1½ hours longer. Using a bulb baster, remove the fat from the pan every 30 minutes.

5. Transfer the goose to a large platter. Remove the rack from the pan and pour off all the fat. Add the onions, carrots and garlic to the pan and set the goose on top of the vegetables. Brush the goose evenly with one-third of the plum ketchup mixture and roast for 20 minutes.

6. Add the chicken stock to the pan and brush the goose with another third of the plum ketchup mixture. Roast for about 15 minutes longer, until an instant-read thermometer inserted in the inner thigh reads 160°. Transfer the goose to the large platter, cover loosely with foil and keep warm.

7. Pour the pan juices into a nonreactive saucepan and add the remaining plum ketchup mixture. Boil the sauce over high heat, skimming occasionally, until reduced by half, about 10 minutes.

8. Meanwhile, in a small bowl, dissolve the cornstarch in the port. Stir this paste into the reduced sauce and let simmer for 3 minutes. Stir in any juices from the goose and season with salt and pepper. Strain the sauce into a serving bowl.

9. Carve the goose at the table and serve the plum sauce alongside.

—*Larry Forgione*

APPALACHIAN DRESSING

Ham and sautéed almonds add toasted, smoky flavors to this dressing, a tasty accompaniment to Roast Goose with Plum Glaze (p. 82).

8 Servings

1 stick (4 ounces) lightly salted butter
1 cup sliced blanched almonds (3½ ounces)
1 pound country ham, finely diced
3 cups crumbled day-old corn bread
1 cup thinly sliced scallions (about 6), white and tender green
2 tablespoons chopped fresh thyme
½ cup chopped flat-leaf parsley
Freshly ground pepper

In a large skillet, melt the butter over moderately high heat. Add the almonds and sauté until golden, 1 to 2 minutes. Stir in the ham, corn bread and scallions. Reduce the heat to moderate and stir in the thyme and parsley. Season with pepper and sauté until all the butter has been absorbed by the corn bread, about 2 minutes longer. Transfer the dressing to a bowl or rimmed platter and serve hot. *(The dressing can be prepared up to 12 hours ahead. Cover and refrigerate, then reheat before serving.)*

—*Larry Forgione*

MUSTARD BARBECUED QUAIL WITH VIDALIA ONION AND BLACK-EYED PEA RELISH

"There are two kinds of barbecue in the South, red or yellow, ketchup or mustard based," explains chef Elizabeth Terry, chef of Elizabeth on 37th in Savannah. Most people are familiar with the red, but she devised this spicy mustard recipe to complement her menu of updated southern food. The quail can be made ahead and served cold or at room temperature. It is a great party dish; the restaurant once prepared it for 1,200 people. Serve it with a green salad and roast corn on the cob.

❖ A 1988 or 1990 Saintsbury Pinot Noir from Napa's Carneros district goes well with the quail and picks up the fruit nicely.

6 Servings

½ pound spicy bulk sausage
½ cup minced Vidalia or other sweet onion
1 Granny Smith apple—peeled, cored and minced
¼ cup grainy mustard
¼ cup fresh lemon juice

A WARMHEARTED HOLIDAY DINNER

Serves 8

New England Cheddar Cheese Soup (p. 45)
❖ *1991 Silverado Sauvignon Blanc*

Winter Greens Salad with Warm Sherry Vinaigrette (p. 120)
Roast Goose with Plum Glaze (at left)
Appalachian Dressing (at right)
Crisp Root-Vegetable Cakes (p. 115)
Winter Fruit and Nut Conserve (p. 245)
❖ *1987 Conn Creek Cabernet Sauvignon*

Baked Pumpkin and Buttermilk Pudding (p. 210)

—*Larry Forgione*

POULTRY

3 garlic cloves, minced
2 tablespoons teriyaki sauce
2 tablespoons minced fresh thyme
2 teaspoons freshly cracked pepper
1 teaspoon minced lemon zest
½ teaspoon salt
½ cup peanut oil
12 partially boned quail
Black-Eyed Pea Relish (p. 247)

1. In a medium skillet, cook the sausage and onion over moderately high heat, stirring constantly to break up the meat, until the sausage is cooked through but not browned, about 4 minutes. Stir in the apple and immediately drain off the fat. Refrigerate to cool slightly, about 5 minutes.

2. In a food processor, combine the mustard, lemon juice, garlic, teriyaki sauce, thyme, pepper, lemon zest and salt. With the machine on, slowly add the peanut oil. The sauce will thicken.

3. Stuff each quail with the chilled sausage mixture and place in a large dish. Cover the quail with the mustard sauce and let marinate for 1 to 2 hours.

4. Preheat the oven to 500°. Arrange the quail without touching on a broiling pan and roast, rotating the pan, for about 20 minutes, until browned and crisp.

5. Spoon the Black-Eyed Pea Relish on 6 dinner plates. Top each portion with 2 quail and serve.

—Elizabeth Terry

ROAST QUAIL WITH TARRAGON

Serve these quail around a mound of brown rice cooked in chicken stock.

8 Servings

1 stick (8 tablespoons) unsalted butter, at room temperature
1 tablespoon chopped fresh tarragon or 1½ teaspoons dried
1 tablespoon chopped parsley
Salt
About ⅓ cup Spanish sherry or Rainwater Madeira
16 whole fresh quail
8 slices smoked bacon, halved crosswise
1¼ cups chicken stock or canned broth
Freshly ground white pepper
Cooked brown rice, for serving

1. In a bowl, blend the butter, tarragon and parsley. Salt lightly. Spoon 1 teaspoon of the sherry and 1 teaspoon of the seasoned butter into the cavity of each quail. Refrigerate the remaining butter.

2. Hold the drumsticks of each quail together and lay a piece of bacon over the legs and across part of the breast. Secure the bacon with a toothpick pushed through the thighs. Arrange the quail side by side but without touching in a large shallow roasting pan or jelly-roll pan.

3. In a small saucepan, boil the chicken stock over high heat until reduced to ⅔ cup, about 10 minutes. *(The recipe can be prepared to this point up to 1 day ahead. Cover and refrigerate the quail and stock separately. Bring the quail to room temperature before proceeding.)*

4. Preheat the oven to 500°. Roast the quail on the top rack of the oven for about 15 minutes, basting once or twice. Remove from the oven and preheat the broiler.

5. Remove the bacon from the quail and sprinkle them with white pepper. Broil the quail for 1 to 2 minutes, rotating the pan as necessary, to crisp the skin.

6. Stir any pan juices from the quail into the reduced stock and simmer over moderate heat for 5 minutes. Remove from the heat and whisk in the reserved seasoned butter, 1 tablespoon at a time. When all the butter has been incorporated, add sherry to taste and season with salt and white pepper.

7. Mound the brown rice on a large round platter and arrange the quail around the rice. Pour the sauce into a warmed sauceboat and pass separately.

—Camille Glenn

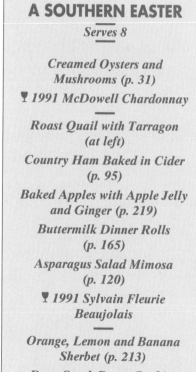

A SOUTHERN EASTER

Serves 8

Creamed Oysters and Mushrooms (p. 31)
🍷 *1991 McDowell Chardonnay*

Roast Quail with Tarragon (at left)
Country Ham Baked in Cider (p. 95)
Baked Apples with Apple Jelly and Ginger (p. 219)
Buttermilk Dinner Rolls (p. 165)
Asparagus Salad Mimosa (p. 120)
🍷 *1991 Sylvain Fleurie Beaujolais*

Orange, Lemon and Banana Sherbet (p. 213)
Deep-South Pecan Cookies (p. 183)
—Camille Glenn

MEAT

POT-ROASTED BEEF BRISKET WITH ANCHO CHILE SAUCE

The heat of dried chiles can vary greatly. Ancho chiles have a sweet, mild flavor with little heat, but once in a while one may have an unusually strong kick. Negro chiles have a richer flavor and considerably more heat than anchos. Use the combination of chiles that appeals to you. The brisket will taste even better if made a day ahead.

For a delicious way to use the leftovers from this brisket, try Beef and Potato Enchiladas (p. 87).

❦ The heat from the chiles as well as the flavor of the meat would be nicely contrasted by a fruity, full-bodied red, such as a 1989 G.D. Vajra Dolcetto d'Alba from Italy or a 1989 Villa Mt. Eden Zinfandel from California.

4 Servings (plus leftovers)

2 to 3 dried ancho chiles
1 to 2 dried negro chiles
¼ cup dried porcini mushrooms (about ⅓ ounce)
1½ teaspoons cumin seeds
5 pounds trimmed beef brisket in one piece
Salt and freshly ground black pepper
2 tablespoons vegetable oil
½ cup red wine
2 tablespoons tomato paste
Two 3-inch strips of orange zest
1 small cinnamon stick
1 bay leaf

6 garlic cloves, peeled
1 large Spanish onion, cut into 8 wedges

1. In a large bowl, cover the ancho and negro chiles with 2 cups of hot water. Cover the bowl with a plate and soak until the chiles soften, about 20 minutes.

2. In a small bowl, cover the dried porcini with ½ cup of hot water. Cover with a small dish and soak until the porcini soften, about 20 minutes.

3. Remove the chiles from the soaking liquid. Pull off the stems and remove as many seeds as possible. Strain and reserve the soaking liquid. Transfer the mushrooms to a small bowl, rinsing any gritty pieces in the soaking liquid. Let the liquid stand so that any grit will settle to the bottom.

4. In a small skillet, toast the cumin seeds over high heat, shaking the pan, until fragrant, about 40 seconds. Transfer the seeds to a work surface to cool completely. Pound them to a coarse powder in a mortar or chop coarsely with a knife.

5. Preheat the oven to 325°. Sprinkle the brisket on both sides with salt and pepper. Rub 1 teaspoon of the cumin on one side of the brisket.

6. In a roasting pan set over 2 burners, heat the oil over moderately high heat. When almost smoking, add the brisket, cumin-side down, and brown well, about 3 minutes. Turn the beef over and brown the other side, about 3 minutes longer. Transfer the brisket to a large plate.

7. Pour the red wine into the roasting pan and reduce the heat to low. Cook, stirring, for 1 minute. Stir in the tomato paste, orange zest, cinnamon stick and bay leaf. Add the reserved chile and mushroom soaking liquids, stopping when you reach the grit at the bottom. Return the brisket to the pan and arrange the garlic cloves, onion wedges, soaked chiles and mushrooms around it. Cover with foil and bake in the middle of the oven for 2 hours.

8. Remove the brisket from the oven, cover and let rest for 15 minutes. Transfer the meat to a large plate to cool. Discard the cinnamon stick, bay leaf and orange zest. Working in batches, puree the contents of the roasting pan in a food processor. Season the sauce with salt, pepper and the remaining ½ teaspoon toasted cumin.

9. Carve the beef in thick slices, allowing 3 to 4 per person. Pour 2 cups of the sauce into a large skillet and lay the sliced beef on top. Warm over low heat, partially covered, for 4 to 5 minutes, turning the meat occasionally. Reserve the remaining meat and sauce for another meal.

—*Marcia Kiesel*

BEEF BRISKET DINNER
Serves 4

Wild Mushroom Salad

Pot-Roasted Beef Brisket with Ancho Chile Sauce (at left)

Hominy and Bell Pepper Sauté (p. 104)

Minted Carrots

❦ *Zinfandel*

Tangerines in Honey Syrup
—*Marcia Kiesel*

BEEF AND POTATO ENCHILADAS

❦ A simple hearty red, such as 1989 Glen Ellen Proprietor's Reserve Cabernet Sauvignon, is one choice, although a full-flavored beer, such as Anchor Steam, would be more refreshing.

6 Servings

1 Idaho potato (about ½ pound), peeled and cut into ⅓-inch dice
1 tablespoon olive oil
½ pound leftover Pot-Roasted Beef Brisket (at left), cut into ⅓-inch dice, plus 1½ cups leftover Ancho Chile Sauce
1 small onion, cut into ⅓-inch dice
2 large garlic cloves, minced
1 cup drained canned Italian peeled tomatoes, chopped
Hot pepper sauce, preferably a Caribbean variety
Twelve 8-inch corn tortillas
1 cup shredded Monterey Jack cheese (4 ounces)
1 cup shredded sharp Cheddar cheese (4 ounces)
3 large scallions, thinly sliced
Sour cream, for serving

1. Preheat the oven to 425°. In a small saucepan, cover the potato with water and bring to a boil over moderately high heat. Cook until tender, about 6 minutes, then drain.

2. In a large skillet, heat the oil. Add the diced beef and cook over high heat, stirring occasionally, until browned, about 2 minutes. Add the onion and garlic, reduce the heat to low and cook, stirring, until fragrant, about 3 minutes. Stir in the diced potato, tomatoes and ½ cup of the leftover Ancho Chile Sauce. Add hot pepper sauce to taste. Simmer until heated through, about 3 minutes.

3. In a medium skillet, warm the remaining 1 cup sauce over low heat. Remove from the heat and dip a corn tortilla in the sauce to coat both sides. Place the tortilla in a 9-by-14-inch baking dish and top with about ⅓ cup of the meat and potato filling. Roll up the enchilada and push it to the end of the dish. Repeat with the remaining tortillas, sauce and filling, packing the enchiladas in a row.

4. Pour any remaining sauce over the enchiladas and scatter the cheeses on top. Bake in the upper third of the oven for about 15 minutes, until bubbling. Sprinkle the scallions over the enchiladas and serve with sour cream.

—Marcia Kiesel

BLANQUETTE OF VEAL VALLEE D'AUGE

6 Servings

1 sweet potato (about ¾ pound), peeled
3 medium-to-large carrots, peeled
About 30 pearl onions (¾ pound)
1 cup fresh shelled peas or frozen petite peas
6 large mushrooms, each cut into 6 wedges
3 pounds very lean veal shoulder, shank or chuck, trimmed of all visible fat and cut into 1½- to 2-inch chunks
1 large onion, peeled and cut into 6 wedges
4 garlic cloves, peeled
Bouquet garni made with 6 parsley sprigs or stems, 3 fresh thyme sprigs and 3 bay leaves tied together with string
Salt and freshly ground pepper
1 cup heavy cream
1 tablespoon potato starch or arrowroot, dissolved in 2 tablespoons Calvados or Cognac

1. Cut the sweet potato into 24 sticks, each about 2 inches long and ¾ inch thick. Using a small sharp knife, round off the edges of each stick to create an oval, football-like shape.

2. Cut the carrots crosswise into 1½-inch chunks. Shape the chunks into ovals to match the sweet potato.

3. In a small pot of boiling water, blanch the pearl onions for 5 seconds; drain and peel.

4. In a large saucepan, bring 4 cups of water to a boil over high heat. Add the pearl onions and boil until tender, about 8 minutes. With a slotted spoon, transfer the onions to a bowl.

5. Bring the water in the saucepan back to a boil. Add the sweet potato and carrots and boil until tender. With the slotted spoon, add the vegetables to the onions in the bowl.

6. Return the water to a boil. Add the fresh peas and boil for 3 minutes. Add the mushrooms and boil for 30 seconds. Remove the peas and mushrooms with the slotted spoon and add them to the other vegetables. There should be about 2½ cups of cooking liquid left. If you have more, boil it down; if less, add water.

7. Place the veal in the liquid and add the onion wedges, garlic, bouquet garni, 1 teaspoon salt and ¼ teaspoon pepper. Bring to a boil and stir well. Cover, reduce the heat and simmer gently until the meat is very tender, about 1¼ hours.

8. With the slotted spoon, transfer the veal to a bowl. Discard the bouquet garni. Strain the cooking liquid through a fine sieve into a bowl, pressing hard on the solids to extract as much liquid as possible. *(The recipe can be prepared to this point up to 1 day ahead. Return the meat to the cooking liquid and let cool. Refrigerate the meat and cooked vegetables separately.)*

9. Rinse the cooking vessel and return the strained liquid to it. You should have 2 cups; if you have more, boil to reduce. Add the cream and ½ teaspoon of salt and bring to a boil. Whisk the dissolved potato starch into the sauce and remove from the heat. Mix well until thick and smooth.

10. Add the meat and all the cooked vegetables to the sauce along with the frozen peas, if using. Bring the stew to a boil, then reduce the heat and simmer gently for 2 minutes. Serve hot.

—*Jacques Pépin*

VEAL AND EGGPLANT ROLLS

At Ristorante Apollinare in Spoleto, this dish is served with vegetables.

4 Servings

*1 large eggplant (1½ pounds), peeled
  and sliced lengthwise in eight
  ⅓-inch-thick slices*
¼ cup olive oil
Salt and freshly ground pepper

*Four 4-ounce slices of veal scaloppine,
  pounded ¼ inch thick*
1 tablespoon fresh lemon juice
2 tablespoons unsalted butter

1. Preheat the broiler. Arrange the eggplant on a large baking sheet and brush both sides with 3 tablespoons of the oil. Season both sides with salt and pepper. Broil the eggplant, turning once, for about 8 minutes, or until deep golden brown. Set aside.

2. Preheat the oven to 450°. On a work surface, season the veal with salt and pepper. Place 2 broiled eggplant slices on each piece of veal. Starting at the narrowest end, roll the veal up into round bundles, folding in the sides as you go. Secure with toothpicks.

3. In a large nonreactive ovenproof skillet, heat the remaining 1 tablespoon olive oil over high heat. When almost smoking, add the veal rolls and brown them well on all sides, about 6 minutes. Put the skillet in the oven and bake for about 5 minutes, or until the veal is barely pink in the center and an instant-read thermometer inserted into a roll registers 140°. Transfer the veal rolls to a platter.

4. Set the skillet over moderate heat. Add the lemon juice and scrape up the browned bits from the bottom of the pan. Turn off the heat and stir in the butter. Season with salt and pepper to taste. To serve, remove the toothpicks, slice the veal rolls crosswise ¼ inch thick and pour the sauce on top.

—*Ristorante Apollinare*

ROASTED PORK LOIN WITH GARLIC

Have your butcher remove the chine bone from the loin to make carving easy.

❢ Pork is mild enough to serve with a light white provided it has sufficient acidity to cut across the fattiness of the meat. A fragrant dry Riesling, such as 1989 Trimbach from Alsace or 1991 Trefethen from California, would also have attractive flavor affinities with the apples and cabbage.

4 Servings

*One 3-pound center-cut pork loin,
  chine bone removed*
3 garlic cloves, thinly sliced
Salt and freshly ground pepper
1 tablespoon vegetable oil

1. Preheat the oven to 425°. Using a small knife, cut deep slits all over the pork and insert a sliver of garlic into each one. Sprinkle the loin on both sides with salt and pepper.

2. Heat the oil in a small roasting pan. Add the pork loin and cook over moderately high heat, turning occasionally, until nicely browned all over, about 5 minutes. Insert a meat thermometer in the center of the pork, making sure it doesn't touch the bone. Roast the pork for about 50 minutes, or until the internal temperature reaches 150°. Transfer to a carving board and let stand for 10 minutes. Carve the pork into ½-inch-thick slices.

—*Stephanie Lyness*

*Roast Quail with Tarragon
(p. 84) and Buttermilk
Dinner Rolls (p. 165).*

Left, Chicken with Raisins and Black Pepper (p. 73). Above, Grilled Chicken Breasts (p. 236) with Caramelized Red Onion Marmalade (p. 236) and Quinoa and Vegetable Pilaf (p. 238).

ROAST FRESH HAM
WITH GARLIC GRAVY

Since most fresh hams will serve 12 to 16 people, it's always nice to have a recipe that will use the leftovers to good advantage. You can use the meat for sandwiches, or try the Pork Barbecue on a Bun (p. 95). Save the ham bone for flavoring the barbecue.

❢ Fresh ham pairs well with both red and white wines; in this case, the garlicky gravy suggests an equally savory, crisp white as the most attractive foil.

6 Servings (plus leftovers)

1 teaspoon olive oil
¼ teaspoon caraway seeds
1 teaspoon salt
1 teaspoon freshly ground pepper
One 10-pound bone-in fresh ham,
*   tough skin removed and fat trimmed*
*   to ¼ inch*
2 medium onions, unpeeled and halved
2 tablespoons unsalted butter
6 medium garlic cloves, very thinly
*   sliced*
⅓ cup dry red wine
2 tablespoons all-purpose flour
1 teaspoon minced fresh rosemary or
*   ½ teaspoon crumbled dried, plus*
*   6 fresh sprigs, for garnish*
1 cup chicken stock or canned
*   low-sodium broth*
2 teaspoons Dijon mustard

1. Preheat the oven to 400°. In a small bowl, mix the olive oil, caraway seeds and ¼ teaspoon each of the salt and pepper. Rub the mixture all over the ham and place it, rounded-side up, in a large heavy roasting pan. Arrange the onions around the ham, cut-sides

Grilled Baby Lamb Chops
with Warm Insalata Tricolore
(p. 96).

down. Insert a meat thermometer deep into the thickest part of the ham, making sure it doesn't touch the bone.

2. Roast the ham for 30 minutes. Reduce the heat to 350° and roast for about 1¾ hours longer, until the internal temperature reaches 160°. Using a large fork and a metal spatula, transfer the ham to a cutting board. Cover loosely with foil and let rest.

3. Pour off any fat from the roasting pan. Discard the crisp outer layers of the onions, leaving the soft portions in the pan. Add the butter and garlic, set the pan over 2 burners and cook over moderately low heat, scraping the onion and browned bits from the bottom of the pan, until the garlic is fragrant and the butter is melted, 1 to 2 minutes.

4. Add the wine and stir for 1 minute. Add 1 cup of water and whisk in the flour, rosemary and the remaining ¾ teaspoon each of salt and pepper until smooth. Whisk in the chicken stock and mustard and bring to a boil over moderately high heat. Boil, whisking occasionally, until thickened, about 4 minutes.

5. Transfer the contents of the roasting pan to a blender and puree until smooth. Pour the gravy into a small saucepan and keep warm over very low heat.

6. Using a large sharp knife, thinly slice the ham, rounded-side up, allowing 3 to 4 slices per person. Reserve the remaining meat on the bone for another meal. Arrange the ham slices on a platter and garnish with the rosemary sprigs. Stir any juices from the meat into the garlic gravy and serve.

—*Tracey Seaman*

BRAISED PORK LOIN
WITH PRUNES AND
CREAM SAUCE

If you have limited oven space, braise this pork loin on top of the stove over very low heat, turning it once or twice during cooking.

6 Servings

18 pitted prunes
2 cups dry white wine
2¼ pounds trimmed boneless pork loin,
*   tied with twine at 1½-inch intervals*
Salt, preferably fine sea salt, and
*   freshly ground pepper*
2 tablespoons olive, canola or peanut
*   oil*
1 tablespoon unsalted butter
¼ cup finely diced onion
¼ cup finely diced carrot
¼ cup finely diced celery
1 tablespoon brandy (optional)
½ cup crème fraîche or ½ cup heavy
*   cream mixed with 1 teaspoon fresh*
*   lemon juice*
Finely chopped flat-leaf parsley or
*   minced chives, for serving*

1. Soak the prunes in the wine until plumped, at least 3 hours or overnight. Transfer the prunes and wine to a small nonreactive saucepan and bring to a gentle boil over moderate heat. Reduce the heat to moderately low and simmer for 10 minutes.

2. Preheat the oven to 325°. Season the pork generously with salt and pepper. In a large heavy flameproof casserole, heat the oil over moderately high heat. When it is hot, add the pork and sear all over until nicely browned,

about 10 minutes; adjust the heat to prevent scorching. Transfer the loin to a plate. Discard all but 1 tablespoon of the fat from the casserole.

3. Add the butter and melt over moderately high heat. Add the onion, carrot and celery and cook, stirring, until golden, about 5 minutes.

4. Strain the prunes and their soaking liquid over the casserole; reserve the prunes. Deglaze the pan with the liquid over low heat, scraping the bottom with a spoon. Return the pork and any accumulated juices to the casserole. Insert a meat thermometer into the center of the loin, cover the casserole and bake in the oven for 45 minutes, or until the internal temperature reaches 145°.

5. Transfer the pork loin to a platter or carving board and cover loosely with foil while finishing the sauce.

6. Strain the cooking liquid through a sieve set over a degreasing pitcher or small bowl, pressing down on the vegetables to extract as much liquid as possible. Reserve the vegetables. Degrease the strained liquid. Return the liquid to the casserole, stir in the brandy and boil over moderately high heat until dark brown and reduced to about ¾ cup, 2 to 3 minutes. Whisk in the crème fraîche and reserved vegetables. Return to a boil, then remove from the heat. Stir in any accumulated juices from the pork roast.

7. Using a blender, puree the sauce until smooth. Transfer the sauce to a small saucepan and stir in the reserved prunes. Season with salt and pepper. Cook over very low heat, stirring, until heated through.

8. Cut the twine off the pork. Slice the meat and serve with the sauce and a sprinkling of parsley.

—*Christopher Kump*

ROSEMARY PORK ROAST

25 to 30 Buffet Servings

Two 3½-pound rolled and tied boneless pork loins
¼ cup dried rosemary plus fresh rosemary sprigs, for garnish
¼ cup plus 2 tablespoons olive oil
2 tablespoons coarsely ground pepper
2 tablespoons balsamic vinegar
2 teaspoons coarse (kosher) salt

1. Preheat the oven to 350°. Place the pork loins side by side, fat-side up,

---

HOLIDAY OPEN HOUSE

Serves 25 to 30

Ricotta, Prosciutto and Basil Spread (p. 22)

Artichoke and Goat Cheese Spread (p. 22)

Crostini (p. 22)

Crudités

🍷 *1991 Preston Cuvée de Fumé*

———

Rosemary Pork Roast (above)

Baked Penne with Roasted Vegetables (p. 154)

Mixed Salad

🍷 *1990 Prosper Maufoux Côtes du Rhône*

———

Chocolate Brownies (p. 182)

Cappuccino Brownies (p. 182)

Fresh Fruit

—*Francine Maroukian*

---

in a large heavy roasting pan. Insert an ovenproof meat thermometer in the center of one of the roasts. Roast the pork for 30 minutes.

2. Meanwhile, in a bowl, crush the rosemary with the olive oil, pepper, vinegar and salt. Spoon the seasoning mixture over the pork. Return the meat to the oven and roast for about 30 minutes longer, until the internal temperature is 160° to 165°. Remove from the oven, cover loosely with foil and let rest for at least 10 minutes. Thinly slice the meat and arrange on platters. Pour any juices over the meat. Garnish with rosemary sprigs. Serve warm or at room temperature.

—*Francine Maroukian*

PORK MEDALLIONS WITH BALSAMIC VINEGAR AND SAGE

4 Servings

1½ pounds pork tenderloin, trimmed
2 tablespoons all-purpose flour
½ teaspoon salt
⅛ teaspoon freshly ground pepper
1 tablespoon unsalted butter
1 tablespoon olive or vegetable oil
⅔ cup balsamic vinegar
¼ cup chicken stock or canned low-sodium broth
1 tablespoon chopped fresh sage or 1 teaspoon dried

1. Cut the tenderloin on a slight angle into eight 1¼-inch medallions. Pound them lightly with the flat side of a large knife to flatten. On a plate, combine the flour with the salt and pepper. Dredge the medallions in the seasoned flour and shake off the excess.

2. In a large nonreactive skillet, melt the butter in the oil over moderately high heat. Add the medallions in 2 batches and cook until nicely browned and medium-rare, 2 to 3 minutes per side. Transfer to a plate, cover with foil and keep warm.

3. Drain the fat from the pan. Add the vinegar and boil, scraping the bottom of the pan with a wooden spoon to release any brown bits, until the mixture is thickened and reduced by about half. Add the chicken stock and any juices that have accumulated on the plate from the pork and boil until reduced to a dark, shiny sauce, about 1 minute. Add the sage and season to taste with salt and pepper. Arrange the medallions on a platter or plates and spoon the sauce on top.

—*Stephanie Lyness*

PORK BARBECUE ON A BUN

Although the ham bone adds extra flavor, it is not strictly necessary to use it. Any cooked pork can be used in this recipe. Serve with spicy black beans and creamy coleslaw.

❦ The spicy flavors here call for a gutsy, full-flavored California red, such as 1987 Louis M. Martini Petite Sirah or 1990 Parducci Bono Sirah (a Charbono/Petite Sirah blend). Of course, full-flavored beer, such as Samuel Adams Boston Lager or Michelob, could also pair well.

6 Servings

About 3½ pounds boneless cooked fresh ham or pork, cut into 3-inch chunks
1 cooked fresh ham leg bone (optional; see Roast Fresh Ham, p. 93)
4 garlic cloves, peeled
¼ cup plus 3 tablespoons cider vinegar
2 teaspoons salt

¾ cup ketchup
3 tablespoons light brown sugar
2 tablespoons Worcestershire sauce
1 tablespoon mild yellow mustard
1½ teaspoons hot pepper sauce, plus more to taste
1 teaspoon freshly ground pepper
6 soft rolls, split

1. In a large heavy nonreactive saucepan or casserole, place the pork chunks, ham bone, garlic, ¼ cup of the vinegar, 1 teaspoon of the salt and 4 cups of water. Bring to a boil over moderately high heat. Reduce the heat to moderately low, cover partially and simmer for 1 hour.

2. Discard the ham bone. Continue simmering until the meat is very tender, about 45 minutes longer. Using a slotted spoon, transfer the pork chunks to a plate. When cool enough to handle, shred the pork.

3. Meanwhile, prepare the barbecue sauce. In a small nonreactive saucepan, combine the remaining 3 tablespoons vinegar and 1 teaspoon salt with the ketchup, brown sugar, Worcestershire sauce, mustard, hot pepper sauce and pepper. Whisk over low heat until the sugar dissolves, about 2 minutes.

4. Return the pork to the large saucepan. Stir in half the barbecue sauce and simmer over moderately low heat until the sauce thickens and coats the pork, about 20 minutes. *(The pork barbecue can be prepared up to 3 weeks ahead and frozen; refrigerate the remaining barbecue sauce. Reheat the pork barbecue and the sauce separately over moderate heat before serving.)* Serve the pork on soft rolls and pass the barbecue sauce separately.

—*Tracey Seaman*

COUNTRY HAM BAKED IN CIDER

The flavor of apple cider is just the right counterpoint to a country ham. Soak the ham for 12 to 48 hours before cooking; the longer it soaks the less salty it will be. After braising, the ham needs to cool overnight before it is finished in the oven. The ham can also be braised up to one week ahead.

You will have a lot of ham left over, but it will keep in the refrigerator for up to two months. Tissue-thin slices make fabulous sandwiches and are delicious with green salads. Thicker slices can be warmed for breakfast. Slivers can be added to scalloped potatoes, bean soups, pastas, egg dishes and stir-fries. Country ham can also be minced or ground and mixed with rice or bread crumbs for stuffing, added to meat loaf or meatballs or simply mixed with mayonnaise for an out-of-this-world ham salad sandwich.

8 Servings (plus leftovers)

1 whole 12-pound smoked country ham (see Note)
1 quart apple cider
2 teaspoons ground cloves
½ cup light brown sugar
1 teaspoon dry mustard
Baked Apples with Apple Jelly and Ginger (p. 219)
Sprigs of watercress, for garnish (optional)

1. Scrub the ham thoroughly all over with a stiff brush. Place the ham in a very large deep roasting pan or stockpot and cover completely with cold wa-

ter. Soak the ham at room temperature for 12 to 48 hours, changing the water a couple of times.

2. Preheat the oven to 300°. Discard the soaking water. Place the ham in a deep roasting pan, fat-side up. Set aside 3 tablespoons of the apple cider. Pour the remainder into the roasting pan and add enough water to barely cover the ham. Set the pan on the lowest rack of the oven and bake the ham for 2 hours. Do not allow the liquid to exceed a quiet simmer at any time, or the ham will be tough.

3. Turn the ham over to insure even cooking. Bake for 2 hours longer. It takes 20 to 25 minutes per pound for a tender cooked ham. An instant-read thermometer inserted into the thickest part of the meat, but not touching the bone, should register 170°.

4. Remove the ham from the oven. Leave it in the liquid to cool overnight in a cool place; this helps to keep the ham moist. *(At this point, the ham can be removed from the cooking liquid, wrapped and refrigerated for up to 1 week. Bring the ham to room temperature before proceeding.)*

5. Preheat the oven to 425°. Remove the ham from the pan and pour off all the liquid if you haven't done so already. Using a sharp knife, remove the skin from the ham. Trim the fat all over to ¼ inch.

6. Return the ham to the roasting pan, fat-side up. Sprinkle the fat with the cloves. Blend the brown sugar with the mustard and the reserved 3 tablespoons apple cider to make a thick paste. Rub the paste over the fat. Roast for 20 to 25 minutes, or until the ham

has a beautiful golden glaze. Let cool.

7. To carve: Cut a thin slice from the bottom of the ham to allow it to sit flat. Turn it over and cut a wedge from the hock end. With a long thin sharp knife, carve very thin vertical slices, then slide the knife horizontally against the bone to release the slices. Surround the ham with the Baked Apples and sprigs of watercress if desired.

NOTE: There are as many country hams to choose from as there are wines in California. The two that follow are favorites, and they're both available by mail: Father's Country Hams, Gatton Farms, P.O. Box 98, Bremen, KY 42325, 502-525-3437; S. Wallace Edwards & Sons, Inc., P.O. Box 25, Surry, VA 23883, 800-222-4267.

—Camille Glenn

GRILLED BABY LAMB CHOPS WITH WARM INSALATA TRICOLORE

This rustic recipe was inspired by the Roman lamb *a scottadito* (burn the finger), in which charred, juicy baby lamb chops are picked up off the hot grill with bare fingers and eaten immediately. As an accompaniment, the traditional salad trio—arugula, radicchio and endive—is quickly sautéed with garlic and crushed red pepper.

6 Servings

1½ tablespoons Dijon mustard
1 tablespoon balsamic vinegar
2 garlic cloves, finely chopped
Salt and freshly ground black pepper
¾ cup extra-virgin olive oil
2 tablespoons slivered fresh basil leaves
20 baby lamb rib chops or 12 rib chops cut 1 inch thick, frenched (see Note)
2 heads of radicchio, coarsely chopped
2 Belgian endives, sliced crosswise ¼ inch thick
2 bunches of arugula, coarsely chopped
Pinch of crushed red pepper

1. In a small nonreactive bowl, whisk the mustard, vinegar, half of the garlic and salt and pepper to taste. Slowly whisk in ½ cup of the olive oil, then add the basil. Arrange the chops in a large shallow glass or ceramic dish and pour the marinade on top. Turn to coat. Marinate the chops for at least 1 hour but not more than 3 hours, turning them every 30 minutes.

2. Light a grill or preheat the broiler. Mix together the radicchio, endives and arugula. In a large skillet, heat the remaining ¼ cup olive oil over low heat. Add the remaining chopped garlic and the crushed red pepper and cook for 2 minutes. Increase the heat to high,

MARVELOUS WINE AND FOOD MENU

Serves 6

Bruschetta Rossa (p. 22)
🍷 *Nino Franco's NV Prosecco Brut*

Roasted Vegetable and Goat Cheese Terrine (p. 30)
🍷 *1990 Matanzas Creek Sauvignon Blanc*

Seared Salmon with Sweet Corn, Shiitakes and Spinach (p. 38)
🍷 *1986 Marqués de Murrieta Rioja Blanco, Reserva*

Grilled Baby Lamb Chops with Warm Insalata Tricolore (at left)
🍷 *1989 Châteauneuf-du-Pape*

Sheep's Milk Cheese and Lemon Fritters with Honey (p. 220)
🍷 *1989 Preston Muscat Brûlé*

add the greens and sauté, tossing constantly, until wilted, 2 to 3 minutes. Season with salt and pepper and remove from the heat. Cover and set aside to keep warm.

3. Season the chops with salt and pepper and grill or broil for 1½ minutes per side for medium-rare. For larger chops, grill for about 3 minutes per side. Arrange the chops on 6 plates and mound the wilted salad alongside.

NOTE: Frenching is a butcher's term for scraping the rib bones clean of meat, fat and gristle.

—*Michael Romano*

CARLOS' RACK OF LAMB

Carlos' is a 10-year-old restaurant on the site of a former butcher shop in Highland Park, Illinois. Chef Don Yamauchi often serves the rack of lamb with black beans flavored with ham. Ask the butcher to french the racks (scrape the meat from the bones) for you.

🍷 A full-bodied Cabernet Sauvignon with good fruit is the classic match for lamb. Try either a 1986 Clos du Bois, Briarcrest Vineyard, or a 1985 Château Lynch-Bages.

4 Servings

8 garlic cloves—7 coarsely chopped, 1 minced
1 tablespoon finely chopped fresh rosemary
1 teaspoon olive oil
2 racks of lamb, each with 8 chops, well trimmed of fat and frenched
3 tablespoons unsalted butter
Salt and freshly ground pepper

¼ cup dry bread crumbs, preferably homemade
1 tablespoon Dijon mustard

1. In a small bowl, mix the coarsely chopped garlic with the rosemary and olive oil. Rub this mixture all over the racks of lamb. Cover and refrigerate overnight.

2. In a small saucepan, melt the butter over low heat. Skim any foam from the surface of the butter. Pour the clarified butter into a large ovenproof skillet, stopping when you reach the milk solids.

3. Preheat the oven to 500°. Heat the clarified butter over high heat. Scrape the garlic off the lamb and season the racks with salt and pepper to taste. Add the racks to the skillet and brown well on all sides. Arrange the racks meat-side up in the skillet and remove from the heat.

4. In a small bowl, mix the remaining minced garlic clove with the bread crumbs. Spread the mustard over the lamb and sprinkle the garlic bread crumbs over the mustard. Put the skillet in the oven and roast the lamb for 12 to 14 minutes, until the meat reaches 120° to 125° on an instant-reading thermometer for rare or medium-rare. Transfer the racks to a carving board and let rest for 10 minutes. Carve the racks and serve 4 chops per person.

—*Don Yamauchi*

GRILLED MARINATED LEG OF LAMB

10 Servings

1 bottle (750 ml) dry red wine
1 cup olive oil
5 garlic cloves, peeled and chopped
2 fresh rosemary sprigs, leaves removed
10 fresh mint leaves
10 fresh basil leaves
9-pound leg of lamb—boned, butterflied and trimmed of excess fat
Salt and freshly ground pepper
Mint Pesto (p. 242)

1. In a blender, combine the wine, olive oil, garlic, rosemary leaves, mint and basil. Blend well. Put the lamb in a shallow glass or ceramic dish large enough for the meat to lie flat. Pour the marinade over the lamb and refrigerate for at least 6 hours or overnight, turning the meat once or twice.

2. Remove the lamb from the marinade and bring to room temperature. Season the meat on both sides with salt and pepper. Grill the lamb over hot coals, turning once, until medium-rare. Each section of the meat will cook a little differently. (Alternatively, broil the lamb, trimmed-side down, until brown and crusty, 8 to 10 minutes. Turn the lamb over and broil until crusty and an instant-read thermometer inserted in the thickest part registers 120° to 125° for rare to medium-rare.) Let the lamb rest for 15 minutes before slicing. Serve with the Mint Pesto.

—*Mary Novak*

ROAST RACK OF LAMB WITH SHIITAKE MUSHROOMS

---

8 Servings

4 garlic cloves, thinly sliced
¼ cup fresh rosemary, coarsely chopped
½ cup olive oil
Freshly ground pepper
4 racks of lamb, frenched (see Note)
Lamb Stock (recipe follows)
1½ cups dry red wine
1 tablespoon unsalted butter
½ pound shiitake mushrooms, stems discarded and caps thickly sliced
1 shallot, minced
Salt

1. In a large baking dish, combine the garlic, rosemary, olive oil and plenty of pepper. Rub the mixture all over the racks of lamb and set them, meaty-side down, in the dish. Marinate for at least 4 hours at room temperature or overnight in the refrigerator.

2. In a large saucepan, boil the Lamb Stock over high heat until reduced to 2 cups, about 1 hour.

3. In a medium nonreactive saucepan, boil the red wine over high heat until reduced by about half, 7 to 10 minutes.

4. In another medium nonreactive saucepan, melt the butter. Add the mushrooms and shallot and cook over moderate heat until softened, about 4 minutes. Add the reduced Lamb Stock and wine and simmer for 5 minutes to

blend the flavors. Season with salt and pepper. *(The recipe can be prepared to this point up to 1 day ahead. Refrigerate the lamb and sauce separately and return the lamb to room temperature before proceeding.)*

5. Preheat the oven to 450°. In a large skillet, heat 1 tablespoon of olive oil from the lamb marinade over high heat until almost smoking. Season the lamb racks with salt and add 2 of them to the skillet, meaty-side down. Brown well on all sides, then place them, rack-side up, in a large roasting pan. Repeat with the remaining 2 racks.

6. Roast the racks in the oven for 10 to 15 minutes, or until an instant-read thermometer reaches 120° to 125° for rare to medium-rare. Transfer the racks to a carving board and let rest for 15 minutes.

7. Just before serving, reheat the sauce. Carve the racks and serve 4 chops per person with the sauce.

NOTE: Frenching is a butcher's term for scraping the rib bones clean of meat, fat and gristle.

—Annie Roberts

LAMB STOCK

Makes About 2 Quarts

5 pounds lamb shanks and/or neck bones
2 medium unpeeled onions, quartered
2 medium carrots, halved
1 bay leaf
2 fresh thyme sprigs
2 fresh parsley sprigs
10 whole black peppercorns

1. Preheat the oven to 500°. Place the lamb shanks in a roasting pan and roast, turning occasionally, until browned on all sides, about 20 minutes. Transfer the lamb to a large stockpot and add the onions, carrots, bay leaf, thyme, parsley and peppercorns.

2. Set the roasting pan over 2 burners. Add 1 quart of water and cook over high heat, scraping up the browned bits from the bottom of the pan. Add the liquid to the stockpot with 3 quarts of water to cover the bones. Bring to a boil and simmer, skimming occasionally, for 6 hours.

3. Strain the stock into a large saucepan. Let cool, then cover and refrigerate for up to 3 days. Remove the congealed fat from the surface of the stock before using.

—Annie Roberts

DINNER WITH THE MONDAVIS
Serves 8

Seared Scallops with Citrus-Ginger Vinaigrette (p. 62)
🍷 *1989 Reserve Chardonnay*

Roast Rack of Lamb with Shiitake Mushrooms (at left)
Risotto Cakes (p. 159)
Sautéed Swiss Chard with Tomatoes (p. 113)
🍷 *1988 Reserve Cabernet Sauvignon*
🍷 *1988 Opus One*

Tarte Tatin with Cinnamon Ice Cream (p. 196)
🍷 *1985 Sauvignon Blanc Botrytis*

VEGETABLES

VEGETABLES

MICHELE'S STUFFED ARTICHOKES

8 Servings

1 loaf of Italian bread (½ pound), sliced ½ inch thick
¾ cup chopped parsley
¾ cup freshly grated Parmesan or Romano cheese
4 medium garlic cloves, minced
1½ to 1⅔ cups olive oil
Salt
8 medium artichokes
1½ cups dry white wine

1. Preheat the oven to 400°. Toast the bread for about 4 minutes, until dry but not brown. Break up the bread and let cool completely. In a food processor, pulse the bread to make coarse crumbs. You should have 2 cups.

2. In a large bowl, mix together the bread crumbs, parsley, grated cheese, garlic and ⅔ cup of the olive oil. Season with salt.

3. Slice off the top third of each artichoke. With scissors, trim the top third off all the leaves. Scrape out the hairy chokes in the center with a spoon. Beginning at the outside of each artichoke and working toward the center, pack the stuffing in between the leaves. When each artichoke is amply filled, press down on the tops to secure the stuffing. *(The recipe can be prepared to this point up to 1 day ahead. Cover and refrigerate the artichokes.)*

4. In a large nonreactive flameproof casserole, heat 1 tablespoon of the olive oil over high heat. Set the artichokes in the pot and sear the bottoms, about 2 minutes. Turn off the heat. Drizzle 1½ to 2 tablespoons of the olive oil over each artichoke and sprinkle them with ½ cup of the wine. Pour the remaining 1 cup wine into the casserole and add enough water to reach 1 inch up the sides of the artichokes. Bring to a boil, cover and simmer gently over low heat until tender, 45 minutes to 1 hour. Check to see that there is enough liquid in the pot during cooking; add more water if necessary. Transfer the artichokes to a platter and serve hot.

—*Evan Jones*

GRILLED ASPARAGUS

10 Servings

3 pounds asparagus
⅓ cup olive oil
Salt and freshly ground pepper

Light a medium hot grill. Place the asparagus on a sheet pan and toss with the olive oil to coat evenly. Grill the asparagus, turning with tongs as necessary, until tender and browned, about 5 minutes. (Alternatively, arrange the asparagus on 2 sheet pans and broil, one pan at a time, until browned and just tender, about 5 minutes.) Arrange the asparagus on a platter and sprinkle with salt and pepper.

—*Mary Novak*

GREEN BEANS WITH BALSAMIC-GLAZED ONIONS

The natural sugar in balsamic vinegar caramelizes the pearl onions with a dark glaze and adds a touch of sweetness to the mustard-vinegar sauce.

8 to 10 Servings

2 pounds fresh pearl onions or 2 bags (16 ounces each) frozen pearl onions, thawed
½ cup balsamic vinegar
2 tablespoons unsalted butter
2 tablespoons vegetable oil
2 teaspoons finely chopped fresh thyme or 1 teaspoon dried
1½ teaspoons freshly ground pepper
1 teaspoon salt
3 pounds fresh green beans, trimmed
¼ cup mild olive oil
1 tablespoon Dijon mustard

1. In a large saucepan of boiling water, blanch the fresh onions for 1 minute. Drain and refresh under cold running water; drain. Using a small, sharp knife, trim the root ends and slip off the skins.

2. Preheat the oven to 400°. In a small nonreactive saucepan, combine ¼ cup of the balsamic vinegar, the butter, vegetable oil, thyme, 1 teaspoon of the pepper and ½ teaspoon of the salt and stir over moderately low heat until the butter is melted.

3. In a medium bowl, toss the fresh or frozen onions with the vinegar mixture to coat. Spread the onions in a single layer on a baking sheet and roast for 35 to 40 minutes, stirring often, until evenly browned.

4. Meanwhile, in a large pot of boiling salted water, blanch the green beans until just tender, about 4 minutes. Drain and refresh under cold running water; drain and set aside. In a large bowl, combine the olive oil, mustard and the remaining ¼ cup balsamic vinegar and ½ teaspoon each of salt and pepper.

5. Add the green beans and the roasted onions to the dressing in the bowl and toss well. Transfer the vegetables to a large casserole. *(The recipe can be prepared to this point up to 1 day ahead; cover the casserole and refrigerate. Return to room temperature before proceeding.)*

6. Preheat the oven to 350°. Cover and bake the green beans and onions for about 20 minutes, or until heated through.

—*Bob Chambers*

WHITE BEANS AND HERBS WITH RED ONION TOPPING

Although freshly cooked white beans are best, you can substitute canned beans; start with Step 3. Handle them with care as they tend to be mushy.

4 Servings

½ pound dried white beans, such as cannellini or Great Northern, rinsed and picked over
3 tablespoons extra-virgin olive oil, plus more for drizzling
3 medium garlic cloves, finely chopped
3 tablespoons chopped flat-leaf parsley
1 tablespoon chopped fresh thyme, sage or rosemary, or a combination
1 bay leaf
¼ to ½ teaspoon crushed red pepper
Pinch of dried oregano
Salt and freshly ground black pepper

4 plum tomatoes—peeled, seeded and very coarsely chopped
1 small red onion, sliced paper thin
⅓ cup fresh basil leaves, torn
Freshly grated Parmesan cheese, for serving

1. In a large saucepan, cover the beans with 2 inches of cold water. Bring to a boil over high heat. Boil for 3 minutes, then remove the beans from the heat and set aside, covered, to soak for 1 hour.

2. Drain and rinse the beans. In a medium saucepan, cover the beans with 1 inch of cold water and bring to a boil over high heat. Reduce the heat to moderately low and simmer until tender, about 50 minutes.

3. In another medium nonreactive saucepan, combine the oil, garlic, parsley, thyme, bay leaf, crushed red pepper and oregano. Cook over low heat for 4 minutes. Add 1 cup of water, season with salt and black pepper and bring to a boil over moderate heat. Cover and simmer for 5 minutes.

4. Stir in the tomatoes, cover and cook for 4 minutes. Gently stir in the beans. Cover and simmer until the beans are heated through, about 5 minutes. Discard the bay leaf.

5. Ladle the beans and their juices into 4 shallow soup bowls. Place a small mound of red onion and some basil in the center of each. Sprinkle Parmesan cheese and, if desired, a few drops of olive oil on top. Serve hot.

—*Viana La Place*

OVEN-ROASTED BEETS WITH WILTED GREENS

8 to 10 Servings

⅓ cup pine nuts (2 ounces)
6 pounds medium beets with greens, trimmed and greens reserved
1½ teaspoons fennel seeds
⅓ cup mild olive oil
⅓ cup extra-virgin olive oil
3 tablespoons fresh lemon juice
2 tablespoons finely grated lemon zest
1 teaspoon salt
½ teaspoon freshly ground pepper
2 pounds Swiss chard, preferably red, trimmed of large ribs

1. Preheat the oven to 350°. Spread the pine nuts in a pan and toast in the oven for 5 minutes, or until golden. Set aside. Increase the temperature to 450°.

2. Place the beets in a single layer on one half of a large sheet of heavy-duty aluminum foil on a baking sheet. Fold the other half of the foil over the beets and crimp the edges to seal. Roast for 1½ hours, or until tender when pierced. Open the foil carefully and let the beets cool slightly.

3. Meanwhile, using a spice grinder or a mortar and pestle, pulverize the fennel seeds. In a small bowl, combine the ground fennel, olive oils, lemon juice, lemon zest, salt and pepper.

4. In a large nonreactive saucepan, heat 1 tablespoon of the flavored oil over high heat. Add half the reserved beet greens and half the Swiss chard and cook until completely wilted, 2 to 3 minutes. Drain in a colander. Repeat the procedure with another 1 table-

spoon of the flavored oil and the remaining beet greens and chard. Season the wilted greens with salt and pepper to taste. Line the sides of a large casserole with the greens.

5. Peel the beets and cut into 1-inch cubes. In a large bowl, toss the beets with the remaining flavored oil. Mound the beets in the center of the casserole. *(The recipe can be prepared to this point up to 1 day ahead; cover the casserole and refrigerate. Return to room temperature before proceeding. Keep the nuts covered at room temperature.)*

6. Preheat the oven to 350°. Cover the casserole and bake for about 15 minutes, or until the vegetables are heated through. Sprinkle the reserved pine nuts over the beets.

—*Bob Chambers*

BROCCOLI WITH SPICY SESAME OIL

4 Servings

1 bunch of broccoli (about 1¼ pounds)
1½ tablespoons Oriental sesame oil
1 small garlic clove, minced
⅛ teaspoon crushed red pepper
2 teaspoons soy sauce
1 scant teaspoon fresh lemon juice

1. Bring a large pot of salted water to a boil. Cut the broccoli into florets. Peel the tough outer layer from the stalks and trim off the woody ends. Cut the stalks diagonally into ¼-inch-thick slices. Add the broccoli to the boiling water and blanch until crisp-tender, about 1 minute. Drain.

2. In a large skillet, warm the sesame oil, garlic and crushed red pepper over low heat for 3 minutes. Stir in the soy sauce and lemon juice. Add the broccoli, toss to coat and serve.

—*Stephanie Lyness*

BROWN-BUTTER BROCCOLI WITH CARAMELIZED CARROTS

Butter that is heated until it turns brown has a rich, nutty taste, which is delicious with many green vegetables, especially broccoli. The carrots provide a colorful nest for the broccoli florets.

6 to 8 Servings

3 pounds broccoli, cut into florets
1 stick (4 ounces) unsalted butter
2 tablespoons mild olive oil
3 pounds carrots, cut into 1½-inch-long matchsticks
1½ teaspoons dill seeds
2 teaspoons sugar
½ teaspoon salt
1 teaspoon freshly ground pepper

1. In a large pot of boiling salted water, blanch the broccoli for 3 minutes. Drain and refresh under cold running water; drain and set aside.

2. In a large deep skillet, melt 1 tablespoon of the butter in the oil over moderately high heat. Stir in the carrots, dill seeds, sugar, salt and ½ teaspoon of the pepper. Cook, stirring frequently, until the carrots are well browned and caramelized, about 15 minutes. Transfer the carrots to a casserole and arrange them around the sides of the dish. Cover to keep warm.

3. Add the remaining 7 tablespoons butter and ½ teaspoon pepper to the skillet and cook over high heat until the butter is fragrant and a deep nutty brown, about 5 minutes. Add the broccoli florets and toss to coat. Place the broccoli in the center of the casserole. *(The recipe can be prepared up to 1 day ahead; cover the casserole and refrigerate. To serve, bring to room temperature and reheat in a 350° oven for 20 minutes, or until hot.)*

—*Bob Chambers*

BRUSSELS SPROUTS WITH MALTED CREAM

This slightly sweet dish will please both fans and non-fans of these baby cabbages. Scoring an "X" in the ends of the brussels sprouts ensures even cooking and speeds up the process.

12 Servings

4 ounces slab bacon, cut into ¼-inch dice
1 large onion, cut into ¼-inch dice (2 cups)
¼ cup malt vinegar
2 cups sour cream
1 teaspoon Worcestershire sauce
Salt and freshly ground pepper
2 pounds brussels sprouts, trimmed

1. Heat a large nonreactive skillet over moderate heat. Add the bacon and cook, stirring occasionally, until just beginning to brown and the fat is rendered, about 5 minutes. Add the onion and cook, stirring, until softened, 8 to 10 minutes.

2. Pour off the excess fat from the skillet. Increase the heat to moderately high, add the malt vinegar and boil until almost evaporated, about 2 minutes. Stir in the sour cream and Worcestershire. Season with salt and pepper and keep warm.

3. In a large saucepan with a steamer basket, bring 3 cups of water to a boil. Meanwhile, score the root ends of the brussels sprouts with an "X." Halve the sprouts if they are large. Steam the brussels sprouts until just tender, 12 to 15 minutes.

4. Transfer the brussels sprouts to a serving bowl. Add the malted cream and toss to coat. Serve hot.

—*Gerry Klaskala*

BRAISED CABBAGE WITH APPLES AND TOASTED CORIANDER

4 Servings

¼ teaspoon ground coriander
1½ tablespoons olive oil
2 medium onions, thinly sliced
1 medium Golden Delicious apple—quartered, cored and thinly sliced
Salt
8 cups shredded cabbage (from a 1¼-pound cabbage)
½ cup dry white wine
½ cup chicken stock or canned low-sodium broth
¼ cup cider vinegar
Freshly ground pepper

1. In a large skillet, toast the coriander over moderate heat, stirring, until fragrant, about 2 minutes. Transfer to a small bowl.

2. Heat the oil in the skillet. Add the onions, apple and ½ teaspoon salt, cover and cook, stirring occasionally, over moderately low heat until the onions are translucent, about 5 minutes. Stir in the shredded cabbage, toasted

coriander, wine, chicken stock, vinegar and ½ teaspoon salt. Bring to a boil. Cover and simmer over low heat until the cabbage is tender, about 20 minutes. Season with pepper and additional salt if needed.

—*Stephanie Lyness*

CELERY ROOT AND APPLE PUREE

This tasty variation on mashed potatoes is inspired by a recipe in *The Cooking of South-West France* by Paula Wolfert, published by The Dial Press.

4 Servings

2 pounds celery root, peeled and cut into ¾-inch cubes
4 large garlic cloves, peeled
1 medium Golden Delicious apple—peeled, cored and cut into 1-inch dice
¾ cup milk
1 tablespoon unsalted butter
1 teaspoon salt
Freshly ground pepper

1. Steam the celery root and garlic in a steamer basket set over boiling water for 10 minutes. Add the apple and continue steaming until the celery root, garlic and apple are very tender, about 5 minutes longer.

2. In a small saucepan, bring the milk to a boil. Transfer the celery root mixture to a food processor or blender, add the hot milk, butter and salt and puree until smooth. Season with freshly ground pepper and serve hot.

—*Stephanie Lyness*

PUREE OF CELERY ROOT WITH LEEKS AND SCALLIONS

Leeks and scallions caramelized in butter provide a contrast to the mild flavor and creamy texture of this puree.

10 to 12 Servings

6 pounds celery root, peeled and cut into 1½-inch chunks
2 pounds baking potatoes, peeled and cut into 1½-inch chunks
1 stick (4 ounces) plus 1 tablespoon unsalted butter
1 tablespoon mild olive oil
8 medium leeks, white part only, halved lengthwise and sliced crosswise ¼ inch thick
6 large scallions, sliced crosswise ¼ inch thick
½ teaspoon salt
¼ teaspoon freshly ground pepper
¾ cup heavy cream

1. In a large saucepan, cover the celery root and potatoes with generously salted water. Bring to a boil over high heat, then reduce the heat to moderate and simmer until the vegetables are tender, about 30 minutes. Drain.

2. Meanwhile, in a large skillet, melt 4 tablespoons of the butter in the oil over moderately high heat. Add the leeks and scallions and cook, stirring often, until well browned, 10 to 12 minutes. Season with the salt and pepper. Set aside.

3. Set a food mill fitted with a medium disk over a large bowl and pass the celery root and potatoes

through it. Alternatively, mash the vegetables with a potato masher.

4. In a small saucepan, melt the remaining 5 tablespoons butter in the heavy cream over moderate heat, stirring occasionally. Using a hand-held electric mixer or a wooden spoon, beat the cream mixture into the celery root puree until fluffy. Season with salt and pepper.

5. Transfer the puree to a large casserole. Spoon the reserved leek-scallion mixture over the top. *(The recipe can be prepared to this point up to 1 day ahead; cover the casserole and refrigerate. Return to room temperature before proceeding.)*

6. Preheat the oven to 350°. Bake the puree, uncovered, for about 15 minutes, or until heated through.

—*Bob Chambers*

HOMINY AND BELL PEPPER SAUTE

4 Servings

1½ tablespoons vegetable oil
1 small onion, thinly sliced
1 small red bell pepper, cut into ½-inch dice
1 small yellow bell pepper, cut into ½-inch dice
Two 16-ounce cans hominy, drained
Salt and freshly ground black pepper

In a medium saucepan, heat the oil. Add the onion and bell peppers, cover and cook over low heat, stirring, until tender, about 8 minutes. Stir in the hominy and 2 tablespoons of water,

cover and cook for 5 minutes. Stir in 2 more tablespoons of water, cover and cook until the hominy is tender, about 5 minutes longer. Season with salt and black pepper and serve.

—*Marcia Kiesel*

CREAMY POLENTA WITH CORN

10 Servings

2 tablespoons olive oil
½ cup minced shallots
6 cups chicken stock or canned low-sodium broth
2½ cups fine cornmeal
2 cups fresh or thawed frozen corn kernels
1½ cups finely grated Asiago cheese (6 ounces)
Salt and freshly ground pepper

1. Warm the olive oil in a large heavy saucepan. Add the shallots and cook over moderate heat, stirring often, until translucent, about 4 minutes. Add the chicken stock and bring to a boil over high heat.

2. Slowly pour in the cornmeal while whisking constantly. When all the cornmeal has been added, reduce the heat to low and stir with a wooden spoon until the polenta thickens and loses its crunch, about 10 minutes. Stir in the corn kernels and cook, stirring, for 3 more minutes.

3. Remove from the heat and stir in the Asiago cheese. Season with salt and pepper. Pour the polenta into a warmed bowl and serve immediately.

—*Mary Novak*

FENNEL GRATIN

4 Servings

2 pounds fennel bulbs (2 to 3) — trimmed, quartered and thinly sliced lengthwise
½ teaspoon salt
¼ teaspoon freshly ground pepper
1½ cups heavy cream
¼ cup dry bread crumbs
¼ cup freshly grated Parmesan cheese
1½ tablespoons unsalted butter

Preheat the oven to 425°. Butter an 8-by-10-inch baking or oval gratin dish. Arrange the fennel slices in the dish. In a small bowl, whisk the salt and pepper into the cream and pour over the fennel. Sprinkle on the bread crumbs and then the Parmesan cheese. Dot with the butter. Cover the gratin with foil and bake for 20 minutes. Remove the foil and continue baking the fennel gratin for about 20 minutes longer, until the cream has reduced and the top is browned.

—*Stephanie Lyness*

LEEK AND POTATO GRATIN

This gratin is so surprisingly light that you can eat lots of it.

6 Servings

3 pounds leeks, white and tender green portions only, thinly sliced crosswise
1¼ teaspoons salt
4 large Idaho potatoes (about 2 pounds), peeled
1 packed cup grated imported Swiss cheese (4½ ounces)
1 teaspoon freshly ground pepper
½ cup heavy cream
1 cup milk

1. Preheat the oven to 400°. Lightly grease a 2½-quart shallow baking dish.

2. In a medium saucepan, combine the leeks with ⅔ cup of water and ½ teaspoon of the salt and bring to a boil over moderately high heat. Cover and cook, stirring occasionally, until tender, 15 to 18 minutes. Drain the leeks, transfer them to a large bowl and let cool.

3. In a food processor fitted with a medium shredding disk, grate the potatoes. Transfer them to a bowl, cover with cold water and stir with your hand to rinse. Drain, rinse under cold running water and drain again. Pat dry with kitchen towels. Add the potatoes, grated cheese, pepper and the remaining ¾ teaspoon salt to the leeks and toss to combine.

4. Spread the leek and potato mixture in the prepared baking dish. Combine the cream and milk and pour evenly over the vegetables. Cover with foil and bake in the upper third of the oven for 20 minutes. Remove the foil and bake for 40 to 45 minutes longer, until brown and crisp on top.

—*Tracey Seaman*

NEAPOLITAN PIZZA

If you don't have a pizza stone and peel, simply assemble and bake the pizzas on a sturdy, flat baking sheet.

Makes Four 12-Inch Pizzas

4½ cups bread flour
6 envelopes active dry yeast (5 tablespoons)
1 teaspoon sugar
1½ cups warm water
1½ teaspoons salt
3 to 4 tablespoons olive oil
Two 35-ounce cans Italian peeled tomatoes, drained

1 large garlic clove, minced
Cornmeal, for sprinkling
½ pound mushrooms, thinly sliced
1 pound mozzarella cheese, cut into ½-inch cubes
¾ cup freshly grated Parmesan cheese (3 ounces)
2 cups fresh basil leaves, torn into large pieces

1. Put the flour in a large bowl and sprinkle the yeast on top. Mix the sugar with the warm water and pour it over the yeast. When the yeast begins to bubble, after 2 to 3 minutes, add the salt and 1 tablespoon of the olive oil. Mix well.

2. Transfer the dough to a lightly floured work surface and knead until smooth and elastic. Put the dough in a lightly oiled bowl and turn to coat. Cover the bowl and let the dough rise until doubled in bulk, about 1 hour.

3. Preheat the oven to 500°. Set a pizza stone on the bottom of the oven to heat. Punch the dough down and cut it into 4 equal pieces. Cover loosely and let rest for 10 minutes.

4. In a food processor, chop the tomatoes until thick but not quite smooth. Pour into a bowl and stir in the garlic.

5. For each pizza, roll and pull 1 piece of the dough into a 12-inch round. Sprinkle a pizza peel with cornmeal. Lay the dough on the peel and lightly brush the rim with olive oil. Spread one-fourth of the tomatoes evenly over the dough and top with one-fourth of the mushrooms, mozzarella, Parmesan and basil. Drizzle a little olive oil over all.

6. Slide the pizza off the peel and onto the pizza stone with a quick jerk. Bake for 8 to 10 minutes, until bubbly and crusty brown on the bottom. Serve immediately.

—*Francis Ford Coppola*

SKEWERED BREAD AND WILD MUSHROOMS WITH PUNGENT HERBS

❡ The earthy, herby, oily tastes here need a tart, crisp, light white, such as 1990 Banfi "Principessa" Gavi, 1990 Château Bonnet Entre-Deux-Mers or 1990 Guenoc Sauvignon Blanc.

2 Servings

Eight ¾-inch-thick slices of country bread
¼ cup extra-virgin olive oil
2 garlic cloves, finely chopped
1 tablespoon finely chopped fresh rosemary
1 teaspoon finely chopped fresh sage
Sea salt
Freshly ground pepper
6 shiitake mushrooms, about 2½ inches in diameter, stems discarded
1 bunch of arugula, leaves only
1 teaspoon fresh lemon juice, or to taste

1. Preheat the oven to 250°. Toast the bread in the oven for 10 minutes.

2. In a small bowl, combine 3 tablespoons of the oil with the garlic, rosemary and sage. Season with sea salt and pepper. Lightly brush the mushroom caps and bread with the herb oil, stuffing the seasonings in the mushroom undersides. Alternately thread 3 mushrooms and 4 slices of bread on a skewer, beginning and ending with a bread slice. Thread another skewer alongside to secure. Repeat the process with the remaining bread and mushrooms. Brush with any remaining herb oil.

3. Light a grill or preheat the broiler. Lightly oil the grill or a baking sheet. Grill or broil the skewers for 3 to 5 minutes, turning, until golden brown on all sides.

4. Lightly dress the arugula leaves with the remaining 1 tablespoon olive oil and lemon juice, sea salt and pepper to taste. Serve the skewered bread and mushrooms with the arugula salad.

—*Viana La Place*

ROASTED ONIONS WITH RED PEPPERS AND GARLIC CROUTONS

In season, small sweet onions are the best to use. Otherwise, red onions work perfectly well. Choose well-shaped, unblemished onions. This dish should be made on the day it is to be served.

8 Servings

8 small onions (about 3 ounces each)
3 large heads of garlic
4 medium red bell peppers (about 1¼ pounds)
½ teaspoon coarse (kosher) salt
½ teaspoon freshly ground black pepper
1 cup extra-virgin olive oil
1 tablespoon fresh marjoram leaves, stems reserved, or 2 teaspoons dried
2 teaspoons fresh thyme leaves, stems reserved, or 2 teaspoons dried
¼ cup chicken stock or water
1 teaspoon Dijon mustard
1½ tablespoons balsamic vinegar

Eight ½-inch-thick slices of sourdough bread or other hearty white bread
4 bunches of mâche (lamb's lettuce)

1. Preheat the oven to 350°. Cut off the root and stem ends of the onions. Brush off any loose skin, but do not peel. Rub any loose skin from the heads of garlic, but do not peel.

2. Place the onions, garlic and red bell peppers in a large heavy roasting pan. Sprinkle the coarse salt and black pepper on top, drizzle ¼ cup of the olive oil over the vegetables and toss to coat. Stand the onions and garlic bulbs on their root ends and lay the bell peppers on their sides, allowing about 1 inch between the vegetables. Bake for 30 minutes.

3. Using tongs, turn the onions and peppers over and add the marjoram and thyme stems or sprinkle 1 teaspoon each of the dried marjoram and thyme over the vegetables. Bake for 30 minutes longer.

4. Remove the peppers and garlic and set aside. Turn the onions over again, setting them in the same spots where the juices have caramelized (don't be alarmed by the blackness of the caramelized juices). Roast the onions until very soft and easily pierced with the tip of a sharp knife, about 20 minutes longer. (Check occasionally; some varieties of onions cook in less time than others.)

5. Cover the roasting pan with foil and set aside for 20 minutes. Transfer the onions to a plate and let cool.

6. Meanwhile, place the pan over moderate heat and add the chicken stock. Bring to a boil, scraping up all the blackened bits on the bottom of the pan, and cook until the caramelized juices have dissolved and the liquid is reduced by half, about 2 minutes. Strain into a medium bowl, add the remaining

1 teaspoon each of dried thyme and marjoram, if using, and let cool.

7. Working over a bowl to catch the juices, remove the stems and cores from the roasted peppers and peel them. Carefully tear each pepper in half lengthwise and scrape the seeds into the bowl. Tear or slice each pepper half into 5 strips and set aside. Strain the pepper juices into the caramelized onion syrup.

8. Separate the garlic cloves and squeeze the pulp into a strainer set over a small bowl. Using a rubber spatula, press the garlic through.

9. In a bowl, whisk the mustard, vinegar and 3 tablespoons of the garlic puree until smooth. Slowly add ½ cup of the olive oil, whisking constantly, and then whisk in the caramelized onion syrup. Add 2 teaspoons of the fresh marjoram and the fresh thyme. Season to taste with coarse salt and black pepper. Set the vinaigrette aside.

10. Preheat a broiler. Lightly brush the bread slices on both sides with 2 tablespoons of the olive oil. Cut each slice into 4 triangles, place on a baking sheet and broil, turning once, until lightly golden on both sides.

11. In a small bowl, combine the remaining garlic puree, 1 teaspoon fresh marjoram and 2 tablespoons olive oil. Season to taste with coarse salt and black pepper. Spread a very thin layer of the garlic mixture on each crouton.

12. Discard the dry and leathery outer layers of the onions. Set the onions on a platter. Cluster the pepper strips, mâche and croutons around the onions. Pass the vinaigrette separately.

—*Andrew Ziobro*

ROASTED PARSNIPS WITH ORANGE ZEST

In this recipe, parsnips are browned in a hot oven, then tossed with sautéed red bell peppers, orange zest and a touch of orange juice.

8 to 10 Servings

6 pounds parsnips, peeled and cut into 1½-inch-long matchsticks
6 tablespoons unsalted butter, melted
1 teaspoon salt
½ teaspoon freshly ground black pepper
2 tablespoons mild olive oil
1 medium onion, thinly sliced
2 red bell peppers, finely diced
½ cup chopped flat-leaf parsley
½ cup fresh orange juice
2 tablespoons finely grated orange zest

1. Preheat the oven to 400°. In a large bowl, toss the parsnips with the melted butter, salt and black pepper. Spread the parsnips in a single layer on 2 baking sheets, preferably nonstick, and roast for 40 to 45 minutes, until tender and well browned.

2. Meanwhile, in a large skillet, heat the oil over moderate heat. Add the onion and cook until softened and translucent, about 4 minutes. Add the diced bell peppers and cook for 2 minutes longer. Remove from the heat and transfer to a large bowl.

3. Add the roasted parsnips, parsley, orange juice and orange zest and toss to mix thoroughly. Transfer the vegetables to a large casserole. *(The recipe can be prepared to this point up to 1 day ahead; cover the casserole and refrigerate. Return to room temperature before proceeding.)*

4. Preheat the oven to 350°. Cover the parsnips and bake for about 20 minutes, or until heated through.

—*Bob Chambers*

ROASTED POTATOES, PARSNIPS AND ONIONS

12 Servings

6 medium yellow potatoes (about 6 ounces each), such as Yellow Finn or Yukon Gold, each cut lengthwise into 6 wedges
12 small flat onions, cipolline or large pearl onions, peeled
6 medium parsnips, halved crosswise
12 medium shallots, peeled
3 medium heads of garlic (7 ounces), separated into cloves, peeled
6 tablespoons unsalted butter, melted
3 sprigs of fresh rosemary
3 sprigs of fresh thyme
1½ teaspoons salt
¾ teaspoon freshly ground pepper

1. Preheat the oven to 375°. In a large roasting pan, about 12 by 18 inches, toss together the potatoes, onions, parsnips, shallots and garlic. Pour the melted butter on top and stir to coat all the vegetables. Scatter the rosemary and thyme sprigs on top and season with the salt and pepper.

2. Roast for about 1 hour, turning the vegetables with a metal spatula every 20 minutes, until crusty brown on the outside and tender on the inside.

—*Gerry Klaskala*

PARSLIED RED POTATOES

4 Servings

Salt
1½ pounds Red Bliss potatoes
2 tablespoons unsalted butter, or more to taste
2 tablespoons chopped parsley
Freshly ground pepper

In a large pot of boiling salted water, cook the potatoes until tender, about 20 minutes. Drain the potatoes and cut them in half lengthwise. Transfer to a serving bowl and toss with the butter and chopped parsley. Season with salt and pepper and serve.

—*Stephanie Lyness*

OVEN-TOASTED POTATO CHIPS

You can use the slicing blade of a food processor to cut the potatoes uniformly. These tend to bake unevenly, so serve the darker chips to those diners who like extra crunch.

4 Servings

1 pound small red potatoes, sliced a generous ⅛ inch thick
2 tablespoons olive oil
½ teaspoon salt

1. Preheat the oven to 500°. In a colander, rinse the sliced potatoes under cold water; pat dry. Toss the potatoes with the oil and ¼ teaspoon of the salt and spread them on a large baking sheet in a single layer.

2. Toast the potatoes on the top rack of the oven, rotating the baking sheet, for 20 to 25 minutes, or until golden brown. Drain on paper towels and sprinkle with the remaining ¼ teaspoon salt. Serve warm.

—*Susan Shapiro Jaslove*

SUMMER SQUASH SAUTE WITH DILL AND TOMATOES

Serve this tasty mélange with pan-fried flounder, sole or snapper.

4 Servings

3 tablespoons unsalted butter
1 medium onion, halved lengthwise and thinly sliced crosswise
1½ pounds yellow summer squash (6 inches long), sliced crosswise into ¼-inch rounds
2 medium tomatoes (¾ pound), peeled and chopped
2 tablespoons chopped fresh dill
Salt and freshly ground pepper

1. In a large nonreactive skillet, melt the butter over low heat. Add the onion, cover and cook, stirring once or twice, until soft but not brown, about 5 minutes. Increase the heat to moderately high, stir in the squash and cook for a minute or two to heat through. Reduce the heat to moderately low, cover and cook, stirring occasionally, until tender, 5 to 8 minutes.

2. Stir in the tomatoes, cover and cook for 1 minute to just heat through. Remove from the heat. Add the dill, season with salt and pepper and serve.

—*Marcia Kiesel*

CANDIED PUMPKIN WITH RUM-PLUMPED CRANBERRIES

Here is a savory vegetable accompaniment that is both sweet and tart.

12 Servings

1 cup sugar
2 tablespoons dark rum
2½ teaspoons finely grated orange zest
2 teaspoons finely grated lemon zest
1 cup cranberries, picked through
4 pounds pumpkin, Hubbard squash or acorn squash—peeled, seeded and cut into 1½-inch cubes
2 tablespoons light corn syrup
¼ teaspoon cinnamon
Pinch of ground mace
Pinch of saffron threads
2 tablespoons unsalted butter

1. In a small saucepan, combine ½ cup of the sugar, the rum, the orange and lemon zests and 1 cup of water. Bring to a boil over moderately high heat. Reduce the heat to moderate and boil for 2 minutes. Remove from the heat and stir in the cranberries. Let stand for at least 1 hour. (*The cranberries can be made up to 1 day ahead; cover and refrigerate. Return to room temperature and proceed.*)

2. In a medium saucepan, barely cover the pumpkin cubes with water. Stir in the corn syrup, cinnamon, mace, saffron and the remaining ½ cup sugar. Bring to a boil over moderately high heat and cook until the pumpkin is just tender, about 15 minutes. Using a large slotted spoon, transfer the pumpkin to a serving bowl. Cover and keep warm.

3. Return the saucepan to the heat and boil the cooking liquid gently until thickened and reduced to 1 cup, about 5 minutes. Stir in the butter and pour the syrup over the cooked pumpkin. Toss to combine.

4. Using a slotted spoon, remove the cranberries from their soaking liquid and scatter them over the pumpkin. Reserve the liquid for another use. Serve the pumpkin warm.

—*Gerry Klaskala*

WINTER SQUASH GRATIN

Any winter squash that peels easily with a knife will be fine in this recipe.

8 Servings

3 pounds winter squash, such as butternut
½ teaspoon cinnamon
¼ teaspoon salt
1 cup heavy cream

1. Preheat the oven to 400°. Peel and halve the squash. Scoop out and discard the seeds. Cut the squash in chunks. In a food processor, coarsely grate the squash. Put the squash in a large bowl and toss with the cinnamon and salt.

2. Spread the squash in a shallow 9-by-12-inch baking dish. Pour the heavy cream evenly over the squash, cover loosely with foil and bake for about 30 minutes, until tender. (*The recipe can be prepared to this point 5 to 6 hours ahead. Reheat in the oven for about 20 minutes before proceeding.*)

3. Preheat the broiler. Broil the gratin for a few minutes to glaze the top. Serve immediately.

—*Evan Jones*

Gratin of Tomatoes and Grilled Peppers with Roasted Polenta (p. 115).

Above, Summer Squash Sauté with Dill and Tomatoes (p. 108). Right, Summer Vegetable Salad with Herb and Shallot Vinaigrette (p. 121).

QUINCE AND APPLE PUREE

The addition of pureed parsnips gives this side dish a deep, earthy flavor and a rich consistency. If you can't find quinces, you can use Bartlett or Comice pears; the result will be a slightly sweeter, lighter puree.

Makes About 4 Cups

1 pound tart apples, such as Granny Smith—peeled, quartered and cored
1 pound quinces—peeled, quartered and cored
3 tablespoons fresh lemon juice
½ cup sugar
2 cinnamon sticks
1 pound parsnips, peeled and cut into ¾-inch dice
4 tablespoons unsalted butter
About 1½ tablespoons apple cider vinegar
Pinch of ground cinnamon
Pinch of salt, preferably fine sea salt

1. In a nonreactive bowl, combine the apples, quinces, 1 tablespoon of the lemon juice and water to cover.

2. In a large nonreactive saucepan, combine 6½ cups of water with the sugar, cinnamon sticks and remaining 2 tablespoons lemon juice and bring to a boil over moderately high heat. Add the parsnips and cook, covered, for 10 minutes.

3. Drain the apples and quinces. Add them to the parsnips in sugar syrup and return to a boil. Reduce the heat to moderately low and weigh down the fruit and parsnips with a heat-proof plate to keep them submerged. Simmer until the fruit and parsnips are

Artichoke and Potato Stew with Mint (p. 45).

tender, about 15 minutes. Strain and set aside. Save the cooking syrup and the cinnamon sticks for another use if you wish.

4. Add the butter to the saucepan and cook over moderate heat until melted. Add the drained fruit and parsnips and cook, stirring to prevent browning, until they are falling apart, about 5 minutes. Add 1 tablespoon of the vinegar and cook over low heat, stirring, for another 5 minutes.

5. Transfer the mixture to a food mill or a food processor and puree. Stir in the ground cinnamon, salt and, if desired, the remaining ½ tablespoon vinegar. (*The puree can be made up to 3 days ahead; cover and refrigerate. Reheat in a double boiler over simmering water or in a casserole in a moderate oven.*) Serve warm.

—*Christopher Kump*

SWEET POTATOES WITH TOASTED ALMONDS

Apple cider reduced to a syrup lends a sweet tang to the roasted potatoes.

6 to 8 Servings

⅔ cup slivered blanched almonds (3¾ ounces)
4 pounds sweet potatoes, peeled and cut into 1-inch cubes
6 tablespoons unsalted butter, melted
1½ teaspoons salt
1 teaspoon freshly ground pepper
3 cups fresh apple cider

1. Preheat the oven to 350°. Spread the almonds on a baking sheet and toast in the oven for about 5 minutes, until golden brown. Set aside. Increase the oven temperature to 450°.

2. In a large bowl, toss the sweet potatoes with the melted butter. Season with the salt and pepper. Spread

the potatoes in a single layer on 1 or 2 baking sheets. Roast for 40 to 50 minutes, stirring occasionally to prevent sticking, until the potatoes are tender when pierced and lightly browned.

3. Meanwhile, in a small nonreactive saucepan, bring the cider to a boil. Reduce the heat to moderately high and boil until the cider is reduced to ½ cup, 25 to 30 minutes.

4. Transfer the potatoes to a large bowl. Add the reduced cider and toss well, then transfer to a large casserole. (*The recipe can be prepared to this point up to 1 day ahead; cover the casserole and refrigerate. Return to room temperature before proceeding.*)

5. Preheat the oven to 350°. Bake the sweet potatoes, uncovered, for about 10 minutes, or until heated through. Sprinkle the toasted almonds on top.

—*Bob Chambers*

SAUTEED SWISS CHARD WITH TOMATOES

8 Servings

2 tablespoons olive oil
1 garlic clove, halved
5½ pounds Swiss chard, stems and large ribs removed and leaves cut into 1-inch pieces
1 cup peeled, chopped fresh or drained canned Italian tomatoes
Salt and freshly ground pepper
About 2 teaspoons red wine vinegar

Heat the olive oil in an enameled cast-iron casserole. Add the garlic and cook

over high heat until fragrant. Add the Swiss chard, a handful at a time, stirring to wilt it before adding more; this will take about 7 minutes. Cover and cook until all the chard is wilted, about 2 minutes longer. Stir in the tomatoes and cook until heated through. Season with salt, pepper and vinegar to taste. Discard the garlic halves and serve hot.

—*Annie Roberts*

SWISS CHARD OMELET

This Provençale omelet, also called a *trucha,* can be eaten warm or at room temperature.

8 Servings

2½ tablespoons extra-virgin olive oil
1 large onion, quartered and thinly sliced crosswise
2 teaspoons chopped fresh thyme
1½ pounds Swiss chard, stems discarded, leaves sliced crosswise into ½-inch strips
Salt and freshly ground pepper
1 medium garlic clove, peeled
8 large eggs, lightly beaten
1 cup grated Gruyère cheese (4 ounces)
⅓ cup thinly sliced scallions, white and some green
⅓ cup chopped fresh basil
¼ cup chopped fresh flat-leaf parsley
2 tablespoons freshly grated Parmesan cheese

1. In a large ovenproof nonstick skillet, heat 1½ tablespoons of the oil. Add the onion and thyme and cook over low heat, stirring occasionally, until the onion is completely soft but not colored, about 12 minutes.

2. Stir in half of the Swiss chard, cover and cook over moderate heat until it starts to wilt. Stir in the remaining chard and cook until the juices have evaporated and the chard is tender, about 10 minutes. Season with salt and pepper.

3. Meanwhile, mash the garlic with a few pinches of salt to make a paste, and place in a large bowl. Add the eggs, Gruyère, scallions, basil, parsley and 1 tablespoon of the Parmesan. Gently whisk to combine.

4. Preheat the broiler. Stir the remaining 1 tablespoon oil into the chard in the skillet. Add the egg mixture and cook over moderately high heat, stirring constantly, for 1 minute. Reduce the heat to low and scramble gently until the eggs begin to set, about 5 minutes. Tilt the pan to spread the eggs evenly and cook until fairly well set but still moist, about 8 minutes longer. Sprinkle the remaining 1 tablespoon Parmesan on top.

5. Broil the omelet, rotating the skillet, until evenly golden, 1 to 2 minutes. Using a spatula, slide the omelet onto a platter and cut into wedges.

—*Deborah Madison*

PAN-WILTED WINTER GREENS WITH FRESH GINGER

6 Servings

2½ tablespoons grated fresh ginger (from a 3-inch piece)
¾ teaspoon salt, preferably fine sea salt
1½ pounds spinach, large stems removed and leaves cut into 1½-inch-wide strips
1 pound kale, stems removed, leaves cut into 1½-inch-wide strips
2 pounds Swiss chard, stems removed, leaves cut into 1½-inch-wide strips

In a very large skillet, combine the ginger, salt and ½ cup of water and bring to a boil over high heat. Add the spinach, kale and Swiss chard, packing them down with the pan lid. Cover and cook over high heat, stirring, until tender, about 5 minutes.

—*Christopher Kump*

BAKED TOMATOES WITH CRUNCHY CRUMBS

8 Servings

2½ pounds plum tomatoes
¼ cup plus 1 teaspoon extra-virgin olive oil
5 garlic cloves, 1 crushed and 4 minced
Salt and freshly ground pepper
¼ cup finely chopped fresh basil
¼ cup finely chopped flat-leaf parsley
1 cup fresh bread crumbs made from Italian bread

1. Halve the tomatoes lengthwise. Working over a strainer in a bowl to catch the juices, core and seed the tomatoes. Set the tomatoes and juices aside. Preheat the oven to 400°.

2. Rub the bottom and sides of a 14-by-10-by-2-inch ovenproof serving dish with 1 teaspoon of the olive oil, then with the crushed garlic clove. Reserve the garlic.

3. Arrange the tomatoes cut-side up in the dish. Sprinkle the reserved tomato juices and the minced garlic on top. Drizzle 2 tablespoons of the oil over the tomatoes and season with salt and pepper. Bake for 20 minutes.

4. Sprinkle the basil on top and bake for 10 minutes longer. Turn off the heat but leave the dish in the oven for 20 minutes to allow the tomatoes to soften completely. *(The tomatoes can be baked up to 6 hours ahead; set aside at room temperature. Reheat briefly in a 400° oven.)*

5. Meanwhile, in a heavy medium skillet, combine the remaining 2 tablespoons olive oil, the reserved crushed garlic clove and the parsley and cook over moderate heat, stirring occasionally, for 5 minutes. Discard the crushed garlic. Add the bread crumbs and cook, stirring, until golden brown and crisp, 7 to 8 minutes. Stir in ¼ teaspoon each of salt and pepper and set aside to cool. *(The bread crumbs can be made 1 day ahead; store in an airtight container at room temperature.)*

6. Sprinkle the bread crumbs over the warm tomatoes and serve.

—*Diana Sturgis*

GRATIN OF TOMATOES AND GRILLED PEPPERS WITH ROASTED POLENTA

4 Servings

½ cup instant polenta
Sea salt
Freshly ground black pepper
1 tablespoon unsalted butter
2 medium red bell peppers
2 medium yellow bell peppers
3 to 4 tablespoons extra-virgin olive oil
2 small garlic cloves, sliced paper thin
4 anchovy fillets, cut into small pieces
½ teaspoon crushed red pepper, or more to taste
6 large plum tomatoes (1½ pounds)— peeled, seeded and cut into small chunks
¼ cup coarsely chopped flat-leaf parsley
12 small green or purple basil leaves

1. Oil an 8-inch pie pan. In a medium saucepan, bring 2 cups of water to a boil. Whisk in the polenta. Reduce the heat to very low and cook, stirring, until the polenta pulls away from the pan, 4 to 5 minutes. Season with sea salt and black pepper to taste and stir in the butter. Pour into the prepared pan and let cool.

2. Roast the peppers directly over a gas flame or under the broiler as close to the heat as possible, turning, until charred all over. Transfer the peppers to a paper or plastic bag, close tightly and let steam for 5 minutes. Using a small sharp knife, scrape off the blackened skin and halve them lengthwise. Remove the cores, seeds and membranes and discard. Slice the peppers into ¾-inch strips.

3. Preheat the oven to 400°. Use a little of the olive oil to coat the bottom of a 9-inch gratin dish. Arrange a layer of the peppers in the bottom of the dish. Sprinkle with a little of the garlic, anchovies, crushed red pepper and some sea salt. Scatter some of the tomatoes over the top, sprinkle with parsley and season again with a little sea salt. Moisten with a few drops of olive oil. Continue layering the ingredients in this way, ending with a layer of peppers. Drizzle the remaining olive oil on top and bake for 20 minutes. Remove from the oven and cover tightly to keep warm.

4. Preheat the broiler. Unmold the polenta and cut it into 4 wedges. Arrange the polenta on a lightly oiled baking sheet and broil for 5 minutes on each side, or until browned at the edges.

5. Place the polenta on 4 plates. Arrange the peppers and tomatoes in a small mound alongside and drizzle a big spoonful of the cooking juices over them. Garnish with the basil leaves.

—*Viana La Place*

SAUTEED TURNIPS

6 Servings

2 pounds large turnips, peeled and cut into ¾-inch dice
2 tablespoons unsalted butter
Salt and freshly ground pepper

1. In a medium saucepan, parboil the turnips in lightly salted water over moderately high heat until fork tender, 12 to 15 minutes. Drain well.

2. In a large nonstick skillet, melt the butter over moderate heat. Add the turnips, season with salt and pepper and cook, tossing, until golden all over, about 15 minutes.

—*Lydie Marshall*

CRISP ROOT-VEGETABLE CAKES

8 Servings

4 tablespoons lightly salted butter, at room temperature
6 medium carrots
1¼ teaspoons salt
½ teaspoon freshly ground pepper
4 Jerusalem artichokes (¾ pound), peeled
3 medium all-purpose potatoes (¾ pound), peeled
2 medium parsnips, peeled
1 medium onion, minced
1 teaspoon fresh lemon juice
½ cup all-purpose flour
2 eggs, lightly beaten

1. Preheat the oven to 375°. Butter

each of two 9-inch pie pans with 1 tablespoon of the butter; refrigerate to set.

2. Coarsely grate the carrots and place in a bowl. Season with ½ teaspoon of the salt and ¼ teaspoon of the pepper. Grate the artichokes, potatoes and parsnips and place in a second bowl. Add the onion and lemon juice and season with the remaining ¾ teaspoon salt and ¼ teaspoon pepper.

3. Sprinkle the carrots with 2 tablespoons of the flour and about 2 tablespoons of the beaten egg. Mix well. Mix the remaining 6 tablespoons flour and beaten egg into the grated Jerusalem artichokes and potatoes.

4. Spread one-fourth of the Jerusalem artichoke mixture on the bottom and up the sides of each prepared pie pan. Layer the carrots on top and cover with the remaining Jerusalem artichoke mixture, making sure the edges are even. Dot with the remaining 2 tablespoons butter.

5. Bake in the center of the oven for 35 to 40 minutes, until the tops are golden brown. Let stand for 2 to 3 minutes, then invert the cakes onto a large baking sheet. *(The recipe can be prepared to this point up to 4 hours ahead. Reheat in a 500° oven for about 20 minutes before proceeding.)*

6. Preheat the broiler. Broil the cakes, for 1 to 2 minutes, rotating the baking sheet as necessary, until the tops are evenly crisp and brown. Slice the cakes into wedges with a serrated knife and transfer to a platter or plates.

—Larry Forgione

FALL VEGETABLE SPIEDINI

For a great main dish with all the colors and tastes of fall, serve these vegetables with piping-hot, soft polenta.

4 Servings

½ pound butternut squash—peeled, seeded and cut into 1-inch dice
16 pearl onions, preferably red, unpeeled
1 red bell pepper, cut into 1-inch squares
1 green bell pepper, cut into 1-inch squares
16 plump cremini or other medium mushrooms, stems removed
3 medium zucchini, cut into 1-inch chunks
¼ cup extra-virgin olive oil
2 teaspoons chopped fresh thyme
2 teaspoons chopped fresh rosemary
2 garlic cloves, thinly sliced
Salt and freshly ground black pepper

1. In a medium saucepan of boiling water, blanch the squash until just tender, about 3 minutes. Drain well. Blanch the onions in the same boiling water until just tender, 2 to 4 minutes. Drain and peel them.

2. In a large bowl, combine the squash, onions, bell peppers, mushrooms and zucchini. Drizzle with the olive oil. Add the thyme, rosemary, garlic and salt and pepper to taste. Toss well. Set aside for at least 1 hour.

3. Light a grill or preheat the broiler. Thread the vegetables onto 8 skewers, alternating them in contrasting colors. Grill or broil for about 5 minutes, turning the skewers, until the vegetables are tender and golden. Brush the vegetables with olive oil if they start to dry out during cooking. Serve immediately or at room temperature.

—Viana La Place

FRIED TOFU WITH HOLY BASIL

This is a vegetarian version of the traditional Thai stir-fried beef with holy basil. It is quick to make, nutritious and full of flavor. Yard-long beans are a Chinese and Southeast Asian favorite. If you can't find them, substitute tender fresh green beans.

3 to 4 Servings

1 tablespoon vegetable oil
2 tablespoons minced garlic (6 cloves)
¼ pound yard-long beans or fresh green beans, trimmed and sliced crosswise into ¼-inch pieces
2 bird chiles, stemmed and minced
1½ pounds firm tofu, cut into 1-inch cubes
1½ tablespoons fish sauce
1 teaspoon salt
1 teaspoon sugar
½ cup coarsely chopped holy basil leaves plus a few whole leaves for garnish or ¾ to 1 cup coarsely chopped sweet basil leaves

1. Set a large heavy skillet or wok over high heat. Add the oil and when it is hot, toss in the garlic and stir-fry until golden, about 30 seconds. Add the beans and chiles and stir-fry for 3 minutes. Add the tofu and stir-fry for 2 minutes; as the tofu breaks up, it will start to look like scrambled eggs.

2. Add the fish sauce, salt and sugar and mix well. Continue to cook until the beans are just tender and bright green, 3 to 4 minutes longer. Add the chopped holy basil and mix thoroughly. Transfer the tofu to a warmed platter, garnish with the whole basil leaves and serve immediately.

—Jeffrey Alford & Naomi Duguid

SALADS

SALADS

HERB SALAD WITH WATERCRESS DRESSING

With its bold, fresh herb flavors, this tangy leaf and blossom salad with a spicy watercress dressing is like a leafy version of a *salsa verde*. Chill all the herbs for the salad before dressing them. Serve with grilled chicken, salmon or bluefish.

4 Servings

2 cups (packed) watercress leaves and tender stems
2 small garlic cloves, chopped
¼ cup chopped onion
1½ tablespoons rice vinegar
⅓ cup extra-virgin olive oil
½ teaspoon salt
½ teaspoon freshly ground pepper
2 cups (packed) flat-leaf parsley leaves
2 cups (packed) fresh chervil sprigs
1 cup (packed) small fresh green or purple basil leaves
½ cup 1-inch chive pieces and/or chive flowers, loosely pulled apart
½ cup small nasturtium leaves and/or flowers
Sage blossoms, borage flowers and mint leaves, for tossing in the salad (optional)

1. Pack the watercress, garlic, onion and vinegar in a blender. Puree on moderate speed, stopping occasionally to scrape down the sides with a rubber spatula. Increase the speed to high and slowly pour in the olive oil to emulsify the dressing. Pour into a bowl and season with the salt and pepper.

2. Just before serving, gently toss all the herbs and flowers with 2 to 3 tablespoons of the dressing and place on plates. Pass the remaining dressing separately.

—*Marcia Kiesel*

SHREDDED LETTUCE AND RADISH SALAD

Iceberg lettuce adds a refreshing crunch to this salad.

6 Servings

2 tablespoons fresh lime juice
2½ tablespoons olive oil
½ teaspoon salt
4 packed cups shredded romaine lettuce (from 1 head)
4 packed cups shredded iceberg lettuce (from 1 head)
6 large radishes, cut into thin matchsticks
¼ cup coarsely chopped fresh coriander (cilantro)

In a small bowl, combine the lime juice, oil and salt. In a large salad bowl, toss the romaine and iceberg lettuces with the radishes and coriander. Pour the dressing over and toss well.

—*Marcia Kiesel*

RED LEAF LETTUCE AND CHICORY SALAD

4 Servings

⅓ cup walnut pieces (1½ ounces), coarsely chopped
½ of a small bunch of red leaf lettuce, torn into bite-size pieces
½ of a medium bunch of chicory, coarsely chopped
1½ tablespoons white wine vinegar
3 tablespoons extra-virgin olive oil
Salt and freshly ground pepper

1. Preheat the oven to 425°. Spread the walnuts on a baking sheet and toast for 7 minutes.

2. In a large bowl, toss the red leaf lettuce and chicory together. In a small bowl, whisk together the vinegar and oil and season with salt and pepper. Just before serving, toss the dressing with the greens and sprinkle with the toasted walnuts.

—*Susan Shapiro Jaslove*

GARDEN LETTUCES WITH LIGHT VINAIGRETTE

10 Servings

1 medium shallot, minced
¼ teaspoon freshly ground pepper
½ teaspoon salt
½ teaspoon Dijon mustard
1 tablespoon chopped fresh herbs, such as chives, flat-leaf parsley and thyme
2 tablespoons white wine
2 tablespoons white wine vinegar
½ cup olive oil
16 packed cups of assorted lettuces torn into bite-size pieces, such as Boston, red leaf, arugula and romaine

1. Combine all the ingredients except the lettuces in a blender and puree. Keep the dressing at room temperature until ready to use.

2. In a very large bowl, toss the lettuces with the vinaigrette and serve at once.

—*Mary Novak*

CUCUMBER SALAD WITH RICE WINE VINEGAR

4 Servings

1 teaspoon sesame seeds
2 medium cucumbers—peeled, halved lengthwise, seeded and thinly sliced crosswise
1 teaspoon rice vinegar
¼ teaspoon salt

1. In a small skillet, toast the sesame seeds over moderate heat until lightly browned, about 1 minute. Set aside.

2. In a medium serving bowl, toss the cucumber slices with the rice vinegar and salt. Cover and refrigerate for 30 to 40 minutes. Sprinkle with the sesame seeds just before serving.

—*Stephanie Lyness*

MIXED FIELD GREENS WITH POTATO SURPRISE AND CAVIAR

In an elegant hotel facing the fountain in Philadelphia's Logan Square, regular customers have made this dish, created by Chef de Restaurant Martin Hamann, a popular standby on the Fountain Restaurant's menu.

❧ For this festive dish, sparkling wine is the right mate. The fizz cuts through the richness of the fried potato, and the crispness pairs well with the food's crunchy, fragile textures. Try a nicely balanced bottle from California, such as nonvintage Domaine Carneros by Taittinger.

4 Servings

4 large baking potatoes, preferably Idaho
Ice water
½ cup sour cream
2 tablespoons finely chopped scallion greens or chives
Salt and freshly ground pepper
2 tablespoons olive oil
1 tablespoon rice vinegar
1 cup all-purpose flour
3 eggs, beaten
1 cup fresh bread crumbs
1 quart vegetable oil, for frying
4 cups bite-size pieces of assorted field greens, such as arugula, mâche and Bibb lettuce
1 tablespoon plus 1 teaspoon beluga, sevruga or osetra caviar

1. Peel and halve the potatoes crosswise. Cut each half into a 1½-inch cube. Using an apple corer, cut out 1 inch of the center all the way through the potato. Save the potato scraps for another use.

2. In a pot of boiling salted water, cook the potato cubes until tender, about 10 minutes. Meanwhile, fill a large bowl with ice water. Drain the potatoes and transfer them to the ice water to stop cooking. Pat the potatoes dry with paper towels and set aside.

3. In a small bowl, mix the sour cream and scallion greens. Season with ¼ teaspoon each of salt and pepper. Using a pastry bag or a spoon, fill each potato cube with the sour cream mixture. Refrigerate for 10 minutes.

4. Meanwhile, in a small bowl, whisk the olive oil, vinegar and ¼ teaspoon each salt and pepper until blended. Set the vinaigrette aside.

5. Dust the potatoes with some of the flour, dip them in the beaten egg to cover thoroughly, then coat them with bread crumbs.

6. In a large deep saucepan, heat the vegetable oil to 375°. Add the potatoes 2 at a time, and fry, turning, until golden, about 4 minutes.

7. To serve, dress the greens with the vinaigrette and arrange on 4 plates. Place 2 potato cubes on top of the greens. Dollop ½ teaspoon of caviar on top of each potato and serve.

—*Martin Hamann*

TOSSED SALAD WITH RADISH SPROUTS AND PARSLEY

Radish sprouts have the peppery bite of radishes but their own pretty look. They're widely available at specialty produce markets and health food stores.

8 Servings

2 large shallots, finely chopped
2 tablespoons red wine vinegar
Salt
⅓ cup olive oil or sunflower oil
1 tablespoon walnut oil, or to taste
About 1¼ pounds mixed greens, such as red leaf lettuce, Treviso chicory, radicchio and romaine—washed, dried and torn into pieces (about 16 lightly packed cups)
1 cup (loosely packed) flat-leaf parsley leaves
Freshly ground pepper
About 2 cups (loosely packed) radish sprouts, preferably pink ones

1. In a small bowl, whisk the shallots, vinegar and ¼ teaspoon salt. Whisk in the olive and walnut oils.

2. In a salad bowl, toss the greens and parsley together with a little addi-

tional salt. Add the vinaigrette and toss to coat. Season with pepper, then sprinkle the radish sprouts over the greens and gently toss again.

—Deborah Madison

WINTER GREENS SALAD WITH WARM SHERRY VINAIGRETTE

8 Servings

2 tablespoons white wine vinegar
1 tablespoon fresh lemon juice
1 tablespoon spicy brown mustard
1 small shallot, minced
1 garlic clove, minced
2 tablespoons cream sherry
½ cup olive oil
2½ tablespoons chopped fresh tarragon or flat-leaf parsley (or a combination)
Salt and freshly ground pepper
10 cups (packed) assorted winter greens—such as tender kale, inner chicory leaves, romaine, turnip greens or beet greens—torn into bite-size pieces
1 small daikon radish (10 ounces), peeled and cut into ¼-inch julienne strips

1. In a small nonreactive saucepan, whisk together the vinegar, lemon juice, mustard, shallot, garlic and sherry. Warm over low heat for about 1 minute. Gradually add the olive oil, whisking until warmed through. Stir in the tarragon and season with salt and pepper. *(The dressing can be made up to 6 hours ahead. Rewarm before using.)*

2. In a large bowl, toss the winter greens with the daikon julienne.

3. Toss the salad with the warm vinaigrette and serve immediately.

—Larry Forgione

ENDIVE AND CARROT SALAD

4 Servings

1 tablespoon yellow mustard seeds
1 garlic clove, minced
½ tablespoon fresh lemon juice
1 teaspoon Dijon mustard
3 tablespoons olive oil
Salt and freshly ground pepper
8 medium Belgian endives, cored and sliced crosswise ½ inch thick
1 large carrot, coarsely grated

1. In a small skillet, toast the mustard seeds over high heat until fragrant and lightly browned, about 1 minute. Transfer the mustard seeds to a plate and let cool.

2. In a small bowl, mix together the garlic, lemon juice, Dijon mustard and olive oil. Season with salt and pepper.

3. In a large bowl, toss the endives and carrot. Add the dressing and toss well. Sprinkle with the mustard seeds and serve.

—Marcia Kiesel

BROCCOLI, ORANGE AND ROASTED PEPPER SALAD

4 Servings

1 small bunch of broccoli (about 1 pound), cut into 2-inch florets
2 medium oranges
⅓ cup bottled roasted red peppers, rinsed and cut into thin strips

2 tablespoons white wine vinegar
1 tablespoon olive oil
¼ teaspoon cayenne pepper
Salt

1. Steam the broccoli florets in a steamer basket until just tender, about 7 minutes. Rinse under cold water and drain well. Set aside in a large bowl.

2. Slice off the tops and bottoms of each orange. Stand the oranges upright on a work surface. Using a small sharp knife, cut away the skin and white pith. Cut between the membranes to release the sections and add them to the broccoli. Mix in the red pepper strips.

3. Just before serving, add the vinegar and oil and toss to combine. Season with the cayenne and ¼ teaspoon salt.

—Susan Shapiro Jaslove

ASPARAGUS SALAD MIMOSA

This salad gets its name from the chopped egg garnish, which resembles the flowers of a mimosa tree.

8 Servings

48 medium asparagus spears (3 pounds), peeled
4 small heads of Bibb lettuce, leaves separated
1 cup extra-virgin olive oil
¼ cup tarragon vinegar
Salt and freshly ground white pepper
3 hard-cooked eggs

1. In a large shallow pot of boiling salted water, cook the asparagus until just tender, 4 to 6 minutes. Drain and cool thoroughly under cold running water. Drain well on paper towels. *(The asparagus can be cooked up to 3 hours ahead and refrigerated.)*

2. Shortly before serving, arrange the lettuce leaves on 8 salad plates. Lay

6 asparagus spears across the center of each plate.

3. In a small bowl, whisk together the oil and vinegar and season with salt and pepper. Drizzle about 2 tablespoons of dressing over each salad. Press the hard-cooked eggs through a coarse sieve over the asparagus and serve the salads.

—Camille Glenn

SPINACH SALAD WITH CHEVRE AND ROASTED SHALLOTS

Crusty peasant bread is a good accompaniment to this goat cheese salad from Odessa Piper at L'Etoile in Madison, Wisconsin. She likes to use the hickory nuts native to her region in place of the pecans.

4 Servings

⅔ *cup light olive oil*
⅓ *cup extra-virgin olive oil*
4 garlic cloves, quartered
4 bay leaves
1 tablespoon coarsely chopped fresh thyme plus 1 teaspoon minced, for garnish
2 teaspoons dried basil
2 teaspoons coarsely chopped fresh rosemary leaves plus one 6-inch sprig of fresh rosemary
1 teaspoon whole black peppercorns
One 12-ounce log of goat cheese, such as Montrachet, cut into 4 equal pieces
1 pound medium shallots, peeled
½ *cup balsamic vinegar*
2 tablespoons water
1 tablespoon sugar
Table salt
Freshly ground pepper
1 cup pecan halves

1 tablespoon vegetable oil
Pinch of coarse (kosher) salt
1½ pounds tender spinach leaves

1. In a deep glass or ceramic dish, combine the olive oils, garlic, bay leaves, coarsely chopped thyme, basil, chopped rosemary and peppercorns. Add the goat cheese, cover and refrigerate for at least 4 hours or overnight.

2. Preheat the oven to 400°. Carefully transfer the cheese to a plate. Strain the oil through a fine sieve set over a nonreactive 9-by-13-inch baking dish. Add the shallots, balsamic vinegar, water, sugar, 1 teaspoon table salt, ½ teaspoon pepper and the rosemary sprig. Cover with foil and bake for about 55 minutes, or until the shallots are tender.

3. Discard the rosemary sprig. Pour the contents of the baking dish through a strainer set over a small nonreactive saucepan. Return the shallots to the baking dish. Season the dressing in the saucepan with table salt and pepper and keep warm over very low heat.

4. In a small bowl, toss the pecans with the vegetable oil and coarse salt. Spread the pecans on a baking sheet and bake for about 7 minutes, or until fragrant and toasted. Let cool.

5. Place the goat cheese in the baking dish with the shallots. Warm in the oven for about 3 minutes, just until heated through; do not let the cheese melt.

6. To serve, mound the spinach on 4 large plates. Set the goat cheese on the spinach. Whisk the dressing and drizzle it over the spinach. Scatter the roasted shallots and toasted pecans on top. Sprinkle with the minced thyme and serve.

—Odessa Piper

SUMMER VEGETABLE SALAD WITH HERB AND SHALLOT VINAIGRETTE

8 Servings

1 pound green beans and/or yellow wax beans
¾ *pound small new potatoes, such as fingerlings, Yellow Finns and Red Dales—peeled if desired and halved (or quartered if large)*
1 medium cucumber—peeled, halved lengthwise and seeded
½ *cup Herb and Shallot Vinaigrette (p. 242)*
Salt and freshly ground pepper
1 cup purple or green basil leaves
¾ *pound red and yellow cherry or pear tomatoes, halved*

1. In a large saucepan of boiling salted water, cook the beans until crisp-tender, about 5 minutes. Drain, pat dry with a kitchen towel and let cool.

2. Steam the potatoes over boiling water until tender, about 12 minutes. Let cool thoroughly. *(The beans and potatoes can be refrigerated separately up to 1 day ahead.)*

3. Cut each cucumber half into 4 lengthwise strips, then slice crosswise 1½ inches thick. In a large bowl, toss the beans, potatoes and cucumber with the Herb and Shallot Vinaigrette. Season well with salt and pepper. Just before serving, add the basil and tomatoes and toss.

—Deborah Madison

SALAD OF SUMMER VEGETABLES

4 Servings

4 large artichokes
1 lemon, halved
¼ cup plus 2 teaspoons fresh lemon juice
Salt
3 cups vegetable oil, for frying
¼ pound very thin green beans, trimmed
8 asparagus spears, tender portion only, cut into four 1-inch lengths
2 medium tomatoes (about 1½ pounds), peeled and very thinly sliced
1 tablespoon minced shallot
6 tablespoons plus 2 teaspoons extra-virgin olive oil
Freshly ground pepper
About ½ pound mesclun or young mixed greens such as mâche, young chicory, oak leaf lettuce and arugula
2 tablespoons finely minced chives
2 tablespoons coarsely chopped chervil
4 fresh mushrooms, thinly sliced

1. With a small sharp knife, cut the leaves from around each artichoke, using a circular motion, until you reach the tender, inner leaves. Cut off the leaves and continue to trim the artichoke hearts down to the base, removing all the tough, fibrous outer skin. Rub the hearts all over with the cut lemon.

2. In a medium saucepan, bring 1½ quarts of water to a boil with 2 tablespoons of the lemon juice and 1 tea-spoon salt. Add 2 of the artichoke hearts and boil until tender, about 30 minutes. Drain and let cool. Scoop out the hairy chokes with a spoon. Cut the artichoke hearts in small wedges and set aside in a bowl.

3. Meanwhile, in a large saucepan or deep fryer, heat the vegetable oil to 350°. Scoop out the chokes of the 2 remaining uncooked artichoke hearts. Using a sharp knife, slice the hearts crosswise as thin as possible. Working in 3 batches, fry the artichoke slices until golden, 2 to 3 minutes. Transfer with a slotted spoon to paper towels to drain. Sprinkle lightly with salt.

4. Bring a large saucepan of salted water to a boil. Add the green beans and cook until tender, 3 to 5 minutes. Using a wire skimmer, transfer the beans to a colander and refresh under cold running water. Drain again; pat dry and add to the bowl with the artichoke wedges.

5. Return the water in the saucepan to a boil. Add the asparagus pieces and cook until tender, about 4 minutes. Drain the asparagus and refresh under cold running water. Pat dry. Add to the bowl with the other cooked vegetables. *(The recipe can be prepared to this point up to 2 hours ahead. Cover and refrigerate the cooked vegetables. Reserve the artichoke chips in a cool, dry place.)*

6. Arrange the tomato slices on 4 plates. Sprinkle the shallot, 1 table-spoon of the lemon juice and 2 table-spoons of the olive oil on top. Sprinkle lightly with salt and pepper.

7. In a bowl, toss the mesclun with the chives and chervil. Add 2 table-spoons of the olive oil and 1 tablespoon of the lemon juice, season with salt and pepper and toss well. Mound the salad greens on the tomatoes.

8. Season the cooked vegetables with 2 tablespoons of the olive oil, 1 teaspoon of the lemon juice and salt and pepper. Toss well and scatter over the salads.

9. Toss the mushrooms with the remaining 2 teaspoons olive oil and 1 tea-spoon lemon juice; season with salt and pepper. Garnish each salad with the mushrooms and the reserved artichoke chips.

—Daniel Boulud

GRILLED GARLIC-STUDDED PORTOBELLO MUSHROOMS WITH TOMATO SALAD AND HERB OIL

Chef Mark Militello's contemporary Floridian cuisine draws crowds of food lovers to Mark's Place, his postmodern mecca on the Gold Coast. He says that people here want a light meal but also want to feel satiated, and that this rustic salad is always popular because it's ideal for a warm climate. The meaty mushrooms can be grilled ahead and put on the arugula at the last minute.

❦ To work with the richness of the mushrooms and garlic, try a clean, crisp Sauvignon Blanc with good fruit flavors, such as 1988 or 1990 St. Clement or Spottswoode, both from the Napa Valley.

4 Servings

Four 6-ounce portobello mushrooms, stems removed
2 large garlic cloves, cut into 40 very thin slices
¾ cup extra-virgin olive oil
1 shallot, coarsely chopped
1 cup (packed) fresh basil leaves
1 cup (packed) flat-leaf parsley leaves
Salt and freshly ground pepper
3 tablespoons balsamic vinegar
1½ teaspoons chopped fresh rosemary
¼ cup plus 2½ tablespoons mild olive oil

1 teaspoon chopped fresh thyme
3 large tomatoes—peeled, seeded and diced
8 cups assorted bite-size greens, such as arugula and Bibb or red leaf lettuce

1. Using a small knife, horizontally slice off the black gills on the underside of the mushrooms and make 10 small but deep incisions in a circular pattern in each mushroom. Stuff a slice of garlic in each incision. Set aside.

2. In a blender, combine the extra-virgin olive oil, shallot, basil and parsley and puree. Strain the herb oil through a fine sieve and season to taste with salt and pepper. Set aside.

3. Pour the balsamic vinegar into a small nonreactive saucepan. Boil over high heat to reduce to 1 tablespoon, about 3 minutes. Scrape into a small dish to cool.

4. In a small bowl, combine 2 teaspoons of the reduced balsamic vinegar and ½ teaspoon of the rosemary. Whisk in 2½ tablespoons of the mild olive oil and season to taste with salt and pepper.

5. Preheat a grill or the broiler. Put the mushrooms on a baking sheet and brush all over with the remaining ¼ cup mild olive oil. Sprinkle with the thyme, the remaining 1 teaspoon rosemary and salt and pepper. Grill or broil the mushrooms, turning once, for about 5 minutes, until browned and just cooked through.

6. Put the tomatoes in a bowl and toss with 1 tablespoon of the balsamic vinaigrette. Put the greens in another bowl and toss with the remaining vinaigrette.

7. Arrange the greens in the center of 4 large plates. Place small mounds of tomato around the greens. Set a portobello cap in the center of each plate. With a small spoon, decoratively drizzle the green herb oil around the plates, in-terspersing it with small drops of the remaining 1 teaspoon reduced balsamic vinegar. Serve immediately.

—*Mark Militello*

VEGETABLE SALAD WITH ARUGULA

4 Servings

6 ounces green beans, halved crosswise
1 small yellow squash, cut into bite-size pieces
1 small red bell pepper, cut into bite-size pieces
2 tablespoons extra-virgin olive oil
1½ tablespoons balsamic vinegar
Salt and freshly ground black pepper
1 small bunch of arugula, leaves torn in large pieces
10 large basil leaves, shredded

1. In a medium saucepan, bring 1 inch of water to a boil over moderately high heat. Add the beans, cover and reduce the heat to moderate. Cook until just tender, about 4 minutes. Drain the beans, refresh under cold water and drain again. Transfer the beans to a large serving bowl. Add the squash and red pepper and toss well.

2. Drizzle the oil over the vegetables and toss to coat evenly. Sprinkle the balsamic vinegar on top and toss again. Season with ¼ teaspoon salt and ⅛ teaspoon black pepper. Just before serving, add the arugula and basil. Toss and serve.

—*Susan Shapiro Jaslove*

WARM MOZZARELLA SALAD WITH SUN-DRIED TOMATO VINAIGRETTE

This salad, from Michael Chiarello of Tra Vigne in St. Helena in California's Napa Valley, calls for lightly salted fresh mozzarella that has not been refrigerated.

♟ You need a fruity wine that is also high in acid for a good pairing with the sun-dried tomato dressing. Try a 1991 Sauvignon Blanc from Duckhorn in Napa or the aromatic 1990 Doro Princic from the Friuli region in northeastern Italy.

4 Servings

1 medium tomato—peeled, seeded and finely chopped
⅓ cup finely chopped drained oil-packed sun-dried tomatoes
1 tablespoon finely chopped fresh basil
½ teaspoon minced garlic
2 tablespoons balsamic vinegar
¼ cup plus 1 tablespoon extra-virgin olive oil
Salt and freshly ground pepper
4 large romaine lettuce leaves
Ice water
One 1-pound ball of lightly salted fresh mozzarella, quartered
2 ounces prosciutto, cut into ⅛-inch dice
6 cups stemmed arugula

1. In a medium bowl, combine the tomato, sun-dried tomatoes, basil and garlic. Whisk in the vinegar, then gradually whisk in ¼ cup of the olive oil. Season well with salt and pepper.

2. Light a grill or preheat the broiler.

SALADS

Bring a large skillet of lightly salted water to a boil. Add 2 of the romaine leaves to the pan and blanch for 30 seconds. Using tongs, transfer the lettuce to a bowl of ice water to stop the cooking. Remove the leaves and pat dry with paper towels. Repeat with the 2 remaining lettuce leaves.

3. Spread the romaine leaves out on a work surface, dark green leafy ends away from you and rib-side down. Gently flatten the center of each leaf with the heel of your hand, taking care not to split the leaves all the way through. Place a piece of mozzarella lengthwise on each leaf. Lightly season the cheese with salt and pepper and sprinkle with the diced prosciutto.

4. To form each package, fold the sides of a romaine leaf against the mozzarella. Fold the rib end over the cheese, then fold the dark green portion of the leaf over to seal the package. Place seam-side up, on a rimmed baking sheet. *(The recipe can be prepared to this point up to 2 hours ahead. Set the packages and dressing aside separately at room temperature.)*

5. Brush the packages lightly with the remaining 1 tablespoon olive oil. Grill or broil, seam-side up, for 2 to 3 minutes, just until the cheese begins to weep and barely melt.

6. Whisk the dressing and spoon 2 tablespoons on each of 4 large plates. In a large bowl, toss the arugula with the remaining dressing. Arrange the greens in a circle on the dressing. Using a metal spatula, set a mozzarella package in the center of each salad and serve immediately.

—*Michael Chiarello*

JAMIE'S FRUIT SALAD

6 Servings

1½ tablespoons raspberry vinegar
1 teaspoon sugar
¼ teaspoon salt
3 tablespoons sour cream
1½ teaspoons finely chopped fresh mint
Pinch of dry mustard
Pinch of ground nutmeg
1 tablespoon vegetable oil
2 medium pears, cored and cut into ½-inch dice
2 cups red grapes, halved
1 large celery rib, finely diced
6 red leaf lettuce leaves, for serving

1. In a bowl, whisk the vinegar, sugar and salt until blended. Whisk in the sour cream, mint, mustard and nutmeg. Whisk in the oil.

2. Add the pears, grapes and celery to the dressing and toss until well coated. Serve on individual leaves of red leaf lettuce.

—*Jamie Davies*

GRAPEFRUIT-KIWI SALAD WITH POPPY SEEDS AND CHICORY

8 Servings

5 large kiwis (1½ pounds)
6 pink or red grapefruits (about 1 pound each)
2 tablespoons fresh lemon juice
2 tablespoons safflower oil
2 tablespoons minced parsley
1 tablespoon poppy seeds
1 tablespoon sugar
1 head of young chicory (about 1 pound), torn into bite-size pieces

1. Peel the kiwis. Halve them length-wise, then slice crosswise ⅛ inch thick and place in a bowl.

2. Peel the grapefruits with a sharp knife, making sure to remove all the bitter white pith. Working over the bowl, cut in between the membranes to release the sections.

3. Squeeze the membranes over a strainer set in a small bowl. Whisk in the lemon juice, oil, parsley, poppy seeds and sugar.

4. Toss half of the dressing with the fruit. In another bowl, toss the chicory with the remaining dressing. Arrange the chicory around a serving platter and mound the fruit in the center.

—*Bob Chambers*

ORANGE-BLUEBERRY SALAD WITH ARUGULA AND TARRAGON

With sweet-tart fruit, peppery arugula and a tangy dressing, this salad is delicious with grilled duck, quail or squab.

6 to 8 Servings

8 navel oranges
2 tablespoons sugar
2 teaspoons Dijon mustard
¼ teaspoon freshly ground pepper
2 teaspoons arrowroot dissolved in ¼ cup cold water
2 teaspoons finely chopped fresh tarragon
1 pint blueberries, rinsed and dried
1 pound arugula, large stems discarded

1. Squeeze the juice from 2 of the oranges into a strainer set over a small nonreactive saucepan. Add the sugar, mustard and pepper to the pan and bring to a boil over high heat. Whisk in the dissolved arrowroot and stir over the heat just until thickened. Transfer the dressing to a small bowl and chill over ice until cool. Stir in the tarragon.

2. Meanwhile, using a sharp knife, peel the 6 remaining oranges, making sure to remove all the bitter white pith. Quarter the oranges lengthwise, then slice them crosswise ¼ inch thick. Place in a medium bowl and add the blueberries. Stir in the dressing.

3. Arrange the arugula on a serving platter, mound the fruit in the center and serve.

—*Bob Chambers*

PEAR AND APPLE SALAD WITH GRUYERE AND TOASTED PECANS

Smoked ham or turkey would go very nicely with this rich and hearty salad. For variety, a firm goat cheese or a pungent blue could stand in for the Gruyère, and walnuts could be used in place of the pecans. For best results, assemble just before serving.

6 to 8 Servings

1½ cups pecan halves (6 ounces)
2 tablespoons balsamic vinegar
1 tablespoon grainy mustard
Salt and freshly ground pepper
¼ cup safflower oil
2 medium Anjou or Comice pears
2 medium Granny Smith apples
3 tablespoons fresh lemon juice
1 pound seedless grapes, halved
*   lengthwise*
5 ounces Gruyère cheese, cut into
*   ⅛-by-1½-inch matchsticks*
1 head of Boston lettuce, leaves
*   separated*

1. Preheat the oven to 350°. Spread the pecans on a baking sheet and toast in the middle of the oven for 8 minutes, until fragrant. Let cool to room temperature, then chop coarsely.

2. In a small bowl, whisk the vinegar and mustard. Season with salt and

pepper. Gradually whisk in the oil.

3. Core the pears and apples and cut them into ½-inch dice. Place in a bowl and toss with the lemon juice. Add the grapes, Gruyère and the dressing and toss.

4. Line a platter with the lettuce leaves and spoon the salad in the center. Sprinkle the toasted pecans on top.

—*Bob Chambers*

MIXED RED BERRIES IN RED WINE SYRUP WITH RADICCHIO

The juicy berries, sweet wine syrup and bitter-crisp radicchio call out for grilled or roasted pork or duck.

6 to 8 Servings

2 pints strawberries, quartered
1 pint raspberries
½ pint fresh red currants, stemmed
½ cup fresh lemon juice
⅓ cup plus 1 tablespoon sugar
3 cups dry red wine
3 whole cloves
2 cinnamon sticks
1 vanilla bean, split lengthwise
1 pound radicchio—quartered, cored
*   and cut into ¼-inch shreds*

1. In a medium bowl, toss the strawberries, raspberries and red currants with 6 tablespoons of the lemon juice and 1 tablespoon of the sugar. Set aside for 30 minutes, tossing occasionally.

2. Meanwhile, in a medium nonreactive saucepan, combine the red wine with the remaining 2 tablespoons lemon juice and ⅓ cup sugar plus the cloves, cinnamon sticks and vanilla bean. Bring to a boil and cook over moderately high heat until reduced to 1½ cups, 8 to 10 minutes. Strain the syrup into a bowl and chill it over ice until cool.

3. In a medium bowl, toss the radicchio with half of the red wine syrup. Add the remaining syrup to the berries and toss. Arrange the radicchio around the edge of a platter, mound the berries in the center and serve.

—*Bob Chambers*

PEACH, PLUM AND CHERRY SALAD WITH CUCUMBER RIBBONS

This salad would be a fine partner for grilled pork or duck. If golden cherries are unavailable, simply use another pound of Bing instead.

8 Servings

1½ pounds medium peaches, sliced
*   into ⅓-inch wedges*
1 pound plums, cut into ¾-inch dice
1 pound Bing cherries, halved and
*   pitted*
1 pound Rainier or Royal Anne
*   cherries, halved and pitted*
½ cup fresh lemon juice
¼ cup sugar
1 tablespoon chopped fresh chervil
¼ teaspoon fresh ground pepper
Pinch of salt
5 large cucumbers

1. In a medium bowl, toss the peaches with the plums and cherries. Add the lemon juice, sugar, chervil, pepper and salt; toss well. Refrigerate for 2 hours, stirring occasionally.

2. Meanwhile, peel the cucumbers and halve lengthwise. Using the vegetable peeler, continue stripping the cucumbers to make thin ribbons, stopping

when you reach the seeds. Place the ribbons in a strainer set over a bowl and refrigerate for up to 2 hours.

3. Shortly before serving, toss the cucumber ribbons with some of the juices from the fruit salad. Arrange the ribbons around the edge of a shallow platter, mound the fruit in the center and serve.

—Bob Chambers

MELON AND MANGO SALAD WITH MINT AND PARSLEY

To turn this salad into a main course, serve plated portions with paper-thin slices of Parma ham.

6 to 8 Servings

1 cantaloupe (about 1½ pounds)
1 honeydew (about 2½ pounds)
2 mangoes (½ pound each)
½ cup plus 3 tablespoons fresh lemon juice
2 tablespoons plus 2 teaspoons sugar
3 tablespoons chopped fresh mint
Pinch of salt
½ teaspoon freshly ground pepper
¼ cup vegetable oil
½ pound flat-leaf parsley, large stems discarded
⅓ cup salted, dry-roasted sunflower seeds

1. Halve the melons crosswise and scoop out the seeds. Set the melon halves on a work surface, cut-sides down, and peel with a sharp knife. Slice the melon halves ½ inch thick. Cut each slice into ½-inch pieces and place in a large bowl.

2. Peel the mangoes and cut the flesh into ½-inch chunks. Add to the melon. Stir in 3 tablespoons of the lemon juice, 2 tablespoons of the sugar, 2 tablespoons of the mint and the salt. Set aside for 10 minutes, tossing occasionally.

3. Meanwhile, in a small bowl, whisk the remaining ½ cup lemon juice, 2 teaspoons sugar, 1 tablespoon mint and the pepper. Whisk in the oil. Toss the parsley with half of the dressing. Stir the remaining dressing into the melon salad.

4. Arrange the parsley around the edge of a large shallow platter and sprinkle with the sunflower seeds. Mound the melon salad in the center and serve.

—Bob Chambers

PINEAPPLE AND JICAMA SALAD WITH RED GRAPES AND BASIL

To cut the jicama, first slice it into ¼-inch rounds, then stack the rounds and slice them into ¼-inch strips. To shred fresh basil, stack the leaves and roll them up lengthwise, then slice the roll crosswise into fine strips. Try this salad with ham or grilled chicken.

6 to 8 Servings

1 fresh pineapple (2½ pounds)
1½ pounds jicama, peeled and cut into 2-by-¼-inch matchsticks
1 pound seedless red grapes, halved lengthwise
1 cup fresh basil leaves, finely shredded
⅓ cup fresh lemon juice
1 tablespoon sugar
¼ teaspoon salt
¼ teaspoon freshly ground pepper

½ cup safflower oil
½ pound red oak leaf lettuce, leaves separated

1. Using a sharp knife, peel the pineapple and remove the eyes. Quarter the fruit lengthwise and cut out the core. Halve each section lengthwise, then slice crosswise ½ inch thick. In a large bowl, toss the pineapple with the jicama, grapes and basil.

2. In a small bowl, whisk the lemon juice with the sugar, salt and pepper. Whisk in the oil. Pour half of the dressing over the fruit and toss well. Refrigerate the salad for 1 to 2 hours.

3. In a bowl, toss the oak leaf lettuce with the remaining dressing. Arrange the lettuce around the edge of a platter, mound the pineapple-jicama salad in the center and serve.

—Bob Chambers

BULGUR SALAD WITH ORANGES, FENNEL AND OLIVES

Buy fine bulgur, which is sold in bulk; the coarse packaged variety is usually cracked wheat, which becomes gluey when squeezed. Add the oranges just before serving. If desired, pair with roasted chicken.

Makes About 4 Cups

1 cup fine bulgur (about 6 ounces)
Boiling water
2 medium navel oranges (about 10 ounces each)
½ of a medium fennel bulb, cored and cut lengthwise into ¼-by-1½-inch strips
⅓ cup Niçoise olives (about 2 ounces), pitted and halved
⅓ cup thinly sliced red onion
2 tablespoons torn fresh basil leaves
3 tablespoons olive oil

2 tablespoons red wine vinegar
½ teaspoon salt
¼ teaspoon freshly ground pepper
2 tablespoons pine nuts
Fresh watercress sprigs, for garnish

1. Place the bulgur in a bowl and pour in boiling water to cover by about 1 inch. Cover the bowl and let steep until plumped and softened, about 40 minutes. Drain in a colander lined with cheesecloth, then twist the cheesecloth around the bulgur and squeeze out any excess water. Transfer to a large bowl.

2. Using a small sharp knife, peel the oranges, removing all the bitter white pith. Holding the oranges over a bowl to catch the juices, cut in between the membranes to release the sections. Squeeze the membranes to extract all the juice. Reserving the juice, drain the orange sections well in a colander; cover and refrigerate. Strain the juice into a small nonreactive saucepan and cook over moderate heat until reduced to about 1 tablespoon. Set aside to cool.

3. Add the fennel, olives, onion and basil to the bulgur. Whisk the oil with the vinegar, reduced orange juice, salt and pepper and pour over the salad. Toss well, cover and refrigerate until cold, at least 1 hour, or up to 5 hours.

4. Meanwhile, in a small skillet, toast the pine nuts over moderate heat, shaking the pan often, until fragrant and golden, 5 to 7 minutes. Let cool.

5. Add the pine nuts to the cold salad and toss gently. Transfer to a wide serving bowl and arrange the orange sections on top. Garnish with the watercress. Serve at once.

—*Stephanie Lyness*

TABBOULEH

A common mistake when making this traditional Middle Eastern salad is to use too much bulgur in proportion to the herbs—it should be a very green salad in which the bulgur garnishes the parsley rather than vice versa.

Makes About 4 Cups

¾ cup medium-grade bulgur
Boiling water
2 cups finely chopped flat-leaf parsley leaves and tender stems
6 medium scallions, white and green, thinly sliced
3 medium tomatoes, cut into ½-inch dice
½ cup finely chopped fresh mint
3½ tablespoons fresh lemon juice
½ cup extra-virgin olive oil
Salt and freshly ground pepper
Large leaves of romaine lettuce, for serving

1. Place the bulgur in a bowl and add enough boiling water to cover by 1 inch. Set aside for about 30 minutes, until softened and plumped.

2. Squeeze out as much water as you can from the bulgur. Turn the grains out into a clean dish towel and twist the towel to squeeze out any remaining water. Each grain of bulgur should be moist and plump but without a trace of liquid.

3. In a large bowl, toss the bulgur with the parsley, scallions, tomatoes and mint. Stir in the lemon juice and then the olive oil. Season with salt and pepper. To serve, arrange overlapping romaine lettuce leaves all around an oval platter and heap the tabbouleh in the middle.

—*Nancy Harmon Jenkins*

JASMINE RICE SALAD WITH ASPARAGUS AND WALNUTS

Serve this salad with grilled or roasted Cornish game hen, quail or chicken.

Makes About 7 Cups

1 cup Jasmine rice
¼ cup walnut pieces
1 pound medium asparagus
2 tablespoons sherry vinegar
2 teaspoons Dijon mustard
¾ teaspoon salt
¼ teaspoon freshly ground pepper
2 tablespoons walnut oil
1 tablespoon olive oil
½ of a small red onion, cut into ¼-inch dice
2 ounces thinly sliced cured ham, such as prosciutto or Black Forest, cut into thin 2-inch-long strips
1 small head of radicchio—halved, cored and sliced crosswise into thin shreds
2 tablespoons slivered fresh basil

1. Place the rice in a bowl, cover with cold water and rub gently between your hands; the water will turn cloudy. Drain and repeat several times until the water is clear. Drain well.

2. Bring 1 cup of water to a boil in a medium saucepan. Add the rice and return to a boil. Turn the heat down to very low, cover and simmer until the rice is tender, about 15 minutes. Let cool.

SALADS

128

3. Meanwhile, preheat the oven to 400°. Spread the walnuts on a baking sheet and toast for about 8 minutes, until fragrant and lightly browned. Coarsely chop.

4. Blanch the asparagus in boiling salted water until just tender, about 3 minutes. Refresh under cold water and drain. Cut the tips from the asparagus and then cut the stems diagonally into ½-inch pieces.

5. In a small bowl, whisk the vinegar, mustard, salt and pepper. Whisk in the walnut and olive oils.

6. In a bowl, toss the rice with the asparagus, walnuts, red onion, ham, radicchio and basil. Add the dressing and toss well. Let stand for 15 minutes or up to 4 hours before serving.

—*Stephanie Lyness*

WILD RICE SALAD WITH GREEN BEANS, MUSHROOMS AND TARRAGON

Don't add the green beans more than 30 minutes before eating the salad; the vinaigrette will turn them an unappetizing olive color. To serve as a main course, add chunks of grilled tuna.

Makes About 6 Cups

1 cup wild rice
Salt
1 cup thinly sliced white mushrooms
1 medium tomato, coarsely chopped
1 tablespoon chopped flat-leaf parsley

2 tablespoons red wine vinegar
1 tablespoon fresh lemon juice
2 teaspoons Dijon mustard
2 garlic cloves, minced
¼ teaspoon freshly ground pepper
3 tablespoons olive oil
1 teaspoon minced fresh tarragon
½ pound green beans

1. Rinse the wild rice, place in a bowl, cover with cold water and let soak for 30 minutes; drain. Place in a medium saucepan with 6 cups of water and 1 teaspoon of salt and bring to a boil. Lower the heat, cover and simmer until plump, split and tender but still chewy, 50 to 60 minutes. Drain and transfer to a bowl. Toss with the mushrooms, tomato and parsley.

2. In a small bowl, whisk the vinegar, lemon juice, mustard, garlic, pepper and ½ teaspoon of salt. Whisk in the oil and tarragon. Pour the dressing over the rice salad and toss. Let stand for 15 minutes, or up to 3 hours.

3. Blanch the beans in boiling salted water until tender, about 5 minutes. Refresh under cold water and drain. Cut the beans into 1-inch pieces and fold them into the salad.

—*Stephanie Lyness*

WILD RICE SALAD

6 Servings

1 cup wild rice
Salt
½ cup walnut halves
¼ cup plus 3 tablespoons vegetable oil
½ pound medium mushrooms, thickly sliced
2 celery ribs, halved lengthwise and thinly sliced crosswise
¾ cup thinly sliced scallions
½ cup coarsely chopped parsley
2 tablespoons sherry vinegar

¼ teaspoon dry mustard
Pinch of cayenne pepper
Freshly ground black pepper
Belgian endive spears, for serving

1. Preheat the oven to 350°. In a heavy medium saucepan, combine the wild rice and 4 cups of water. Season with salt and bring to a boil. Cover, lower the heat and simmer until tender, about 45 minutes. Uncover, fluff with a fork and cook gently for 5 minutes longer. Drain off any excess liquid and let cool.

2. While the rice is cooking, spread the walnuts on a small baking sheet and roast for 7 to 8 minutes, until fragrant and lightly toasted. Let cool and then coarsely chop.

3. In a large skillet, heat 1 tablespoon of the vegetable oil over moderately high heat. Add the mushrooms and cook, stirring occasionally, until browned, about 5 minutes. Transfer to a large bowl. Add the celery, scallions, parsley, wild rice and walnuts and toss well.

4. In a small jar, combine the vinegar, mustard, cayenne and ¼ teaspoon each of salt and black pepper. Shake until blended. Pour in the remaining ¼ cup plus 2 tablespoons oil and shake vigorously until creamy.

5. Toss the rice salad with the vinaigrette and season with salt and pepper. Transfer to a bowl and surround with the endive spears to use as scoops.

—*Jamie Davies*

Lobster Coleslaw with Basil, Tarragon and Chives (p. 138).

Left, Grilled Chicken Salad with Frizzled Tortillas (p. 139).
Above, Herb Salad with Watercress Dressing (p. 118).

MOROCCAN MILLET SALAD

Japanese eggplants are very slender, have fewer seeds and are less bitter than the larger variety.

Makes About 8 Cups

1 cup millet
¾ teaspoon cumin
¼ teaspoon ground coriander
¼ cup rice vinegar
3 tablespoons dried currants
1 bunch of medium scallions
1 large carrot, peeled and thinly sliced crosswise
2 small zucchini, cut into ½-inch dice
3 tablespoons olive oil
Salt and freshly ground pepper
1 medium Japanese eggplant, cut into ½-inch dice
1 cup canned red kidney beans, rinsed
2 tablespoons chopped flat-leaf parsley
Pinch of cinnamon

1. In a medium skillet, toast the millet over moderate heat until it pops and is golden brown, 3 to 4 minutes. Transfer to a saucepan, add 2 cups of water and bring to a boil. Lower the heat, cover and simmer until chewy but not crunchy, 18 to 20 minutes. Transfer to a large bowl.

2. Toast the cumin and coriander in the skillet over moderate heat, stirring often, until fragrant, 1 to 2 minutes. Transfer to a small bowl.

3. In a medium bowl, combine the vinegar and currants and set aside to macerate for at least 15 minutes or until you are ready to dress the salad.

4. Thinly slice enough of the scallion greens to make ¼ cup. Cut the remaining scallions into ¾-inch pieces.

Asparagus Salad Mimosa (p. 120).

5. Place the carrot in a skillet. Add ¼ cup water and simmer over moderate heat until the water has evaporated, 3 to 5 minutes. Add the zucchini and 1 tablespoon of the olive oil. Season with salt and pepper and cook over moderately high heat, stirring often, until the zucchini is golden, about 5 minutes. Transfer the vegetables to the millet.

6. Add 1 more tablespoon oil to the skillet. Add the eggplant and the scallion pieces and cook, stirring occasionally, until nicely browned, about 5 minutes. Transfer the eggplant and scallions to paper towels to drain, then add to the millet along with the kidney beans and parsley and toss.

7. Whisk the toasted cumin and coriander, the cinnamon and 1¼ teaspoons salt into the vinegar and currants. Whisk in the remaining 1 tablespoon oil and toss with the salad. Let stand for at least 15 minutes or up to 5 hours. Toss with the sliced scallion greens just before serving.

—*Stephanie Lyness*

BARLEY SALAD WITH ROASTED CORN AND PEPPERS

You can turn this salad into a main course by adding shrimp. Skewer one pound of cleaned shrimp and grill it along with the corn and peppers, or simply sauté it. If you don't add the papaya until just before serving, you can make the salad one day ahead.

Makes About 6 Cups

1 cup medium pearl barley
Salt
2 ears of corn, husked
1 medium red bell pepper
1 medium poblano pepper
3 scallions, thinly sliced crosswise

½ of a medium papaya—peeled, seeded and cut into ⅓-inch dice
2 tablespoons chopped fresh coriander (cilantro)
¾ teaspoon ground cumin
¼ cup fresh lime juice
1 tablespoon cider vinegar
⅛ teaspoon freshly ground black pepper
3 tablespoons olive oil

1. Place the barley in a bowl, cover with warm water and rub gently between your hands; the water will turn cloudy. Drain and repeat several times until the water is clear. Drain well.

2. Bring 8 cups of water to a boil in a large saucepan. Add 2 teaspoons of salt and the barley and return to a boil. Lower the heat, cover and simmer until tender, about 30 minutes. Drain and rinse the barley with cold water. Drain well and transfer to a bowl.

3. Meanwhile, roast the corn on a grill, in the broiler or on a sturdy rack set over a gas flame, turning the ears often, until tender and many of the kernels are browned, about 5 minutes. Using a sharp knife, slice the kernels from each cob. Add to the barley.

4. Roast the red bell pepper and poblano pepper over a grill or gas flame or under the broiler as close to the heat as possible, turning often, until charred all over. Transfer the peppers to a paper bag and set aside to steam for 10 minutes. Using a small sharp knife, scrape off the blackened skins and remove the cores, seeds and ribs. Rinse the peppers and pat dry. Cut the peppers into ¼-inch dice. Add to the barley and corn, along with the scal-

lions, papaya and coriander; toss well.

5. In a small dry skillet, toast the ground cumin over moderate heat, stirring, until fragrant, 1 to 2 minutes. In a small bowl, whisk the lime juice and vinegar with the cumin, 1 teaspoon of salt and the black pepper. Whisk in the oil. Pour the dressing over the salad and toss. Let stand for 15 to 30 minutes before serving.

—Stephanie Lyness

QUINOA "TABBOULEH"

Two people can make a very substantial meal of this salad along with hummus, pita bread and tossed greens.

Makes About 5 Cups

1 cup quinoa (about 6½ ounces)
Salt
¼ cup shelled raw unsalted pumpkin seeds
½ pint cherry tomatoes, quartered
½ cup finely diced seeded cucumber
½ cup finely chopped onion
¼ cup coarsely chopped flat-leaf parsley
1 tablespoon coarsely chopped fresh mint
1 tablespoon coarsely chopped fresh coriander (cilantro)
¼ cup crumbled feta cheese (optional)
3 tablespoons olive oil
2 tablespoons fresh lemon juice
½ teaspoon freshly ground pepper
*Available at health food stores

1. Place the quinoa in a bowl, cover with warm water and rub between your hands; the water will turn cloudy. Drain and repeat several times until the water is clear. Drain well. Transfer the quinoa to a large nonstick skillet and toast over moderate heat, stirring, until light golden, about 4 minutes.

2. Bring 2 cups of water to a boil in a heavy medium saucepan. Add 1 teaspoon of salt and the toasted quinoa and return to a boil. Lower the heat, cover and simmer gently until the quinoa is tender but not mushy, about 12 minutes. Transfer to a fine strainer and rinse with cold water. Drain well.

3. In a skillet, toast the pumpkin seeds over moderate heat, stirring, until puffed, about 5 minutes.

4. In a large bowl, toss the quinoa with the toasted pumpkin seeds, tomatoes, cucumber, onion, parsley, mint, coriander and feta cheese. Whisk the oil with the lemon juice, pepper and 1 teaspoon salt. Pour the dressing over the salad and toss well. Let stand for 20 minutes before serving.

—Stephanie Lyness

CURRIED COUSCOUS SALAD

Serve this tangy, multiflavored salad with rich robust food such as grilled lamb or beef. You can make the salad one day ahead, but add the pistachios and coconut just before serving.

Makes 6 Cups

1½ cups water
1 cup couscous
¼ cup sweetened shredded coconut
¼ cup shelled unsalted pistachios
1 teaspoon curry powder
½ cup fresh orange juice
3 tablespoons fresh lime juice
1 tablespoon grated fresh ginger
1 teaspoon finely grated lime zest
1 teaspoon salt
¼ teaspoon freshly ground pepper

2 tablespoons olive oil
1 teaspoon Oriental sesame oil
1 cup shredded green cabbage
3 small carrots, finely grated
⅓ cup thinly sliced scallion greens

1. In a small saucepan, bring the water to a boil. Stir in the couscous, remove from the heat, cover and let stand for 5 minutes. Fluff with a fork and let stand, covered, for 5 minutes longer. Let cool.

2. Preheat the oven to 350°. Spread the coconut on a baking sheet and toast for about 4 minutes, until lightly browned. Spread the pistachios on another baking sheet and toast for about 7 minutes, until fragrant; coarsely chop.

3. In a skillet, toast the curry powder over moderate heat, stirring, for about 2 minutes. Transfer to a bowl and add the orange juice, lime juice, ginger, lime zest, salt and pepper. Whisk in the olive and sesame oils.

4. In a serving bowl, toss the couscous with the cabbage, carrots, scallions and pistachios. Add the curry vinaigrette and toss to coat. Let stand for 15 to 30 minutes. Sprinkle the toasted coconut on top and serve.

—Stephanie Lyness

SALADE NICOISE

I've always adored *salade niçoise* for lunch and am often lured by false hope into ordering one in a restaurant. There are those who pile all the various elements in a large salad bowl. They pour on the dressing and toss everything together with stylish abandon, often with their bare hands and with that archly playful look of "ain't I the naughty one?" This is certainly quick boarding-house service, but what a shame to make a mess of such beautiful ingredients. I like a plattered arrangement so that I can see and admire, make my own choice and toss or not, as I wish.

The freshness and quality of every ingredient is the key to a first-class salad. And I am frankly against innovations, such as substituting seared fresh tuna for canned tuna. No. A real *niçoise* is made with canned tuna: Fresh tuna does not have the traditional, classic taste!

6 Servings

GREEN BEANS:
6 quarts water
2 tablespoons salt
1½ pounds crisp, young, stringless green beans, ends snapped off

FRENCH POTATO SALAD:
1½ pounds red-skinned or Yukon Gold potatoes (2 inches in diameter), scrubbed
⅓ cup dry white wine
⅓ cup cold water
1 tablespoon minced shallots
3 to 4 tablespoons excellent olive oil (see Note)
Salt and freshly ground pepper

DRESSING:
Grated zest of ½ lemon
Salt and freshly ground pepper
½ tablespoon Dijon mustard
½ tablespoon very finely minced shallot or scallion
1 tablespoon fresh lemon juice
½ cup excellent olive oil (see Note)

1 large head of Boston lettuce, leaves separated, rinsed and spun dry
6 large hard-boiled eggs
Salt
3 or 4 beautifully ripe red tomatoes, quartered lengthwise

8 to 10 ounces oil-packed chunk white tuna
Fresh lemon juice
Freshly ground pepper
2-ounce can or jar of anchovy fillets packed in olive oil
2 tablespoons fine fat capers
A handful of small, brine-packed Italian or French black olives
Chopped fresh parsley

1. *Cook the green beans:* In a large kettle, bring the water to a boil with the salt. Drop in the beans, cover and return to a boil. (The large amount of boiling water and rapid cooking seizes the color.) Uncover at once and boil slowly for 3 or 4 minutes. The beans are done when just tender with the slightest crunch. Drain immediately. Return the beans to the kettle at once and run cold water into it to cool them rapidly, adding a tray or two of ice cubes if you have them. When chilled, drain again, pat dry and refrigerate.

2. *Prepare the potato salad:* Place the potatoes in a steamer basket in a saucepan containing 2 inches of water and bring to a boil. Lower the heat to moderate, cover tightly and steam for about 20 minutes, or until cooked through; taste one to check. Peel while still hot (cooks need asbestos hands!), halve and slice ¼ inch thick.

3. Meanwhile, in a medium bowl, blend together the wine, water, shallots, 3 tablespoons of the olive oil, ½ teaspoon salt and a few grindings of pepper. Gently place the potatoes in the bowl and, using a bulb baster so as not to break the slices, baste the potatoes with the dressing. Taste for seasoning, adding more salt, pepper and olive oil. Baste several times as the potatoes cool.

4. *Prepare the dressing:* In a screw-topped jar, mix the lemon zest, ¼ teaspoon salt, several grindings of pepper,

the mustard, shallot and lemon juice. Pour in the oil and shake vigorously. Taste for seasoning, adding more lemon juice, salt and pepper if needed.

5. Shortly before serving, toss the lettuce leaves in a large bowl with just enough dressing to coat them. Halve the eggs lengthwise. Toss the green beans with a spoonful of dressing. Lightly salt the cut surfaces of the tomatoes and dribble a little dressing on top. Drain the tuna, flake gently and season with lemon juice and pepper.

6. Arrange the largest lettuce leaves around the sides of a large platter and make a bed of the remaining leaves in the center, where you will pile the potatoes. Arrange the eggs on the platter and decorate with crossed or rolled anchovies and a sprinkling of capers. Divide the beans, tomatoes and tuna into portions, and place at strategic intervals around the potatoes. Survey the platter, scattering black olives and chopped parsley wherever needed. Serve as soon as possible.

NOTE: On olive oils: Virgin oil is supposed to be from the first cold pressing of the olives and can be very good indeed. Extra-virgin, the trendy olive oil of the moment, is the first cold pressing, presumably from specially selected olives, and it can be extravagantly expensive. Is it really what it says on the bottle? Is it worth its stiff price? That depends on who makes it and how. Taste carefully before you buy, or get advice from a knowing friend. For salads, you want the best.

—*Julia Child*

THAI SEAFOOD SALAD

In this Thai classic called *yam thalae,* quickly poached fish, shrimp and squid are tossed in a distinctive dressing made with chiles, lime and a hint of sugar.

Begin with cleaned and filleted fish and seafood. Cut back on the chiles if you don't like heat, or increase them for greater authenticity. In Thailand this salad is usually very hot, made with at least double the number of chiles called for here. Serve the salad with steamed rice and a plate of sliced fresh tomatoes and cucumbers.

4 Servings

3 large garlic cloves, chopped
2 serrano chiles, stemmed and finely chopped
2 tablespoons chopped fresh coriander (cilantro) roots plus ½ cup coarsely chopped fresh coriander leaves
1 teaspoon sugar
3 tablespoons fish sauce
6 small shallots, peeled and thinly sliced
¼ cup plus 1 tablespoon fresh lime juice
4 cups lightly salted water
½ pound cleaned squid, bodies sliced crosswise ¼ inch thick
½ pound medium shrimp, shelled and deveined
½ pound monkfish, orange roughy or sea bass fillets, sliced crosswise ½ inch thick
Freshly ground black pepper

1. Make the dressing in a mortar by pounding together the garlic, chiles, co-riander roots and sugar until a paste forms. Stir in the fish sauce. (Alternatively, mince the garlic, chiles and coriander roots very finely, then stir in the sugar and fish sauce.) Transfer to a serving bowl and stir in the chopped coriander leaves, shallots and ¼ cup of the lime juice.

2. In a large nonreactive saucepan, combine the water with the remaining 1 tablespoon lime juice and bring to a boil over high heat. Add the squid, shrimp and fish and simmer just until the squid and fish are white and the shrimp are pink and loosely curled, 2 to 3 minutes. Using a slotted spoon, transfer the seafood to the dressing and stir well to coat. Sprinkle with black pepper and serve warm or at room temperature.

—Jeffrey Alford & Naomi Duguid

NEO-CLASSIC SEAFOOD SALAD

When serving this towering salad at Gotham Bar & Grill in New York City, chef Alfred Portale adds thinly sliced octopus to the seafood mélange.

❦ Since shellfish are sweet and olive oil is smooth, the salad needs a medium-bodied wine with a hint of sweetness and firm acidity, typified by the 1990 Albariño Morgadio from Galicia, Spain.

4 Servings

¼ cup fresh lemon juice
1 tablespoon red wine vinegar
½ teaspoon Dijon mustard
¾ cup extra-virgin olive oil
Salt and freshly ground white pepper
Pinch of cayenne pepper
One 1½-pound lobster
6 ounces medium sea scallops
6 ounces cleaned squid
18 small mussels, scrubbed and debearded
1 large shallot, minced
1 tablespoon finely chopped fresh basil
1 tablespoon finely chopped flat-leaf parsley
1 tablespoon minced fresh chives
1 avocado
1 small head of frisée, separated into whole leaves
1 small head of red oak leaf lettuce, separated into whole leaves
Very thin strips of lemon zest, for garnish (optional)

1. In a small bowl, whisk together the lemon juice, vinegar and mustard. Slowly whisk in the oil and season with salt, white pepper and cayenne.

2. Bring a large saucepan of water to a boil. Plunge the lobster in head first and cook over high heat for 10 minutes. Using tongs, transfer the lobster to a bowl and let cool.

3. Steam the scallops in a steamer basket set over boiling water until tender and almost white, about 3 minutes. Transfer to a plate and let cool. Add the squid to the steamer and cook until tender, about 3 minutes; transfer to a bowl and let cool. Repeat with the mussels, steaming them until they open, about 3 minutes.

4. Break off the claws from the lobster, crack them open and remove the meat. Twist the lobster body to remove the tail section. Crack the underside of the tail and remove the meat. Slice the claw and tail meat ½ inch thick. Place the claw meat in a large bowl and the tail meat in a small bowl.

5. Slice the scallops horizontally ¼ inch thick. Cut the squid bodies crosswise into ¼-inch rings; if the tentacles are large, cut them into smaller pieces. Remove the mussels from their shells. Add the scallops, squid and mussels to the lobster claw meat. Stir in the shallot, basil, parsley, half of the chives and ⅓ cup of the vinaigrette. Season with salt and pepper.

6. Mound the seafood in the center of 4 large plates. Peel and quarter the avocado. Thinly slice each section lengthwise, keeping the slices attached at one end. Brush each quarter with 1 tablespoon of the vinaigrette. Toss the lobster tail meat with 2 tablespoons of the vinaigrette and arrange 2 to 3 slices on one side of the seafood. Arrange the avocado quarters on the other side.

7. In the large bowl, toss the frisée and red oak leaf lettuce with about ¼ cup of the vinaigrette. Anchor the lettuce leaves in the seafood salad so that they stand straight up. Sprinkle the remaining ½ tablespoon chives and the lemon zest over the salads and serve. Pass the remaining dressing alongside.

—Alfred Portale

SEARED SEA SCALLOP SALAD WITH CITRUS VINAIGRETTE

The wine-glazed onions that garnish this salad from Charles Palmer of Aureole in New York City contrast nicely with the sage and citrus in the dressing. ♟ This salad needs a wine with a great balance of fruit and acidity to complement and balance the sage and citrus. A good choice is 1991 Iron Horse Vineyards Chardonnay from Sonoma.

4 Servings

2 medium red onions, cut lengthwise into ⅓-inch wedges
1½ cups chicken stock or canned low-sodium broth
1 cup fruity red wine, such as Burgundy or Pinot Noir
¼ cup plus 2 tablespoons extra-virgin olive oil
1 garlic clove, smashed

Salt and freshly ground pepper
½ cup fresh orange juice
3 tablespoons fresh lemon juice
2 tablespoons minced fresh sage
1½ teaspoons finely grated orange zest
¾ teaspoon finely grated lemon zest
2 tablespoons safflower or other neutral vegetable oil
16 large sea scallops (1½ pounds)
8 cups mâche or other delicate greens
4 cups bite-size pieces of frisée

1. Place the onion wedges in a large skillet. Add ½ cup of the chicken stock, the wine, 2 tablespoons of the olive oil and the garlic and bring to a boil over high heat. Reduce the heat to moderately low and simmer, stirring occasionally, until the onions are tender and the liquid has reduced, about 12 minutes. Season with salt and pepper.

2. In a medium bowl, combine the remaining ¼ cup olive oil with the orange juice, lemon juice, sage, orange zest and lemon zest.

3. In a large nonreactive skillet, heat 1 tablespoon of the vegetable oil until almost smoking. Season the scallops with salt and pepper and add half of them to the skillet in a single layer without crowding. Sear the scallops over high heat, turning once, until nicely browned and just cooked through, 1 to 2 minutes per side. Transfer to a large plate. Repeat with the remaining oil and scallops.

4. Add the remaining 1 cup chicken stock to the skillet and boil over high heat until reduced to ⅓ cup, about 4 minutes. Add the lemon-orange vinaigrette, remove from the heat and season the dressing with salt and pepper.

5. In a large bowl, combine the mâche and frisée. Whisk any accumulated scallop juices into the dressing. Add about one-third of the dressing to the greens and toss to coat. Mound the greens on 4 large plates and arrange the scallops on top. Remove the onions from the glaze and scatter them around the salads. Serve the remaining dressing alongside.

—Charles Palmer

TOMATO SALAD WITH SEA SCALLOPS, MAUI ONIONS, PICCOLO BASIL AND OLIVE OIL DRESSING

German chef Martin Woesle characterizes his fare at Mille Fleurs in Rancho Santa Fe, California, as "European common food," built around whatever fresh produce he finds at nearby Chino Ranch. This salad makes a refreshing summer lunch or light dinner appetizer.

Piccolo basil is sharply flavored and has tiny leaves. If unavailable, use regular basil.

♟ For this salad, try a rich white French Burgundy, such as 1989 Meursault Les Charmes, or a California Chardonnay, such as 1990 Clos du Bois Proprietor's Reserve from Sonoma County.

4 Servings

¼ cup plus 2 teaspoons extra-virgin olive oil
1 tablespoon tarragon vinegar
1 garlic clove, minced
Salt and freshly ground pepper

SALADS

6 large red and yellow tomatoes, peeled
    and sliced ¼ inch thick
1 pound large sea scallops
1 large Maui or other sweet onion,
    thinly sliced
½ cup (lightly packed) Piccolo basil
    leaves, coarsely chopped

1. In a small bowl, whisk ¼ cup of
the oil with the vinegar, garlic, ½ teaspoon salt and ¼ teaspoon pepper; set
aside. Arrange the sliced tomatoes on
4 cold plates.

2. Heat a large nonstick skillet until
hot. Add the remaining 2 teaspoons oil
and the scallops in a single layer and
cook over high heat, turning once, until
well seared and opaque, about 2 minutes per side.

3. Arrange the scallops over the
tomatoes. Scatter the onion and basil
on top. Drizzle the reserved dressing
over the tomatoes and sea scallops and
serve.

—*Martin Woesle*

LOBSTER COLESLAW WITH BASIL, TARRAGON AND CHIVES

Ask your fishmonger for female lobsters for this dish. Once the lobsters are
cooked, you'll find bright red eggs,
called coral, where the body separates
from the tail. When pushed through a
strainer and separated, these beautiful
little eggs add striking dots of color and
a mild sea flavor to this salad. Serve
with sliced beefsteak tomatoes.

🍷 A fruity, light Chardonnay, such as
1991 Parducci or 1991 Mâcon-Lugny

"Les Charmes," would have enough
depth and roundness to underscore the
rich, creamy textures and mild seafood
flavors of this dish.

4 Servings

Two 1½-pound lobsters, preferably
    female
1 small onion, halved lengthwise and
    thinly sliced crosswise
1 cup mayonnaise
¼ cup chopped fresh basil
3 tablespoons minced fresh chives
1 tablespoon chopped fresh tarragon
2½ teaspoons Dijon mustard
2½ teaspoons fresh lemon juice
8 cups finely shredded green cabbage
Salt and freshly ground pepper

1. Bring a large pot of water to a
boil over high heat. Plunge the lobsters
in head first, cover and cook the lobsters for 10 minutes. The lobsters are
done when they are red all over. Using
tongs, remove the lobsters to a large
bowl.

2. When cool enough to handle,
twist each lobster to detach the bodies
from the tails. If there is red roe inside,
push it through a coarse strainer to separate the eggs. (If the roe is only partially cooked—it will be greenish
black—simmer it gently in the cooking
water until it turns red.) Remove all the
lobster meat from the shells and slice it
thickly. Cover and set aside.

3. In a small bowl, cover the onion
with cold water and set aside for 5 minutes to remove any harsh taste. Drain.

4. In a large bowl, mix together the
onion, mayonnaise, basil, chives, tarragon, mustard and lemon juice. Stir in
the cabbage, lobster meat and roe. Season with salt and pepper and serve, or
refrigerate for up to 3 hours.

—*Marcia Kiesel*

COCONUT SHRIMP WITH LEMON GRASS VINAIGRETTE

If you cannot find fresh lemon grass,
Binh Duong, of La Truc in Boca Ra-
ton, suggests substituting one-half teaspoon of finely grated lemon zest.

4 Servings

COCONUT SHRIMP:

3 red Thai, or bird, chiles or 1 large
    serrano chile, coarsely chopped
¾ cup coarsely chopped fresh coriander
    (cilantro)
4 garlic cloves, coarsely chopped
1 large shallot, coarsely chopped
2½ teaspoons sugar
1½ teaspoons curry powder
½ teaspoon turmeric
¼ teaspoon salt
¼ teaspoon freshly ground pepper
¾ cup unsweetened coconut milk,
    skimmed from an undisturbed
    14-ounce can (see Note)
3 tablespoons light olive oil or
    vegetable oil
1½ pounds large shrimp, shelled and
    deveined

SALAD:

2 tablespoons minced fresh lemon grass
    (tender white bulb only)
1 tablespoon fresh lemon juice
1 small garlic clove, minced
½ teaspoon sugar
¼ teaspoon salt
⅛ teaspoon freshly ground pepper
⅛ teaspoon Oriental chili oil, or to
    taste
2 tablespoons extra-virgin olive oil
1 pound medium asparagus
8 medium radicchio leaves
2 medium Belgian endives, separated
    into spears
4 lemon wedges, for serving

1. *Prepare the coconut shrimp:* In a food processor, combine the chiles, coriander, garlic, shallot, sugar, curry powder, turmeric, salt and pepper and process to a coarse paste. Transfer the paste to a large bowl and stir in the coconut milk and oil. Add the shrimp and stir to coat. Cover and set aside to marinate at room temperature for 30 minutes or for up to 2 hours in the refrigerator.

2. *Prepare the salad:* In a small bowl, combine the lemon grass, lemon juice, garlic, sugar, salt, pepper and chili oil. Whisk in the olive oil.

3. In a large skillet of boiling salted water, cook the asparagus until just tender, 3 to 5 minutes. Drain, refresh under cold running water and pat dry with paper towels.

4. Light a grill or preheat the broiler. Remove the shrimp from the marinade and thread them on 4 to 6 bamboo skewers so that they fit snugly. Grill or broil the shrimp, turning once, until lightly browned and cooked through, about 2 minutes per side.

5. In a large bowl, toss the asparagus with 2 tablespoons of the dressing. Arrange the asparagus spears in 3 piles on each plate. Toss the radicchio and endives with the remaining dressing. Place 2 to 3 endive spears in between each asparagus bundle. Place 2 radicchio leaves in the center of each plate. Arrange the grilled shrimp in the radicchio leaves, garnish with a lemon wedge and serve.

NOTE: Use the rich, thick coconut milk that rises to the surface as the can sits.

—*Binh Duong*

GRILLED CHICKEN SALAD WITH FRIZZLED TORTILLAS

This chicken salad from chef Vincent Guerithault, whose Phoenix restaurant bears his name, goes well with chewy sourdough rolls.

❦ Try a slightly sharp and fruity California Chardonnay, such as 1985 or 1987 Sonoma-Cutrer Les Pierres or 1985 or 1987 Grgich Hills.

4 Servings

½ cup plus 2 tablespoons olive oil
Six 6-inch blue or yellow corn tortillas, cut into ¼-inch strips
Salt
¼ cup red bell pepper dice (¼ inch)
¼ cup green bell pepper dice (¼ inch)
¼ cup yellow bell pepper dice (¼ inch)
¼ cup finely chopped fresh basil
2 tablespoons minced fresh ginger
3 tablespoons sherry vinegar
Freshly ground black pepper
Four 6-ounce skinless, boneless chicken breast halves
10 cups bite-size pieces of mixed lettuces, such as red oak leaf, arugula, watercress and mâche
1 medium tomato, cut into ½-inch dice

1. In a large skillet, heat ½ cup of the oil until ripples appear. Add half of the tortilla strips and fry over moderately high heat, stirring, until crisp, about 2 minutes. Transfer to paper towels and sprinkle with salt. Repeat with the remaining strips. Strain the oil through a fine sieve and reserve.

2. In a large bowl, combine the red, green and yellow bell peppers, basil and ginger. Stir in the vinegar, 1 teaspoon salt and ½ teaspoon black pepper. Whisk in the reserved tortilla oil.

3. Light a grill or heat a large heavy skillet until almost smoking. Brush the chicken with the remaining 2 table-

spoons oil and sprinkle both sides with salt and pepper. Grill or sear the chicken, turning once, until browned and just cooked through, about 5 minutes per side. Transfer to a cutting board.

4. Add the greens and diced tomato to the dressing and toss to coat. Add two-thirds of the fried tortilla strips, toss again and season with salt and pepper. Mound the salad on 4 large plates. Slice the chicken breasts diagonally across the grain. Fan 1 sliced breast half on top of each salad and drizzle any accumulated juices over the chicken. Garnish with the remaining tortilla strips and serve.

—*Vincent Guerithault*

MINCED CHICKEN SALAD WITH FRESH HERBS

This salad, known as *laab gai*, is a quickly prepared dish of poached minced chicken tossed with herbs in a lime-based dressing. It is traditionally served with sticky rice. Diners make balls of rice with their hands and then use the rice and lettuce leaves to scoop up the salad.

Laab is generally associated with the cuisine of northeast Thailand, where it is made with beef. This version is flavored with Vietnamese coriander, called *rau ram* in Vietnam. If you cannot find it, substitute a mixture of chopped fresh coriander and mint.

SALADS

140

❦ The welter of assertive tastes here—lime juice, fish sauce, coriander—will dominate any wine. Serve a chilled, off-dry wine for simple refreshment: a white Zinfandel or other blush wine, a blend, such as Trefethen Eschol White, or a fruity Sauvignon Blanc, such as 1990 Gallo.

3 to 4 Servings

1 tablespoon raw long-grain jasmine rice or sticky rice
2½ cups water
1 pound skinless, boneless chicken, trimmed and minced
4 small shallots, peeled and thinly sliced
2 dried red chiles, stemmed and finely chopped
¼ cup fresh lime juice
3 tablespoons fish sauce
1 teaspoon sugar
¼ teaspoon freshly ground black pepper
½ cup coarsely chopped Vietnamese coriander leaves or ¼ cup each chopped fresh mint and coriander leaves
1 head of Boston, red leaf or other soft lettuce, leaves separated
Sticky Rice, for serving (p. 158)

1. In a small heavy skillet, dry roast the raw rice over moderate heat, stirring often, until browned, 3 to 4 minutes. Remove the rice to a plate to cool, then grind it to a fine powder in a blender, spice mill, clean coffee grinder or a mortar.

2. In a small saucepan, bring the water to a boil over high heat. Add the chicken and stir until it turns white, about 3 minutes. Drain the chicken and save the stock for another use.

3. In a bowl, mix together the shallots, chiles, lime juice, fish sauce, sugar and black pepper. Add the chicken and mix well. Stir in the coriander.

4. Line a plate with the lettuce leaves and mound the chicken salad on top. Sprinkle the ground, roasted rice on top. Serve with Sticky Rice.

—*Jeffrey Alford & Naomi Duguid*

CHICKEN AND GOAT CHEESE SALAD WITH JALAPENO-CILANTRO LIME SALSA

Michael's in Santa Monica was one of the originators of the new California cuisine, and it continues to excel with surprising combinations of fresh, native California ingredients. This light entrée was an impromptu creation by the chef and owner Michael McCarty when he and his wife, Kim, were entertaining friends on the patio of their Malibu home.

❦ A full-bodied and very rich white wine is just the ticket to stand up to this hearty salad. Try a 1989 Chardonnay from Chalone Vineyard in Monterey County.

6 Servings

12 small boneless chicken breast halves, with the skin left on
One 12-ounce log of creamy fresh goat cheese, sliced ¼ inch thick
Salt and freshly ground black pepper
3 red bell peppers, cut lengthwise into ¾-inch strips
3 yellow bell peppers, cut lengthwise into ¾-inch strips

1 large or 2 medium, sweet onions, such as Maui, sliced ⅓ inch thick
2 tablespoons olive oil
2 heads of Bibb or limestone lettuce, torn into bite-size pieces
3 bunches of mâche (lamb's lettuce), leaves separated
1 bunch of arugula, leaves only, torn into bite-size pieces
1 head of baby red leaf lettuce, leaves torn into bite-size pieces
1 head of baby radicchio, leaves torn into bite-size pieces
Balsamic Vinaigrette (p. 242)
Tomato Concassée (recipe follows)
Jalapeño-Cilantro Lime Salsa (p. 247)
1 bunch of chives, finely chopped

1. Light a grill or preheat the broiler. Gently separate the skin from the chicken breasts to form a pocket, keeping it attached on one side. Insert the slices of goat cheese under the breast skin, overlapping them slightly. Season the breasts with salt and black pepper.

2. Toss the red and yellow bell pepper strips and the onion slices with the olive oil and season to taste with salt and black pepper.

3. Grill the bell pepper and onion slices in a grill basket (or broil them on a rack set over a baking sheet). Set aside.

4. Grill the chicken breasts, skin-side down, for 3 to 5 minutes, until browned. Then turn them and grill for 5 to 7 minutes longer, until the juices run clear when the meat is deeply pierced. Alternatively, bake the chicken at 500° for about 10 minutes until cooked through and the juices run clear. Broil for about 2 minutes to brown the skin.

5. In a large bowl, toss all the salad greens with about ½ cup of the Balsamic Vinaigrette. Add more dressing if desired. Arrange the salad on large serving plates.

6. Cut each chicken breast crosswise in 4 or 5 slices. Place 2 sliced breasts in the center of each salad. Garnish each serving with the Tomato Concassée and the grilled peppers and onions. Spoon the Jalapeño-Cilantro Lime Salsa over the chicken. Garnish with the chives and serve immediately.

—Michael McCarty

TOMATO CONCASSEE

Makes About 1¾ Cups

2 medium tomatoes—peeled, seeded and cut into ¼-inch dice
½ cup olive oil
2 tablespoons sherry vinegar
1½ teaspoons finely chopped shallot
1 tablespoon finely shredded fresh basil
Salt and freshly ground pepper

Combine all the ingredients in a bowl; season with salt and pepper to taste. Stir well to combine. Cover and refrigerate for at least 30 minutes before serving.

—Michael McCarty

COMPOSED TURKEY SALAD WITH CRANBERRY VINAIGRETTE

4 Servings

½ pound thin green beans
2 medium navel oranges
½ cup jellied cranberry sauce
1 tablespoon red wine vinegar
¼ cup mild olive oil
1½ teaspoons chopped fresh thyme
Salt and freshly ground pepper
1 pound sliced leftover turkey, preferably white meat
1 large Belgian endive

4 cups bite-size pieces of Boston lettuce (from 1 medium head)
4 cups bite-size pieces of red leaf lettuce (from 1 medium head)
8 cherry tomatoes, halved crosswise
¼ cup minced fresh chives

1. In a medium saucepan, bring 1 inch of water to a boil over moderately high heat. Add the green beans, cover and cook until crisp-tender, about 4 minutes. Refresh under cold water until cool, then drain and pat dry.

2. Working over a plate to catch the juice, trim the tops and bottoms off the oranges with a paring knife, exposing the flesh. Cutting downwards, remove the peel and all the bitter white pith from the oranges. Slice in between the membranes to release the orange sections into a small bowl. Gently squeeze the membranes over the plate to extract a total of 2 tablespoons of orange juice.

3. Pour the juice into a blender. Add the cranberry sauce and vinegar and blend at medium speed until smooth. With the machine on, pour in the oil in a fine stream and blend until incorporated. Add the thyme, ¾ teaspoon salt and ½ teaspoon pepper and blend briefly. Pour the dressing into a bowl.

4. Arrange the beans in 4 bundles on each dinner plate like the spokes of a wheel. Arrange the sliced turkey between the bean bundles.

5. Separate and stack the endive spears, then slice them lengthwise as thin as possible. In a large bowl, toss the endive with the Boston and red leaf lettuces. Add 3 tablespoons of the dressing and toss. Mound the greens in the center of the plates. Drizzle about 1

tablespoon of dressing over each serving of turkey and beans. Place alternating orange sections and tomato halves around the greens, sprinkle with chives and serve.

—Tracey Seaman

WOK-SEARED DUCK SALAD

Barbara Tropp's duck salad, from China Moon Cafe in San Francisco, packs a triple punch of fresh ginger: There's crushed ginger in the marinade, ginger juice in the dressing and fried strips for the garnish.

❢ This salad calls for a full-bodied red with lots of fruit and little tannin. Try a 1990 Robert Mondavi Pinot Noir Reserve, 1990 Duckhorn Merlot or 1990 Matanzas Creek Merlot.

4 Servings

DUCK SALAD:

1 cup corn or peanut oil
¼ cup thin matchsticks of fresh ginger (from a 2-inch piece), plus 3 nickel-size slices, smashed
¼ cup sliced blanched almonds
¼ cup soy sauce
2 tablespoons mushroom soy sauce
¼ cup rice wine or dry sherry
1 scallion, cut into 1-inch lengths
1 tablespoon finely chopped fresh coriander (cilantro) leaves and stems
4 skinless, boneless duck breast halves (about 4 ounces each)

SALADS

GINGER DRESSING:

*1 tablespoon plus 1 teaspoon finely
    grated fresh ginger (from a 2-inch
    piece)*
2 tablespoons fresh orange juice
1 tablespoon balsamic vinegar
¾ teaspoon finely grated orange zest
½ teaspoon soy sauce
¼ teaspoon coarse (kosher) salt
Freshly ground pepper

*10 cups bite-size pieces of mixed
    lettuces, such as frisée, mizuna and
    radicchio*

1. *Prepare the duck salad:* In a wok
or deep heavy skillet, heat the oil over
moderate heat to 375°. Remove from
the heat, add the ginger matchsticks
and stir with chopsticks just until
golden, about 10 seconds. Using a slotted spoon, transfer the ginger to paper
towels to drain. Strain the oil and set
aside.

2. Preheat the oven to 400°. Spread
the almonds on a baking sheet and
toast for about 4 minutes, or until
golden brown. Let cool.

3. In a shallow glass or ceramic dish,
combine the smashed ginger slices, soy
sauce, mushroom soy, rice wine, scallion and fresh coriander. Add the duck
breasts in a single layer and turn to
coat. Cover and marinate at room temperature for 1 hour, turning once.

4. *Prepare the ginger dressing:* Put
the ginger in a fine strainer set over a
small bowl and press firmly to extract
the juice (you should have about 2 teaspoons). Whisk in ½ cup of the reserved ginger oil, the orange juice,
balsamic vinegar, orange zest, soy
sauce and coarse salt. Season with
pepper.

5. Heat a wok or large heavy skillet
until a bead of water evaporates on
contact. Add 2 teaspoons of the reserved ginger oil, swirl to coat the pan
and place over high heat just until the
oil begins to smoke. Remove the duck
breasts from the marinade and add
them to the wok in a single layer. Sear
the duck until the undersides are nicely
browned, about 2 minutes. Turn and
sear the other side, about 1 minute.
Turn the breasts again and cook until
medium-rare, about 2 minutes longer.
Transfer the duck breasts to a plate and
let stand for 3 minutes.

6. Slice the duck breasts diagonally
across the grain into ¼-inch strips and
transfer to a medium bowl. Whisk the
dressing, add 2 tablespoons to the duck
and toss to coat. In a large bowl, toss
the greens with about ¼ cup of the
dressing. Mound the salad on 4 large
plates and arrange the duck strips on
top. Sprinkle with the toasted almonds
and fried ginger matchsticks. Pass the
remaining dressing alongside.

—*Barbara Tropp*

FILLET OF BEEF SALAD WITH BLUE CHEESE DRESSING AND SESAME SEEDS

At An American Place in New York
City, Larry Forgione uses beef from the
tail end of the fillet in this meaty salad.
❦ With this beef salad you can go red
or white. A soft red Merlot, such as
1989 Duckhorn, Hogue Cellars or Clos
du Val would accent the flavor of
sesame seeds. For a white, try a good
full-bodied Chardonnay, such as 1990
Freemark Abbey or 1989 Neyers, both
from Napa.

4 Servings

*3 ounces blue cheese, preferably
    Maytag, crumbled (⅓ cup)*
2 tablespoons hot water
⅓ cup mayonnaise
⅓ cup sour cream
Freshly ground pepper
¼ teaspoon hot pepper sauce
½ pound snow peas, trimmed
*8 cups bite-size mixed greens, such as
    arugula, Bibb, red leaf, endive and
    radicchio*
2 tablespoons Oriental sesame oil
*One 1-pound piece fillet of beef, cut
    across the grain into ½-inch strips*
Salt
*2 medium carrots, cut into 2-by-⅛-inch
    matchsticks*
1 tablespoon white sesame seeds
1 tablespoon rice vinegar
1 medium tomato, cut into ⅓-inch dice
*1 tablespoon black sesame seeds
    (optional)* *
Available at Asian markets

1. Place the cheese in a small bowl. With a fork, stir in the hot water until nearly smooth. Stir in the mayonnaise, sour cream, pepper and hot sauce. *(The dressing can be refrigerated for up to 3 days. Let stand at room temperature for 30 minutes before serving.)*

2. Blanch the snow peas in a small saucepan of boiling salted water until bright green, about 45 seconds. Drain, refresh under cold running water and drain again. Place the salad greens in a large bowl.

3. In a large heavy nonreactive skillet, heat the sesame oil until nearly smoking. Add half of the beef to the pan in a single layer. Sprinkle with salt and pepper and sear over moderately high heat, turning once, until browned, 1 to 2 minutes. Transfer to a plate and keep warm in a very low oven. Repeat with the remaining beef.

4. Remove the skillet from the heat and add the carrots, white sesame seeds and blanched snow peas. Stir in the vinegar and add to the greens in the bowl. Season well with salt and pepper and toss.

5. Mound the salad on 4 large plates. Arrange one-fourth of the warm beef strips on each salad and top with the diced tomato. Drizzle each salad with 2 tablespoons of blue cheese dressing and sprinkle with the black sesame seeds. Serve immediately, passing the remaining dressing separately.

—*Larry Forgione*

GRANDE SALADE AUX COTES D'AGNEAU

Composed salads are certainly not new—there are hundreds attributed to Escoffier and dozens are listed in *Larousse Gastronomique*—but they have been enjoying a revival in fashionable restaurants in recent years. Made with greens, fresh herbs and everything from raw and cooked vegetables to fish, shellfish, poultry and meat, these salads are attractive, nutritious alternatives to more traditional entrées.

With so many ingredients to enjoy in these salads, a little meat goes a long way. In the recipe that follows, for example, one lamb chop per person is sufficient. The salad itself is made with such a great variety of fresh herbs and vegetables—potatoes, mushrooms, asparagus, tomatoes, Belgian endives and lettuce—that it could just as well be served on its own without the meat.

For those with an appetite for meat, I've included the option of adding lamb kidneys (which came with my racks when I was testing the recipe, but they are also available separately). I cut the kidneys into pieces, sauté them over high heat at the last minute and serve them as a garnish. If kidneys are not to your liking, however, they can be left out.

❦ A glass of cold Sauvignon Blanc would go well with this salad for lunch. For dinner, you might try a more substantial wine—perhaps a Côtes du Rhône or a light red like a California Syrah or Zinfandel.

6 Servings

1½ tablespoons red wine vinegar
1 tablespoon Worcestershire sauce
Salt and freshly ground pepper

SALADS

143

5 tablespoons extra-virgin olive oil
1 potato (about ¾ pound), peeled and cut into 2-by-½-inch sticks
2 cups water
12 asparagus spears (about ¾ pound), peeled and cut into 1-inch pieces
1 tablespoon peanut or canola oil
6 large mushrooms, washed and cut into ½-inch dice
3 lamb kidneys (optional)
¾ teaspoon herbes de Provence (see Note)
6 double-cut lamb chops from the rack, rib bones frenched (see Note)
1 tablespoon plus 1 teaspoon mild olive oil
2 tomatoes—halved, seeded and cut into ½-inch pieces
3 Belgian endives, cored and sliced crosswise 1 inch thick
6 cups (loosely packed) assorted salad greens, torn into 2-inch pieces
4 cups (loosely packed) mixed fresh herbs, such as chervil, parsley and basil leaves and snipped chives

1. In a small bowl, mix the vinegar, Worcestershire sauce, ¾ teaspoon salt and ½ teaspoon pepper. Gradually whisk in the extra-virgin olive oil. Set the dressing aside.

2. In a medium skillet, cover the potato sticks with the water and bring to a boil. Boil until just tender, 6 to 7 minutes. Drain the potato sticks and place in a large bowl.

3. In the same skillet, steam the asparagus pieces over boiling water until barely tender, about 2 minutes. Drain well. Dry the skillet.

4. Heat the peanut oil in the skillet until hot but not smoking. Add the asparagus and mushrooms and sauté over high heat until just tender, about 2 minutes. Add the vegetables to the potatoes in the bowl.

5. Place the lamb kidneys flat on a cutting board and, holding your knife blade parallel to the board, cut through the rounded side of each kidney to divide it in half. Cut out and discard the fatty white centers. Cut each kidney half into 3 pieces.

6. In a small bowl, mix the *herbes de Provence* with ½ teaspoon each of salt and pepper. Sprinkle the lamb chops and the kidneys with the *herbes de Provence* and rub the chops on both sides with 2 teaspoons of the mild olive oil.

7. Light a very hot grill or preheat the broiler. About 15 minutes before serving, grill the chops for about 3 minutes on each side for medium-rare. Alternatively, broil the chops or sauté them in a large cast-iron skillet over high heat for 3 to 4 minutes per side. Transfer the chops to a plate and set aside in a warm place for 10 minutes, uncovered, to rest and continue cooking in their own residual heat.

8. Meanwhile, in a medium skillet, heat the remaining 2 teaspoons mild olive oil until hot but not smoking. Add the kidney pieces and sauté over high heat until nicely browned all over, about 1½ minutes. Transfer to a colander to drain.

9. Add the tomatoes, endives and dressing to the vegetables in the bowl and toss well. In another bowl, toss the salad greens with the fresh herbs. Spread the greens on 6 large plates. Mound the vegetable salad on top of the lettuces.

10. Butterfly the lamb chops, splitting them in half and opening them like a book. Place a lamb chop on each salad and garnish with the kidneys. Serve immediately.

NOTE: Herbes de Provence, a blend of dried herbs often used in the cooking of southern France, is available at many specialty food shops. If you are unable to find it, make your own by combining equal amounts of dried thyme, savory, marjoram and oregano.

Frenching, a term used by butchers, refers to scraping exposed chop bones completely clean for a more attractive presentation.

—Jacques Pépin

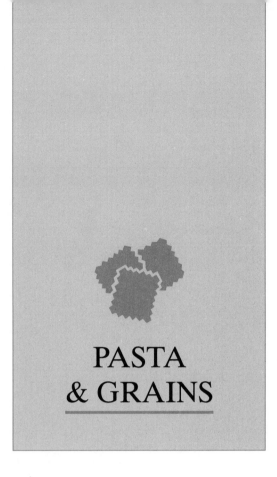

PASTA
& GRAINS

ORZO WITH GREEN AND BLACK OLIVES

4 Servings

1½ cups orzo (about 10 ounces)
One 2¼-ounce jar pitted Spanish green olives, drained and chopped
½ cup Calamata olives, pitted and coarsely chopped
1 tablespoon olive oil

Bring a large pot of salted water to a boil. Add the orzo and cook until al dente. Drain well, add the green and black olives and the olive oil and toss. Serve at once.

—Bob Chambers

ORZO WITH DILL

4 Servings

8 ounces orzo (about 1¼ cups)
1 tablespoon olive oil
2 teaspoons finely grated lemon zest
2 tablespoons finely chopped fresh dill
Salt and freshly ground pepper

1. In a large pot of boiling salted water, stir in the orzo, return to a boil and cook until just tender, about 8 minutes. Drain.

2. Return the orzo to the dry saucepan and stir in the olive oil. *(The recipe can be made to this point up to 1 day ahead. Rewarm over moderately low heat before proceeding.)* Stir in the lemon zest, dill, and ¼ teaspoon each salt and pepper and serve at once.

—Susan Shapiro Jaslove

FETTUCCINE WITH BASIL AND ALMONDS

The dramatic setting of Rex in a downtown Los Angeles Art Deco building rivals its Italian *nuova cucina.* This recipe, called *fettuccine con pesto alla trapanese* on Rex's menu, was discovered by the chef Odette Fada on a trip to Sicily; she recommends making it with fresh rather than dried pasta.

🍷 To go with this very full-bodied pasta, try a full-bodied white Sicilian wine, such as 1990 Regaleali, Nozze, d'Oro.

4 Servings

1 pound fresh fettuccine
⅓ cup extra-virgin olive oil
4 garlic cloves, minced
2 tablespoons fresh bread crumbs
¼ cup finely chopped natural almonds (1 ounce)
1½ pounds plum tomatoes— peeled, seeded and cut into ¼-inch strips
½ cup coarsely chopped fresh basil
Salt

1. Bring a large pot of salted water to a boil over high heat. Stir in the pasta and cook until al dente, about 4 minutes. Drain and set aside.

2. Meanwhile, in a very large nonreactive skillet, combine ¼ cup of the oil, the garlic, bread crumbs and almonds and cook over moderate heat, stirring, until the mixture is golden, about 3 minutes.

3. Stir in the tomatoes, basil and the remaining 1 tablespoon plus 1 teaspoon oil and cook for 1 minute to blend. Toss the cooked pasta in the sauce until well coated and heated through, about 2 minutes. Season to taste with salt and serve immediately.

—Odette Fada

FRESH PASTA WITH ARUGULA, TOMATOES AND SHAVED PARMESAN

This recipe comes from Arancio d'Oro in Florence; there the dish is prepared with *tonnarelli,* a square-shaped homemade spaghetti, but you can use any fresh pasta noodle. If arugula is not available, substitute fresh watercress.

🍷 With this pasta, we drank a young Dolcetto d'Alba, from Piedmont. Its smoothness proved a perfect match for a dish that is quite delicate despite the peppery flavor of arugula.

4 to 6 Servings

2-ounce chunk of Parmigiano-Reggiano cheese
4 cups (loosely packed) stemmed arugula leaves (1 large bunch)
4 plum tomatoes (½ pound), coarsely chopped
¼ cup extra-virgin olive oil
3 tablespoons sea salt
1 pound fresh pasta, such as tagliarini, tagliatelle or fettuccine
Freshly ground pepper

1. In a large pot, bring 5 quarts of water to a rolling boil over high heat. Meanwhile, using a vegetable peeler, shave the Parmesan cheese into long thick strips into a large warmed serving bowl. Add the arugula, tomatoes and oil and toss to blend.

2. Stir the sea salt and pasta into the boiling water and cook, stirring to prevent sticking, until al dente, 2 to 3 minutes. Drain the pasta in a colander. Add to the arugula mixture and toss. Season to taste with sea salt and plenty of freshly ground pepper and serve hot.

—Patricia Wells

PESTO FETTUCCINE WITH CHICKEN AND VEGETABLES

Since commercially prepared pestos vary, use the amount given in the recipe as a guide, adding more or less to taste.

4 Servings

2 tablespoons olive oil
1 medium red bell pepper, cut into thin strips
1 medium yellow bell pepper, cut into thin strips
½ pound medium asparagus, cut into 1-inch pieces
8 oil-packed sun-dried tomato halves, thinly sliced
1 pound small boneless chicken breast halves, sliced crosswise into ½-inch-thick strips
Salt and freshly ground black pepper
About ¾ cup prepared pesto (7½ ounces), excess oil drained (see Note)
6 tablespoons freshly grated Parmesan cheese plus more for serving
1 pound dried fettuccine

1. Bring a large pot of salted water to a boil. In a large nonreactive skillet, heat 1 tablespoon of the olive oil. Add the bell peppers and asparagus and cook over moderately high heat, stirring, until lightly charred and softened, about 10 minutes. Transfer to a large bowl and add the sun-dried tomatoes.

2. Wipe out the skillet and heat the remaining 1 tablespoon oil. Season the chicken pieces with salt and pepper and add them to the skillet. Cook over moderately high heat, stirring occasionally, until just cooked through, about 3 minutes. Transfer to the bowl with the vegetables. Toss with about ⅓ cup of the pesto and 2 tablespoons of the Parmesan and season with salt and pepper.

3. Cook the fettuccine in the boiling water until al dente. Drain, return to the pot and toss with the remaining pesto and Parmesan, salt and pepper.

4. To serve, mound the fettuccine on 4 dinner plates. Spoon the chicken and vegetables on top and pass the additional Parmesan separately.

NOTE: "Food & Wine" recently conducted a tasting of nationally available prepared pesto sauces. DiGiorno, a pesto sauce found in the refrigerated section of supermarkets, was the favorite with the freshest flavor. Contadina, also found in the refrigerated section, was our second choice.

—Susan Shapiro Jaslove

HERB RAVIOLI WITH BASIL OIL AND TOMATO COULIS

This recipe makes about 96 ravioli. Serve about 6 to 8 per person and save the rest; they are great to have on hand for a quick meal, or wrap and freeze any uncooked ravioli between sheets of parchment paper for up to one month.

4 Servings

RAVIOLI DOUGH:
2½ cups all-purpose flour
¾ cup semolina flour
5 eggs
½ teaspoon salt

FILLING:
1½ teaspoons olive oil
1 medium onion, finely chopped
2 teaspoons fresh rosemary leaves, finely chopped
2 teaspoons fresh thyme leaves, finely chopped
1 teaspoon finely minced garlic
Pinch of freshly grated nutmeg

Salt
1¾ pounds Swiss chard, thick white ribs discarded
1 large bunch of arugula, stemmed
¾ pound fresh spinach, stemmed
2 bunches of watercress, stemmed
1 small bunch of chervil, stemmed
¼ cup (loosely packed) dill sprigs
3 tablespoons minced chives
3 tablespoons fresh tarragon leaves
¼ cup (loosely packed) fresh coriander (cilantro) leaves
3 tablespoons fresh ricotta cheese
2 tablespoons mascarpone cheese
2 tablespoons freshly grated Parmesan cheese
Freshly ground pepper
1 egg beaten with 1 tablespoon water

ACCOMPANIMENTS:
Basil Oil (p. 242)
Tomato Coulis (p. 243)
Freshly grated Parmesan cheese

1. *Prepare the ravioli dough:* In a food processor, combine the all-purpose flour, semolina flour, eggs and salt. Process until the dough begins to form a ball, about 2 minutes. Transfer to a lightly floured working surface and knead briefly by hand until well combined. Wrap the dough in plastic wrap and refrigerate for at least 1 and up to 8 hours.

2. *Prepare the filling:* In a small skillet, heat the olive oil over moderate heat. Add the onion, rosemary, thyme, garlic and nutmeg and cook, stirring frequently, until the onion softens, about 8 minutes. Do not let brown. If necessary, add a few tablespoons of water. Set aside to cool.

3. Meanwhile, in a large saucepan, combine 3 quarts of water with 1½ teaspoons of salt and bring to a boil over moderately high heat. Add the Swiss chard and boil for 2 minutes. Add the arugula and boil for another 2 minutes. Add the spinach and watercress and boil for 3 minutes longer. Drain the greens and refresh them under cold running water. Squeeze firmly to remove as much liquid as possible.

4. In a medium bowl, toss together the chervil, dill, chives, tarragon and coriander. Transfer the cooked greens to a food processor. Add the reserved cooked onion mixture, three-fourths of the mixed fresh herbs and the ricotta, mascarpone and Parmesan. Process until very smooth, scraping down the sides of the bowl as necessary. Season with salt and pepper to taste. Scrape the filling into a sturdy plastic bag, seal and refrigerate until needed. Cover the remaining mixed fresh herbs and refrigerate until serving time.

5. *Prepare the ravioli:* Sprinkle a work surface and rolling pin with flour. Cut the dough in 8 equal pieces. Flatten one piece, keeping the others covered with a towel, and roll it through a hand-crank pasta machine on the widest setting. Continue rolling the dough through each successively smaller setting to the last setting. The pasta sheet will be very thin and about 26 inches long.

6. Repeat with a second piece of dough. Cut off the tip of one of the bottom corners of the plastic bag containing the pureed greens. Lay a strip of the rolled pasta dough on a work surface and brush it with the egg wash. Pipe tea-spoon-size mounds of the pureed greens 1 inch apart in 2 rows of 12 to make 24 ravioli. Cover with the second sheet of dough. Press all around each mound to seal, then cut the ravioli apart with a fluted pastry wheel. Repeat with the remaining dough and filling.

7. In a stockpot, bring 1 gallon of water with 1 tablespoon of salt to a boil over high heat. Add the ravioli in batches and boil until just tender, 3 to 4 minutes. Gently drain the ravioli, then toss them in the pot with the Basil Oil.

8. Spoon the warm Tomato Coulis on 8 warm plates. Place the ravioli on the *coulis* and sprinkle the reserved mixed fresh herbs on top. Pass the grated Parmesan separately.

—*Daniel Boulud*

FRESH THAI RICE NOODLES WITH MEAT AND GREENS

These noodles are served with a mild chile-and-vinegar condiment that brings out the full flavor of the dish, as does the fresh white pepper that is sprinkled on top before serving.

❡ The soy flavor and mild tart taste in this dish would be nicely complemented by a California Gewürztraminer, such as 1991 St. Francis or 1992 Alexander Valley Vineyards.

2 Servings

1 pound fresh rice noodles
2 tablespoons vegetable oil
3 tablespoons soy sauce
2 tablespoons minced garlic (6 cloves)
½ pound boneless pork or chicken, trimmed of all fat and thinly sliced across the grain
¾ pound Chinese kale, bok choy or broccoli, cut into 1-inch pieces (4 cups)
1 tablespoon fish sauce
1 tablespoon sugar
1½ cups chicken stock or canned broth
1 tablespoon cornstarch dissolved in ¼ cup cold water
1 teaspoon freshly ground white pepper
Vinegar-Chile Sauce, for serving (p. 243)

1. If your fresh rice noodles come in uncut folded sheets, slice them into ¾-inch ribbons. Place the noodles in a colander and rinse under hot water for about 1 minute, then shake to drain and to help separate the strands.

2. Set a wok over high heat. When it is very hot, add 1 tablespoon of the oil and swirl to coat the wok. Add the noodles and stir-fry for about 1 minute, tossing constantly to separate the strands. Add 1 tablespoon of the soy sauce and stir-fry for 30 seconds. Turn the noodles out on a platter.

3. Rinse out the wok and wipe it dry. Return it to high heat, add the remaining 1 tablespoon oil and swirl to coat the wok. Toss in the garlic and stir-fry until golden, about 30 seconds. Add the meat and stir-fry until it turns white, about 2 minutes. Add the greens and stir-fry until softened, 3 to 4 minutes.

4. Add the remaining 2 tablespoons soy sauce, the fish sauce and sugar and mix well. Pour in the chicken stock and bring to a vigorous boil. Cook for 3 minutes. Add the dissolved cornstarch and cook, stirring, until the sauce thickens, about 2 minutes.

5. Remove from the heat and pour over the noodles. Sprinkle the white pepper on top and serve in deep bowls. Pass the Vinegar-Chile Sauce separately.

—*Jeffrey Alford & Naomi Duguid*

Country Bread Rolls (p. 165).

Left, Baked Spaghetti with Artichokes and Peas (p. 153).
Above, Asparagus, Shrimp and Penne with Saffron Sauce (p. 153).

PENNETTE WITH MUSHROOMS AND CREAM

This dish from Le Tre Vaselle in Torgiano, Italy, is cooked like risotto.

4 Servings

3 tablespoons olive oil
½ pound white or cremini
mushrooms, sliced
2 garlic cloves, minced
3 tablespoons minced parsley
Salt and freshly ground pepper
1 cup canned low-sodium beef broth
diluted with 3½ cups of water
12 ounces pennette or tubettini pasta
(2 cups)
1 tablespoon dry sherry
½ cup heavy cream
1 cup freshly grated Parmesan cheese

1. In a small skillet, heat 2 tablespoons of the olive oil over moderate heat. Add the mushrooms, garlic and 2 tablespoons of the parsley and cook, stirring, until the mushrooms are tender, about 2 minutes. Season with salt and pepper and set aside.

2. In a medium saucepan, bring the diluted beef broth just to a simmer over low heat.

3. In a large saucepan, heat the remaining 1 tablespoon olive oil over high heat. Add the *pennette* and cook, stirring, until the pasta turns deep golden brown, 3 to 4 minutes. Add the sherry and cook until evaporated. Reduce the heat to moderately high and add enough of the hot stock to barely

A perfect accompaniment for roast chicken: Couscous Timbales with Asparagus and Corn (p. 160).

cover the pasta. Cook, stirring frequently and adding more stock to just keep the pasta covered, until it is al dente, about 12 minutes. There should be just enough liquid to coat the cooked pasta. Stir in the heavy cream and cook for 1 minute.

4. Remove from the heat and stir in the Parmesan cheese, reserved mushrooms and the remaining 1 tablespoon parsley. Season with salt and pepper to taste and serve at once.

—*Le Tre Vaselle*

ASPARAGUS, SHRIMP AND PENNE WITH SAFFRON SAUCE

4 to 6 Servings

⅔ cup dry white wine
¼ teaspoon (lightly packed) saffron
threads
2 pounds medium asparagus, peeled
and cut diagonally into 1-inch
pieces
1 pound penne
2 tablespoons vegetable oil
1 pound medium shrimp, shelled and
deveined
¼ cup minced shallots
1½ cups heavy cream
¾ cup chicken stock or canned
low-sodium broth
Salt and freshly ground pepper
¼ cup minced fresh chives or fresh
chervil

1. In a small bowl, combine the wine and saffron threads and let steep for at least 20 minutes. In a medium skillet, bring 1 inch of salted water to a boil. Add the asparagus pieces and cook until just fork-tender, about 3 minutes. Drain well.

2. Bring a large pot of salted water to a boil. Add the penne and cook until

al dente. Drain and transfer to a large bowl.

3. Meanwhile, heat the oil in a large skillet. Add the shrimp and cook over moderately high heat, stirring occasionally, until bright pink, about 3 minutes; do not overcook. Transfer the shrimp to a plate; reserve the skillet.

4. Add the shallots and saffron wine to the reserved skillet and bring to a boil. Boil over moderately high heat until almost all the liquid evaporates, 3 to 4 minutes. Stir in the cream and chicken stock and simmer over moderate heat, stirring occasionally, until reduced by half, about 7 minutes. Stir in the asparagus and shrimp and simmer for 2 minutes. Season with salt and pepper, add to the pasta and toss to combine. Garnish the pasta with the chives and serve hot.

—*Jeannette Ferrary & Louise Fiszer*

BAKED SPAGHETTI WITH ARTICHOKES AND PEAS

6 to 8 Servings

7 tablespoons unsalted butter
3 tablespoons all-purpose flour
2½ cups hot milk
¾ cup freshly grated Parmesan cheese
(3 ounces)
Salt and freshly ground pepper
2 garlic cloves, minced
Two 9-ounce packages frozen artichoke
hearts—thawed, patted dry and
quartered
One 10-ounce package frozen petite
peas, thawed

1½ pounds plum tomatoes—peeled, seeded and cut into eighths
⅓ cup chopped parsley
1 pound thick green or white spaghetti, such as perciatelli or bucatini
¾ cup shredded Italian Fontina cheese (3 ounces)

1. Make the béchamel sauce. In a heavy medium saucepan, melt 4 tablespoons of the butter over moderate heat. Off the heat, whisk in the flour. Return to the heat and cook, stirring, without coloring, for 2 minutes. Remove from the heat and gradually whisk in the hot milk, beating well to avoid lumps. Return to the heat and bring to a boil. Reduce the heat to moderately low and simmer gently for 10 minutes, stirring often. Stir in ¼ cup of the Parmesan cheese and season with salt and pepper. Remove from the heat, cover and keep warm.

2. In a large nonreactive skillet, cook the garlic in the remaining 3 tablespoons butter over moderately high heat, stirring, until golden, about 1 minute. Add the artichoke hearts and cook until lightly colored, about 5 minutes. Add the peas and cook for 3 minutes. Stir in the tomatoes and parsley and cook until the tomatoes are tender but not broken down, about 6 minutes. Season with salt and pepper.

3. Preheat the oven to 350°. Cook the pasta in a large amount of rapidly boiling salted water until barely al dente, about 5 minutes. Drain.

4. Spread one-third of the béchamel in the bottom of a buttered shallow 3-quart baking dish. Spread half the pasta in the dish and cover with half the vegetable mixture. Spread another third of the béchamel on top and sprinkle with half the Fontina and half the remaining Parmesan. Repeat the layering in the following order: pasta, vegetable mixture, béchamel, Fontina and Parmesan. Bake the pasta for 20 to 25 minutes, until piping hot.

—*Nancy Verde Barr*

BAKED PENNE WITH ROASTED VEGETABLES

Makes 25 to 30 Buffet Servings

6 pounds red, orange and yellow bell peppers, cut into ½-by-1-inch strips
About 1¼ cups extra-virgin olive oil
3 pounds Japanese eggplants, cut into ¾-inch dice
4½ pounds zucchini, halved lengthwise and sliced crosswise ½ inch thick
1½ tablespoons coarse (kosher) salt
1½ tablespoons freshly ground black pepper
3 pounds dried penne rigate (with ridges)
¾ cup plus 3 tablespoons finely chopped flat-leaf parsley
Tomato Sauce (p. 244)
3 pounds mozzarella cheese, shredded
3⅓ cups freshly grated Parmesan cheese (about ¾ pound)

1. Preheat the oven to 500°. In a bowl, toss the bell pepper strips with ⅓ cup of the olive oil. Put the peppers on a large baking sheet with sides or in a shallow roasting pan and roast in the oven for about 35 minutes, stirring occasionally, until softened. Transfer to a very large bowl.

2. Place the eggplant cubes on the baking sheet and toss with ½ cup of the oil. Roast for about 20 minutes, stirring occasionally, until softened. Transfer to the bowl with the peppers. Repeat the process with the zucchini, using as much of the remaining oil as necessary and baking for about 25 minutes, until softened. Add to the other vegetables. Season with the salt and black pepper and toss well.

3. Preheat the broiler. Spread one-fourth of the vegetables on the baking sheet and broil for about 5 minutes, rotating the pan, until the vegetables are lightly charred. Broil the remaining vegetables in three batches.

4. Bring two large pots of salted water to a boil over moderately high heat. Add the pasta and cook, stirring frequently, until al dente. Drain well and let cool.

5. Meanwhile, lightly grease three large ovenproof glass or ceramic baking dishes, either 10-by-15-inch ovals or 9-by-13-inch rectangles.

6. Add the ¾ cup parsley to the vegetables and toss. Add the pasta and toss well. Stir in the Tomato Sauce and then the mozzarella and half of the Parmesan. Divide the pasta evenly between the baking dishes. *(The pasta can be prepared to this point up to 1 day ahead and refrigerated overnight. Bring to room temperature before proceeding.)*

7. About 1 hour before serving, preheat the oven to 375°. Sprinkle the remaining Parmesan cheese and 3 tablespoons parsley over the pasta. Bake for 35 to 40 minutes, until bubbly.

—*Francine Maroukian*

BAKED SHELLS WITH FRESH SPINACH AND PANCETTA

6 to 8 Servings

4 tablespoons unsalted butter
2 cups heavy cream
½ cup tomato puree
½ cup freshly grated Parmesan cheese (2 ounces)
Salt and freshly ground pepper
⅓ pound pancetta or prosciutto, finely diced
1 pound fresh spinach, rinsed and stemmed, leaves torn
1 pound medium pasta shells

1. In a heavy, medium nonreactive saucepan, melt 2 tablespoons of the butter. Add the heavy cream and tomato puree and bring to a boil over high heat. Reduce the heat to moderately low and simmer until reduced to 2¼ cups, about 15 minutes. Remove from the heat and stir in ¼ cup of the Parmesan cheese. Season with salt and pepper.

2. In a large skillet, cook the pancetta in the remaining 2 tablespoons butter over moderately high heat until slightly crisp, 3 to 4 minutes. Add the spinach in batches and cook, tossing, until wilted. Season with salt and pepper.

3. Preheat the oven to 350°. Cook the pasta shells in a large pot of rapidly boiling salted water until barely al dente, about 7 minutes. Drain.

4. Toss the pasta with the creamy tomato sauce and the spinach. Spoon it into a 3-quart shallow buttered baking dish. Sprinkle the remaining ¼ cup Parmesan cheese on top and bake for 15 to 20 minutes, until piping hot.

—*Nancy Verde Barr*

BAKED ZITI WITH SAUSAGE AND PEPPERS

I always like to peel bell peppers with a vegetable peeler. Peeled peppers tend to cook faster and more evenly, and there won't be any tough, shriveled skins in the finished dish.

6 to 8 Servings

1 pound sweet or hot Italian sausage
2 tablespoons olive oil
3 garlic cloves, finely chopped
1 green bell pepper, cut into ½-inch slices
2 red bell peppers, cut into ½-inch slices
Salt
¼ teaspoon crushed red pepper
Two 28-ounce cans Italian peeled tomatoes, drained and finely chopped
½ cup dry red wine
2 teaspoons paprika
1 pound ziti
1¼ cups shredded mozzarella cheese (6 ounces)
¾ cup grated ricotta salata (dried ricotta) or Pecorino Romano cheese (3 ounces), plus more for serving

1. Heat a large nonreactive skillet. Add the sausage and cook over moderately high heat, turning, until nicely browned, about 10 minutes. Prick the sausage as it cooks to release the juices. Remove the sausage from the skillet and let cool slightly.

2. Reduce the heat to moderately low. Add 1 tablespoon of the oil and the garlic to the skillet and cook, stirring, until golden, about 1 minute. Stir in the bell peppers, ½ teaspoon salt and the crushed red pepper and cook until the bell peppers just begin to soften, about 10 minutes.

3. Meanwhile, cut the sausage into ½-inch slices. (The sausage will not

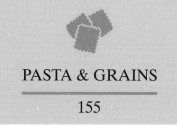
be cooked all the way through.) Add the sausage slices, tomatoes, red wine and paprika to the skillet and bring to a boil. Reduce the heat to moderately low and simmer for 15 minutes.

4. Preheat the oven to 375°. Cook the ziti in a large pot of rapidly boiling salted water until barely al dente, about 7 minutes. Drain and toss with the remaining 1 tablespoon olive oil.

5. Spread 1 cup of the sausage and pepper mixture in the bottom of a 3-quart shallow baking dish. Cover with one-third of the pasta, 1½ more cups of the sausage and pepper mixture and one-third of the mozzarella and ricotta *salata*. Continue to layer the remaining ingredients, ending with the cheeses. Bake for 20 minutes, or until piping hot.

—*Nancy Verde Barr*

BAKED PENNE RIGATE WITH EGGPLANT

8 Servings

1 large eggplant (about 1¼ pounds), cut into ½-inch dice
Salt
¼ cup plus 2 tablespoons olive oil
1 large onion, coarsely chopped
3 garlic cloves, minced
One 35-ounce can Italian peeled tomatoes, chopped, juices reserved
½ cup brine-cured Italian black olives, pitted and chopped
2 tablespoons capers, rinsed
½ teaspoon crushed red pepper
⅓ cup chopped parsley
1¼ cups fresh ricotta cheese (10 ounces)

1 pound penne rigate (with ridges)
2½ cups shredded or finely chopped fresh mozzarella (¾ pound)
½ cup freshly grated Pecorino Romano cheese (2 ounces)

1. Place the eggplant cubes in a colander and toss with 2 teaspoons of salt. Put a plate in the colander on top of the eggplant and weight the plate. Let the eggplant drain for 45 minutes. Rinse well under cool water, drain and pat dry.

2. In a large nonreactive skillet, heat ¼ cup of the oil over moderately high heat. Add the eggplant and cook, tossing occasionally, until softened and browned, about 10 minutes. Stir in the remaining 2 tablespoons oil and the onion and garlic, reduce the heat to moderate and cook until the onion softens, about 7 minutes. Stir in the tomatoes and their juices, the olives, capers and crushed red pepper and simmer for 15 minutes. Stir in the parsley and cook for 5 minutes more. Remove from the heat.

3. Preheat the oven to 350°. Using a rubber spatula, push the ricotta through a strainer into a large bowl.

4. Cook the pasta in a large pot of rapidly boiling salted water until barely al dente, about 8 minutes. Stir ¼ cup of the pasta cooking water into the ricotta. Drain the pasta and stir it into the ricotta cheese.

5. Scatter one-fourth of the eggplant in the bottom of a shallow 3-quart baking dish. Spread one-third of the pasta on top. Add another layer of eggplant and top with one-third of the mozzarella and Pecorino cheeses. Make 2 more layers of pasta, eggplant, mozzarella and Pecorino. Bake for 20 minutes, until piping hot.

—*Nancy Verde Barr*

BAKED PENNE WITH ZUCCHINI

❧ The browned zucchini and tangy tomato sauce require a crisp, assertive white that can stand up to—and set off—the flavors here. A California Fumé Blanc, such as 1990 Chimney Rock or 1991 De Loach, would work particularly well.

6 to 8 Servings

2 pounds small zucchini
½ cup vegetable oil or olive oil, for frying
5 tablespoons extra-virgin olive oil
1 small onion, coarsely chopped
2 garlic cloves, minced
One 35-ounce can Italian peeled tomatoes, lightly drained
Salt and freshly ground pepper
4 tablespoons unsalted butter
¼ cup all-purpose flour
2 cups hot milk
¾ cup freshly grated Parmesan cheese (3 ounces)
Freshly grated nutmeg
1 pound penne
1 cup (loosely packed) fresh basil leaves, torn into large pieces

1. Halve the zucchini crosswise, then cut each half into very thin lengthwise slices. In a large skillet, heat 1½ tablespoons of the vegetable oil over moderately high heat. Add a layer of zucchini slices and cook, turning once, until slightly browned, about 3 minutes. Drain on paper towels. Repeat with the remaining vegetable oil and zucchini.

2. In a medium nonreactive saucepan, combine 3 tablespoons of the extra-virgin olive oil with the onion and garlic. Cook over moderate heat, stirring, until softened but not browned, about 7 minutes. Add the tomatoes and break them up with a wooden spoon. Add ½ teaspoon each of salt and pepper and cook, stirring occasionally, until the sauce is very thick, about 30 minutes.

3. Meanwhile, make the béchamel sauce. In a heavy, medium saucepan, melt the butter over moderate heat. Remove from the heat and whisk in the flour. Return to the heat and cook, stirring, without coloring, for 2 minutes. Remove from the heat and gradually whisk in the hot milk, beating well to avoid lumps. Return to the heat and bring to a boil. Reduce the heat to moderately low and simmer the sauce gently for 10 minutes. Add ¼ cup of the Parmesan cheese and season with salt, pepper and nutmeg. Remove the sauce from the heat, cover and keep warm.

4. Preheat the oven to 400°. Cook the pasta in a large pot of rapidly boiling salted water until barely al dente, about 8 minutes. Drain and toss with the remaining 2 tablespoons extra-virgin olive oil.

5. Spread ⅓ cup of the tomato sauce in the bottom of a 3-quart shallow baking dish and spread 2 generous cups of the penne on top. Dot with ¾ cup of the béchamel and ½ cup of the tomato sauce and cover with one-third of the zucchini and basil. Sprinkle 2 tablespoons of the Parmesan on top. Repeat this layering two more times, ending with the zucchini and basil. Sprinkle the remaining ¼ cup Parmesan on top and bake until heated through, about 20 minutes.

—*Nancy Verde Barr*

NEAPOLITAN CARNIVAL LASAGNA

This traditional southern Italian lasagna is made with meatballs, sausage and sliced hard-cooked eggs.

6 to 8 Servings

½ pound ground beef
½ cup fresh bread crumbs
1 egg, lightly beaten
Salt and freshly ground pepper
3 tablespoons olive oil
½ pound Italian sausage, casings removed
One 9-ounce package precooked lasagna noodles (see Note)
3½ cups Nonna's Ragù (p. 244)
2 hard-cooked eggs, thinly sliced crosswise
1 pound fresh ricotta cheese
1¼ cups shredded mozzarella cheese (6 ounces)
½ cup freshly grated Parmesan cheese (2 ounces)

1. In a bowl, mix together the ground beef, bread crumbs, egg and ½ teaspoon each salt and pepper until well blended. Form the mixture into 12 meatballs about 1 inch in diameter.

2. In a heavy, medium skillet, heat 2 tablespoons of the olive oil. Add the meatballs and fry over moderately high heat, turning as necessary, until browned all over, about 6 minutes. Drain on paper towels.

3. Add the sausage meat to the skillet and fry, stirring occasionally, until nicely browned and cooked through, 4 to 5 minutes. Remove the meat with a slotted spoon and drain on paper towels.

4. Preheat the oven to 375°. Brush a 9-by-13-by-2½-inch baking dish with the remaining 1 tablespoon olive oil. Cover the bottom of the dish with one-third of the noodles, overlapping them

slightly. Spread 1 cup of Nonna's Ragù over the noodles, then top with half the meatballs, sausage meat and sliced eggs. Dot with half the ricotta. Sprinkle one-third of the mozzarella and Parmesan cheeses on top. Repeat the layering once, then end with a final layer of noodles, sauce, mozzarella and Parmesan.

5. Cover the baking dish tightly with foil and bake the lasagna for 30 minutes. Uncover and bake for 20 to 25 minutes longer, until golden brown and bubbly. Let rest for 10 minutes before serving.

NOTE: Precooked dried lasagna noodles are available at supermarkets nationwide. These noodles are used dry and reconstitute during baking. They are thinner and more delicate than the traditional, ripple-edged lasagna noodles.
—*Nancy Verde Barr*

VEGETABLE FRIED RICE

Thai-style fried rice is a light and nourishing meal that can be varied in many ways depending on what you have on hand. If you like, add one-quarter pound of chicken or pork, thinly sliced or in strips, or a few oyster mushrooms and baby corns.

Whatever you add, be sure to start with fragrant Thai jasmine rice, to brown the garlic first and to use fish sauce; these are the elements that make this dish unique and good. If you are using freshly cooked rice, spread it on a plate and refrigerate uncovered until chilled before stir-frying.

2 Servings

3 tablespoons vegetable oil
8 garlic cloves, finely chopped
2 cups coarsely chopped kale
2 cups sliced mushrooms

4 cups cold cooked Plain Jasmine Rice (recipe follows)
2 medium tomatoes, seeded and cut into small pieces
4 teaspoons light soy sauce
4 teaspoons fish sauce
1 teaspoon sugar
½ cup fresh coriander (cilantro) leaves
Freshly ground white pepper
Lime wedges, scallions and thinly sliced cucumbers, for garnish
Fish Sauce with Hot Chiles, for serving (p. 243)

1. Set a wok over high heat. When it is hot, add the oil and swirl to coat the wok. Add the garlic and stir-fry until lightly browned, about 30 seconds.

2. Add the kale and mushrooms and stir-fry until the mushrooms begin to soften, 2 to 3 minutes. Add the rice, breaking it up with your fingers as you toss it in. Using a spatula, stir-fry the rice for 1½ to 2 minutes; it may stick at first, but scoop and toss the rice and soon it will be more manageable. Add the tomatoes, soy sauce, fish sauce and sugar. Stir well and cook for another minute or two. Spoon the rice onto a platter or plates and sprinkle lightly with the coriander leaves and white pepper. Arrange the lime wedges, scallions and overlapping cucumber slices around the rice. Squeeze the lime on the rice as you eat it. Serve with Fish Sauce with Hot Chiles; the salty-hot sauce brings out the full flavor of the rice.

—*Jeffrey Alford & Naomi Duguid*

PLAIN JASMINE RICE

Many Thais still measure the rice-to-water ratio the old-fashioned way: After thorough rinsing, the rice is placed in a pot, and water is added to cover it by about three-quarters of an inch. The depth is then measured by resting the tip of an index finger on the rice; the water should just reach the first joint. For those who prefer more precise measurements, instructions are provided below.

4 Servings

2 cups Thai jasmine rice
2 cups cold water

1. In a bowl, rinse the rice thoroughly under cold running water, rubbing it between your fingers until the water is clear. Drain well.

2. Place the rice in a heavy medium pot and add the water. Bring to a boil, then cover the pot tightly and turn the heat to the lowest setting. Cook the rice without lifting the lid for 14 minutes, then remove from the heat and stir. If you have time, cover the rice again and let it stand for 5 to 10 minutes before serving.

—Jeffrey Alford & Naomi Duguid

STICKY RICE

If you have access to a Thai or Laotian grocery, ask about a special basket used for steaming sticky rice. The instructions here call for a Chinese bamboo steamer, but the Asian baskets made specifically for the purpose are attractive and easy to use. The rice must soak for at least two hours before steaming, so plan accordingly.

4 Servings

2 cups sticky rice
5 cups water, for soaking

1. Soak the rice for 2 hours in hot water or for 8 hours or more in cold water. Drain the rice.

2. Place 3 inches of water in a wok or a large saucepan and bring to a boil over high heat. Line a bamboo steamer with cheesecloth, then spread the rice on the cheesecloth. Cover and steam over the boiling water for 25 to 30 minutes, checking once or twice to ensure that the pan isn't dry. The rice is done when it's tender, shiny and somewhat sticky. Turn it out into a large bowl and serve.

—Jeffrey Alford & Naomi Duguid

RICE PILAF WITH BAY LEAF

4 Servings

2 cups chicken stock or canned low-sodium broth
1½ tablespoons unsalted butter
1 medium onion, finely chopped
1 cup arborio rice
1 bay leaf
¼ teaspoon salt
Freshly ground white pepper

1. In a medium saucepan, bring the chicken stock to a simmer over moderate heat.

2. Meanwhile, in a medium skillet, melt the butter over moderate heat. Add the onion and cook, stirring, for 2 minutes. Stir in the rice and bay leaf and cook until the onion is soft and the rice is translucent, about 5 minutes.

3. Add the hot chicken stock and the salt to the skillet. Reduce the heat to low, cover and simmer gently until the liquid is absorbed and the rice is tender but still firm in the center, 18 to 20 minutes. Discard the bay leaf. Season the rice with white pepper to taste and serve hot.

—Stephanie Lyness

LEMON RISOTTO

This creamy risotto was inspired by one served at Milan's Casa Fontana. Remember three important rules for making perfect risotto. Do not add too much liquid at once; do not add more liquid until previous additions have been absorbed; and stir, stir, stir.

♈ Serve this risotto with a pale, golden Vernaccia from the hilltop village of San Gimignano in Tuscany.

4 Servings

5 cups chicken stock, preferably homemade
1 teaspoon chopped fresh mint
1 teaspoon chopped fresh sage
1½ teaspoons finely grated lemon zest
4 tablespoons unsalted butter
1 tablespoon extra-virgin olive oil
2 shallots, minced
Sea salt
1½ cups arborio rice
2 tablespoons fresh lemon juice

½ cup freshly grated Parmesan cheese
(2 ounces), plus more for serving
Freshly ground pepper

1. Heat the stock in a medium saucepan and keep it simmering over very low heat. In a small bowl, toss the mint, sage and lemon zest together. Set aside.

2. In a large heavy nonreactive saucepan, combine 2 tablespoons of the butter with the oil, shallots and a sprinkling of sea salt. Cook over moderate heat, stirring, until the shallots are soft and translucent but not brown, about 3 minutes. Add the rice and stir until the grains are well coated with fat, glistening and semitranslucent, 1 to 2 minutes.

3. Stir ½ cup of the hot stock into the rice and stir constantly until most of the stock has been absorbed, 1 to 2 minutes. Add another ½ cup of the simmering stock and stir until it has been absorbed. Keep the heat at moderate to maintain a simmer. The rice should always be just barely covered with stock. Repeat this process, stirring frequently and tasting regularly, until the rice is almost tender but firm to the bite, about 17 minutes total. The risotto should have a creamy, porridge-like consistency.

4. Remove the saucepan from the heat. Stir in the remaining 2 tablespoons butter, the reserved lemon zest and herbs, the lemon juice, ½ cup of the Parmesan and sea salt and pepper to taste. Cover and let stand for 2 minutes to allow the flavors to blend. Serve immediately, with additional cheese passed separately.

—*Patricia Wells*

RISOTTO CAKES

These cakes can be made, shaped and cooked one day ahead, cutting down on all the last-minute details.

Makes 16 Cakes

*4½ cups chicken stock or canned
    low-sodium broth*
6 tablespoons unsalted butter
1 medium onion, finely chopped
1½ cups arborio rice
1 cup dry white wine
½ cup freshly grated Parmesan
1 large egg, lightly beaten
½ cup all-purpose flour
2 tablespoons olive oil

1. In a medium saucepan, bring the chicken stock to a simmer over moderate heat. Butter a 9-by-13-inch glass baking dish.

2. Melt 4 tablespoons of the butter in a large nonreactive saucepan. Add the onion and cook over moderate heat, stirring occasionally, until softened, about 5 minutes. Add the rice and stir until coated with butter, 1 to 2 minutes. Raise the heat to moderately high and pour in the wine. Cook, stirring, until almost all the wine is absorbed, about 4 minutes.

3. Add about 1 cup of the simmering stock (enough to just cover the rice) and cook, stirring constantly, until the stock is absorbed. Continue adding stock, about 1 cup at a time; stir constantly until the stock is absorbed before adding more. The rice is done when it is just cooked through and lightly bound with creamy liquid, after about 15 minutes.

4. Remove from the heat and stir in the Parmesan cheese. Let cool slightly, then stir in the egg. Spread the risotto evenly in the prepared baking dish. Cover and refrigerate until very firm, at least 4 hours or overnight.

5. Cut the risotto into 16 squares. Shape each square into a disk, about 2½ inches in diameter and ½ inch thick. Coat the disks with flour and refrigerate on a baking sheet until firm, about 20 minutes.

6. In a large skillet, melt 1 tablespoon of the butter in 1 tablespoon of the olive oil. Add 8 of the cakes to the skillet and cook over moderately high heat, turning once, until browned and warmed through, about 3 minutes per side. Transfer the cakes to a serving platter, cover and keep warm in a low oven. Wipe out the pan and repeat with the remaining butter, oil and risotto cakes. *(The risotto cakes can be fried up to 1 day ahead. To serve, warm them in a 450° oven for about 10 minutes, or until heated through.)*

—*Annie Roberts*

BARLEY AND MILLET PILAF WITH WILD MUSHROOMS

6 to 8 Servings

3 tablespoons unsalted butter
2 tablespoons vegetable oil
*1 pound shiitake mushrooms, stemmed,
    caps sliced ¼ inch thick*
*1 pound cremini mushrooms, stemmed,
    caps sliced ¼ inch thick*
1 cup dry white wine
2 tablespoons mild olive oil
1 medium onion, finely chopped
2 cups pearl barley
1 cup millet
2 teaspoons salt

1. In a large nonreactive skillet, melt 1 tablespoon of the butter in 1 tablespoon of the vegetable oil over high heat. Add the shiitake mushrooms and cook, stirring, until softened and lightly browned, 4 to 5 minutes. Transfer the shiitakes to a plate.

2. Add 1 more tablespoon of the butter and the remaining 1 tablespoon vegetable oil to the skillet. When hot, add the cremini mushrooms and cook, stirring, until softened and lightly browned, about 5 minutes. Return the shiitakes to the pan and stir in the white wine. Cook for 1 minute, then transfer the mushrooms to a bowl.

3. In a large saucepan, melt the remaining 1 tablespoon butter in the olive oil over high heat. Add the onion and cook, stirring occasionally, until softened and golden, 3 to 4 minutes. Add the barley and millet and cook, stirring, for 1 minute. Stir in the mushrooms.

4. Add 6 cups of water and the salt to the mushroom-barley mixture, stir well and bring to a boil over high heat. Reduce the heat to moderately low, cover and simmer until the grains are tender, 20 to 25 minutes. Fluff with a fork and serve immediately.

—*Bob Chambers*

COUSCOUS TIMBALES WITH ASPARAGUS AND CORN

Molding the couscous in timbales dresses up this tasty side dish for a dinner party.

4 Servings

3 tablespoons unsalted butter, softened
1 pound medium asparagus—trimmed, peeled and cut into ¼-inch pieces
½ cup fresh or thawed frozen corn kernels
3 tablespoons chopped red onion
1 teaspoon minced fresh thyme or ½ teaspoon dried
1½ cups chicken stock or canned low-sodium broth
1 cup couscous
2 tablespoons minced flat-leaf parsley
2 tablespoons minced fresh chives
Salt and freshly ground pepper

1. Lightly butter six ¾-cup timbale molds or ramekins with 1 tablespoon of the butter. Melt the remaining 2 tablespoons butter in a medium saucepan. Add the asparagus, corn, onion and thyme and cook over moderately high heat, stirring occasionally, for 2 minutes.

2. Add the chicken stock and bring to a boil. Stir in the couscous, cover and remove from the heat. Let stand until the stock is absorbed, about 5 minutes. Fluff lightly with a fork.

3. Stir the parsley, chives, 1 teaspoon salt and ¾ teaspoon pepper into the couscous. Pack the mixture into the prepared molds. *(The timbales can be made up to 2 hours ahead. Cover with a damp cloth and let stand at room temperature.)* Unmold the timbales on warmed serving plates and serve.

—*Jeannette Ferrary & Louise Fiszer*

GREEN LENTILS AND BULGUR WITH FRESH HERBS

Nutty-flavored bulgur makes a good side dish for lamb, especially when combined with lentils and other vegetables. This recipe is tasty enough to stand alone as a meatless main course.

6 Servings

1 tablespoon extra-virgin olive oil
1 large onion, finely chopped
3 medium carrots, finely chopped
2 celery ribs, finely chopped
1 cup bulgur, preferably organic (about 6½ ounces)
1 cup green or brown lentils (about 5½ ounces), picked over
Salt and freshly ground pepper
1 imported bay leaf
¼ cup finely chopped Italian flat-leaf parsley
2 tablespoons finely chopped fresh coriander (cilantro)
2 tablespoons finely chopped fresh mint

1. In a heavy medium saucepan, heat the olive oil. Add the onion, carrots and celery and cook over moderate heat, stirring, until the onion is slightly soft but not brown, about 8 minutes.

2. Add the bulgur, lentils, 1 teaspoon salt, ¼ teaspoon pepper, the bay leaf, 1 tablespoon of the parsley and 3 cups of water. Bring to a boil over high heat, then reduce the heat to low, cover tightly and cook until the liquid is absorbed, about 30 minutes.

3. Stir in the fresh coriander, mint and the remaining 3 tablespoons parsley. Taste for seasoning and serve warm.

—*Diana Sturgis*

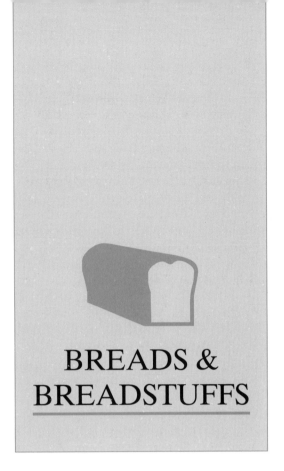

BREADS &
BREADSTUFFS

WHOLE WHEAT BERRY PANCAKES

Serve the light and fluffy cakes with butter, warm maple syrup, sliced bananas and strawberries.

6 Servings

⅔ cup whole wheat berries*
2 large eggs, separated
2 cups milk
¼ teaspoon pure vanilla extract
1 cup whole wheat flour
1 cup unbleached all-purpose flour
1 tablespoon baking powder
1½ tablespoons sugar
Pinch of salt
1½ tablespoons clarified butter
*Available at specialty food markets
    and health food stores

1. In a medium saucepan, cover the wheat berries with 1 inch of water and bring to a boil. Cover and simmer over moderately low heat until chewy, about 30 minutes. Drain and let cool.

2. In a medium bowl, whisk the egg yolks until thick and light in color. Whisk in the milk and vanilla. Sift the whole wheat and all-purpose flours, baking powder, sugar and salt over the egg yolks and stir to blend.

3. In another medium bowl, whisk the egg whites until soft peaks form. Fold the whites into the batter just until combined. Fold in the wheat berries.

4. Heat a large cast-iron skillet or griddle over moderate heat. Brush the bottom with a little of the clarified butter. For each pancake, drop ¼ cup of the batter into the skillet, allowing room for it to spread to 4 inches. Cook until tiny bubbles cover the surface, then flip and cook until golden brown, about 2 minutes per side. Transfer to a large heatproof plate and keep warm in a low oven. Brush the skillet with clarified butter between batches.

—Sarabeth Levine

CORNMEAL WAFFLES

These waffles, made in a Belgian waffle maker, are crisp on the outside and soft inside and can be served with an assortment of mix-and-match accompaniments. Savory toppings include chunks of cooked chicken, crab or lobster, sautéed mushrooms, roasted bell peppers and Creamy Wine Sauce (p. 243). For sweet waffles, there are fresh peach slices, strawberries and raspberries, Baked Apples (p. 219), Plum-Yum Sauce (p. 244) and Raspberry Sauce (p. 245). Maple syrup, crème fraîche, plain yogurt and toasted pecans can also be offered, as well as cooked breakfast sausages and bacon.

Serve the waffles hot with as many toppings as you like.

Makes Eight 8-Inch Waffles

1 cup all-purpose flour
1 teaspoon baking soda
3 extra-large eggs, separated
1 cup sour cream
3 cups buttermilk
¾ cup yellow or white cornmeal
4 tablespoons lightly salted butter,
    melted
2 tablespoons vegetable oil

1. Grease and preheat a Belgian waffle maker. In a small bowl, combine the flour and baking soda. In a large bowl, using an electric mixer, beat the egg yolks and sour cream on low speed. Beat in the flour mixture. Add the buttermilk, 1 cup at a time, beating well after each addition. Beat in the cornmeal, then add the melted butter and oil and mix until thoroughly incorporated.

2. In a medium bowl, beat the egg whites until stiff peaks form. Stir half of the egg whites into the batter. Gently fold in the remaining whites with a rubber spatula.

3. Spoon about 1 cup of the batter into the prepared waffle maker and cook until golden brown and crisp. Repeat with the remaining batter. Serve the waffles as they are made.

—Molly Chappellet

LEMON-POPPY SEED BISCUIT STICKS

These tender, fragile breadsticks are a cross between shortbread and biscuits, with just a hint of sweetness.

Makes About 3 Dozen

2 cups unbleached all-purpose flour
3 tablespoons confectioners' sugar
1 tablespoon baking powder
1½ teaspoons poppy seeds
1 teaspoon salt
1 teaspoon finely grated lemon zest
1 stick (8 tablespoons) cold unsalted
    butter, cut into ½-inch pieces
1 egg
½ cup buttermilk
1 teaspoon pure vanilla extract

1. Preheat the oven to 400°. In a food processor, pulse the flour with the confectioners' sugar, baking powder, poppy seeds, salt and lemon zest just to combine. Add the butter and pulse until the mixture resembles fine meal.

2. In a small bowl, beat the egg with the buttermilk and vanilla. Add the egg mixture to the food processor and pulse just until a dough forms.

3. On a lightly floured surface, roll the dough into a rectangle ¼ inch thick. Using a sharp knife, cut the dough into long, ¼-inch-wide strips. Arrange the strips ½ inch apart on nonstick baking sheets or cookie sheets lined with parchment paper.

4. Bake the biscuit sticks for 6 minutes on the upper and lower racks of the oven. Switch the pans and bake for 5 to 6 minutes longer, or until the sticks begin to brown. Let cool on the sheets for 10 minutes before transferring them to a rack to finish cooling. *(These biscuit sticks can be stored in an airtight tin for up to 3 days.)*

—*Bob Chambers*

SARABETH'S ENGLISH MUFFINS

These airy muffins tower over commercial varieties and are well worth the time it takes to make them. Start making them at least one day ahead so that the dough can rise overnight.

Makes 12 Muffins

1 cup milk
1 cup water
2 tablespoons sugar
½ teaspoon salt
2½ tablespoons unsalted butter
1 large egg, lightly beaten
1 tablespoon active dry yeast

4 cups all-purpose flour
Cornmeal, for sprinkling

1. In a medium saucepan, bring the milk, water, sugar and salt to a boil. Stir in the butter and let cool to lukewarm. Beat in the egg.

2. In a large bowl, combine the yeast and flour. Using an electric mixer, gradually beat in the liquid until smooth with a loose, sticky consistency. Cover and refrigerate overnight.

3. Butter the inside of 12 English muffin rings (see Note). Dip each ring in cornmeal and place on a large baking sheet sprinkled with cornmeal.

4. Stir down the dough with a rubber spatula to release air; the dough will be sticky and elastic. With a large sharp knife, cut the dough into 12 equal portions. Fill the muffin rings with the pieces of dough and sprinkle the tops lightly with cornmeal. Cover loosely and let rise in a draft-free spot until doubled in bulk, about 45 minutes.

5. Preheat the oven to 400°. Bake the muffins in the lower third of the oven for about 25 minutes, or until lightly browned. Let cool on the baking sheet on a rack for 15 minutes.

6. Remove the rings, transfer the muffins to a rack and let cool. *(The muffins can be frozen for up to 1 month.)* Toast them before serving.

NOTE: Muffin rings measure 3 inches across and 1⅜ inches high and are available at kitchen-supply stores. You can also use 7½-ounce pineapple cans with the tops and bottoms removed or any other similarly sized can.

—*Sarabeth Levine*

PECAN CORN BREAD MUFFINS

Halve these muffins and layer them with slices of Sage-Roasted Rolled Turkey (p. 78) for a real treat.

Makes 2 Dozen Muffins

4 strips of bacon, cut into 1-inch lengths
¾ cup pecan halves, chopped (3 ounces)
1¾ cups all-purpose flour
1½ cups cornmeal
½ cup sugar
3 eggs, lightly beaten
1¼ cups milk
2 sticks (8 ounces) unsalted butter, melted

1. Preheat the oven to 350°. Heat a medium skillet over moderate heat. Add the bacon and cook, stirring occasionally, until the fat is rendered and the bacon is golden brown, about 5 minutes. Pour off the fat from the skillet, add the chopped pecans and cook over moderate heat, stirring often, until lightly toasted, about 4 minutes. Transfer the bacon and pecans to a plate to cool.

2. In a large bowl, toss together the flour, cornmeal and sugar. Beat in the eggs, then the milk and ½ cup of the melted butter until smooth. Stir in the bacon and pecans.

3. Divide the remaining ½ cup melted butter between two 12-cup muffin tins, placing 1 teaspoon in each cup. Heat the muffin tins in the oven for 4 minutes, until the butter bubbles. Remove the tins from the oven and fill each cup half full of batter. Bake the muffins for 20 to 25 minutes, or until a cake tester inserted in the center comes out clean and the tops are cracked and golden brown. Let the muffins cool in the tins for at least 1 hour before turning out. Serve warm or at room temperature. (*The muffins can be made up to 5 hours ahead; keep them at room temperature.*)

—*Gerry Klaskala*

WHIPPING-CREAM BISCUITS

These rich biscuits have flaky exteriors and soft centers. They are delicious as a counterpoint to a salad of mixed greens.

Makes 1 Dozen Biscuits

2 cups all-purpose flour
1 tablespoon baking powder
1½ teaspoons sugar
1 teaspoon salt, preferably fine sea salt
4 tablespoons unsalted butter, cut into bits and frozen
1 cup plus 2 tablespoons heavy cream

1. Preheat the oven to 425°. In a large bowl, toss together the flour, baking powder, sugar and salt. Using a pastry cutter, 2 knives or your fingertips, cut in the butter until the mixture is rough textured with particles the size of peas. Using a fork, stir in the heavy cream until just incorporated. Immediately turn the dough out on a lightly floured surface and knead about 10 times. (It's okay if small lumps of butter are still visible.)

2. Roll out the dough to a 7-inch square and, using a large sharp knife, cut into 12 rectangular biscuits. Place the biscuits on an ungreased baking sheet and bake for 20 minutes, or until golden brown.

—*Christopher Kump*

BUTTERMILK SPOONBREAD

Spoonbread is sometimes known as soft corn bread or cornmeal soufflé. It goes with chicken, turkey, ham and game, sits nicely beside a dark stew or a creamy fricassee and is wonderful all by itself with butter and salt. What's left can be chilled overnight, then sliced, fried golden in butter and served with syrup or honey to start the next day right.

4 to 6 Servings

3 tablespoons unsalted butter, slightly softened
1 cup white cornmeal
1½ teaspoons baking powder
1 teaspoon sugar
½ teaspoon baking soda
Coarse (kosher) salt
2 cups buttermilk
1 cup milk
3 large eggs, lightly beaten

1. Preheat the oven to 375°. Butter a 2-quart soufflé dish or casserole with 1 tablespoon of the butter. Cut the remaining 2 tablespoons butter into 8 pieces and set aside.

2. In a large heatproof bowl, combine the cornmeal, baking powder, sugar, baking soda and 1½ teaspoons coarse salt.

3. In a heavy nonreactive saucepan, heat the buttermilk and milk over moderate heat until steaming but not simmering. (The mixture may separate but this will not affect the spoonbread.) Add the hot milk mixture to the cornmeal in a steady stream, stirring vigorously. Stir in the butter until melted, then gradually stir in the eggs.

4. Pour the batter into the prepared soufflé dish and bake in the middle of the oven for 45 minutes, until set and golden. Serve at once.

—*Leslie Newman*

ITALIAN BREADSTICKS

These long breadsticks, or *grissini* in Italian, look quite dramatic. The thinner you make them, the crisper they bake. For variety, you can add any of the following ingredients to the dough at the end of kneading: 2 tablespoons Parmesan cheese, ¼ cup chopped fresh herbs or 1 onion, chopped and sautéed.

Makes 20 to 24 Breadsticks

1¼ cups lukewarm water (105° to 115°)
1 envelope active dry yeast
1 teaspoon barley malt* or honey
2 tablespoons olive oil, plus more for brushing
1½ teaspoons salt
About 3½ cups all-purpose flour

About ¾ *cup sesame seeds or poppy*
   seeds (optional)
*Available at health food stores

1. In a large bowl, combine the lukewarm water and yeast. Stir in the malt and set aside until bubbly, about 10 minutes. Stir in the 2 tablespoons oil, the salt and 3 cups of the flour. Turn the dough out on a floured work surface and knead until smooth and elastic, about 8 minutes, kneading in as much of the remaining ½ cup flour as necessary to prevent the dough from sticking; let rest for about 5 minutes.

2. Roll or pat the dough into an 18-by-4-inch rectangle. Brush with olive oil, loosely cover with plastic wrap and let rise until doubled in bulk, about 1 hour.

3. Preheat the oven to 375°. If desired, gently brush a little more oil over the dough and sprinkle the sesame or poppy seeds on top. Using a pizza wheel or a large sharp knife, cut the dough crosswise in ¾-inch-wide strips. Pick up 1 strip and gently and evenly stretch it into a thin rope about 15 inches long. Pinch the ends slightly and place on an ungreased baking sheet. Repeat with the remaining dough strips, placing them about 2½ inches apart. Bake for about 20 minutes, until golden brown. Transfer to racks to cool. (*The breadsticks will keep for up to 3 days. Store in a paper bag or wrap in aluminum foil.*)

—*Peggy Cullen*

BUTTERMILK DINNER ROLLS

In the South, biscuits are served for breakfast or supper, but for dinner or a special occasion, buttermilk yeast rolls are the bread of choice. These light, springy rolls are not overly sweet.

Makes About 40 Rolls

1 envelope active dry yeast
¼ cup warm water (110° to 115°)
4½ cups sifted all-purpose flour
3 tablespoons sugar
1 teaspoon salt
3 tablespoons vegetable shortening or
   lard
1½ cups buttermilk
3 tablespoons melted unsalted butter,
   plus more for brushing if desired

1. In a small bowl, dissolve the yeast in the water.

2. Sift the flour, sugar and salt into a large bowl. Cut in the shortening using a pastry blender or 2 knives. Add the dissolved yeast and buttermilk and mix the dough thoroughly with a wooden spoon.

3. Transfer the dough to a well-floured surface and knead for a few seconds. The dough will be soft and sticky. Place the dough in a lightly greased bowl and turn to grease the top. Cover with plastic wrap and put in a warm, draft-free place to rise until doubled in bulk, about 1 hour.

4. Turn the dough out on a lightly floured surface. Roll it into a 22-by-14-inch rectangle about ¼ inch thick. With a 2-inch biscuit cutter, cut out about 40 rounds or as many as you can. Don't reroll the scraps.

5. Lightly dip each side of the rounds into the melted butter. Fold the 2 sides of each round into the center and pinch together firmly. Arrange the

rolls side by side in rows on a lightly greased baking sheet; they should be touching to prevent them from springing open.

6. Cover the rolls with plastic wrap and set aside in a warm place until doubled in bulk, about 45 minutes.

7. Preheat the oven to 400°. Bake the rolls in the middle of the oven for 5 minutes, then lower the heat to 375° and bake until light golden, 15 to 20 minutes longer. For soft, buttery rolls, brush them with melted butter as soon as they come out of the oven. Serve at once. (*Alternatively, the rolls can be cooled, wrapped in foil and set aside overnight. Rewarm before serving.*)

—*Camille Glenn*

COUNTRY BREAD ROLLS

To make good bread, start with flour that has at least 12 percent protein; it is always listed on the bag. I like to buy yeast at health food shops and store it in the freezer to keep it fresh.

If you don't bake all the dough at once, keep whatever's left in the refrigerator. During the week you can bake more rolls or make a pizza; one cup of dough makes a 10-inch pizza.

Makes 16 Rolls

Two envelopes active dry yeast
3¼ cups warm water (110° to 115°)
1 tablespoon plus 2 teaspoons salt
About 8 cups unbleached all-purpose
   flour

Cornmeal
1 tablespoon olive oil

1. Sprinkle the yeast in a very large warmed bowl and pour ¼ cup of the lukewarm water over it. Let stand for 15 minutes to soften.

2. With a wooden spoon, stir in the remaining 3 cups water and the salt. Start incorporating 7 cups of the flour, 1 cup at a time. When the dough becomes difficult to stir, turn it out on a lightly floured work surface. Knead the dough, gradually adding the remaining 1 cup flour until the dough is smooth and only slightly tacky, about 15 minutes.

3. Transfer the dough to a lightly greased bowl. Snip the top of the dough with scissors. Cover the bowl tightly with plastic wrap and let the dough rise in a warm place until tripled in volume, 1 to 3 hours. (Alternatively, let the dough rise overnight in the refrigerator and skip the next step.)

4. Gently punch down the dough. Cover and refrigerate it for 2 hours to chill; it is easier to shape the rolls when the dough is cold.

5. Punch down the dough and flour it lightly. Quarter it and cut each piece into 4 wedges for a total of 16 pieces. With floured hands, shape each piece into a round roll.

6. Lightly sprinkle cornmeal on 2 large baking sheets. Arrange 8 rolls on each sheet and slash the top of each one with a small sharp knife. In a small bowl, mix the olive oil with a pinch of salt and brush the oil on each roll. Loosely cover the rolls with wax paper and set aside in a warm place until they rise to 1½ times their size, about 1 hour.

7. Preheat the oven to 425°. Place a baking sheet in the hot oven to heat for 5 minutes. With a metal spatula, transfer half of the rolls to the hot baking sheet. Using a plant sprayer filled with water, spray the oven. Bake the rolls for 30 minutes, spraying the oven twice more during baking. Transfer the hot rolls to a rack and bake the second batch.

—Lydie Marshall

ROSEMARY-POTATO FOCACCIA LOAVES

Makes 4 Small Round Loaves

2 large baking potatoes, peeled and halved
1 cup warm water
1 teaspoon sugar
2 envelopes active dry yeast
1 cup olive oil
2 tablespoons coarse (kosher) salt
2 tablespoons rosemary, finely chopped
8 cups unbleached all-purpose flour
1 egg beaten with 3 tablespoons water

1. In a medium saucepan, cover the potatoes with cold water and bring to a boil over high heat. Boil until tender, about 15 minutes. Pour off the water and return the pan to the heat. Shake the pan to completely dry out the potatoes, about 30 seconds. Pass the hot potatoes through a ricer or a food mill. Let cool.

2. In the bowl of a standing mixer fitted with a paddle, combine the 1 cup warm water with the sugar. Sprinkle the yeast on the water and let stand for a few minutes until it bubbles up. Add the olive oil, salt and rosemary to the bowl; then add the potatoes.

3. Turn the mixer to low speed and beat in 2 cups of the flour. Add the remaining flour, 2 cups at a time. When the dough becomes difficult to knead, replace the paddle with the dough hook. Knead the dough for 15 minutes; it should be fairly soft. Remove the bowl from the mixer, cover and let the dough rise until doubled in bulk, about 2 hours.

4. Turn the dough out on a floured surface and knead lightly. Cut the dough into 4 equal pieces and shape each piece into a round. Set the rounds on 2 baking sheets, cover with kitchen towels and let rise until doubled, about 45 minutes.

5. Preheat the oven to 400°. Place one rack in the middle of the oven and one on the lowest shelf. Brush the loaves with the beaten egg wash and bake for about 25 minutes, switching the pans at half time. The loaves are done when they are well browned and sound hollow when tapped on the bottom. Cool the loaves on a rack.

—Mary Novak

SPICED CRANBERRY ROLLS

Makes About 2 Dozen Rolls

1 cup milk
4 tablespoons unsalted butter
¼ cup plus 2 tablespoons sugar
½ teaspoon salt
2 envelopes active dry yeast
¼ cup warm water (110° to 115°)
2 eggs at room temperature, lightly beaten
½ teaspoon ground ginger
½ teaspoon freshly grated nutmeg
4½ cups plus 2 tablespoons all-purpose flour
⅔ cup chopped fresh cranberries

1. In a small saucepan, bring the milk to a boil over moderately high heat. Remove from the heat and stir in the butter, ¼ cup of the sugar and the salt until dissolved. Let the milk mixture cool to lukewarm.

2. In a large bowl, sprinkle the yeast over the warm water. Set aside for 5 minutes. Whisk in the warm milk mixture, beaten eggs, ginger and nutmeg. With a wooden spoon, stir in 4 cups of the flour until incorporated.

3. Dust a work surface with ¼ cup of the flour. Turn out the dough and knead for about 6 minutes, adding about ¼ cup more flour by tablespoons to make a smooth, slightly sticky dough.

4. On the work surface, sprinkle the remaining 2 tablespoons flour and 2 tablespoons sugar over the cranberries and quickly knead them into the dough. The dough will be sticky and wet. Transfer the dough to a lightly greased large bowl and cover with plastic wrap. Let rise in a warm place until doubled in bulk, about 40 minutes.

5. Lightly butter 2 large baking sheets. Turn the dough out onto a well-floured surface and roll it out ½ inch thick. With a 2½-inch biscuit cutter, cut into rounds. Reroll the scraps and cut out more rounds. Plump each round into a ball by pulling the edges under and pinching the dough at the bottom. Place the rolls seam-side down on the prepared baking sheets, 1 inch apart. Cover with a kitchen towel and let rest for 30 minutes.

6. Preheat the oven to 350°. Set the racks in the upper and lower thirds of the oven. Bake the rolls for 10 minutes, then switch the baking sheets and bake for 6 to 8 minutes longer, until nicely browned. Serve warm. *(The rolls can also be cooled completely, sealed in sturdy plastic bags and frozen for up to 1 month. Thaw before reheating.)*
—Evan Jones

PECAN STICKY BUNS

This dough is based on Paula Peck's Rich Sour Cream Dough from her book *The Fine Art of Baking* (Galahad Books). Start the sticky buns at least one day ahead to allow time for the dough to rise.

Makes 12 Sticky Buns

DOUGH:
2 tablespoons plus 2 teaspoons warm water (110° to 115°)
2 tablespoons plus 2 teaspoons sugar
1 tablespoon active dry yeast
2 tablespoons plus 2 teaspoons milk
⅓ cup sour cream
1½ teaspoons fresh lemon juice
¼ teaspoon pure vanilla extract
1 egg yolk
½ teaspoon salt
About 2 cups all-purpose flour
1 stick (8 tablespoons) unsalted butter, at room temperature

TOPPING AND FILLING:
⅓ cup dried currants
¼ cup dark rum
2 sticks (½ pound) unsalted butter, at room temperature
½ cup plus 1 tablespoon granulated sugar
½ cup (packed) dark brown sugar
¼ cup honey

1⅓ cups pecan halves plus 1⅓ cups chopped pecans (about 10 ounces total)
2 teaspoons cinnamon

1. *Prepare the dough*: In a large bowl, whisk together the warm water, sugar and yeast. Let stand for 5 minutes. Mix in the milk, sour cream, lemon juice, vanilla, egg yolk and salt until smooth. Stir in 1½ cups of the flour. Work in the butter. Turn the dough out on a lightly floured surface and knead, gradually adding the remaining ½ cup of flour as necessary, until the dough is smooth and elastic, about 7 minutes; it will be slightly sticky. Transfer to a clean bowl, cover and refrigerate overnight.

2. *Prepare the topping and filling*: In a small saucepan, warm the currants and rum over moderate heat until hot. Set aside.

3. In a medium bowl, combine 13 tablespoons of the butter with 7 tablespoons of the granulated sugar, the brown sugar and the honey. Beat until creamy. Place a rounded tablespoon of the mixture in the bottom of each cup of a 12-cup muffin tin. Press about 6 pecan halves into each cup.

4. On a lightly floured surface, roll out the dough to a 10-by-12-inch rectangle. Rub the remaining 3 tablespoons butter over the dough, leaving a 1-inch border on the closer long edge. Drain the rum-soaked currants and sprinkle them over the buttered dough. Mix the remaining 2 tablespoons granulated

sugar with the cinnamon and sprinkle over the dough. Top with the chopped pecans.

5. Fold in ½ inch of each short side of dough and gently press down. Starting from a long end, roll up the dough. Lightly moisten the bottom edge with water and press to seal the cylinder. Roll the cylinder back and forth until it is 12 inches long.

6. Using a sharp heavy knife, cut the roll into twelve 1-inch-thick slices. Place a slice in each muffin cup, cut-side up, and press in gently. Cover with a kitchen towel and set aside until the buns have risen ½ inch above the top of the pan, about 2½ hours.

7. Preheat the oven to 375°. Place the muffin tin on a baking sheet to catch the drippings and bake in the lower third of the oven for about 35 minutes, or until the buns feel springy and look caramelized. Immediately invert the muffin tin onto the baking sheet to release the buns. Let cool for at least 15 minutes before serving. *(The sticky buns can be wrapped in foil and frozen for up to 2 weeks. Rewarm them in their foil wrapping in a 350° oven.)*

—Sarabeth Levine

CAKES &
COOKIES

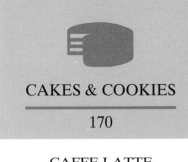

CAFFE LATTE CHEESECAKE

This variation on the cream cheese cake theme has the flavor of cappuccino. Be sure the cream cheese and eggs are at room temperature before you begin, and bake the cake at least 24 hours before serving to let the flavors develop fully.

12 Servings

CRUST:

⅔ cup plus ¼ cup graham cracker crumbs
5 teaspoons sugar
1 teaspoon instant espresso powder
¼ teaspoon cinnamon
4 tablespoons unsalted butter, melted

FILLING:

1½ pounds cream cheese, at room temperature
1¼ cups plus 2 tablespoons sugar
1½ teaspoons fresh lemon juice
½ teaspoon pure vanilla extract
2 large eggs, at room temperature
1 tablespoon very hot water
1½ tablespoons instant espresso powder

1. *Make the crust:* Preheat the oven to 375°. In a food processor, pulse the ⅔ cup graham cracker crumbs with the sugar, espresso powder and cinnamon. Pour the melted butter over the crumbs and process briefly to blend. Press the crumb mixture firmly and evenly over the bottom of an 8-by-3-inch springform pan. Bake for 10 to 15 minutes, until the crust begins to color. Transfer the pan to a wire rack to cool. Lower the oven temperature to 325°. Lightly grease the sides of the pan.

2. *Make the filling:* Using an electric mixer, beat the cream cheese until smooth. Gradually beat in the 1¼ cups sugar at high speed until fluffy. Beat in the lemon juice and vanilla, then the eggs 1 at a time, beating well after each addition.

3. Pour 1½ cups of the batter into a glass measure. Pour the remaining batter into the cooled crust. In a small bowl, combine the hot water, espresso powder and the remaining 2 tablespoons sugar. Stir this mixture into the 1½ cups batter. Using a spoon, dollop the espresso-flavored batter in a thick ring on top of the plain batter about ½ inch in from the edge of the pan. Swirl, or marble, the batters together with the spoon. Do not overblend.

4. Bake the cheesecake in the lower third of the oven for 1 hour, until set. Remove the cake from the oven. To prevent the cheesecake from cracking as it cools, run a thin sharp knife carefully around the edge of the pan to loosen the cake; transfer the pan to a rack and cover with a large inverted bowl. Let cool completely. Cover and refrigerate the cake overnight or for up to 4 days.

5. To serve, remove the sides of the springform pan. With your palm, gently pat the remaining ¼ cup graham cracker crumbs around the sides of the cake, being careful not to get crumbs on top. Transfer to a platter and serve.

—*Alice Medrich*

CRANBERRY SWIRL CHEESECAKE

Fresh cranberry puree provides a tart contrast in this sweet, creamy, crustless cheesecake. Prepare this cake a day ahead so that it will have time to chill and set completely.

12 Servings

1 bag (12 ounces) cranberries
1⅓ cups plus 2 tablespoons sugar
2 pounds cream cheese at room temperature, cut into 8 pieces
2 teaspoons pure vanilla extract
4 eggs, at room temperature
1 pint sour cream, at room temperature

1. In a medium nonreactive saucepan, combine the cranberries and ¾ cup of water. Bring to a boil over moderate heat and boil, stirring occasionally, until the cranberries burst and the mixture reduces to 1¼ cups, about 12 minutes. Remove from the heat and stir in ⅓ cup of the sugar until dissolved. Strain the mixture through a coarse sieve and let the puree cool completely.

2. Preheat the oven to 275°. Butter and flour a 9-by-2¾-inch springform pan. In a large bowl, using an electric mixer, beat the cream cheese with the remaining 1 cup plus 2 tablespoons sugar and the vanilla at low speed until smooth. Beat in the eggs one at a time, beating until just blended. Stir in the sour cream.

3. Spoon half of the cream cheese mixture into the prepared pan. Drop 8 or 9 rounded teaspoons of the cranberry puree randomly over the top. Spoon half of the remaining cheesecake mixture evenly over the first layer and dot with half of the remaining puree.

Repeat with the remaining cheesecake mixture and puree. (Avoid dropping puree in the center of more than 1 layer.) With a blunt knife, cut through the batter in a swirling motion to distribute the cranberry puree.

4. Place the pan on a baking sheet and bake in the lower part of the oven for 1 hour. Turn the oven off and leave the cheesecake in for 1 hour longer. Transfer the cake to a rack and let cool to room temperature. Cover and refrigerate overnight before serving.

—Diana Sturgis

MRS. McGREGOR'S CARROT CAKE

Makes One 9-Inch Two-Layer Cake

2 sticks (½ pound) unsalted butter, at room temperature
1⅓ cups sugar
4 large eggs, at room temperature
2 cups sifted unbleached all-purpose flour
1 tablespoon cinnamon
1 teaspoon baking soda
1 teaspoon baking powder
1 teaspoon salt
2½ cups (packed) grated carrots (about 8 medium)
1 cup walnut or pecan halves, coarsely chopped (about 4 ounces)
Orange Frosting (recipe follows)
Coarsely grated orange zest, for garnish

1. Preheat the oven to 350°. Grease two 9-by-1½-inch round cake pans, then line the bottoms with parchment or wax paper.

2. Using an electric mixer at medium speed, cream the butter with the sugar. Beat in the eggs, 1 at a time, mixing well after each addition.

3. Over a large bowl, sift together the flour, cinnamon, baking soda, baking powder and salt. Beat the dry ingredients into the butter-egg mixture. Stir in the carrots and nuts. Pour the batter into the prepared pans. Bake for about 35 minutes, until the center springs back after a gentle touch.

4. Transfer to a rack to cool for 10 minutes, then invert the layers on the rack to cool to room temperature. Peel off the paper.

5. Transfer 1 layer, bottom-side up, to a cake platter. Using a spreading spatula, spread about 1 cup of the Orange Frosting over the layer. Place the second cake layer right-side up on top. Spread the remaining frosting over the top and sides of the cake. Sprinkle orange zest over the top.

—Lila Jaeger

ORANGE FROSTING

Makes About 2 Cups

1½ sticks (12 tablespoons) unsalted butter, at room temperature
3 cups confectioners' sugar
1½ teaspoons finely grated orange zest
2 tablespoons fresh orange juice

In a large bowl, using an electric mixer at medium speed, beat the butter until soft. Beat in the sugar, orange zest and juice until fluffy.

—Lila Jaeger

QUICK APPLE CAKE

The recipe for this Latvian dessert came from Karolyn Nelke, a friend in New York. This is barely a cake at all. It's more like an instant apple pie—a simple batter is poured over apples in a pie dish and baked until crusty and golden. Browning the butter adds a toasty flavor, but if you don't want to bother, just melt it. Serve with vanilla ice cream or plain or vanilla yogurt.

8 Servings

1½ sticks (12 tablespoons) unsalted butter, cut into pieces
3 large tart apples, such as Granny Smith, Winesap or Mutsu (about 1½ pounds)—peeled, quartered, cored and sliced about ¼ inch thick
1 teaspoon fresh lemon juice
¾ cup plus 1 tablespoon sugar
2 teaspoons cinnamon
2 eggs, lightly beaten
1 cup unbleached all-purpose flour, sifted

1. Preheat the oven to 350°. Generously butter a 9½- or 10-inch glass pie dish.

2. In a medium skillet, cook the butter over moderate heat until golden, about 10 minutes. Watch carefully to avoid burning. (Alternatively, microwave at full power in a bowl covered with plastic wrap for about 6 minutes.) Pour the butter into a bowl, leaving behind any solids.

3. While the butter is cooking, toss the apple slices in a bowl with the lemon juice. Stir in 1 teaspoon of the

sugar and the cinnamon. Spread the apples evenly in the prepared dish.

4. Stir ¾ cup of the sugar into the browned butter. Gently stir in the eggs and then the flour just until blended. Spread the batter evenly over the apples. Sprinkle the remaining 2 teaspoons sugar over the top.

5. Bake the cake for about 50 minutes, or until the surface is golden and crusty. Transfer to a wire rack to cool. Cut in wedges and serve warm or at room temperature.

—*Richard Sax*

APPLE-RAISIN SPICE CAKE WITH CARAMEL SAUCE AND PECAN ICE CREAM

This down-home dessert with its contrasting textures and flavors is so popular that Stephan Pyles, co-owner and chef of Dallas's Routh Street Cafe, has kept it on the menu since the restaurant opened in 1983. "I would get hate mail if I took it off," he says, proud of a recipe he developed from his grandmother's cooking. The cake will keep for up to three days if well wrapped.

❦ If you don't overdo it with the caramel sauce, a good pairing for this dessert is a sparkling wine that's not too fruity and has some residual sugar, such as Schramsberg Crémant from Napa County or Veuve Clicquot Demi-Sec.

12 Servings

¾ cup pecan halves (2½ ounces)
¾ cup raisins
¼ cup bourbon

1 cup cake flour
1 cup all-purpose flour
1½ teaspoons baking soda
½ teaspoon salt
½ teaspoon freshly grated nutmeg
½ teaspoon cinnamon
⅛ teaspoon ground cloves
⅛ teaspoon mace
2 cups sugar
1 cup vegetable oil
2 eggs
2 large unpeeled Granny Smith apples, cut into ⅓-inch dice (3½ cups)
Caramel Sauce (p. 245)
Pecan Ice Cream (p. 212)

1. Preheat the oven to 400°. Spread the pecans on a baking sheet and toast in the middle of the oven for about 5 minutes, until fragrant and golden brown. Chop coarsely and set aside. Reduce the oven temperature to 325°.

2. In a small bowl, combine the raisins and bourbon and set aside to macerate for 30 minutes.

3. Butter and flour a 10-by-3-inch springform pan. In a medium bowl, sift together the cake flour, all-purpose flour, baking soda, salt, nutmeg, cinnamon, cloves and mace. Set aside.

4. In a large bowl, using an electric mixer, beat the sugar and vegetable oil at medium speed for 5 minutes. Add the eggs 1 at a time, beating well after each addition. Add the dry ingredients all at once and stir with a wooden spoon until thoroughly incorporated; the batter will be very thick.

5. Drain the raisins. Using a spatula, stir them into the batter along with the apples and toasted pecans until well distributed. Scrape the batter into the prepared pan and bake for 1 to 1½ hours, or until a knife inserted in the center comes out dry. Transfer the

pan to a rack to cool slightly; then turn the cake out of the pan and let cool completely. Drizzle the cake with the Caramel Sauce and serve with the Pecan Ice Cream.

—*Stephan Pyles*

POLENTA CAKE

Cornmeal adds crunch to the "true grit" desserts that have come into vogue in recent years—cakes, cookies, tart crusts and even puddings.

Andrea Hellrigl—chef-owner of Palio in New York and Villa Mozart in Merano, Italy—gets even more crunch in his recipe for this simple dense cake by adding chopped, unskinned almonds. He offsets the dryness of the cake by serving it with whipped cream and berries. In the winter months, try a sauce of cranberries cooked with sugar; in the summer months, serve it with fresh berries.

6 Servings

½ cup plus ¼ teaspoon sugar
1 stick (8 tablespoons) unsalted butter, softened
2 egg yolks, at room temperature
1 teaspoon finely grated orange zest
½ teaspoon finely grated lemon zest
½ of a vanilla bean, split, or 1 teaspoon pure vanilla extract
⅔ cup natural almonds (about 4 ounces)
½ cup yellow cornmeal
¼ cup potato starch or cornstarch
½ teaspoon baking powder
4 egg whites, at room temperature
1 to 2 teaspoons confectioners' sugar
Lightly sweetened whipped cream, for serving

1. Preheat the oven to 325°. Generously butter an 8-by-1-inch square baking pan.

2. In a large bowl, combine ½ cup of the sugar and the butter, egg yolks and orange and lemon zests. Using the tip of a knife, scrape the seeds from the vanilla bean into the mixture or add the vanilla extract. Using an electric mixer, beat at high speed until smooth, light and creamy, about 2 minutes.

3. In a food processor, finely grind the almonds with the cornmeal, potato starch and baking powder.

4. In a medium bowl, using an electric mixer, beat the egg whites with the remaining ¼ teaspoon sugar until they form soft peaks. Gently fold the dry ingredients and half of the beaten egg whites into the butter mixture; then fold in the remaining whites just until incorporated.

5. Gently scrape the batter evenly into the prepared pan and bake for about 30 minutes, or until the top of the cake is golden and a cake tester inserted in the center comes out clean. Transfer the pan to a wire rack to cool for 10 minutes; then invert the cake on the rack and let cool completely. Sprinkle the confectioners' sugar over the top of the cake, cut into 6 rectangles and serve with the whipped cream (see headnote).

—*Richard Sax*

COCONUT-PECAN CAKE

🍷 Rich late-harvest whites, such as 1988 Château Climens Sauternes or 1989 Ferrari-Carano Eldorado Gold Late Harvest Sauvignon Blanc Alexander Valley.

6 Servings

GINGER CAKE:
1¼ cups all-purpose flour
1 teaspoon baking powder
1 teaspoon baking soda
1 tablespoon ground ginger
2 teaspoons cinnamon
½ teaspoon salt
½ teaspoon freshly grated nutmeg
¼ teaspoon ground cloves
1 cup sugar
1 tablespoon instant coffee granules
¼ cup unsulphured molasses
3 tablespoons unsalted butter
1 large egg
¼ cup minced candied ginger
¼ cup finely chopped pecans

COCONUT FILLING:
½ cup heavy cream
1 large egg yolk
¼ cup sugar
2 tablespoons unsalted butter
½ teaspoon pure vanilla extract
½ cup plus 2 tablespoons medium-shred unsweetened coconut
½ cup finely chopped pecans

1. *Make the cake:* Preheat the oven to 350°. Butter an 8-by-3-inch springform pan and line it with wax paper. Butter and lightly flour the paper. In a medium bowl, whisk together the flour, baking powder, baking soda, ginger, cinnamon, salt, nutmeg and cloves.

2. In a small nonreactive saucepan, bring 1 cup of water and the sugar to a boil. Remove from the heat and stir in the coffee, then the molasses and butter. Let the syrup cool slightly.

3. Lightly beat the egg. Whisk a small amount of the syrup in a thin stream into the egg. Whisk the egg into the remaining warm syrup. Whisk this mixture into the dry ingredients.

4. Pour the batter into the prepared pan and bake for 35 to 40 minutes, until nearly set but loose in the center.

5. Open the oven and gently distribute the ginger and pecans on top of the cake. Bake for 15 to 20 minutes longer, until a cake tester inserted halfway between the center and the edge of the pan comes out clean and the center of the cake is set but moist. Transfer to a rack to cool for 15 minutes. Remove the sides of the pan and cool completely. Remove the bottom of the pan and the wax paper.

6. *Make the filling:* In a small saucepan, whisk the heavy cream, egg yolk and sugar and bring to a boil over moderately high heat. Cook, whisking, until the mixture thickens, about 2 minutes. Remove from the heat and stir in the butter. Stir in the vanilla, then the coconut and pecans. Set aside to cool. *(The recipe can be made to this point up to 3 days ahead. Wrap the cake well and store at room temperature; refrigerate the filling.)*

7. Using a sharp serrated knife, halve the cake horizontally. Spread the coconut filling on the bottom layer and cover with the top layer.

—*Peggy Cullen*

BUTTERY NUT CAKE

Whether you make this cake with almonds, pecans, walnuts, hazelnuts or just about any nut, it never fails to please. Use the same nut to garnish the cake to let people know what flavor it is. Grind nuts in a food processor fitted with a metal blade, pulsing repeatedly until coarsely ground. Scrape down the bowl and pulse until the nuts are finely ground, scraping occasionally. Do not overprocess, or the nuts may become pasty.

Frost the layers with Chocolate Ganache (p. 178), Whipped Cream (p. 178) or Spirited Buttercream (p. 178) flavored with a nut-based liqueur, such as Frangelico.

8 to 10 Servings

2 cups all-purpose flour
1 cup finely ground nuts (about 5 ounces)
1 teaspoon baking powder
1 teaspoon baking soda
1½ sticks (12 tablespoons) unsalted butter, softened
1½ cups (firmly packed) light brown sugar
3 large eggs
1 cup milk or buttermilk

1. Preheat the oven to 350°. Butter two 9-by-1½-inch round cake pans. Line the bottoms with parchment or wax paper.

2. In a medium bowl, toss together the flour, ground nuts, baking powder and baking soda.

3. In a large bowl, using an electric mixer, beat the butter and sugar at medium speed until light and fluffy. Beat in the eggs, 1 at a time, stopping to scrape the bowl and beaters with a rubber spatula after each addition.

4. At low speed, beat in the dry ingredients alternately with the milk in 4 parts, beginning and ending with the dry ingredients. Stop to scrape the bowl and beaters frequently.

5. Pour the batter into the prepared pans and smooth with a spatula. Bake in the middle of the oven for 25 to 30 minutes, or until a cake tester inserted in the center comes out clean.

6. Transfer the pans to a rack to cool for 5 minutes, then invert the cakes onto the rack, peel off the parchment paper and let cool completely.

NOTE: This recipe makes a 9-inch layer cake but it can also be baked as a 13-by-9-inch sheet cake, which needs an extra 5 minutes of baking time. The cake can be frosted when cooled, or the layers can be refrigerated for up to one week or frozen for up to two months. Wrap them tightly in plastic wrap and return them to a clean cake pan for storage.
—Nick Malgieri

LIGHTNING CAKE

"Mrs. Farback's *Blitzen Kuchen*" was inscribed in a spidery handwriting on an old recipe card handed down to my friend Sue Crouse by her grandmother. *Blitzen,* which means "lightning," refers to the use of baking powder instead of yeast, which rises more slowly. This cake is golden with eggs (about twice as many as in most yellow cakes in proportion to the butter and flour) and is just about the best plain butter cake you can imagine.

6 Servings

1 stick (8 tablespoons) unsalted butter, softened
1 cup plus 1 tablespoon sugar
4 eggs, at room temperature
1 tablespoon fresh lemon juice
½ teaspoon finely grated lemon zest
1 cup all-purpose flour
1 teaspoon baking powder
¼ cup coarsely chopped almonds, hazelnuts or pecans (about 1½ ounces)

1. Preheat the oven to 350°. Butter and flour an 8-by-2-inch round cake pan; set aside.

2. In a medium bowl, using a hand-held electric mixer, cream the butter with 1 cup of the sugar at medium-high speed until very light, about 3 minutes. Beat in the eggs 1 at a time, beating well after each addition, until well combined. Beat in the lemon juice and lemon zest.

3. In a small bowl, toss the flour with the baking powder. Using the electric mixer, beat the flour mixture into the butter mixture at low speed just until combined. Scrape the batter evenly into the prepared pan and sprinkle the nuts and the remaining 1 tablespoon sugar over the top.

4. Bake for 30 to 35 minutes, or until the top of the cake is lightly golden and a cake tester inserted in the center comes out clean. Transfer to a wire rack to cool slightly, then invert to remove the pan. Cut the cake into 6 equal wedges and serve warm or at room temperature.

—Richard Sax

MEXICAN CHOCOLATE CAKE

Chocolate suffused with cinnamon and coffee adds an exotic and appealing note to this cake.

10 to 12 Servings

CAKE:

1 cup sifted all-purpose flour
½ cup sifted unsweetened cocoa powder
½ teaspoon salt
¼ teaspoon baking powder
¼ teaspoon baking soda
1 tablespoon instant espresso powder
1½ tablespoons hot water
½ cup buttermilk, at room temperature
1½ sticks (12 tablespoons) unsalted butter, softened
1⅓ cups sugar
1 teaspoon pure vanilla extract
3 large eggs, at room temperature

FILLING:

10 ounces milk chocolate, finely chopped
¾ cup heavy cream
1 tablespoon light corn syrup
1 tablespoon plus 1 teaspoon instant espresso powder dissolved in a few drops of hot water
⅛ teaspoon cinnamon

GLAZE:

6 ounces bittersweet or semisweet chocolate, finely chopped
1 stick (8 tablespoons) unsalted butter, cut up
1 tablespoon light corn syrup

GARNISH:

12 walnut or pecan halves, lightly toasted, or chocolate-covered espresso beans

1. *Make the cake:* Preheat the oven to 350°. Lightly grease the bottom and sides of an 8-by-2-inch round cake pan or 8-inch springform pan. Line the bottom with a round of parchment paper.

2. In a medium bowl, sift together the flour, cocoa, salt, baking powder and baking soda. In a small bowl, dissolve the espresso powder in the hot water. Stir in the buttermilk.

3. In a large bowl, using an electric mixer, cream the butter. Gradually add the sugar and vanilla and beat until fluffy. Add the eggs 1 at a time, beating well after each addition. At medium speed, beat in the dry ingredients in 3 parts alternating with the buttermilk mixture, beginning and ending with the dry ingredients. Scrape the batter into the prepared cake pan and smooth the surface.

4. Bake on the lower rack of the oven for 50 to 60 minutes, until a cake tester inserted in the center comes out clean. Transfer the pan to a rack to cool for 5 minutes. Run a thin sharp knife around the edges of the pan and invert to unmold the cake. Peel off the parchment and turn the cake right-side up again on the rack. Let cool completely. *(The cooled cake can be wrapped well and kept at room temperature for 2 to 3 days or frozen for up to 3 months. Let frozen cake return to room temperature before continuing.)*

5. *Make the filling:* Place the chocolate in a medium bowl. In a small saucepan, bring the heavy cream and corn syrup to a simmer. Stir in the dissolved espresso and the cinnamon. Pour the liquid over the chocolate and let sit for about 1 minute. Then stir until the mixture is completely smooth. Let cool to room temperature.

6. *Make the glaze:* In a medium bowl, combine the chocolate, butter

and corn syrup. Place the bowl in a skillet of barely simmering water and stir until the glaze is nearly smooth. Remove from the heat and stir occasionally until completely smooth.

7. Place the cooled cake upside down on an 8-inch cardboard cake circle. Using a long serrated knife and a gentle sawing motion, halve the cake horizontally. Set the top layer aside.

8. Using an electric mixer, whip the cooled filling at high speed until light in color and slightly stiff; do not overbeat. (If necessary, refrigerate it briefly to achieve a spreadable consistency.) Using an offset or regular icing spatula, spread a little more than half of the filling on the bottom cake layer. Cover with the top layer. Spread the remaining filling on the top and sides of the cake. Smooth the top completely with the spatula. Refrigerate for 10 minutes to set.

9. Set the bowl of glaze in a pan of barely simmering water. With a wooden spoon, stir gently until smoothly combined and barely warm. Center the cake on a cake turntable or a large upturned bowl. Pour all the glaze on the top of the cake. Holding a metal icing spatula with the flat blade almost parallel to the top of the cake and rotating the cake carefully as you work, spread the glaze in just a few sweeping strokes so that it coats the top of the cake and runs down and completely coats all sides. Try not to overwork the glaze with the spatula. Transfer the cake to a wire rack until the glaze has set.

10. Place the nuts or espresso beans around the top edge of the cake. Transfer the cake to a platter. *(The cake can*

be stored, covered, at room temperature for up to 1 day or refrigerated for up to 2 days; return to room temperature before serving.)

—*Alice Medrich*

CHOCOLATE ANGEL FOOD CAKE WITH MOCHA FROSTING

The frosting will keep the cake moist overnight at room temperature. However, if you want to save on calories, sift a little confectioners' sugar and cocoa powder over the top and serve the cake the day it's made.

12 Servings

¾ cup cake flour

½ cup unsweetened cocoa powder, preferably Dutch process

1½ cups superfine sugar

2 cups egg whites (about 14 large or 12 jumbo), at room temperature

1½ teaspoons cream of tartar

¼ cup hot water

1 tablespoon freeze-dried instant coffee granules

1 stick (8 tablespoons) plus 2 tablespoons unsalted butter

6 ounces semisweet chocolate, chopped

1. Preheat the oven to 350°. In a large bowl, sift the flour, cocoa and ¾ cup of the sugar 3 times.

2. In another large bowl, using an electric mixer, beat the egg whites at high speed until thickened and foamy. Add the cream of tartar and beat until the egg whites have almost tripled in volume, about 1½ minutes. Sprinkle 6 tablespoons of the sugar over the whites and beat until just incorporated. Beat in the remaining 6 tablespoons sugar until the whites are glossy and hold stiff peaks when the beaters are lifted, about 1 minute.

3. Sprinkle one-third of the flour mixture over the egg whites and, using a balloon whisk, large slotted spoon or large rubber spatula, gently fold in until just combined. Fold in the remaining flour mixture in 2 additions until no streaks of flour remain.

4. Scrape the batter into an ungreased 10-by-4-inch tube pan with a removable bottom. Bake for 45 minutes, or until a cake tester inserted in the center comes out clean.

5. Invert the pan over a narrow-necked bottle and let the cake cool completely, about 1½ hours. Run a thin knife between the cake and the sides and center tube of the pan, remove the pan and invert the cake on a platter.

6. In a small saucepan, combine the hot water and coffee granules; stir to dissolve the granules. Add 1 stick of the butter and about three-quarters of the chopped chocolate and melt over moderately low heat, stirring, until smooth, about 5 minutes.

7. Remove from the heat, add the remaining 2 tablespoons butter and chocolate and stir until smooth. Scrape the frosting into a small bowl and refrigerate, stirring occasionally, until spreadable, about 45 minutes. (Alternatively, place the bowl in a larger bowl filled with ice water and stir with a rubber spatula, scraping the bottom and sides of the bowl, until the frosting is spreadable, about 5 minutes.)

8. Frost the sides and top of the cake with a metal spreading spatula.

—*Diana Sturgis*

CLASSIC CHOCOLATE CAKE

This classic chocolate cake works well with any number of frostings. Try it with Chocolate Ganache (p. 178), Chocolate-Coffee Buttercream (p. 178) or cinnamon-flavored Whipped Cream (p. 178).

8 to 10 Servings

3 ounces unsweetened chocolate, coarsely chopped

⅓ cup water

2 large eggs

1 stick (8 tablespoons) unsalted butter, softened

1½ cups (firmly packed) dark brown sugar

2 cups all-purpose flour

1½ teaspoons baking powder

½ teaspoon baking soda

¼ teaspoon salt

¾ cup sour cream

1. Preheat the oven to 350°. Butter two 9-by-1½-inch round cake pans. Line the bottoms with parchment or wax paper.

2. In a medium heatproof bowl, combine the chocolate and water and place over a pan of hot, but not simmering, water. Stir occasionally just until the chocolate melts. Set the bowl aside and let the chocolate cool slightly. Whisk in the eggs.

3. In a large bowl, using an electric mixer, beat the butter and brown sugar at medium speed until light and fluffy. Add the chocolate mixture. Stop to scrape the bowl and beaters with a rubber spatula, then beat until smooth.

4. In a medium bowl, toss together the flour, baking powder, baking soda and salt. Beat half the dry ingredients into the batter at low speed, then scrape the bowl and beaters. Beat in the sour cream, then beat in the remaining dry ingredients.

5. Spoon the batter into the prepared pans and smooth with a spatula. Bake in the middle of the oven for about 35 minutes, or until a cake tester inserted in the center comes out clean.

6. Transfer the pans to a rack to cool for 5 minutes, then invert the cakes onto the rack, peel off the parchment paper and let cool completely.

NOTE: This recipe makes a 9-inch layer cake but it can also be baked as a 13-by-9-inch sheet cake, which needs an extra 5 minutes of baking time. The cake can be frosted when cooled, or the layers can be refrigerated for up to one week or frozen for up to two months. Wrap them tightly in plastic wrap and return them to a clean cake pan for storage.
—Nick Malgieri

CLASSIC WHITE CAKE

The fine moist crumb of this vanilla cake makes it an ideal background for any frosting. Try Raspberry Buttercream (at right), Chocolate Ganache (p. 178) or Whipped Cream (p. 178) flavored with liqueur.

8 to 10 Servings

2 cups all-purpose flour
2 teaspoons baking powder
¼ teaspoon salt
6 large egg whites, at room temperature
¾ cup milk
2 teaspoons pure vanilla extract
1½ sticks (12 tablespoons) unsalted butter, softened
1½ cups sugar

1. Preheat the oven to 350°. Butter two 9-by-1½-inch round cake pans. Line the bottoms with parchment or wax paper.

2. In a medium bowl, stir together the flour, baking powder and salt. In another bowl, beat the egg whites, milk and vanilla just to combine.

3. In a large bowl, using an electric mixer, beat the butter and sugar at medium speed until light and fluffy. At low speed, beat in the dry ingredients alternately with the egg white mixture in 4 parts, beginning and ending with the dry ingredients. Stop to scrape the bowl and beaters with a rubber spatula after each addition.

4. Pour the batter into the prepared pans and smooth with a spatula. Bake in the middle of the oven for 25 to 30 minutes, or until a cake tester inserted in the center comes out clean.

5. Transfer the pans to a rack to cool for 5 minutes, then invert the cakes onto the rack, peel off the parchment paper and let cool completely.

NOTE: This recipe makes a 9-inch layer cake but it can also be baked as a 13-by-9-inch sheet cake, which needs an extra 5 minutes of baking time. The cake can be frosted when cooled, or the layers can be refrigerated for up to one week or frozen for up to two months. Wrap them tightly in plastic wrap and return them to a clean cake pan for storage.
—Nick Malgieri

EASY MERINGUE BUTTERCREAM

One of the best light buttercreams is also the easiest to make. Just be sure the meringue has cooled to room temperature before adding the butter. If the meringue is too warm and it melts the butter, stir the soupy buttercream over ice water, then beat over ice water with an electric mixer until smooth, thick and spreadable. If the buttercream separates—it will look like soft scrambled eggs—briefly warm the bowl in hot tap water, then beat until smooth.

Makes About 3½ Cups

4 large egg whites
1 cup sugar
Pinch of salt
3 sticks (¾ pound) unsalted butter, softened
Flavoring of choice (see below)

1. In a large heatproof bowl, combine the egg whites, sugar and salt. Place the bowl over a pan of simmering water and stir constantly with a spatula until the sugar dissolves and the mixture reaches 140° to 150°, about 4 minutes. Remove the bowl from the pan of water.

2. Using an electric mixer, beat the egg whites at high speed until thick and cooled to room temperature, about 5 minutes. Add the butter, a little bit at a time, and beat until the buttercream is smooth, thick and spreadable. *(The buttercream can be made up to 5 days ahead; cover and refrigerate. Before using, bring the buttercream to room temperature and beat with an electric mixer until smooth.)*

3. Right before using, beat in the flavoring, a little at a time, until smooth.

RASPBERRY BUTTERCREAM:
Press 10 ounces of defrosted frozen raspberries in light syrup through a fine strainer into a small nonreactive saucepan. Cook over moderately low heat, stirring, until reduced to about ⅓ cup. Skim off any foam, cover and cool the syrup to room temperature before adding it to the Easy Meringue Buttercream in Step 3.

CHOCOLATE-COFFEE BUTTERCREAM:
Finely chop 4 ounces of bittersweet or semisweet chocolate and place in a heatproof bowl. Add 1½ tablespoons instant espresso powder and 3 tablespoons hot water. Set over a pan of hot, but not simmering, water and stir occasionally until melted and smooth. Let cool completely before adding to the Easy Meringue Buttercream in Step 3.

SPIRITED BUTTERCREAM:
Add 2 to 3 tablespoons of liqueur, such as Grand Marnier, or liquor, such as rum, to the Easy Meringue Buttercream in Step 3.

—Nick Malgieri

CHOCOLATE GANACHE

This classic chocolate frosting of Swiss origin is similar in texture to the center of a chocolate truffle.

Makes About 3 Cups

1 cup heavy cream
¼ cup light corn syrup
1 pound semisweet or bittersweet chocolate, coarsely chopped
4 tablespoons unsalted butter, softened
1 tablespoon liqueur (optional)

1. In a medium saucepan, bring the cream and corn syrup to a boil over moderate heat. Remove from the heat and add the chocolate and butter. Shake the pan and set aside for about 4 minutes, then whisk until smooth. Whisk in the liqueur.

2. To use the ganache immediately, scrape it into a bowl set in a larger bowl of ice water. Stir until cooled and thickened to a spreading consistency. *(Alternatively, cover and refrigerate the ganache for up to 1 week; bring to room temperature before proceeding.)*

3. Before frosting, whisk the ganache vigorously by hand or beat briefly with an electric mixer to lighten it slightly. Do not overbeat or the ganache will separate.

—Nick Malgieri

WHIPPED CREAM

The key to successful whipped cream is making sure that the cream, bowl and beaters are ice cold. In hot weather, pour the cream into the bowl and place it in the freezer for 10 to 15 minutes before attempting to whip the cream, or whip the cream in a bowl set in a larger bowl half-filled with ice water.

You can flavor the whipped cream with one tablespoon of liqueur or a dash of cinnamon or other spice.

To frost a cake with whipped cream, apply it generously. Serve any extra on the side.

Makes About 6 Cups

2½ cups chilled heavy cream
⅓ cup sugar
2 teaspoons pure vanilla extract

In a large bowl, beat the cream with the sugar and vanilla until thick and smooth. *(The whipped cream can be made up to 1 day ahead and refrigerated, covered. Lightly whip again before using.)*

—Nick Malgieri

HAZELNUT TORTE WITH MAPLE BUTTERCREAM FROSTING

Unfrosted, this flourless nut cake keeps well in the refrigerator overnight.

10 to 12 Servings

1 pound hazelnuts (about 3½ cups)
1 cup granulated sugar
6 eggs, at room temperature
¾ cup pure maple syrup
1½ sticks (12 tablespoons) unsalted butter, at room temperature
About ⅓ cup sifted confectioners' sugar

1. Preheat the oven to 350°. Butter a 9-by-2¾-inch springform pan and line the bottom with wax paper. Butter the paper and flour the pan.

2. Spread the hazelnuts on a baking sheet and toast in the oven for about 10 minutes, until the skins are blistered. Wrap the hot nuts in a kitchen towel and vigorously rub them together to remove most of the skins. Let the nuts cool completely.

3. In a food processor, combine the nuts and ¼ cup of the granulated sugar. Pulse just until finely ground; do not overprocess.

4. Place the eggs and the remaining ¾ cup sugar in a large heatproof bowl. Set the bowl over a large saucepan one-quarter filled with simmering water. Over low heat, using a handheld electric mixer, beat the eggs at high speed until thickened and warm to the touch, about 5 minutes. Remove the bowl from the heat and beat the eggs at high speed until the mixture is pale yellow, has tripled in volume and holds a ribbon on the surface for 10 seconds when the beaters are lifted, about 5 minutes.

5. Sprinkle one-third of the ground nuts over the eggs and, using a large rubber spatula, quickly and lightly fold the nuts into the eggs. Fold in the remaining nuts until evenly incorporated; do not overmix. Scrape the batter into the prepared pan. Bake in the middle of the oven for 35 to 40 minutes, until the cake begins to shrink away from the sides of the pan and a cake tester inserted in the center comes out clean. Transfer the pan to a rack and let the cake cool to room temperature.

6. In a small, heavy saucepan, bring the maple syrup to a boil over moderately low heat. Boil gently until reduced to about ½ cup, about 10 minutes. Set the reduced syrup aside to cool completely, stirring occasionally.

7. In a medium bowl, using an electric mixer, combine the butter and ⅓ cup confectioners' sugar and beat until creamy. Beat in the cooled maple syrup until spreadable, adding a little more confectioners' sugar if necessary. *(The recipe can be made to this point up to 1 day ahead, wrap the cake in plastic wrap and cover the frosting; refrigerate both. Bring to room temperature and stir the frosting before proceeding.)*

8. Invert the cake onto a serving platter or large plate. Using a large metal spreading spatula, frost the sides and top of the cake. If desired, use the tines of a fork to make a simple design of concentric circles or another pattern on the top of the cake.

—*Diana Sturgis*

LEMON MOUSSE CAKE

To make the lemon mousse, you will need a microwave oven for the Safe Meringue (see p. 210).

10 Servings

2 large eggs, separated, at room temperature
4½ tablespoons superfine sugar
1¼ teaspoons pure vanilla extract
⅛ teaspoon cream of tartar
½ cup sifted cake flour
3 tablespoons dark rum
Lemon Mousse (p. 209)
5 tablespoons minced unsalted pistachios
½ cup heavy cream, chilled
2 teaspoons granulated sugar

1. Preheat the oven to 400°. Using a dark pen or pencil, trace two 8-inch circles on a sheet of parchment paper. Invert the traced parchment onto a large baking sheet.

2. In a nonreactive bowl, using an electric mixer, beat the egg yolks with 2 tablespoons of the superfine sugar and ¾ teaspoon of the vanilla until thick and pale.

3. In a small bowl, using clean beaters, beat the egg whites with the cream of tartar at high speed until soft peaks form. Gradually beat in the remaining 2½ tablespoons superfine sugar until the whites are stiff but not dry.

4. Using a rubber spatula, fold one-third of the beaten whites into the yolk mixture. Scrape half of the remaining whites on top and sift half of the flour over the whites. Fold in gently until barely combined. Scrape the remaining whites over the batter and sift the remaining flour on top. Fold together quickly and gently.

5. Pour the batter onto the 2 traced circles and spread it evenly with an icing spatula to make 8-inch rounds. Bake in the middle of the oven for 8 minutes, until golden; rotate the pan about halfway through the baking time. Transfer to a rack to cool. Invert the pan and peel the parchment paper off the cooled sponge layers. (The layers will be thin but will swell when soaked and assembled.)

6. If necessary, trim the layers to fit in the bottom of an 8-by-3-inch springform pan. Using a pastry brush, moisten the tops of the layers with half of the rum. Place 1 layer, moistened side up, in the pan. Moisten the bottom of the second layer with the remaining rum and set it aside.

7. Scrape half of the Lemon Mousse into the springform pan and spread it evenly over the sponge cake layer with a rubber spatula. Place the second layer on top and press gently. Scrape the remaining mousse into the pan and spread evenly to the edges. Smooth the top. Cover with plastic wrap and refrigerate for at least 3 hours or up to 1 day.

8. Warm the sides of the pan for about 30 seconds with a hot damp towel. Run a thin, sharp knife around the edges of the cake and carefully remove the sides of the pan. Sprinkle one-third of the minced pistachios evenly over the top of the cake, letting

the mousse show through. Press the remaining pistachios around the sides of the cake.

9. In a small bowl, beat the heavy cream until it begins to thicken. Beat in the granulated sugar and the remaining ½ teaspoon vanilla until stiff. Scrape the whipped cream into a pastry bag fitted with a star tip and pipe 10 small rosettes or stars to indicate the portions. Serve immediately or refrigerate for up to 3 hours.

—Alice Medrich

CHOCOLATE-WALNUT GANACHE TORTE

This remarkably simple dessert—layers of thin chocolate-nut meringue and ganache—is light textured, rich and pretty without being fussy. If you like, substitute almonds or hazelnuts for the walnuts. Allow enough time to refrigerate this torte overnight to let the meringue soften. You can decorate the top with a stencil design of confectioners' sugar or cocoa.

10 to 12 Servings

CHOCOLATE GANACHE:
1½ cups heavy cream
6 ounces bittersweet or semisweet chocolate, finely chopped

CHOCOLATE-WALNUT LAYERS:
¾ cup sugar
½ cup plus 2 tablespoons chopped walnuts (2¼ ounces)
2 tablespoons plus 2 teaspoons unsweetened cocoa
1 teaspoon instant espresso powder

2 teaspoons brandy
3 tablespoons lightly beaten egg whites (about 1½)
Confectioners' sugar and unsweetened cocoa powder, for dusting

1. *Make the chocolate ganache:* In a heavy, medium saucepan, bring the heavy cream to a simmer. Remove from the heat and add the chocolate. Set aside for 1 minute, then stir until completely smooth. Let the ganache cool completely, stirring occasionally to prevent a skin from forming. Stir, cover and refrigerate for several hours or up to 5 days before using (the ganache will not whip properly if it is not well chilled).

2. *Make the chocolate-walnut layers:* Using a dark pen or pencil, draw three 8-inch circles on 2 or 3 pieces of parchment paper. Invert the parchment onto 2 or 3 baking sheets. Position the oven racks in the lower and upper thirds of the oven. Preheat the oven to 300°.

3. In a food processor, combine the sugar, walnuts, cocoa, espresso powder and brandy. Process until thoroughly incorporated. With the machine on, drizzle in the egg whites to form a thick, sticky batter.

4. Spoon the batter into the center of each traced circle. Spread it evenly with an offset or regular icing spatula to make 8-inch rounds about ¼ inch thick. Smooth the edge of each disk with your fingertip. Bake for 25 to 30 minutes, until the layers puff and the tops look dry. Switch the pans after 15 minutes for even baking. Transfer the pans to a rack to cool completely, then invert the layers and peel the parchment paper off carefully; it may be sticky.

5. Using an electric mixer, beat the chilled chocolate ganache at high speed until light and stiff; do not overbeat.

Scrape the ganache into a pastry bag fitted with a star tip.

6. Reserve the best-looking chocolate-walnut layer for the top. Place 1 layer on a serving platter and pipe a decorative border of ganache around the edge. Continue piping in concentric circles to cover the layer with half of the ganache. Top with the second chocolate-walnut layer and pipe on the remaining ganache as before. Place the reserved layer on top. Cover and refrigerate overnight. Just before serving, sift a light dusting of confectioners' sugar or a mixture of confectioners' sugar and cocoa over the torte.

7. To serve, slice the torte with a long, thin, sharp knife. Dip the knife in hot water and wipe it dry before cutting each slice.

—Alice Medrich

CHOCOLATE APRICOT TORTE

This torte tastes best when baked at least one day ahead. Serve the cake at room temperature with chilled whipped cream.

10 to 12 Servings

3 tablespoons minced dried apricots (about 10), preferably California
¼ cup brandy
⅛ teaspoon pure almond extract
6 ounces bittersweet or semisweet chocolate, coarsely chopped
1 stick (8 tablespoons) unsalted butter, cut into pieces
3 eggs, separated
½ cup plus 3 tablespoons granulated sugar
¼ cup all-purpose flour
3½ ounces blanched almonds, finely ground (⅔ cup)

⅛ teaspoon cream of tartar
1 tablespoon confectioners' sugar
1 tablespoon unsweetened cocoa
    powder
Caramelized Dried Apricots (p. 245)
Unsweetened whipped cream

1. Preheat the oven to 375°. Lightly grease an 8-by-2-inch round cake or springform pan. Line the bottom with parchment or wax paper; lightly grease the paper.

2. In a small bowl, combine the minced apricots, brandy and almond extract; set aside to macerate.

3. In a double boiler, melt the chocolate and butter over moderate heat, stirring occasionally. (Alternatively, microwave on MEDIUM—50%—power for about 2 minutes, then stir until completely melted.) Let cool slightly.

4. In a large bowl, using an electric mixer, beat the egg yolks with ½ cup of the granulated sugar until pale and thick. Stir in the chocolate mixture, flour and ground almonds. Stir in the apricots and their soaking liquid.

5. In a large bowl, using clean beaters, beat the egg whites until foamy. Add the cream of tartar and beat at medium speed until soft peaks form. Gradually add the remaining 3 tablespoons granulated sugar and beat at high speed until stiff but not dry.

6. Using a rubber spatula, fold about one-fourth of the whites into the chocolate batter. Fold in the remaining whites until just mixed.

7. Scrape the batter into the prepared pan. Bake the torte for 30 to 40 minutes, or until puffed, the center is just barely set and a cake tester inserted about 1 inch from the edge of the torte shows moist crumbs.

8. Set the pan on a rack and let the torte cool completely; it will sink in the center. *(The cake can be made to this*

point up to 1 day ahead; cover and store at room temperature.) Invert the torte onto a serving plate. Sift the confectioners' sugar and then the cocoa on top. Decorate with the Caramelized Dried Apricots. Serve with whipped cream.

—Alice Medrich

RUM BABA

Use a ring pan, such as a savarin mold, for this light, rum-soaked yeast cake.

12 Servings

¼ cup dried currants
1 cup dark rum
2 cups all-purpose flour
1 envelope active dry yeast
1¼ cups plus 1 teaspoon granulated
    sugar
⅔ cup warm milk (110° to 115°)
4 eggs, at room temperature
1 stick (8 tablespoons) plus 2
    tablespoons softened unsalted
    butter, cut into 10 pieces
1 cup heavy cream, chilled
1 tablespoon confectioners' sugar
1½ teaspoons pure vanilla extract

1. In a small saucepan, combine the currants and ¼ cup of the rum. Heat over low heat just until the rum is hot. Remove from the heat and set aside until the currants are plump, about 30 minutes.

2. Meanwhile, place the flour in a large bowl. Make a well in the center and sprinkle the yeast and 1 teaspoon of the granulated sugar into the well. Pour in the warm milk and set aside in a warm spot for 30 minutes.

3. Butter and flour a 6-cup ring mold. Drain the currants.

4. Using a wooden spoon, beat the eggs into the yeast mixture in the bowl of flour and gradually incorporate the flour until the dough is smooth and silky. Using your cupped hand or the spoon, slap or beat 2 pieces of the butter into the dough. Repeat until all the butter has been incorporated, beating well after each addition. The dough should be smooth and elastic. Beat in the currants until evenly distributed.

5. Evenly drop large spoonfuls of the dough into the prepared ring mold. Set aside in a warm place until the dough rises almost to the top of the pan, about 45 minutes.

6. Preheat the oven to 425°. Place the ring mold in the middle of the oven and reduce the heat to 400°. Bake for 30 minutes, or until the cake is well risen, springy to the touch and golden brown on top.

7. In a small saucepan, combine the remaining 1¼ cups sugar and 1 cup of water. Bring to a boil over moderate heat, stirring to dissolve the sugar. Boil for 1 minute. Remove the sugar syrup from the heat and stir in the remaining ¾ cup rum.

8. Invert the cake onto a wire rack set over a large platter. Pour the hot syrup evenly over the cake. As the syrup accumulates on the platter, spoon it over the cake until most of it has been absorbed. Let the baba cool completely. Reserve any remaining syrup that has collected; transfer the baba to the platter. *(The baba can be made up to 1 day ahead. Cover with plastic wrap and refrigerate. Let come to room temperature before proceeding.)*

9. In a medium bowl, beat the heavy

cream with the confectioners' sugar and vanilla until stiff. Drizzle the reserved rum syrup, if any, on top of the baba and pile the cream in the center.

—Diana Sturgis

CHOCOLATE BROWNIES

This recipe comes from the food writer Jim Fobel. When I first made these brownies, I accidentally overbeat and underbaked them. They were so soft that we had to freeze them and cut them cold, but they had a wonderful truffle-like texture. Now, we never make them any other way. These brownies must be baked in 8-inch foil baking pans to facilitate removal.

Makes 80 Bite-Size Brownies

4 sticks (1 pound) unsalted butter
12 ounces unsweetened chocolate, finely chopped
8 eggs
2 teaspoons salt
4 cups sugar
3 tablespoons pure vanilla extract
2 cups all-purpose flour

1. Preheat the oven to 375°. Lightly grease four 8-inch square foil cake pans.

2. In a large heavy saucepan, melt the butter over moderate heat. Remove from the heat. Add the chocolate and stir until melted.

3. In a large bowl, using an electric mixer, beat the eggs with the salt. Gradually beat in the sugar, then beat at high speed until the mixture is thick and pale, about 3 minutes. At medium

speed, beat in the vanilla and then gradually add the melted chocolate mixture, beating until blended. On low speed, beat in the flour.

4. Pour the batter into the prepared pans. Bake in the middle of the oven for about 28 minutes, until barely set. Let cool on a rack, then cover and refrigerate overnight. *(The brownies can be made up to 1 month ahead. Turn the cold brownies out of the pans, wrap the squares in plastic and foil and freeze. Defrost the brownies in the refrigerator overnight.)*

5. To serve, cut each cold brownie square into 20 pieces.

—Francine Maroukian

CAPPUCCINO BROWNIES

Makes 80 Bite-Size Brownies

2 pounds milk chocolate chips or chopped milk chocolate
¼ cup instant coffee granules
2 sticks (½ pound) unsalted butter, at room temperature
2 cups sugar
8 eggs
3 tablespoons pure vanilla extract
1 teaspoon cinnamon
1 teaspoon salt
2 cups all-purpose flour

1. Preheat the oven to 375°. Lightly grease four 8-inch square foil cake pans.

2. Place the chocolate and coffee in a double boiler over simmering water. Stir occasionally until the chocolate melts.

3. In a large bowl, using an electric mixer, beat the butter until fluffy. Gradually beat in the sugar, scraping

down the sides as necessary. Beat in the eggs, 2 at a time, beating until the mixture is pale yellow, about 3 minutes. Stir in the vanilla, cinnamon and salt, then carefully beat in the melted chocolate and coffee mixture until combined. Beat in the flour; you may have to finish this by hand.

4. Scrape the batter into the prepared pans. Bake for 35 minutes, until puffed, cracked and slightly resistant to the touch. Let cool on a rack, then cover and refrigerate overnight. *(The brownies can be made up to 1 month ahead. Turn the cold brownies out of the pans, wrap the squares in plastic and foil and freeze. Defrost them in the refrigerator overnight.)*

5. To serve, cut each cold brownie square into 20 pieces.

—Francine Maroukian

PEANUT CRISPS

Makes About 4 Dozen Cookies

1 cup unsalted dry-roasted peanuts (5 ounces)
1 stick (4 ounces) unsalted butter, softened
¾ cup sugar
1 egg, lightly beaten
¾ cup all-purpose flour
1 teaspoon baking powder
2 ounces bittersweet chocolate, melted and cooled

1. Preheat the oven to 375°. In a food processor, pulse the peanuts until finely ground.

2. In a large bowl, beat the butter and sugar together until fluffy. Beat in the egg well. Stir in the ground peanuts, then stir in the flour and baking powder until just combined.

3. Drop heaping teaspoons of the batter about 2 inches apart on large ungreased cookie sheets. Bake the cookies, 1 sheet at a time, for about 8 minutes, until golden brown. Let the cookies cool on the sheets for 2 minutes, then transfer them to a rack to cool completely.

4. Drizzle the melted chocolate over the cooled cookies. Refrigerate until ready to serve

—*Gerry Klaskala*

PECAN CARAMEL TRIANGLES

This recipe was inspired by the chocolate-covered caramel nut candies called turtles. You don't need a thermometer to test the caramel filling for doneness.

Makes 4 Dozen Triangles

2 cups all-purpose flour
½ teaspoon salt
1 stick (8 tablespoons) cold unsalted butter, cut into pieces
1 egg
1 tablespoon plus 1 teaspoon ice water
1½ cups fresh bread crumbs
1 cup heavy cream
1 cup (packed) dark brown sugar
1 teaspoon pure vanilla extract
2½ cups pecan halves (½ pound)
4 ounces bittersweet or semisweet chocolate, melted

1. Preheat the oven to 400°. In a large bowl, stir the flour and salt. Using your fingertips, a pastry blender or 2 knives, cut the butter into the flour until it is in pea-size pieces. Then rub the mixture between your palms until it resembles coarse meal. In a small bowl, combine the egg and ice water and beat with a fork until blended. Pour over the flour mixture and stir to combine. Shape the dough into a flat rectangle about 6 by 5 inches.

2. Between sheets of wax paper, roll the dough into a 15-by-11-inch rectangle. Remove the top layer of wax paper and invert the dough into a 13-by-9-by-½-inch metal baking pan. Remove the wax paper. Fit the dough evenly into the pan and trim off any overhang. Prick the dough at 1-inch intervals with a fork. Scatter the bread crumbs evenly over the dough.

3. In a medium saucepan, combine the heavy cream, brown sugar and vanilla. Bring to a boil over moderately high heat, stirring to dissolve the sugar. Reduce the heat to moderately low and boil, stirring occasionally, for 5 minutes.

4. Drizzle the caramel evenly over the pastry. Arrange the pecans, flat-sides down, on the caramel, covering it completely. Bake in the lower third of the oven for 25 minutes, or until the crust is golden brown and the caramel is bubbling. Transfer to a rack to cool to room temperature.

5. Drizzle the melted chocolate over the pecans. Refrigerate for 30 minutes, or until the chocolate is set. Cut into 24 squares, then transfer the squares to a work surface and halve them diagonally to make 48 triangles.

—*Diana Sturgis*

DEEP-SOUTH PECAN COOKIES

For the pecan flavor to thoroughly permeate the dough, refrigerate it overnight before shaping and baking. These cookies will keep for a week in an airtight tin.

Makes About 2 Dozen Cookies

1½ sticks (12 tablespoons) unsalted butter, softened
6 tablespoons confectioners' sugar plus more for rolling (see Note)
½ teaspoon salt
2 cups sifted all-purpose flour

1½ teaspoons pure vanilla extract
1 tablespoon water
2 cups pecan halves (7 ounces), finely chopped

1. In a large bowl, beat the butter with an electric mixer until light and fluffy. Add the 6 tablespoons confectioners' sugar and the salt and beat at medium speed until blended. Add the flour, vanilla and water and blend until you have a smooth soft dough. Stir in the pecans by hand until thoroughly incorporated. Cover with foil and refrigerate overnight.

2. Remove the dough from the refrigerator 15 minutes before forming the cookies. Preheat the oven to 300°.

3. Shape the dough with your hands into small fingers about 2 inches long and ½ inch wide. Place the cookies about ½ inch apart on a large, lightly greased or nonstick cookie sheet. Bake for 30 to 40 minutes, or until the bottoms are golden but the cookies are very pale otherwise. Roll the warm cookies in confectioners' sugar and let cool. Shortly before serving, roll the cookies in confectioners' sugar once more.

NOTE: For additional flavor, cut a whole vanilla bean in half lengthwise and bury it in ½ pound confectioners' sugar in a jar with a tight-fitting lid. Store for several weeks so that the vanilla flavor will be absorbed. Use the vanilla sugar in the cookie dough and for rolling.

—*Camille Glenn*

CAKES & COOKIES

MEXICAN TEA CLOUDS

Makes 30 Cookies

1 cup all-purpose flour
1 teaspoon baking powder
1 stick (8 tablespoons) unsalted butter,
   at room temperature
½ cup coarsely chopped walnuts
½ cup confectioners' sugar

1. Preheat the oven to 350°. Sift the flour and baking powder together over a medium bowl. Using your fingers, work the butter into the flour until completely blended. Mix in the nuts.

2. Pinch off a piece of dough and roll it into a ball about ¾ inch in diameter. Repeat with the remaining dough to make 30 balls, placing them about ½ inch apart on a cookie sheet. Bake for about 30 minutes, or until lightly browned. Transfer the cookie sheet to a rack.

3. Spread the confectioners' sugar on a large, flat plate. When the cookies are cool enough to handle, gently roll each one in the sugar. Place on the rack to cool completely. Gently roll each cookie in the sugar once more before serving.

—Virginia Ibarra

POLENTA COOKIES

These crunchy, crumbly cookies almost melt in your mouth.

Makes About 4 Dozen Cookies

2 sticks (½ pound) unsalted butter,
   softened
1 cup confectioners' sugar
1½ teaspoons pure vanilla extract
1½ teaspoons finely grated lemon
   zest
¼ teaspoon salt
1 large whole egg
1 large egg yolk
2 cups all-purpose flour
1 cup yellow cornmeal, plus ½ cup
   extra for rolling

1. Preheat the oven to 350°. Lightly grease 2 large baking sheets.

2. In a large bowl, using an electric mixer, cream the butter and sugar until pale and fluffy. At low speed, beat in the vanilla, lemon zest and salt. Beat in the whole egg and the egg yolk until well blended. Beat in the flour and 1 cup of the cornmeal until smooth.

3. Spread the remaining ½ cup cornmeal on a plate. Pinch off a piece of dough and form it into a ¾-inch ball, then roll it in the cornmeal until well dusted and place on a baking sheet. Repeat with the remaining dough, leaving about 2 inches between the balls. Using your palm, pat each ball into a 2-inch round, about ¼ inch thick. Bake for 22 to 25 minutes, until lightly browned around the edges.

4. Using a spatula, transfer the cookies to a rack to cool completely. *(The cookies can be frozen in an airtight container for up to 1 week.)*

—Deborah Madison

PINE NUT-BROWN SUGAR SHORTBREAD

Makes 12 to 16 Wedges

1 stick (8 tablespoons) unsalted butter,
   at room temperature
⅓ cup confectioners' sugar plus extra
   for dusting
3 tablespoons light brown sugar
½ teaspoon pure vanilla extract
1 cup plus 1 tablespoon all-purpose
   flour
½ teaspoon cinnamon
¼ teaspoon salt
⅓ cup pine nuts

1. Preheat the oven to 325°. In a large bowl, cream the butter with the confectioners' sugar and brown sugar until light and fluffy. Beat in the vanilla, then the flour, cinnamon and salt until crumbly but well blended. Press the dough evenly into the bottom of a 9-inch fluted tart pan with a removable bottom. Lightly score the edge with the tines of a fork and press the pine nuts all over the center of the dough.

2. Bake the shortbread for about 35 minutes, until nicely browned and fairly firm. Let cool in the pan for 15 minutes. While still warm, carefully score into 12 to 16 wedges. Let cool in the pan completely. Dust with confectioners' sugar before serving.

—Deborah Madison

Cranberry Swirl Cheesecake
(p. 170).

Near right,
Deep-South
Pecan Cookies
(p. 183).
Below, Mexican
Chocolate
Cake (p. 175).
Far right,
Apple-Raisin
Spice Cake with
Caramel Sauce
and Pecan
Ice Cream
(p. 172).

CHOCOLATE COOKIE DOUGH

Use small cut-outs of Ginger Cookie Dough (at right) as appliqué decorations before baking these cookies.

Makes About 6 Dozen Cookies

3¼ cups all-purpose flour
1 teaspoon baking powder
½ teaspoon salt
2 sticks (½ pound) unsalted butter, softened
1⅔ cups superfine sugar
⅔ cup unsweetened cocoa powder
2 eggs, at room temperature

1. In a medium bowl, whisk together the flour, baking powder and salt.

2. In a large bowl, using an electric mixer, cream the butter and sugar until light and fluffy. Add the cocoa and beat until incorporated, scraping down the bowl with a rubber spatula. Beat in the eggs, one at a time. On low speed, gradually add the dry ingredients until thoroughly combined.

3. Cut the dough in thirds and pat into disks. Wrap well and refrigerate until firm, at least 2 hours or overnight.

4. Preheat the oven to 350°. On a lightly floured surface, roll out the dough about 1/16 inch thick. Cut with cookie cutters. Transfer the cookies to ungreased cookie sheets and bake on the upper and lower racks of the oven for about 10 minutes, switching the pans after 5 minutes. The cookies are done as soon as they can be lifted from the sheet; do not overbake, or they will be bitter. Let the cookies cool on the sheet until firm, then transfer to a rack to cool completely.

—Peggy Cullen

GINGER COOKIE DOUGH

This simple cookie dough can be decorated in a variety of ways before or after baking. Before baking, cut the dough out into interesting shapes, or press patterns on the rolled out cookie dough. Or, after baking, decorate with royal icing or colored sugar.

Makes About 6 Dozen Cookies

4 cups all-purpose flour
1 tablespoon unsweetened Dutch process cocoa powder
1 tablespoon ground ginger
2 teaspoons ground cloves
2 teaspoons cinnamon
¾ teaspoon baking soda
½ teaspoon salt
2 sticks (½ pound) unsalted butter, softened
1 cup superfine sugar
1 egg, at room temperature
½ cup unsulphured molasses

1. In a medium bowl, whisk together the flour, cocoa, ginger, cloves, cinnamon, baking soda and salt.

2. In a large bowl, using an electric mixer, cream the butter and sugar until light and fluffy. Add the egg and beat thoroughly. Beat in the molasses. On low speed, gradually add the dry ingredients until thoroughly combined; you may need to use a rubber spatula to mix them in at the end.

3. Cut the dough in thirds and pat into disks. Wrap well and refrigerate until firm, at least 2 hours or overnight.

4. Preheat the oven to 350°. On a lightly floured surface, roll out the dough about 1/16 inch thick. Cut with cookie cutters. Transfer the cookies to ungreased cookie sheets and bake on the upper and lower racks of the oven

for about 10 minutes, switching the pans after 5 minutes. The cookies are done when the edges begin to brown. Let the cookies cool on the sheets until firm, then transfer to a rack to cool completely.

—Peggy Cullen

LEMON SHORTBREAD

Makes 8 Large Wedges

1¼ cups all-purpose flour
¼ cup plus 1 tablespoon sugar
1½ teaspoons finely grated lemon zest
⅛ teaspoon salt
1 stick (8 tablespoons) cold unsalted butter, cut into small pieces

1. Preheat the oven to 325°. Lightly butter a 9-inch pie pan.

2. In a large bowl, combine the flour, sugar, lemon zest and salt. Using your fingers, work in the butter until the mixture is crumbly. Press the dough together to form a ball, place in the pie pan and flatten to evenly cover the bottom of the pan. Make a decorative border around the edge of the dough with the back of a fork and prick the bottom all over.

3. Bake the shortbread for about 35 minutes or until lightly browned around the edges. Cut into 8 large wedges while still warm. Let cool in the pan.

—Susan Shapiro Jaslove

Peanut Crisps (p. 182).

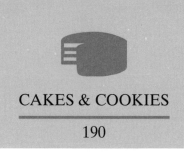

BUTTER SPRINKLE COOKIES

Makes About 32 Cookies

1 stick (8 tablespoons) unsalted butter, at room temperature
⅓ cup sugar
1 egg at room temperature, beaten
½ teaspoon pure vanilla extract
¼ teaspoon finely grated lemon zest
¾ cup all-purpose flour
Colored sugar, for sprinkling

1. Preheat the oven to 375°. Grease a cookie sheet. In a large bowl, using an electric mixer at medium speed, cream the butter with the sugar. Beat in the egg, then beat in the vanilla, lemon zest and flour. The dough will be soft. Cover and refrigerate for 4 hours or overnight to firm up.

2. Using a small spoon, scoop ½-inch rounds of dough and place about 1 inch apart on the prepared cookie sheet. Bake for 10 to 12 minutes, until the edges are lightly browned. Transfer them to a wire rack and immediately sprinkle the colored sugar lightly over the cookies. Let cool completely.

—Lila Jaeger

CASHEW-COFFEE BISCOTTI

Makes About 3 Dozen Biscotti

1½ cups unsalted cashews
1¾ cups all-purpose flour
½ teaspoon baking powder
¼ teaspoon salt
⅔ cup plus ½ teaspoon sugar
4 tablespoons cold unsalted butter, cut into small dice
2 tablespoons instant coffee granules
2 large eggs
½ teaspoon pure vanilla extract

1. Preheat the oven to 350°. Spread the cashews on a large baking sheet and toast in the oven for 10 to 12 minutes, until golden brown. Transfer to a medium bowl to cool.

2. Meanwhile, in a food processor, combine the flour, baking powder, salt and ⅔ cup of the sugar. Add the diced butter and pulse until the mixture resembles coarse meal.

3. Add the mixture to the cashews and toss. Mix in the coffee granules. Using a fork, lightly beat the eggs with the vanilla. Stir into the flour mixture; mix with your hands until just blended. Pat into a disk.

4. Lightly butter the baking sheet. On a lightly floured work surface, quarter the disk into 4 equal wedges. Using your hands, roll each wedge into an 8-inch log. Place the logs 2 inches apart on the prepared baking sheet and flatten with the heel of your hand to a width of 2 inches; sprinkle the tops with the remaining ½ teaspoon sugar. Bake for about 20 minutes or until golden brown. Using 2 metal spatulas, carefully transfer the logs to a rack to cool slightly, 5 to 10 minutes.

5. Place the logs on a work surface. Using a sharp knife in a quick motion, slice each log on the diagonal ¾ inch thick. Place the biscotti cut-side down on the baking sheet and bake for 5 to 7 minutes, just until they begin to color. Transfer to a rack to cool completely. *(The biscotti will keep in an airtight container for up to 2 weeks.)*

—Peggy Cullen

RASPBERRY TROLLS

These are thumbprint butter cookies filled with raspberry preserves.

Makes 24 Trolls

1 stick (8 tablespoons) unsalted butter, at room temperature
⅓ cup confectioners' sugar
1¼ teaspoons cinnamon
1 teaspoon pure vanilla extract
1 cup cake flour, sifted
About 2 tablespoons raspberry preserves

1. Preheat the oven to 400°. In a large bowl, using an electric mixer at medium speed, cream the butter with the sugar. Beat in the cinnamon and vanilla. Stir in the flour.

2. Using floured hands, pinch off a piece of dough and roll into a ball about 1 inch in diameter. Make 24 balls, placing them 1 inch apart on a large baking sheet. With your thumb, make a dent in the top of each ball. Dollop a heaping ¼ teaspoon raspberry preserves in each dent.

3. Bake the cookies for about 12 minutes, until the dough is set and the preserves are bubbly. Cool for 10 minutes on the cookie sheet, then transfer to a rack to cool completely.

—Lila Jaeger

PIES, TARTS & TURNOVERS

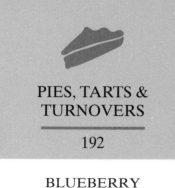
BLUEBERRY TURNOVERS

Ducky, a friend who cooks on wind-jammer sailing vessels that cruise Maine's Penobscot Bay in the summertime, bakes these turnovers in an old, wood-fired ship's stove.

Makes 1 Dozen Turnovers

1 cup sugar, plus more for sprinkling
⅓ cup instant tapioca
8 cups blueberries (about 2½ pounds)
2 teaspoons fresh lemon juice
2 pounds puff pastry (preferably all-butter), well chilled
1 egg white beaten with 1 teaspoon water

1. In a small bowl, toss the sugar with the tapioca. Pour the blueberries into a large nonreactive saucepan and sprinkle the sugar and tapioca on top; mix well. Add 2 tablespoons water, cover and cook over moderate heat until the berries begin to bubble, about 3 minutes. Gently stir the blueberries and cook until the sugar has dissolved, about 3 minutes longer. Remove from the heat and stir in the lemon juice. Scrape the blueberries into a bowl and set aside, stirring once or twice, until thickened and cooled to room temperature, about 30 minutes.

2. On a lightly floured surface, roll out half of the puff pastry to a 20-inch square, about 1/16 inch thick. Cut the pastry into six 6-inch squares. Transfer the squares to a baking sheet and refrigerate until firm. Repeat with the re-maining puff pastry and another baking sheet.

3. Preheat the oven to 375°. To assemble the turnovers, lightly brush the rim of each pastry square with some of the beaten egg white. Put ⅓ cup of the blueberry filling in the center of each square and bring the four corners into the center, pinching firmly along the edges to seal. Pull the tips of the corners back about ½ inch to make a steam vent.

4. Lightly brush the outside of the turnovers with egg white and sprinkle with sugar. Bake in the middle of the oven for 30 to 35 minutes, or until browned and crisp. Let cool before serving.

—*Nancy Harmon Jenkins*

GINGER-PLUM TURNOVERS

If desired, these turnovers can be frosted with Sugar Glaze (p. 196).

Makes 9 Turnovers

¾ pound red, purple or Italian prune plums, pitted and coarsely chopped
3 tablespoons minced crystallized ginger
2 tablespoons sugar, plus more for sprinkling
1½ teaspoons instant tapioca
Pinch of salt
Cream Cheese Dough (p. 196)
2 tablespoons cold unsalted butter, cut into small bits
1 egg, lightly beaten with 1 tablespoon water

1. In a small bowl, toss the chopped plums with the ginger, sugar, tapioca and salt. Set aside.

2. On a lightly floured work surface, roll out the Cream Cheese Dough to a 16-inch square, 1/16 inch thick. Using a sharp knife, cut the dough into nine 5-inch squares.

3. Spoon 2 tablespoons of the plum mixture in the center of each square and dot with the butter. Lightly moisten the edges of the squares with water. Bring up the 4 corners of the squares to meet in the center, enclosing the plum filling. Pinch the seams together to seal, forming square packets. Transfer the turnovers to a heavy baking sheet and refrigerate for at least 15 minutes.

4. Preheat the oven to 425°. Brush the turnovers with the egg wash. Using a sharp knife, cut 2 small slits in the top of each turnover to vent steam. Sprinkle additional sugar on top if desired.

5. Bake the turnovers in the middle of the oven for 10 minutes. Move them to the upper rack and bake for 8 to 10 minutes longer, or until the turnovers are deep golden brown. Let cool on a rack.

—*Carl Parisi*

PINEAPPLE AND DRIED SOUR CHERRY TURNOVERS

If desired, these turnovers can be frosted with Sugar Glaze (p. 196).

Makes 9 Turnovers

½ cup dried sour cherries (2½ ounces)
2 tablespoons kirsch or water
1 tablespoon unsalted butter
2 cups diced fresh pineapple (⅓-inch pieces)
1 to 2 tablespoons sugar, depending on the sweetness of the fruit
1 teaspoon instant tapioca
Cream Cheese Dough (p. 196)
1 egg, lightly beaten with 1 tablespoon water

1. In a small bowl, toss the dried cherries with the kirsch and set aside.

2. In a medium nonreactive skillet, melt the butter over moderate heat. Add the diced pineapple and cook until it begins to color, about 5 minutes.

3. Stir in the sugar and continue cooking for 1 minute, then stir in the cherries and their soaking liquid. Remove from the heat and stir in the instant tapioca. Set aside.

4. On a lightly floured work surface, roll out the Cream Cheese Dough to a 16-inch square, ¹⁄₁₆ inch thick. Using a sharp knife, cut the dough in nine 5-inch squares.

5. Spoon the fruit mixture on a triangular half of each square to within ½ inch of the edge. Lightly moisten the edges of each square with water and fold the dough over the filling to form triangles. Press down on the edges to seal, first with your fingers and then with the tines of a fork. Using the back of a small knife, press into the sealed edges at ½-inch intervals to create a scalloped effect. Transfer the turnovers to a heavy baking sheet and refrigerate for at least 15 minutes.

6. Preheat the oven to 425°. Brush the turnovers with the egg wash. Using a sharp knife, cut 2 small slits in the top of each turnover to vent steam.

7. Bake the turnovers in the middle of the oven for 10 minutes. Move them to the upper rack and bake for 8 to 10 minutes longer, or until the turnovers are a deep golden brown. Let cool on a rack.

—*Carl Parisi*

LEMON CURD TURNOVERS

If desired, these turnovers can be frosted with Sugar Glaze (p. 196).

Makes 9 Turnovers

6 tablespoons unsalted butter, melted
3 egg yolks
3 whole eggs
¾ cup sugar, plus more for sprinkling
2 teaspoons finely grated lemon zest
¼ cup fresh lemon juice
Pinch of salt
Cream Cheese Dough (p. 196)

1. In a nonreactive double boiler or a stainless steel bowl set over simmering water, melt the butter. Whisk in the egg yolks, 2 of the whole eggs, the ¾ cup sugar, lemon zest, lemon juice and salt. Whisk continuously over moderate heat until the mixture reaches 185° and thickly coats the back of a spoon, 10 to 12 minutes. Remove from the heat and let cool completely. Cover the curd and refrigerate until cold before proceeding.

2. On a lightly floured work surface, roll out the Cream Cheese Dough to a 16-inch square, ¹⁄₁₆ inch thick. Using a sharp knife, cut the dough into nine 5-inch squares.

3. Spoon 2 tablespoons of the lemon curd in the center of each square. Lightly moisten the edges of the squares with water. Bring up the 4 corners of the squares to meet in the center, enclosing the curd filling. Pinch the seams together to seal, forming square packets. Transfer the turnovers to a baking sheet and refrigerate for at least 15 minutes.

4. Preheat the oven to 400°. Beat the remaining 1 egg with 1 tablespoon of water. Brush the turnovers with the egg wash. Using a sharp knife, cut 2

small slits in the top of each turnover to vent steam. Sprinkle additional sugar on top.

5. Bake the turnovers in the middle of the oven for 20 to 22 minutes, or until deep golden brown. Let cool on a rack.

—*Carl Parisi*

DRIED FRUIT TURNOVERS

The spiced fruit filling in these semicircular turnovers is reminiscent of mincemeat. If desired, these turnovers can be frosted with Sugar Glaze (p. 196).

Makes 10 Turnovers

⅔ cup dark raisins
½ cup golden raisins
½ cup dried currants
½ cup dried apricots, chopped
⅔ cup orange juice
2½ tablespoons orange liqueur (optional)
1 tablespoon unsalted butter, melted
1 tablespoon sugar, plus more for sprinkling
1 teaspoon finely grated lemon zest
¼ teaspoon cinnamon
Pinch of freshly grated nutmeg
Cream Cheese Dough (p. 196)
1 egg, beaten with 1 tablespoon water

1. In a bowl, combine the dark and golden raisins, currants, apricots, orange juice and orange liqueur. Set aside to macerate for several hours, stirring occasionally. Alternatively, microwave the mixture on medium for 2 to 3 minutes, then let cool.

2. Add the melted butter, sugar, lemon zest, cinnamon and nutmeg to the dried fruit mixture and stir to blend.

3. On a lightly floured work surface, roll out the Cream Cheese Dough to an 18-by-20-inch rectangle, ¹⁄₁₆ inch thick. Using a bowl or a plate as a guide, cut out eight 6-inch rounds. Gather and reroll the scraps, then cut out 2 additional rounds.

4. Spoon 2 tablespoons of the dried fruit mixture in the center of each of the 10 rounds. Lightly moisten the edges with water and fold the dough over the filling to form semicircular turnovers. Press down on the edges to seal, first with your fingers and then with the tines of a fork. Using the back of a small knife, press into the sealed edges at ½-inch intervals to create a scalloped effect. Transfer the turnovers to a baking sheet and refrigerate for at least 15 minutes.

5. Preheat the oven to 425°. Brush the turnovers with the egg wash. Using a sharp knife, cut 2 small slits in the top of each to vent steam. Sprinkle additional sugar on top of the turnovers.

6. Bake the turnovers in the middle of the oven for about 20 minutes, until deep golden brown. Let cool on a rack.

—Carl Parisi

PEAR AND CRANBERRY TURNOVERS WITH BLACK PEPPER

Black pepper provides a balancing accent to the fragrant pears and tart cranberries. If you can find Tellicherry peppercorns, use them here—their aromatic flavor is somewhat like cloves or allspice. The pears for this recipe should be medium-ripe and not overly soft. If desired, these turnovers can be frosted with Sugar Glaze (p. 196).

Makes 9 Turnovers

2 medium pears (about 1 pound)— peeled, cored and cut into small dice
¼ teaspoon freshly ground pepper
2 tablespoons plus 2 teaspoons sugar, plus more for sprinkling
1 teaspoon fresh lemon juice
2 tablespoons cranberry juice
3 tablespoons cold unsalted butter— 1 tablespoon cut in small bits
Pinch of salt
½ teaspoon arrowroot, mixed with 1 teaspoon water
½ cup coarsely chopped fresh cranberries
½ tablespoon pear or apple brandy, or Cognac
Cream Cheese Dough (p. 196)
1 egg, beaten with 1 tablespoon water

1. In a bowl, toss half of the pears with the pepper and 2 teaspoons of the sugar. Sprinkle with the lemon juice and toss to coat. Cover and set aside.

2. In a medium nonreactive saucepan, combine the remaining pears with the cranberry juice, 2 tablespoons of the butter, the remaining 2 tablespoons sugar and the salt. Bring to a simmer over moderate heat, stirring occasionally. Cook until the pears are almost tender but still hold their shape, about 5 minutes.

3. Stir in the dissolved arrowroot and the chopped cranberries and cook until the cranberries just begin to soften and the mixture is thickened, about 5 minutes longer. Remove from the heat and stir in the brandy. Transfer the fruit mixture to a bowl and let cool, then refrigerate until cooled completely.

4. On a lightly floured work surface, roll out the Cream Cheese Dough to a 16-inch square, ¹⁄₁₆ inch thick. Using a sharp knife, cut the dough into nine 5-inch squares.

5. Spread 1 tablespoon of the cooked fruit mixture on a triangular half of each square to within ½ inch of the edge. Place 1 tablespoon of the reserved uncooked pear mixture on top of the cooked fruit and dot with the remaining 1 tablespoon butter bits. Lightly moisten the edges of each square with water and fold the dough over the filling to form triangles. Press down on the edges to seal, first with your fingers and then with the tines of a fork. Using the back of a small knife, press into the sealed edges at ½-inch intervals to create a scalloped effect. Transfer the turnovers to a heavy baking sheet and refrigerate for at least 15 minutes.

6. Preheat the oven to 425°. Brush the turnovers with the egg wash and sprinkle them lightly with additional sugar. Using a sharp knife, cut 2 small slits in the top of each turnover to vent steam.

7. Bake the turnovers in the middle of the oven for 12 minutes. Move them to the upper rack and bake for about 8 minutes longer, or until the pastry is deep golden brown and the filling begins to bubble. Let cool on a rack before serving.

—Carl Parisi

ALL-AMERICAN APPLE TURNOVERS

These turnovers are best when made with at least two varieties of firm cooking apples, such as Granny Smith, Jonathan, Winesap and Golden Delicious, for differences in texture and acidity. The sweet spices below are optional. If desired, these turnovers can be frosted with Sugar Glaze (p. 196).

Makes 10 Turnovers

2 tablespoons unsalted butter
3 large apples (about 1½ pounds)— peeled, cored and cut into ¼-inch dice (3 cups)
½ cup apple cider or unsweetened apple juice
2 tablespoons sugar
2 teaspoons fresh lemon juice
Pinch of salt
¼ cup unsweetened apple butter
2 tablespoons dried currants (optional)
1 teaspoon finely grated lemon zest
¼ teaspoon cinnamon (optional)
Pinch of ground cloves (optional)
Pinch of ground allspice (optional)
Cream Cheese Dough (p. 196)
1 egg, beaten with 1 tablespoon water

1. Melt the butter in a large nonreactive skillet over moderately high heat. Add 2 cups of the diced apples and cook, stirring frequently, until they begin to color, about 5 minutes.

2. Stir in the cider, sugar, lemon juice and salt; reduce the heat to moderate and cook until the liquid is reduced and the apples appear almost dry but still retain their shape, about 5 minutes longer.

3. Remove the skillet from the heat and stir in the apple butter, currants, lemon zest, cinnamon, cloves and allspice, along with the remaining 1 cup of raw chopped apple. Transfer the apple mixture to a medium bowl and refrigerate, uncovered, until cooled completely.

4. On a lightly floured work surface, roll out the Cream Cheese Dough to an 18-by-20-inch rectangle, ¹⁄₁₆ inch thick. Using a 6-inch plate or bowl as a guide, cut out eight 6-inch rounds as close together as possible. Gather and reroll the dough scraps, then cut out 2 additional rounds.

5. Spoon the cooled apple filling on the lower half of each of the rounds. Lightly moisten the edges of the rounds with water and fold the dough over the filling to form semicircular turnovers. Press down on the edges to seal, first with your fingers and then with the tines of a fork. Using the back of a small knife, press into the sealed edges at ½-inch intervals to create a scalloped effect. Transfer the turnovers to a heavy baking sheet and refrigerate for at least 15 minutes.

6. Preheat the oven to 425°. Brush the turnovers with the egg wash. Using a sharp knife, cut 2 small slits in the top of each turnover to vent steam.

7. Bake the turnovers in the middle of the oven for 10 minutes. Move them to the upper rack and bake for 8 to 10 minutes longer, or until the pastry is a deep golden brown and the filling begins to bubble. Let cool on a rack.
—*Carl Parisi*

APPLE FRANGIPANE TURNOVERS

Apples and almonds have a natural affinity. With almond paste in the filling and sliced almonds on top, these turnovers taste like a sophisticated flaky French pastry but are much simpler to prepare. If desired, these turnovers can be frosted with Sugar Glaze (p. 196).

Makes 9 Turnovers

3 ounces almond paste
1 tablespoon unsalted butter, softened
1 tablespoon sugar, plus more for sprinkling
1 egg, lightly beaten
1 teaspoon all-purpose flour
1 very large or 2 small firm, tart apples (about ¾ pound)—peeled, quartered, cored and thinly sliced crosswise
1 teaspoon fresh lemon juice
Cream Cheese Dough (p. 196)
1 ounce sliced blanched almonds (generous ⅓ cup)

1. In a small bowl, beat the almond paste with the butter, ½ tablespoon of the sugar, half of the beaten egg and the flour until smooth. Set the frangipane aside.

2. In another bowl, toss the apple slices with the lemon juice and ½ tablespoon of the sugar.

3. On a lightly floured work surface, roll out the Cream Cheese Dough to a 16-inch square, ¹⁄₁₆ inch thick. Using a sharp knife, cut the dough into nine 5-inch squares.

4. Spread the frangipane on a trian-

gular half of each square to within ½ inch of the edge. Press the apple slices into the frangipane. Lightly moisten the edges of each square with water and fold the dough over the filling to form triangles. Press down on the edges to seal, first with your fingers and then with the tines of a fork. Using the back of a small knife, press into the sealed edges at ½-inch intervals to create a scalloped effect. Transfer the turnovers to a heavy baking sheet and refrigerate for at least 15 minutes.

5. Preheat the oven to 425°. Brush the turnovers with some of the remaining beaten egg. Using a sharp knife, cut 2 small slits in the top of each to vent steam. Sprinkle the sliced almonds and additional sugar on top.

6. Bake the turnovers in the middle of the oven for 10 minutes. Move them to the upper rack and bake for 8 to 10 minutes longer, or until the turnovers are deep golden brown. Let cool on a rack.

—Carl Parisi

CREAM CHEESE DOUGH

This is enough dough for nine square or triangular turnovers or 10 semicircular ones.

Makes About 1¼ Pounds

1½ cups all-purpose flour
½ cup cake flour
1 teaspoon sugar
½ teaspoon salt

1½ sticks (12 tablespoons) cold unsalted butter, cut into ½-inch slices
4 ounces cold cream cheese, pinched into small pieces
1 egg yolk, lightly beaten
3 to 4 tablespoons ice water

1. In a food processor, combine the all-purpose and cake flours, sugar and salt and process until blended. Add the butter and cream cheese and pulse 10 to 12 times, until the butter is coated with flour and is the size of small peas.

2. Combine the egg yolk with 3 tablespoons of the ice water. Pour this mixture through the feed tube and continue pulsing several times, until the dough just begins to clump together, but before it forms a ball on the blade. (Use the remaining 1 tablespoon ice water if the dough seems too dry.)

3. Using floured hands, pat the dough into a ball, then press it into a 4-by-6-inch rectangle, about 1½ inches thick. Dust the dough lightly with flour and wrap in wax paper. Refrigerate for at least 30 minutes before rolling out.

—Carl Parisi

SUGAR GLAZE

This glaze can be used on any of the semicircular or triangular turnovers (see recipes, pages 192-195). It should be made shortly before using, since it hardens quickly on contact with air.

Makes Enough Glaze for 10 Turnovers

½ cup confectioners' sugar
¼ teaspoon pure vanilla extract

1. Sift the confectioners' sugar into a small bowl. Sprinkle 2 teaspoons of warm water and the vanilla over the

sugar and stir until smooth. If the glaze seems stiff, add a little more water, drop by drop, until it reaches drizzling consistency.

2. To use the glaze, drizzle it over the cooled turnovers with a fork. Alternatively, scrape the glaze into a sturdy plastic bag; snip off a tiny portion of one corner and use the bag to pipe the glaze decoratively on the turnovers.

—Carl Parisi

TARTE TATIN WITH CINNAMON ICE CREAM

8 Servings

PASTRY DOUGH:

1 cup all-purpose flour
1 tablespoon sugar
1 stick (8 tablespoons) cold unsalted butter, cut into 1-inch pieces
About 3 tablespoons ice water

APPLES:

2 tablespoons unsalted butter
½ cup sugar
2 pounds Granny Smith apples— peeled, cored and cut into eighths

Cinnamon Ice Cream (p. 212)

1. *Make the pastry dough:* In a food processor, pulse the flour and sugar together to combine. Add the butter and pulse until coarse crumbs form. Add the water, 1 tablespoon at a time, pulsing just until the dough comes together. Transfer the dough to a lightly floured surface and gather it into a ball. Pat into a disk, wrap tightly in plastic wrap and refrigerate until chilled, at least 20 minutes.

2. On a lightly floured surface, roll out the dough into a 10-inch circle, about ¼ inch thick. Transfer the dough to a lightly floured baking sheet, cover and refrigerate.

3. *Prepare the apples:* Preheat the oven to 400°. Melt the butter in a 9-inch cast-iron skillet. Add the sugar and cook over moderately high heat, stirring, until a rich brown caramel forms, about 5 minutes. Remove from the heat. Pack the apple pieces in the skillet, rounded-sides down but slightly leaning, in concentric circles.

4. Lay the pastry round on top of the apples, pressing gently to fit it in the pan. Bake the tart for about 35 minutes, or until the pastry is golden brown. Let cool slightly, then carefully invert the pan on a large serving plate. Serve the tart warm or at room temperature accompanied by the Cinnamon Ice Cream.

—Annie Roberts

THE CLAREMONT DINER COCONUT CREAM PIE

This pie is almost like my childhood favorite from The Claremont Diner except that I've eliminated the whipped cream between the filling and the coconut topping.

8 Servings

2⅔ cups sweetened shredded coconut (7 ounces)
3 cups milk
1 envelope (¼ ounce) unflavored gelatin
½ cup sugar
¼ cup cornstarch
1 whole egg
3 egg yolks
2 tablespoons unsalted butter
1 tablespoon pure vanilla extract
Pinch of salt

¾ cup heavy cream, well chilled
Basic Prebaked Pie Shell (recipe follows)

1. Preheat the oven to 350°. Spread half the coconut on a baking sheet and toast in the middle of the oven, stirring once or twice, for about 9 minutes, until golden brown. Watch carefully to prevent burning. Transfer to a wire rack to cool.

2. In a heavy nonreactive saucepan, bring 2⅔ cups of the milk nearly to a boil over moderately high heat.

3. Meanwhile, pour the remaining ⅓ cup cold milk into a medium bowl. Sprinkle the gelatin on top, stir once or twice and set aside to soften for about 5 minutes. Whisk in the sugar, cornstarch, whole egg and egg yolks until well blended. Gradually whisk in a little of the hot milk. Whisk all the gelatin mixture into the hot milk in the saucepan and bring to a boil over moderately high heat. Cook, whisking until very thick, about 2 minutes.

4. Strain the pastry cream into a clean bowl and whisk in the butter, vanilla, salt and the untoasted coconut until incorporated. Set the bowl of hot pastry cream in a larger bowl of ice water and stir frequently until the mixture reaches room temperature.

5. Whip the chilled heavy cream just until stiff and gently fold it into the pastry cream.

6. Pour the filling into the Basic Prebaked Pie Shell, mounding it in the center. Sprinkle the toasted coconut evenly over the top. Refrigerate the pie until the filling has set, for at least 2 and up to 6 hours.

—Richard Sax

BASIC PREBAKED PIE SHELL

Makes One 9-Inch Pie Shell

1⅓ cups unbleached all-purpose flour
1 teaspoon sugar
½ teaspoon salt
3 tablespoons cold unsalted butter, cut into small pieces
4 tablespoons chilled vegetable shortening, cut into small pieces
About 4 tablespoons ice water

1. In a food processor, pulse the flour, sugar and salt to combine. Add the butter and shortening and pulse until coarsely textured.

2. Add 3 tablespoons of the ice water, 1 tablespoon at a time, pulsing briefly after each addition to incorporate. Add 1 more tablespoon of ice water if the dough is too dry and pulse just until the dough barely comes together.

3. Transfer the dough to a lightly floured work surface and gather it into a smooth ball. Flatten the dough into a 6-inch disk, wrap tightly in wax paper and refrigerate until cold, at least 30 minutes. *(The dough can be made up to 1 day ahead. Let the dough soften at room temperature for a few minutes before rolling out.)*

4. Preheat the oven to 350°. On a lightly floured surface, roll the dough out to a 12-inch round. Transfer the dough to a 9-inch pie pan and fit it evenly against the bottom and sides without stretching. Trim the overhang to ½ inch from the rim, then fold the extra dough under and crimp decoratively.

5. Bake the shell for about 35 minutes, until golden brown, pricking any air bubbles with a fork after 10 minutes. Transfer to a wire rack and let cool completely. *(The pie shell can be baked up to 1 day ahead and kept covered at room temperature.)*

—*Richard Sax*

ALMOND-RASPBERRY TART

6 Servings

CRUST:
**1 cup plus 2 tablespoons all-purpose
    flour**
1 teaspoon sugar
⅛ teaspoon salt
**1 stick (8 tablespoons) cold unsalted
    butter, cut into pieces**
¼ cup very cold water

FILLING:
⅓ cup sliced almonds
1 cup whole natural almonds
⅔ cup sugar
¼ teaspoon pure almond extract
**1 stick (8 tablespoons) plus 1
    tablespoon unsalted butter, softened**
3 large eggs
½ cup all-purpose flour
½ cup raspberry preserves

GLAZE:
½ cup raspberry preserves
2 tablespoons sugar

1. *Make the crust:* Preheat the oven to 400°. In a large bowl, toss together the flour, sugar and salt. Using a pas-

try blender or two knives, cut in the butter to form a coarse meal. With a fork, stir in the cold water until the dough forms a ball. Pat the dough into a smooth disk.

2. On a well-floured surface, roll out the dough into a 12-inch round. Roll the dough onto the rolling pin and unroll over a 9-by-1-inch fluted tart pan with a removable bottom. Fit the dough evenly into the pan without stretching, leaving 1 inch of overhanging dough. Fold in the extra dough and press it into the fluted edge, smoothing the top rim. Prick the bottom of the pastry all over with a fork. Freeze until firm, about 10 minutes.

3. Line the pastry with foil and fill with pie weights, dried beans or rice. Bake for 20 minutes, then remove the foil and weights. Bake the crust for another 20 minutes, or until golden and set in the center.

4. *Make the filling:* Spread the sliced almonds on a small baking sheet and toast for about 6 minutes, until golden. Set aside to cool. Spread the whole almonds on the baking sheet and toast for 8 minutes. Let cool.

5. In a food processor, finely grind the whole almonds. Add ⅓ cup of the sugar and the almond extract. Process to blend. Pour in 2 tablespoons of water and process to make a paste.

6. In a large bowl, using an electric mixer, beat the softened butter with the remaining ⅓ cup sugar until fluffy. Beat in the almond paste in 3 additions. Beat in the eggs 1 at a time. Mix in the flour.

7. Spread the raspberry preserves in the bottom of the crust. Spoon the almond filling over the preserves and smooth the surface. Bake for 35 minutes until firm in the center.

8. *Make the glaze:* In a small nonreactive saucepan, stir together the preserves, sugar and 2 tablespoons of water. Bring to a boil and boil gently for 3 minutes. Press through a fine sieve to remove the seeds.

9. Brush some of the warm glaze over the warm tart. Repeat with the remaining glaze 10 minutes later, rewarming the glaze if necessary. Scatter the toasted sliced almonds all over the top of the tart. Let cool completely before serving.

—*Jamie Davies*

PEAR AND CUSTARD TART

This tart tastes best the day it is made, but the pastry shell can be baked a day ahead. Wrap the shell well in foil or plastic wrap and store overnight at room temperature.

8 Servings

1 whole egg
3 egg yolks
½ cup plus 1 tablespoon sugar
1 cup heavy cream
½ cup crème fraîche
¼ teaspoon ground cardamom
Pinch of salt
**1⅔ pounds firm-ripe pears (about
    4)—peeled, halved, cored and
    sliced lengthwise ⅛ inch thick**
Prebaked Tart Shell (recipe follows)

1. Preheat the oven to 325°. In a large bowl, whisk the whole egg, egg yolks and sugar. Whisk in the cream, crème fraîche, cardamom and salt. Set the custard aside.

2. Arrange the sliced pears in a circular pattern in the Prebaked Tart Shell. Carefully and evenly pour the custard over the pears. Bake for about 25 minutes, or until the custard is just set in the center and the surface is lightly golden. Transfer the tart to a rack to cool. Serve at room temperature.

—*Emily Luchetti*

PREBAKED TART SHELL

Makes One 11-Inch Tart Shell

2 cups unbleached all-purpose flour
1½ tablespoons sugar
Pinch of salt
2 sticks (½ pound) cold unsalted butter, cut up
2 tablespoons ice water

1. In a food processor, combine the flour, sugar and salt and pulse to blend. Add the butter and pulse until it is the size of small peas. With the machine on, add the ice water through the feed tube and process until the dough barely begins to form a ball, 25 to 30 seconds. Pat the dough into a disk, wrap in wax paper and refrigerate until firm, at least 30 minutes.

2. On a lightly floured surface, roll out the dough to a 15-inch round. Gently place the dough in an 11-by-1-inch tart pan with a removable bottom, fitting it evenly into the pan without stretching. Trim the overhanging dough to 1 inch, then fold in against the inside of the pan to make a double-thick rim, pressing it even with the top of the pan. With a fork, prick the bottom of the tart shell at 1-inch intervals. Refrigerate the shell for 15 minutes to set.

3. Preheat the oven to 350°. Line the tart shell with parchment paper and fill with pie weights, uncooked rice or dried beans. Bake for about 15 minutes, or until the edges of the shell are golden brown. Remove the paper and weights, reduce the oven temperature to 325° and bake for about 15 minutes

longer, or until the inside of the tart shell is golden brown. (If the tart shell cracks during baking, make a thick paste out of a little flour and water and use it to seal the crack. Place the shell back in the oven for a few minutes to dry the seal.)

—*Emily Luchetti*

FRESH BLUEBERRY TART

Makes One 9-Inch Tart

1 cup all-purpose flour
¼ cup plus 1 tablespoon sugar
1 stick (8 tablespoons) cold unsalted butter, cut into ½-inch pieces
½ teaspoon pure vanilla extract
3 cups blueberries
Confectioners' sugar, for dusting

1. Preheat the oven to 425°. In a food processor, place the flour and ¼ cup of the sugar and process briefly to combine. Add the butter and pulse until the mixture resembles coarse meal. Add the vanilla and process until the dough begins to form a ball, about 1 minute. Transfer the dough to a surface and knead gently to gather into a ball.

2. Crumble the dough into a 9-inch springform pan and press it evenly over the bottom of the pan to the edge. Do not press the dough up the sides.

3. In a bowl, toss the blueberries with the remaining 1 tablespoon sugar. Pour the berries into the pan, mounding them slightly in the center. Bake the tart for about 50 minutes, until bubbly and golden. Transfer to a rack and let cool for at least 30 minutes.

4. Loosen the edge of the tart with a small, sharp knife. Remove the springform. Sift confectioners' sugar over the tart just before serving.

—*Susan Shapiro Jaslove*

BUTTERY APPLE TART

10 to 12 Servings

1⅔ cups all-purpose flour
⅓ cup plus 4 teaspoons sugar
¼ teaspoon salt
1½ sticks (12 tablespoons) cold unsalted butter
3 to 4 tablespoons ice water
4 large Golden Delicious apples (about 1¾ pounds)
2 tablespoons plus 1 teaspoon fresh lemon juice
2 tablespoons apple jelly

1. In a medium bowl, stir together the flour, 4 teaspoons of the sugar and the salt. Cut 1 stick plus 2 tablespoons of the butter into small pieces. Using your fingertips, a pastry blender or 2 knives, cut the butter into the flour until it resembles coarse meal. Drizzle 3 tablespoons of the ice water on top and, using a fork, stir until a piece of the dough just holds together when pinched, adding up to 1 tablespoon more ice water if necessary. Shape the dough into a disk; wrap well and refrigerate for at least 1 hour. *(The dough can be made up to 1 day ahead.)*

2. On a lightly floured surface, roll out the dough into a 13½-inch round. Fit the pastry into an 11-by-1-inch fluted tart pan with a removable bottom, pressing it gently into the pan without stretching. Trim off any overhanging pastry. Using a fork, prick the bottom of the tart shell at 1-inch intervals. Refrigerate the tart shell for 15 minutes to firm up.

3. Preheat the oven to 450°. Peel,

halve and core the apples. Toss them with 2 tablespoons of the lemon juice to prevent discoloring. Place 1 apple half cut-side down on a work surface and cut it crosswise into about 20 thin slices. Using a metal spatula, transfer the apple, without separating the slices, and place it close to the edge of the pastry shell. Repeat with 5 more apple halves. Then, with your fingers, fan each apple toward the center of the tart.

4. Chop the remaining 2 apple halves into ½-inch pieces and sprinkle between the fanned apples to completely cover any exposed dough. Sprinkle the remaining ⅓ cup sugar over the apples. Cut the remaining 2 tablespoons butter into thin slices and scatter over the apples.

5. Bake on the lowest rack of the oven for 45 minutes, or until the crust is golden brown and the apples are tender when pierced with the tip of a sharp knife. If the crust begins to brown too quickly, loosely cover the tart with aluminum foil. Transfer to a rack.

6. In a small nonreactive saucepan, combine the apple jelly and the remaining 1 teaspoon lemon juice. Melt over low heat, stirring, until smooth, 1 to 2 minutes. Brush the warm apple jelly evenly over the apples. Serve the tart warm or at room temperature.

—*Diana Sturgis*

APPLE-ALMOND CUSTARD TART

We often finish a celebratory meal with this sweet and splendid tart, inspired by one in *Simca's Cuisine.* We've used jam made from our own gooseberries instead of apricot jam, and we've also substituted local butternuts for almonds with delicious results.

8 Servings

PASTRY:
1⅓ cups all-purpose flour
⅓ cup cake flour
2 tablespoons sugar
Pinch of salt
1 stick (8 tablespoons) plus 1 tablespoon cold unsalted butter, cut into small pieces
1 egg yolk, beaten with 2 tablespoons cold water

FILLING:
2 large tart cooking apples
½ of a lemon
4 egg yolks
½ cup sugar
Pinch of salt
½ cup ground almonds (3 ounces)
⅓ cup raisins
½ teaspoon cinnamon
⅓ cup apricot jam
3 tablespoons unsalted butter, melted

1. *Prepare the pastry:* Put the all-purpose flour, cake flour, sugar and salt in a food processor and pulse to mix. Add the butter and pulse quickly 6 or 7 times. Pour the beaten egg yolk through the spout and process for 3 seconds. If the dough has not formed a mass, sprinkle in a little water and pulse once. Turn the dough out on a lightly floured work surface and smear the dough out with the heel of your hand, one-third at a time. Gather the dough together, flour it lightly and form it into

a smooth disk. Wrap in plastic wrap and refrigerate until chilled, at least 30 minutes.

2. On a lightly floured surface, roll out the dough to an 11-inch circle. Line a 9½-by-1-inch tart shell with the dough. Prick the dough all over with a fork and freeze the shell until firm, about 20 minutes.

3. Preheat the oven to 350°. Line the tart shell with a sheet of foil and fill it with pie weights or dried beans. Bake the shell for 15 minutes. Remove the foil and weights and bake for about 25 minutes longer, until golden. Let cool slightly. Leave the oven on.

4. *Prepare the filling:* Peel and core the apples and rub them with the lemon. Grate the apples and put them in a strainer to drain.

5. In a large bowl, using an electric mixer, beat the egg yolks. Gradually beat in the sugar and salt; continue beating until the eggs are thick and lemon colored, about 3 minutes. Stir in the grated apples, ground almonds, raisins and cinnamon.

6. Spread the apricot jam in the pastry shell. Fill the shell with the apple mixture and bake for 20 minutes. Increase the heat to 375° and remove the tart from the oven. Prick the top of the filling in several places and pour in the melted butter so that it seeps down. Return the tart to the oven, turn the heat down to 350° and bake for 20 minutes longer, until the filling is set and pale gold around the edge. Let cool on a rack and serve at room temperature. *(The tart can be made 1 day ahead; cover and refrigerate. Rewarm slightly before serving if desired.)*

—*Evan Jones*

BLACK BOTTOM BANANA TART

This is an elegant banana cream pie with a chocolate twist.

8 Servings

3 tablespoons sugar
1 tablespoon all-purpose flour
1 tablespoon cornstarch
3 large egg yolks
1 cup milk
1 teaspoon pure vanilla extract
2 ounces bittersweet or semisweet chocolate, finely chopped
¼ cup heavy cream
Sweet Tart Shell (recipe follows)
4 firm-ripe medium bananas
Melted and strained apricot jam, for glazing
Melted chocolate, for drizzling (optional)

1. In a small bowl, combine the sugar with the flour and cornstarch. Using an electric mixer, beat in the egg yolks until the mixture is pale and thick.

2. Scald the milk in a medium non-reactive saucepan. Gradually whisk the hot milk into the beaten yolks. Wash the saucepan and pour in the custard mixture. Whisk briskly over moderate heat, scraping all over the bottom and sides of the pan, until the custard is hot and thick and has lost its raw taste, about 3 minutes. Strain the custard into a clean bowl. Whisk in the vanilla. Let cool, stirring occasionally to prevent a skin from forming. *(The custard can be made up to 3 days ahead; press a piece of plastic wrap directly over the custard and refrigerate.)*

3. In a small saucepan, melt the chopped chocolate in the heavy cream over moderate heat, stirring until smooth. Let cool to room temperature, stirring occasionally.

4. Pour the chocolate cream into the Sweet Tart Shell, tilting the shell to cover the bottom evenly. Refrigerate for 10 minutes.

5. Slice 3 of the bananas ¼ inch thick. Arrange the slices in the tart shell in concentric circles, overlapping them slightly. Spoon the custard over the bananas and spread gently to cover evenly. Refrigerate the tart for at least 3 hours or up to 6 hours.

6. Shortly before serving, cut the remaining banana on the diagonal into ½-inch slices. Garnish the rim of the tart with the slices. Brush them all over with the apricot jam. If desired, drizzle melted chocolate over the bananas. Remove the tart from the pan and serve.

—*Alice Medrich*

SWEET TART SHELL

Makes One 9-Inch Tart Shell

1 large egg yolk
2 tablespoons sugar
¼ teaspoon pure vanilla extract
1⅓ cups all-purpose flour
⅛ teaspoon salt
1 stick (8 tablespoons) cold unsalted butter, cut up

1. In a small bowl, mix the egg yolk, sugar and vanilla with a fork.

2. In a food processor, pulse the flour with the salt. Add the butter and pulse until the mixture resembles coarse meal. Add the egg yolk mixture and pulse until the dough starts to gather into a mass.

3. Remove the dough and pat gently into a smooth flat disk. Wrap it and refrigerate until firm, about 45 minutes. *(The dough can be refrigerated for up to 2 days or frozen for up to 6 months. Remove the dough from the refrigerator about 15 minutes before rolling out.)*

4. Roll out the dough between 2 sheets of wax paper into a 13-inch round. Remove the top sheet of wax paper and invert the dough over a 9-by-1-inch fluted tart pan with a removable bottom. Peel off the wax paper and ease the dough into the pan without stretching. Run the rolling pin over the rim of the pan to trim off the extra dough. If necessary, patch the sides of the tart shell with excess bits of dough to make an even thickness. (If the pastry becomes too soft to handle at any point, refrigerate until firm.) Prick the shell all over with a fork and freeze for 15 minutes.

5. Preheat the oven to 400°. Bake the tart shell for about 20 minutes, until golden brown. Transfer to a rack to cool thoroughly.

—*Alice Medrich*

THREE-CHEESE TART WITH LEMON CURD AND BERRIES

Makes One 11-Inch Tart

PECAN CRUST:
1½ cups all-purpose flour
½ cup pecans
1 teaspoon sugar
Pinch of salt
1 stick (8 tablespoons) plus 1 tablespoon cold unsalted butter, cut into small pieces
3 to 4 tablespoons ice water

CHEESE FILLING:
8 ounces mascarpone (1 cup), at room temperature
8 ounces cream cheese, at room temperature
3 ounces mild goat cheese, at room temperature
⅓ cup sugar
2 large eggs
2 teaspoons pure vanilla extract
3 tablespoons blackberry or raspberry preserves, warmed

LEMON CURD:
¼ cup plus 3 tablespoons sugar
4 tablespoons unsalted butter
¼ cup fresh lemon juice
1 large egg
½ tablespoon finely grated lemon zest

GARNISH:
2 to 3 cups assorted fresh berries

1. *Make the crust:* In a food processor, pulse the flour, pecans, sugar and salt until the nuts are finely ground. Add the butter and pulse until the mixture resembles small peas. Add 3 tablespoons of the water and pulse just until the dough comes together; add another tablespoon of water by teaspoons if the dough seems dry. Scrape the dough out onto a piece of wax paper and flatten into a disk. Wrap and refrigerate for 20 minutes.

2. With moistened fingers, press the dough evenly into an 11-inch tart pan with a removable bottom. Refrigerate for 20 minutes.

3. Preheat the oven to 375°. Bake the crust for about 40 minutes, until golden brown and cooked through. Let cool. Lower the oven temperature to 350°.

4. *Make the cheese filling:* In a large bowl, combine the mascarpone, cream cheese, goat cheese and sugar. Beat with a hand-held mixer until the cheeses are smooth and creamy. Add the eggs, one at a time, then beat in the vanilla.

5. Brush the bottom of the crust with the blackberry preserves. Spread the cheese filling in the crust and bake for 30 to 35 minutes, until set and just starting to brown on top. Transfer the tart to a rack and let cool completely.

6. *Make the lemon curd:* In a medium nonreactive saucepan, combine the sugar, butter, lemon juice and egg. Whisk constantly over moderate heat until the curd thickens and coats the back of a spoon, about 7 minutes; do not let it boil, or it will curdle. Strain the curd and stir in the lemon zest. Let cool completely.

7. Gently spread the lemon curd over the tart and refrigerate briefly until set. To decorate the top of the tart, cover it completely with berries in any pattern you wish. Serve the tart at room temperature.

—*Mary Novak*

DESSERTS

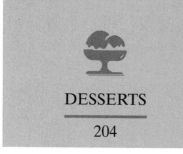

DESERTS

ORANGE TRIFLE

This version of the classic English dessert includes walnuts, almond meringues and orange slices. The separate components can be prepared in stages over a period of several days. Assemble the trifle a day ahead and add the whipped cream shortly before serving.

10 to 12 Servings

4 egg yolks
½ cup granulated sugar
¼ cup all-purpose flour
1 tablespoon cornstarch
2½ cups milk
1 tablespoon (packed) finely grated
*   orange zest*
5 large navel oranges
Almond Meringues (at right)
1 cup chopped walnuts (4 ounces)
Eighteen 3-inch ladyfingers
½ cup seedless raspberry jam
6 tablespoons medium-dry sherry, such
*   as Harveys Bristol Cream*
2 cups cold heavy cream
1 tablespoon confectioners' sugar
2 teaspoons pure vanilla extract

1. In a medium heatproof bowl, whisk the egg yolks with the granulated sugar, flour and cornstarch until thoroughly blended. In a heavy medium saucepan, combine the milk and the orange zest and bring just to a boil over moderate heat. Gradually whisk the boiling milk into the egg mixture.

2. Clean the saucepan and strain the custard into it. Bring to a boil over moderate heat, whisking constantly, about 3 minutes. Reduce the heat to moderately low and cook, whisking constantly, for 2 minutes longer. Pour the custard into a clean bowl and whisk until slightly cooled, about 1 minute. Let cool to room temperature, whisking occasionally to prevent a skin from forming. Cover and refrigerate for at least 2 hours. *(The custard can be made up to 2 days ahead.)*

3. Using a small sharp knife, peel the oranges, making sure to remove all the bitter white pith. Working over a bowl, cut between the membranes to release the sections. You should have 3 cups of orange sections and juice. *(The oranges can be prepared up to 2 days ahead; cover and refrigerate.)*

4. Set aside 12 of the Almond Meringues and ¼ cup of the walnuts for garnish. Spread 1 side of each ladyfinger with the raspberry jam.

5. In a deep 4-quart nonreactive serving bowl, preferably glass, arrange one-third of the ladyfingers in a single layer, jam-side up. Sprinkle 2 tablespoons of the sherry over the ladyfingers. Scatter one-third of the orange sections, with their juice, on top. Scatter one-third of the remaining meringues between the ladyfingers and sprinkle with one-third of the remaining walnuts. Spread one-third of the custard evenly on top. Repeat the layering of ladyfingers, sherry, orange sections, meringues, walnuts and custard 2 more times. Cover the trifle and refrigerate overnight.

6. In a large bowl, whip the heavy cream with the confectioners' sugar and vanilla until stiff. Spread or pipe the whipped cream over the top of the trifle. Refrigerate until serving time. *(The trifle can be prepared to this point up to 4 hours ahead.)*

7. Just before serving, arrange the reserved meringues over the top of the trifle and sprinkle the remaining ¼ cup walnuts on top.

—*Diana Sturgis*

ALMOND MERINGUES

Make these on a dry day, since meringue mixtures do not fare well in humid weather. Stored airtight, the cookies will keep for a week.

Makes About 4½ Dozen
Small Cookies

2 egg whites
½ cup sugar
½ cup ground almonds (see Note)

1. Preheat the oven to 325°. Butter and flour a large baking sheet or line with parchment paper.

2. In a medium bowl, using an electric mixer, beat the egg whites at medium speed until they hold soft peaks. Gradually beat in the sugar until the whites are stiff and glossy. Fold in the ground almonds.

3. Drop rounded ½ teaspoons of the meringue mixture about ½ inch apart on the prepared baking sheet.

4. Place in the oven and reduce the heat to 250°. Bake for about 1 hour, or until the meringues are barely colored and somewhat dry to the touch. Turn the oven off and leave the meringues in until completely dry to the touch.

NOTE: If you are unable to find ground almonds, place 2 ounces (about ½ cup) blanched almonds in a food processor with 1 tablespoon of the sugar called for in the recipe and pulse just until finely ground.

—*Diana Sturgis*

Buttery Apple Tart (p. 199).

**Left, Apple-Almond Custard Tart (p. 200).
Above (left to right), Chocolate Apricot Torte
(p. 180) and Pear and Custard Tart (p. 198).**

FROZEN PEACH SOUFFLE WITH FRESH PEACHES AND PLUM WINE NECTAR

In only three years New York's Aureole has vaulted to the top under the helm of the chef and owner Charles Palmer, who serves what he describes as "American food with a French classical flair." Use the ripest peaches possible for this dessert. For the garnish, slice several peaches just before serving and gently toss them in a bit of lemon juice to keep them from turning brown.

❦ What's needed here is a nice spiciness to complement the ginger and plum and a refreshing acidity to cut the sweetness. The answer is a 1989 Delice du Sémillon from Joseph Phelps Vineyards in Napa.

8 Servings

2¼ pounds peaches, quartered but not peeled, plus sliced fresh peaches for garnish
1¼ teaspoons fresh lemon juice
⅛ teaspoon pure vanilla extract
1 cup sugar
4 egg whites, at room temperature
1 cup mascarpone cheese
Plum Wine Nectar (recipe follows)

1. Line a 2-quart soufflé dish or terrine with plastic wrap, smooth the surface and set aside.

2. In a food processor, puree the peach quarters and 1 teaspoon of the lemon juice until smooth, scraping down the sides of the bowl once or twice. Transfer the puree to a large, heavy, nonreactive saucepan. Stir in the vanilla and bring to a boil over moderate heat. Cover partially and simmer, stirring occasionally, until the puree has reduced by half, about 40 minutes.

3. Using a rubber spatula, press the peach puree through a fine sieve set over a bowl and set aside until cool, about 30 minutes.

4. In a small saucepan, stir together the sugar, the remaining ¼ teaspoon lemon juice and ½ cup of water. Bring to a boil over moderately high heat and cook until the syrup reaches 240° on a candy thermometer and just starts to color, about 7 minutes.

5. In a large bowl, using an electric mixer, beat the egg whites at medium speed until frothy. Increase the speed to high and slowly pour in the hot sugar syrup. Beat the meringue until cool to the touch, about 6 minutes.

6. In a large bowl, using a large rubber spatula, stir the mascarpone cheese gently to soften. Gradually pour in the peach puree, stirring until incorporated. Whisk gently to break up any remaining tiny lumps of mascarpone.

7. Using the spatula, stir about one-fourth of the meringue into the peach mixture to lighten it. Gently fold in the remaining meringue until just blended. Scrape the mixture into the prepared soufflé dish, cover lightly with plastic wrap and freeze for at least 6 hours or overnight.

8. To serve, dip the soufflé dish in several inches of hot water for about 10 seconds to loosen the bottom. Run a thin knife around the inside of the dish and invert the soufflé onto a platter. Peel off the plastic wrap. Cut the soufflé in 8 slices. Garnish with the sliced fresh peaches and the Plum Wine Nectar.

—*Charles Palmer*

Blueberry Turnovers (p. 192) are the perfect ending to a picnic lunch that also includes a colorful Black Bean Salsa (p. 246) and crackers.

DESSERTS

PLUM WINE NECTAR

Makes About 1½ Cups

1 cup Japanese plum wine
½ cup sugar
1½ teaspoons minced fresh ginger

Combine all the ingredients in a medium nonreactive saucepan and bring to a simmer over moderate heat. Cook until slightly reduced, about 5 minutes. Cover and set aside to let the flavors combine for about 10 minutes. Strain through a fine-mesh sieve and let cool completely before serving. *(The recipe can be made up to 4 hours ahead; cover and set aside at room temperature.)*

—*Charles Palmer*

LEMON MOUSSE

4 Servings

1¼ teaspoons unflavored gelatin
2½ tablespoons cold water
3 large egg yolks
3 medium lemons
⅓ cup sugar
¾ teaspoon pure vanilla extract
¾ cup heavy cream, chilled
Safe Meringue (recipe follows)

1. Sprinkle the gelatin over the water in a small cup. Let soften without stirring for at least 5 minutes.

2. Place the egg yolks in a small bowl near the stove to keep warm. Finely grate the zest of 1 lemon. Juice all 3 lemons until you have ½ cup juice.

3. In a small nonreactive sauce-

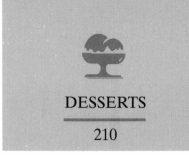
pan, bring the lemon zest, lemon juice and sugar to a simmer. Gradually whisk the hot lemon syrup into the yolks. Pour the mixture back into the saucepan and cook over moderately low heat, whisking constantly to avoid scorching, until it begins to simmer around the edge. Cook, whisking, for 30 seconds more.

4. Strain the hot lemon curd into a large bowl. Whisk in the gelatin and the vanilla. Set the bowl in a larger bowl of ice water and stir until cool. Remove from the ice water.

5. Using an electric mixer, beat the heavy cream until it holds its shape. Fold half of the cooled lemon curd into the Safe Meringue. Scrape the mixture on top of the remaining lemon curd, add the whipped cream and fold it all together. Use immediately.

—*Alice Medrich*

SAFE MERINGUE

I've come up with a simple technique that employs the microwave oven to take the risk out of using uncooked meringue. The egg whites are heated in stages until they reach 160°—the temperature at which salmonella bacteria are destroyed—and then beaten to a stable, creamy meringue.

Near the microwave oven, have ready a hand-held mixer, an instant-read or microwave thermometer (available in cookware and hardware stores), a medium strainer set over a 6- to 8-cup bowl, a fork and a cup of boiling water.

Makes About 1 Cup

⅜ teaspoon cream of tartar
1 tablespoon water
⅓ cup sugar
3 large egg whites

1. In a small microwavable bowl, dissolve the cream of tartar in the water. Stir in the sugar and the egg whites. Using the hand-held electric mixer, beat at high speed for 15 seconds just to homogenize the ingredients and break up clots. Let the mixture sit for 10 minutes or longer to dissolve the sugar and let the foam settle. (The cream of tartar, water and sugar protect the egg whites from actually cooking during the heating process.)

2. Whisk the mixture briefly with the fork; dip the fork in the boiling water for a few seconds and set aside. Microwave the whites on HIGH for exactly 40 seconds. Remove from the oven; beat with the fork to break up the foam. Return to the oven and microwave on HIGH for 20 seconds more. Meanwhile dip the fork in the boiling water again. Remove the egg whites and stir again. Tilt the bowl and insert the thermometer so that at least 2½ inches of the stem is immersed. If the mixture has reached at least 160°, skip to Step 3 now. If the mixture is under 160°, return it to the oven for additional 10-second intervals, dipping the fork and thermometer in boiling water before each round. Stir the mixture well to even out the hot and cool spots before reading the temperature.

3. Pour the hot egg white mixture into the strainer set over a bowl. There may be lots of foam. Rap the strainer down sharply several times against the bowl until the foam passes through. Discard the tiny bits of overcooked egg white left in the strainer. Using an electric mixer, beat the whites at high speed for 4 minutes until glossy, stiff and com-

pletely cool. The meringue is stable enough to hold for 15 minutes or longer; it remains creamy and easy to fold without weeping or deflating.

—*Alice Medrich*

BAKED PUMPKIN AND BUTTERMILK PUDDING

Bake this pudding in a pretty oven-to-table serving dish.

8 Servings

*1½ cups canned unsweetened
  pumpkin puree*
2½ cups buttermilk
*¾ cup plus 1 tablespoon granulated
  sugar*
½ cup brown sugar
*5 tablespoons unsalted butter, melted
  and slightly cooled*
3 eggs, beaten
1½ cups all-purpose flour
1½ teaspoons baking soda
1½ teaspoons baking powder
1 teaspoon cinnamon
1 teaspoon freshly grated nutmeg
½ teaspoon salt
Sweetened whipped cream, for serving

1. Preheat the oven to 450°. Lightly butter a shallow 9-by-13-inch baking dish.

2. In a large bowl, combine the pumpkin and buttermilk and beat until smooth. Stir in ¾ cup of the granulated sugar, the brown sugar and 4 tablespoons of the melted butter. Add the eggs and mix until blended.

3. Sift together the flour, baking soda, baking powder, cinnamon, nutmeg and salt. Add the dry ingredients to the pumpkin mixture a little at a time, whisking lightly but thoroughly after each addition.

4. Pour the batter into the prepared baking dish and place the dish in a large roasting pan. Add enough hot water to the pan to reach halfway up the sides of the dish. Bake in the center of the oven for 15 minutes. Reduce the oven temperature to 350° and bake for 25 to 30 minutes longer, until a toothpick inserted in the center comes out clean.

5. Remove the pudding from the oven. Brush with the remaining 1 tablespoon melted butter and sprinkle the remaining 1 tablespoon granulated sugar on top. Serve warm, with sweetened whipped cream.

—Larry Forgione

SWEET POTATO CUSTARD WITH A BROWN SUGAR CRUST

For a thin, crisp, evenly caramelized crust, dry the brown sugar overnight. It will be easier to sprinkle and less likely to form clumps.

12 Servings

¼ cup light brown sugar
1 large sweet potato (about ½ pound)
9 egg yolks
½ cup granulated sugar
½ cup half-and-half
Half a vanilla bean, split
2½ cups heavy cream
Pinch of cinnamon

1. Sprinkle the brown sugar evenly on a plate. Let stand uncovered overnight to dry. In a food processor, grind the dried brown sugar until fine and set aside. (*The brown sugar can be prepared 1 month ahead and kept in an airtight container.*)

2. Preheat the oven to 400°. Bake the sweet potato for 1 hour, until tender. Let cool, then peel it. Place the potato in a food mill or ricer set over a bowl and puree it. Measure out ½ cup

of the puree; reserve any remaining puree for another use. (*The potato puree can be made up to 1 day ahead; cover and refrigerate. Return to room temperature and proceed.*) Reduce the oven temperature to 300°.

3. In a medium bowl, using an electric mixer, beat the egg yolks and granulated sugar until pale and thick, about 4 minutes.

4. In a heavy medium saucepan, bring the half-and-half and vanilla bean to a boil over moderate heat. Gradually whisk the hot liquid into the beaten egg yolks. Strain the custard into a medium bowl and whisk in the heavy cream, cinnamon and potato puree.

5. Pour the custard into a 10-inch ceramic quiche dish set in a jelly-roll pan. Pour enough hot water into the pan to reach halfway up the sides of the quiche dish. Bake for about 35 minutes, until the custard is just set but still wobbly to the touch. Do not let the top brown.

6. Remove the quiche dish from the water bath and let cool to room temperature. Refrigerate until cold, at least 3 hours or overnight.

7. Preheat the broiler. Sprinkle the dried brown sugar evenly over the top of the custard. Broil for about 1 minute, until the sugar is lightly caramelized. Serve at once.

—Gerry Klaskala

CHOCOLATE CUSTARDS

6 Servings

1 cup heavy cream
1 cup milk
1 vanilla bean, split, or 1½ teaspoons pure vanilla extract
4 ounces semisweet chocolate, coarsely chopped
2 whole eggs

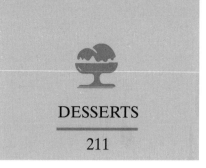
2 egg yolks
⅓ cup sugar

1. In a heavy medium saucepan, bring the heavy cream, milk and vanilla bean to a simmer over moderate heat. Set aside to steep for 30 minutes. Omit this step if using vanilla extract.

2. Return the mixture to a simmer. Remove from the heat and whisk in the chocolate until smooth.

3. In a medium bowl, whisk the whole eggs, egg yolks and sugar. Slowly whisk in the chocolate mixture; stir in the vanilla extract if using. Strain the mixture through a coarse sieve.

4. Preheat the oven to 300°. Place six ⅔-cup custard cups in a shallow baking dish. Fill each cup about ¾ full with the chocolate cream. Place the pan in the center of the oven and carefully pour in hot water to reach about halfway up the custard cups.

5. Bake for 25 to 30 minutes, until the custards are set but still slightly wobbly in the center and the temperature reads 160° on an instant-read thermometer. Remove the custards from the water bath and let cool to room temperature on a wire rack. Refrigerate the custards for at least 2 hours before serving.

—Richard Sax

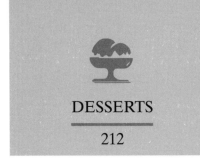

DESSERTS

CHOCOLATE ICE CREAM

Makes About 5 Cups

**4 ounces semisweet chocolate, coarsely
  chopped**
**1 ounce unsweetened chocolate,
  coarsely chopped**
2 cups heavy cream
1 cup half-and-half
¾ cup sugar
6 large egg yolks
1 teaspoon pure vanilla extract

1. In a large bowl set over a medium saucepan with 1 inch of simmering water, melt the semisweet and unsweetened chocolates, stirring until smooth. Set aside to cool.

2. In a medium saucepan, combine the heavy cream, half-and-half and sugar. Cook over moderate heat, stirring occasionally, until the mixture is hot and the sugar has dissolved, 5 to 6 minutes.

3. In a large bowl, whisk the egg yolks to break them up. Gradually whisk the hot cream into the eggs. Return the mixture to the saucepan and cook over moderate heat, stirring constantly, until the custard coats the back of a spoon and reaches 170° on a candy thermometer, 1 to 2 minutes. Gradually whisk the custard into the melted chocolate, strain into a bowl and stir in the vanilla. Refrigerate until cold, about 3 hours.

4. Freeze the ice cream in 2 batches: Pour half of the custard into an ice cream maker and freeze according to the manufacturer's instructions. Transfer the ice cream to a chilled container, cover and freeze until firm, at least 4 hours or for up to 4 days. Repeat with the remaining custard.

—*Lindsey Shere*

CINNAMON ICE CREAM

Makes About 5 Cups

3 cups heavy cream
¾ cup milk
1 cup sugar
1 teaspoon cinnamon
5 egg yolks

1. In a medium saucepan, combine the cream, milk, sugar and cinnamon and cook, stirring occasionally, until heated through.

2. In a large bowl, whisk the egg yolks. Gradually whisk in half of the hot cream mixture to temper the yolks, then whisk the mixture back into the saucepan. Cook over moderate heat, stirring constantly with a wooden spoon, until the mixture thickens and coats the back of the spoon, about 5 minutes; do not boil or the custard will curdle (an instant-read thermometer dipped in the custard should register 170°).

3. Strain the custard into a medium bowl and let cool. Cover and refrigerate until chilled.

4. Freeze the custard in an ice cream maker according to the manufacturer's instructions. *(The cinnamon ice cream can be made up to 2 days ahead and kept frozen.)*

—*Annie Roberts*

PECAN ICE CREAM

Makes About 1 Quart

1 cup pecan halves (3 ounces)
2 cups milk
1 vanilla bean, split
⅔ cup sugar
6 egg yolks
Ice water
**¾ cup cold heavy cream or crème
  fraîche**

1. Preheat the oven to 400°. Spread the pecans on a baking sheet and toast in the middle of the oven for about 5 minutes, until fragrant and golden brown. Chop coarsely and set aside.

2. In a medium saucepan, combine the milk, pecans and vanilla bean and bring to a boil over moderate heat. Remove from the heat, cover and set aside to infuse for 15 minutes.

3. Meanwhile, in a medium bowl, using an electric mixer, beat the sugar into the egg yolks until the yolks thicken and lighten in color, about 3 minutes.

4. Return the milk mixture to a boil over moderate heat. Slowly pour the milk through a strainer into the egg yolk mixture, whisking occasionally. Discard the pecans and vanilla bean, or save for another use.

5. Pour the custard into the saucepan and cook over moderately low heat, stirring constantly with a wooden spoon and scraping the sides and bottom of the pan to prevent scorching, until the custard thickens and reaches 175° on a candy thermometer; do not boil. Immediately set the saucepan in a bowl of ice water. Stir in the heavy cream until thoroughly incorporated. Chill in the ice-water bath, stirring, for about 30 minutes. Pour the custard into an ice cream maker and freeze according to the manufacturer's instructions.

—*Stephan Pyles*

ROASTED BANANA ICE CREAM

Campton Place in San Francisco celebrates American regional cooking, and the pastry chef Sherry Yard developed this recipe as part of her update on the classic ice cream sandwich. The banana is baked in its skin to retain its natural juices and enhance its flavor. Although she serves the ice cream between slices of walnut cake in a ring of caramel walnut sauce with zigzags of piped chocolate, it is delicious on its own or as a sundae sprinkled with walnuts and any warm topping.

Makes About 2 Quarts

4 large bananas (about 2 pounds), 3
*   unpeeled, 1 peeled and coarsely*
*   chopped*
2 cups milk
2 cups heavy cream
1 cup sugar
8 egg yolks
1 tablespoon rum

1. Preheat the oven to 350°. Using a small sharp knife, make 6 holes in each of the 3 unpeeled bananas and place them on a small baking sheet. Roast for 10 minutes, until black and split. Let cool, then peel and coarsely chop.

2. In a medium, nonreactive, saucepan, stir together the milk, cream and sugar. Add the roasted bananas and simmer over moderate heat for about 8 minutes.

3. In a large bowl, whisk the egg yolks to break them up. Whisk in half of the hot milk and cream, then whisk the mixture into the saucepan to blend. Cook over moderate heat, stirring constantly with a wooden spoon, until the custard thickens and reaches 185°, about 4 minutes; do not boil. Remove from the heat. Stir in the uncooked banana along with the rum.

4. In a blender, puree the custard in 2 batches and transfer to a large stainless steel bowl. Let cool, then cover and refrigerate for at least 2 hours or overnight. (Alternatively, set the bowl in a larger bowl of ice and chill, stirring occasionally, about 45 minutes.)

5. Working in 2 batches, transfer the custard to an ice cream maker and freeze according to the manufacturer's instructions. *(The ice cream will keep for up to 5 days; freeze in an airtight container.)*

—Sherry Yard

PLUM ICE CREAM

Makes About 2 Quarts

1 pound Santa Rosa or other tart
*   plums, quartered and pitted*
¼ cup water
2 cups heavy cream
1 cup half-and-half
1 cup sugar
6 large egg yolks
¼ teaspoon pure vanilla extract

1. In a medium nonreactive saucepan, combine the plums and water. Cover and cook over moderately low heat, stirring occasionally, until the plums are very tender, 15 to 18 minutes. Transfer to a food processor or blender and puree, then strain into a large bowl.

2. In another medium saucepan, cook the heavy cream, half-and-half and sugar over moderate heat, stirring occasionally, until the mixture is hot and the sugar dissolves, 5 to 6 minutes.

3. In a large bowl, whisk the egg yolks to break them up. Gradually whisk in the hot cream, then return the mixture to the saucepan. Cook over moderate heat, stirring constantly, until the custard coats the back of a spoon

and reaches 170° on a candy thermometer, 1 to 2 minutes.

4. Strain the custard into the plum puree, stir in the vanilla and refrigerate until cold, about 3 hours.

5. Freeze the ice cream in 2 batches: Pour half of the custard into an ice cream maker and freeze according to the manufacturer's instructions. Transfer to a chilled container, cover and freeze until firm, at least 4 hours or for up to 4 days. Repeat with the remaining custard.

—Lindsey Shere

ORANGE, LEMON AND BANANA SHERBET

Makes About 1½ Quarts

1½ cups sugar
¾ cup water
3 medium bananas
⅔ cup fresh lemon juice
2½ cups fresh orange juice (from
*   about 8 oranges)*

1. In a small saucepan, combine the sugar and water and bring to a boil. Continue cooking until the syrup is clear, 1 to 2 minutes. Let cool.

2. In a large nonmetallic bowl, mash the bananas until smooth, gradually pouring in the lemon juice. Stir in the orange juice and then the cooled sugar syrup. Refrigerate until cold, at least 1 hour.

3. Freeze half of the mixture at a time in an ice cream maker according to the manufacturer's instructions. Transfer the sherbet to a plastic con-

tainer and freeze for up to 3 days. Let soften in the refrigerator for about 30 minutes before serving.

—*Camille Glenn*

RED WINE-RASPBERRY SHERBET

Serve this sherbet with sweetened mixed berries, sliced peaches or a scoop of vanilla ice cream.

4 Servings

2½ cups water
2 cups fruity red wine, such as red Zinfandel or Beaujolais
¾ cup plus 2 tablespoons sugar
½ pint raspberries

1. In a medium nonreactive saucepan, bring the water, wine and sugar to a boil over moderately high heat. Lower the heat and gently simmer until the liquid is reduced to 3 cups, about 20 minutes.

2. Transfer the wine syrup to a large bowl and stir in the raspberries. Let cool, then cover and macerate in the refrigerator for at least 3 hours or overnight.

3. Using a slotted spoon, transfer the raspberries to a food processor and puree. Strain the puree into the macerating liquid and stir to combine. Pour into an ice cream maker and freeze according to the manufacturer's instructions. Serve the sherbet at once or transfer to a chilled container, cover tightly and freeze for up to 3 days.

—*Lindsey Shere*

VANILLA ICE CREAM WITH COFFEE GRANITA AND CANDIED ORANGE

8 Servings

COFFEE GRANITA:
¾ cup hot brewed espresso or strong coffee
3 tablespoons granulated sugar
¾ cup water

VANILLA ICE CREAM:
2 cups heavy cream
1 cup half-and-half
⅔ cup granulated sugar
½ of a vanilla bean
6 large egg yolks
½ teaspoon pure vanilla extract

ASSEMBLY:
½ cup heavy cream
1 tablespoon confectioners' sugar
½ teaspoon pure vanilla extract
1 tablespoon finely chopped candied orange peel, for garnish*
**Available at specialty food stores*

1. *Make the coffee granita:* In a medium bowl, stir the hot coffee with the sugar until the sugar dissolves. Stir in the water and let cool to room temperature. Cover and freeze until solid, at least 6 hours or overnight.

2. Dip the bottom of the bowl in hot water and quickly turn the coffee ice out onto a chopping board. Finely chop the ice into a granular slush, then return it to the bowl. Cover and return to the freezer for up to 4 days.

3. *Make the vanilla ice cream:* In a medium saucepan, combine the cream, half-and-half and sugar. Scrape the seeds from the vanilla bean half into the saucepan and add the bean. Cook over moderate heat, stirring occasionally, until the cream is hot and the sugar dissolves, 5 to 6 minutes.

4. In a large bowl, whisk the egg yolks to break them up. Gradually whisk in the hot cream, then return the mixture to the saucepan. Cook over moderate heat, stirring constantly, until the custard lightly coats the back of a spoon and reaches 170° on a candy thermometer, 1 to 2 minutes.

5. Strain the custard into a bowl and add the vanilla bean and vanilla extract. Refrigerate the custard until cold, at least 2 hours.

6. Remove the vanilla bean. Pour the custard into an ice cream maker and freeze according to the manufacturer's instructions. Transfer the ice cream to a chilled container, cover and freeze until firm, at least 4 hours or for up to 4 days.

7. *Assemble the dessert:* In a medium bowl, using an electric mixer, whip the heavy cream with the confectioners' sugar until soft peaks form. Beat in the vanilla extract.

8. Scoop the vanilla ice cream into 8 bowls. Break up the granita crystals with a fork and sprinkle about ¼ cup over each bowl of ice cream. Top with a dollop of whipped cream, sprinkle with the chopped candied orange peel and serve.

—*Lindsey Shere*

GINGERSNAP-PLUM ICE CREAM SANDWICHES

This recipe doesn't use quite all of the Plum Ice Cream recipe. There may be as much as 2 cups left over.

Makes About 30 Sandwiches

1½ sticks (12 tablespoons) unsalted butter, softened
1 cup sugar
¼ cup unsulphured molasses
1 large egg
½ teaspoon pure vanilla extract

2 cups all-purpose flour
1¾ teaspoons baking soda
¾ teaspoon cinnamon
¾ teaspoon ground ginger
½ teaspoon salt
Plum Ice Cream (p. 213)

1. In a large bowl, using an electric mixer, beat the butter on high speed until fluffy. Add ¾ cup plus 2 tablespoons of the sugar, and beat until light. On low speed, beat in the molasses, egg and vanilla.

2. In a medium bowl, sift the flour with the baking soda, cinnamon, ginger and salt. Stir the dry ingredients into the butter mixture just until blended.

3. Divide the dough in half and place each half on a large piece of parchment or wax paper. Wrap the dough and shape each package into a log about 8 by 1¾ inches. Refrigerate until firm, at least 3 hours or overnight. If the rolls have flattened, reshape them and freeze until firm.

4. Preheat the oven to 350°. Unwrap the dough and cut each log into scant ¼-inch slices. Arrange the slices about 1 inch apart on 2 large baking sheets. Sprinkle the tops lightly with the remaining 2 tablespoons sugar and bake for about 15 minutes, or until golden brown and sunken. Transfer the cookies to wire racks to cool.

5. To assemble the sandwiches, arrange 6 of the gingersnaps, bottom-side up, on a work surface. Scoop about 2 tablespoons of the Plum Ice Cream onto each gingersnap and top with a right-side-up cookie. Transfer the assembled sandwiches to a serving platter and store in the freezer; repeat with the remaining cookies and ice cream.

6. Serve the ice cream sandwiches at once or wrap them in parchment or wax paper and freeze for up to 3 days.

—Lindsey Shere

MOCHA-CHOCOLATE FLOAT

Make the chocolate ice cream at least one day ahead to be sure that it will be firm enough.

8 Servings

1½ cups strong brewed coffee
1 cup sugar
About 2 quarts chilled club soda or sparkling water
1 cup cold heavy cream
Chocolate Ice Cream (p. 212)

1. In a medium nonreactive saucepan, bring the coffee and sugar to a boil over moderately high heat. Reduce the heat and simmer for 5 minutes. Remove the syrup from the heat and let cool to room temperature, then cover and refrigerate until cold, about 1 hour. (The coffee syrup can be refrigerated for up to 1 week.)

2. For each serving, mix ¾ cup of the club soda, 2 tablespoons of the heavy cream and 3 tablespoons of the coffee syrup in a tall glass. Gently add ½ cup of the Chocolate Ice Cream in scoops, adding up to ¼ cup more seltzer if desired. Serve with a straw.

—Lindsey Shere

STRAWBERRY SALAD WITH LEMON-PEPPER PETALS

The wafers serve as little scoops for the salad. For best results, avoid baking them in humid weather because they won't stay crisp.

6 Servings

LEMON-PEPPER COOKIES:
4 tablespoons unsalted butter, very soft
¼ cup plus 2 teaspoons superfine sugar
2 large egg whites, at room temperature

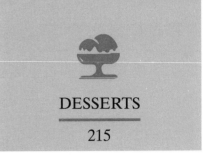

½ cup all-purpose flour, sifted
2 tablespoons grated lemon zest
2 teaspoons strained fresh lemon juice
Scant teaspoon freshly ground pepper

STRAWBERRY SALAD:
2 tablespoons strained fresh lemon juice
4 teaspoons superfine sugar
¾ teaspoon pure almond extract
2 pints ripe strawberries—rinsed, patted dry and hulled
Fresh mint sprigs, for garnish
Julienne strips of lemon zest, for garnish

1. Make the cookies: Preheat the oven to 350°. In a medium bowl, beat the butter and sugar until light and fluffy.

2. In a small heatproof bowl or double boiler over simmering water, break up the egg whites with your finger or a fork and stir until slightly warm to the touch. Whisk the whites into the butter mixture thoroughly in four additions. With a few quick strokes, whisk in the flour, lemon zest, lemon juice and pepper.

3. Lightly butter and flour a large cookie sheet. Drop teaspoons of the batter 2 inches apart on the prepared sheet in 3 rows of three. Moving the tip of your finger in a circular motion, spread each dollop of batter into a thin 2¼-inch round. Bake for about 10 minutes, until the edges are brown and the centers are golden.

4. Open the oven door and rest the cookie sheet on the door. (The warmth of the oven will keep the cookies pliable while you're working.) Hold a

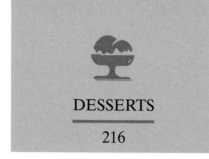

DESSERTS

sturdy cotton kitchen towel in one hand. Using a metal spatula, transfer a cookie to the towel-covered hand. Using your fingers, pinch part of the edge of the cookie together, then tilt the rounded edge back a little to form a rose petal. Set aside and continue quickly with the remaining cookies. Repeat the procedure with the remaining batter in 3 more batches. *(The cookies can be made 1 day ahead; store in an airtight container.)*

5. *Make the salad:* In a large bowl, whisk the lemon juice, sugar and almond extract. Halve or quarter the strawberries, add to the syrup and toss. Refrigerate for at least 30 minutes or up to 2 hours.

6. Spoon the strawberries onto 6 large dessert plates. Arrange 5 petal cookies around each portion. Garnish with the mint and lemon zest.

—*Peggy Cullen*

PEACHES WITH HONEY ZABAGLIONE

For this recipe, use the same wine you will be drinking. Both the dessert and the wine leave a light impression.

6 Servings

2 tablespoons whole natural almonds
4 large egg yolks
1½ tablespoons strongly flavored honey, such as wildflower
⅓ cup ice wine or other sweet Riesling
½ of a vanilla bean, split
½ cup heavy cream
3 large peaches, preferably freestone

1. Preheat the oven to 350°. Spread the almonds on a baking sheet and roast for 10 to 12 minutes, until fragrant. Transfer the nuts to a work surface to cool, then coarsely chop.

2. In a medium heatproof bowl or double boiler, whisk the yolks and honey. Gradually whisk in the wine until incorporated. Scrape down the sides of the bowl with a rubber spatula. Cook over simmering water, whisking constantly, until the mixture is pale, thick and holds a ribbon for 10 seconds (175° on a candy thermometer). Remove the zabaglione from the heat and whisk for 2 minutes to cool slightly; refrigerate. *(The recipe can be made to this point up to 3 hours ahead.)*

3. Using the tip of a small knife, scrape the seeds from the vanilla bean into a medium bowl. Stir in the heavy cream and whisk to soft peaks. Gently fold the whipped cream into the zabaglione. Refrigerate for at least 1 or up to 4 hours.

4. Halve and pit the peaches. Cut each half into 8 slices and arrange in a fan pattern on 6 dessert plates. Spoon about ⅓ cup of the zabaglione at the base of each fan and sprinkle the almonds over the zabaglione.

—*Peggy Cullen*

FIGS IN SNOW

6 Servings

4 cups milk
1 cup sugar
16 large fresh spearmint leaves plus 2 teaspoons finely chopped spearmint and 6 fresh sprigs, for garnish
4 large eggs, unshelled and at room temperature
Pinch of cream of tartar
2 tablespoons water

12 ripe medium figs, stemmed and cut into bite-size wedges
Cognac (optional), for serving

1. In a medium saucepan, combine the milk, ¾ cup of the sugar and the 16 spearmint leaves and bring just to a boil, stirring occasionally, over moderate heat. Remove from the heat, cover and let steep for 30 minutes. Refrigerate until thoroughly chilled, about 2 hours.

2. In a large bowl, cover the eggs with hot but not boiling water and warm them for 5 minutes. Separate the eggs and transfer the whites to a large bowl; reserve the yolks for another use. Using an electric mixer, beat the whites until foamy. Add the cream of tartar and beat until soft peaks form. Set aside in a draft-free area.

3. Strain the milk mixture into a medium bowl; discard the mint. In a small saucepan, stir together the remaining ¼ cup sugar and the water. Boil over moderately high heat until the mixture reaches 240° on a candy thermometer, about 5 minutes. Immediately beat the syrup into the whites in a thin steady stream. Continue beating until cool, then slowly beat in the milk mixture. Pour into an ice cream maker and freeze according to the manufacturer's instructions. Transfer to a chilled container and fold in the chopped spearmint. Cover and freeze until firm, at least 1 hour or for up to 2 days.

4. In a medium bowl, toss the figs with a sprinkle of Cognac, if desired. Scoop the mint-flavored ice milk into 6 parfait glasses or bowls and arrange the figs on top. Garnish with sprigs of spearmint and serve.

—*Lindsey Shere*

PEARS WITH DRIED CHERRIES AND STILTON

❦ Sweet reds, such as Graham's Six Grapes Porto or Warre's Warrior Porto

6 Servings

¼ cup red port
1 tablespoon sugar
½ cup dried cherries (2½ ounces)
3 ripe Bosc pears
*1½ cups crumbled Stilton cheese
    (5 ounces)*

1. In a small nonreactive saucepan, bring the port, sugar and ½ cup of water to a boil over moderately high heat. Remove from the heat and add the cherries. Set aside to plump for at least 2 hours or overnight.

2. Strain the cherries. Return the liquid to the saucepan and simmer gently over moderately high heat until reduced slightly, 5 to 8 minutes. Remove from the heat and return the cherries to the syrup.

3. Meanwhile, quarter the pears lengthwise and core them. Thinly slice each quarter lengthwise, leaving the slices attached at the stem end. Fan out 2 pear quarters on each plate. Spoon about 1½ tablespoons of the cherries and cherry sauce and ¼ cup of cheese over each portion.

—*Peggy Cullen*

SPICED RED WINE FRUIT SOUP WITH CANDIED ORANGE

This elegant dessert offers a change from the traditional cakes and pies of the holiday season.

6 to 8 Servings

1 small pineapple
*8 small thin-skinned seedless oranges
    or tangerines (see Note)*
About 1¼ cups sugar
Half a vanilla bean, split
1 star anise pod
2 tablespoons orange liqueur
3 medium pears, such as Bartlett
4 cups dry red wine
*Bouquet garni made with 12 fresh mint
    leaves or 2 teaspoons high-quality
    peppermint tea leaves, 1 cinnamon
    stick, 1 teaspoon whole black
    peppercorns and ½ teaspoon
    cardamom seeds tied in
    cheesecloth*
*1 tablespoon plus 1 teaspoon
    cornstarch*
½ cup crème fraîche
About ¼ cup heavy cream
Fresh mint leaves, for garnish

1. Using a large sharp knife, trim off the top and bottom of the pineapple and slice off the skin. Using the tip of a vegetable peeler, remove the eyes. Quarter the pineapple lengthwise and core it. Slice each quarter crosswise ½ inch thick, then cut enough slices into bite-size pieces to make 1 cup. Reserve the rest of the pineapple for another use.

2. In a large saucepan of simmering water, scald the oranges for 5 seconds. Refresh under cold running water and pat dry. Pick out the orange with the nicest skin. Using a sharp knife, cut it crosswise into very thin slices, saving any juices. Using a vegetable peeler, strip the zest from 3 of the remaining oranges and cut it into very thin strips; set aside.

3. Juice the 3 zested oranges. Add enough water to make 1¼ cups and pour into a medium nonreactive saucepan. Stir in the 1¼ cups sugar and the orange slices and their juices. Scrape the seeds out of the vanilla bean with the tip of a knife and set aside. Add the

bean and star anise pod to the saucepan and bring to a simmer over high heat, stirring to dissolve the sugar. Cover, reduce the heat to low and simmer very gently until the white of the orange slices begins to turn translucent and the syrup takes on a rich amber color, about 1 hour. Add a few tablespoons of water if the syrup thickens too much before the slices are translucent. Strain the syrup and add enough water to make ¾ cup. Reserve the orange slices and orange syrup separately; discard the star anise and vanilla bean.

4. While the orange slices are cooking, using a small sharp knife, peel the remaining 4 oranges, removing all the bitter white pith. Working over a nonreactive bowl, cut in between the membranes to release the orange sections. Squeeze the membranes to extract all the juice. Add the cut pineapple and orange liqueur. Set aside to macerate until ready to assemble the soup.

5. Peel, halve and core the pears. Slice them crosswise ⅓ inch thick.

6. In another medium nonreactive saucepan, boil the red wine over high heat until reduced to 2½ cups, about 12 minutes. Stir in the reserved orange syrup and orange zest and the bouquet garni. Bring to a simmer over moderately low heat. Add the pears and poach until wine colored and tender when pierced with a knife, about 5 minutes. Using a slotted spoon, transfer the pears to a plate to cool.

7. If desired, add another teaspoon or so of sugar to the wine mixture. Dissolve the cornstarch in 2 tablespoons of water and whisk into the wine. Return

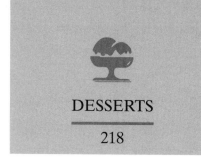

to a boil over high heat and boil for 1 minute to thicken. Pour the soup into another nonreactive container and let cool slightly; then refrigerate to cool completely. Squeeze the bouquet garni gently and discard.

8. In a food processor, puree the reserved candied orange slices and vanilla bean seeds. Add the crème fraîche and blend. Thin with the heavy cream to a semiliquid consistency.

9. To assemble the soup: Place the poached pear slices in chilled shallow bowls. Scatter the orange sections and pineapple pieces evenly on top. Ladle ¼ cup of the soup over each serving. Place a dollop of the crème fraîche mixture in the center of each bowl and garnish with a mint leaf.

NOTE: If you buy organic oranges or tangerines, you need not follow the scalding procedure in Step 2.

—Christopher Kump

PEACH FRAPPE

If you're using large ice cubes, use two heaping cups.

2 Servings

2 medium peaches (about 5 ounces each), peeled and sliced
2 cups small ice cubes (about 7 ounces)
1 tablespoon plus 1 teaspoon sugar
⅔ cup cold milk
⅛ teaspoon pure vanilla extract

In a blender, combine the peach slices, ice, sugar, milk and vanilla. Begin blending at low speed, then increase to high speed and blend until smooth and thick, 30 to 40 seconds. Pour into 2 tall glasses and serve immediately with straws.

—Lindsey Shere

PAN-ROASTED PEACHES AND BLACKBERRIES WITH GINGER AND CARAMEL ICE CREAM

4 Servings

ICE CREAM:
7 egg yolks
¾ cup plus 2 tablespoons sugar
1-inch piece of fresh ginger, peeled and thinly sliced
2 cups cold heavy cream
2 cups cold milk

CANDIED GINGER:
2-inch piece of fresh ginger—peeled, thinly sliced and cut into thin matchsticks
¼ cup sugar

ROASTED PEACHES AND BLACKBERRIES:
6 firm-ripe peaches
1 tablespoon unsalted butter
1 tablespoon sugar
1-inch piece of fresh ginger, peeled and thinly sliced
1 pint blackberries

1. *Prepare the ice cream:* In a large heatproof bowl, beat the egg yolks with 1 tablespoon of the sugar until foamy.

2. In a large saucepan, combine the remaining ¾ cup plus 1 tablespoon sugar, the ginger and 1 tablespoon of water. Cook over moderate heat without stirring until the sugar is dark amber, about 10 minutes. Carefully and quickly whisk in the cold cream and milk (it will splatter) and bring to a boil over moderately high heat until smooth, 2 minutes.

3. Whisk the caramel cream into the egg yolks. Pour the mixture into the saucepan and cook over low heat, stirring with a wooden spoon, until it thickens and reaches 175° on a candy thermometer. Do not let it boil. Strain the custard into a clean bowl and let cool, then refrigerate until cold, at least 2 hours or overnight. (Alternatively, set the bowl in a larger bowl of ice and chill, stirring, for 30 minutes.)

4. Transfer the mixture to an ice cream machine and freeze according to the manufacturer's instructions. Pack the ice cream into a covered container and freeze for up to 3 days.

5. *Prepare the candied ginger:* In a small saucepan, combine the ginger, sugar and ¾ cup of water and bring to a boil over moderate heat. Reduce the heat to moderately low and simmer until the syrup becomes very thick, about 25 minutes.

6. Preheat the oven to 350°. Drain the candied ginger and, using tongs, transfer to a lightly greased baking sheet and spread out in an even layer. Bake the ginger for 5 to 8 minutes, until dry but not brittle. Using a metal spatula, transfer to a plate and set aside to cool.

7. *Prepare the roasted peaches and blackberries:* Bring 2 quarts of water to a boil in a large saucepan. Plunge the whole peaches in and boil for 1 minute. Transfer the peaches to a colander and refresh under cold running water. Pat the peaches dry and carefully peel them with a small knife. Halve and pit the peaches.

8. In a large nonreactive skillet, melt the butter over moderate heat. Add the sugar, ginger slices and peach halves, cut-sides down. Cook until lightly caramelized, about 5 minutes, then turn the peaches and add 1 tablespoon of water. Cook for 5 minutes longer (add a touch more water if the pan looks too dry). Transfer the peaches to a plate and cover to keep warm.

9. Add the blackberries to the skillet and toss over moderately high heat until slightly soft, 2 to 3 minutes. Remove from the heat and discard the ginger slices.

10. To serve, spoon the warm blackberries and a little of their juice onto 4 dessert plates. Arrange 3 warm peach halves, cut-sides up, on the berries. Scoop 1 small spoonful of caramel ice cream into each peach cavity and sprinkle with the candied ginger. Serve at once, while the fruit is still warm.

—*Daniel Boulud*

HARVEST FRUIT PARFAIT

❦ Heavy brown wines, such as González Byass Noé Pedro Ximénez and Pedro Domecq Pedro Ximénez

6 Servings

BUTTERSCOTCH SAUCE:
½ cup light brown sugar
¼ cup dark corn syrup
2 tablespoons unsalted butter
5 tablespoons heavy cream
FRUIT COMPOTE:
1 cup moist light-colored dried figs, such as Calimyrna, halved or quartered if large
¼ cup golden raisins
¼ cup dark raisins
½ cup pitted prunes, halved
⅓ cup granulated sugar
1½ pints vanilla ice cream

1. *Make the sauce:* In a small saucepan, stir together the brown sugar, corn syrup, butter and 1 tablespoon of the heavy cream. Bring to a boil over moderately high heat, washing down the sides of the pan occasionally with a wet pastry brush. Cook, stirring occasion-

ally, until the sauce reaches 250° on a candy thermometer, 5 to 7 minutes. Remove from the heat and gradually whisk in the remaining ¼ cup heavy cream until thoroughly incorporated. (*The sauce can be made up to 3 days ahead and refrigerated.*)

2. *Make the compote:* Combine the figs, raisins and prunes. In a small saucepan, bring the granulated sugar and ¾ cup of water to a boil. Pour the syrup over the dried fruit and set aside to macerate at room temperature for at least 4 hours or overnight.

3. To assemble the dessert, strain the fruit compote over the pan of butterscotch sauce. Cook the sauce over low heat, stirring occasionally, until warm, about 3 minutes. Scoop the ice cream into parfait glasses or dessert dishes. Spoon about ⅓ cup of the soaked fruit over each portion and drizzle about 2 tablespoons of the warm butterscotch sauce over the fruit. Serve at once.

—*Peggy Cullen*

BAKED APPLES WITH APPLE JELLY AND GINGER

8 Servings

8 medium Golden Delicious apples, peeled and cored almost all the way through
24 thin slivers of candied ginger
¾ cup apple jelly

1. Preheat the oven to 350°. Arrange the apples in a glass baking dish. Place 3 slivers of ginger and 1½ tablespoons of the jelly in each cored apple. Pour about ⅓ inch of water into the baking dish and bake in the middle of the oven for 45 to 50 minutes, basting occasionally with the pan

juices, until the apples are tender when pierced. (*The apples can be made up to 1 day ahead and refrigerated. Rewarm before proceeding.*)

2. To serve, baste the apples with the pan juices and transfer to a platter with a slotted spatula or spoon.

—*Camille Glenn*

PEAR BROWN BETTY

6 Servings

1½ cups soft fresh white or whole wheat bread crumbs
⅓ cup light brown sugar
¼ cup granulated sugar
¾ teaspoon allspice
6 firm-ripe medium Bosc pears (about 2½ pounds)—peeled, quartered, cored and sliced crosswise about ½ inch thick
1 teaspoon fresh lemon juice
3 tablespoons cold unsalted butter, cut into small pieces
Unsweetened whipped cream, for serving

1. Preheat the oven to 375°. Butter a 9-inch pie dish or shallow cake pan.

2. In a small bowl, toss together the bread crumbs, brown and granulated sugars and allspice. In a medium bowl, toss the sliced pears with the lemon juice.

3. Scatter 1 or 2 tablespoons of the crumb mixture into the bottom of the pie dish. Cover with half the pears. Drizzle 2 tablespoons of water on top, then scatter slightly less than half the crumb mixture over the pears. Dot with

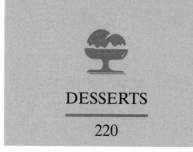
half the butter. Top with the remaining fruit, crumb and butter mixture.

4. Place the dish on a baking sheet. Bake for about 40 minutes, or until the crumbs are nicely browned and the pears are tender and bubbling. Transfer to a wire rack to cool slightly. Serve warm with whipped cream.

—Richard Sax

BAKED PEARS WITH GINGER

4 Servings

2 tablespoons unsalted butter
1½ teaspoons minced fresh ginger
4 Bartlett pears
¼ cup sugar
¼ cup dry white wine
Plain yogurt or sour cream

1. Preheat the oven to 400°. Smear the bottom of an 8-inch square nonreactive baking dish with half the butter; sprinkle the ginger on top.

2. Peel, halve and core the pears. Place them cut-side down in a single layer in the prepared pan. Sprinkle the sugar on top, pour the wine over the pears and dot with the remaining butter. Cover tightly with foil and bake for about 30 minutes, until the pears are tender (the time will vary depending on their ripeness). Let cool slightly.

3. Place the pears on 4 dessert plates and spoon the juices over the pears. Serve warm or at room temperature with a dollop of yogurt.

—Stephanie Lyness

SHEEP'S MILK CHEESE AND LEMON FRITTERS WITH HONEY

This traditional Sardinian dessert is made with slight variations in scores of tiny villages throughout the island. Although all recipes contain sheep's milk cheese and honey (for an exquisite salty-sweet contrast), Union Square Cafe's favorite version includes a touch of vanilla and tangy lemon zest.

6 Servings

1½ cups all-purpose flour
¼ cup cake flour
¼ cup granulated sugar
1 teaspoon baking powder
1¼ tablespoons cold unsalted butter, diced
1¼ tablespoons chilled vegetable shortening
¼ cup plus 2 tablespoons ice water
½ pound semisoft sheep's milk cheese, shredded on a box grater
1½ teaspoons freshly grated lemon zest
1 vanilla bean, split
1 egg, beaten
1 quart vegetable oil, for deep-frying
2 tablespoons confectioners' sugar
½ cup bitter honey, such as chestnut honey from Badia a Coltibuono

1. Sift together the all-purpose and cake flours, granulated sugar and baking powder into a bowl. Using a pastry cutter or 2 knives, cut in the butter and shortening until the mixture resembles coarse meal. Gradually add the ice water until the dough just holds together. Transfer the dough to a work surface and knead until smooth. Wrap the dough in plastic wrap and refrigerate for at least 3 hours.

2. Meanwhile, place the cheese and lemon zest in a bowl. Carefully scrape the inside of the vanilla bean into the cheese and toss well to blend. Reserve the bean for later use. Form the cheese mixture into 6 round patties, 2 inches in diameter and ½ inch thick. Cover and refrigerate until ready to use.

3. After the dough has rested, divide it in half. On a very lightly floured work surface, roll out each piece of dough into a 6-by-24-inch rectangle. (If you have a manual pasta machine, you can roll the dough through the number 3 setting on the machine.) Lightly brush one of the strips of dough with the beaten egg. Arrange the cheese patties at equal intervals on the egg-brushed strip of dough. Cover with the second sheet of dough. Using a 3½-inch fluted cookie cutter, stamp out the fritters, making sure that the cutter is centered over the cheese mixture. Using your fingers, gently press around the rim of each fritter to seal.

4. In a large saucepan, heat the vegetable oil to 375°. (If you don't have a thermometer, a small piece of bread dropped into the fat will float almost immediately and brown at this temperature.) Carefully slip half of the fritters into the hot oil and fry, turning once, until golden brown, 2 to 3 minutes. Drain well on paper towels. Repeat with the remaining fritters.

5. Place each fritter on a plate and sift the confectioners' sugar on top. Generously drizzle with honey and serve immediately.

—Michael Romano

LOW-CALORIE COOKING

EGGPLANT AND GARLIC DIP

4 Servings

1 head of garlic
1 large eggplant (about 1¼ pounds)
1 teaspoon salt
¼ cup coarsely chopped flat-leaf parsley plus 1 sprig for garnish
1 tablespoon fresh lemon juice
1 tablespoon extra-virgin olive oil
Four 6-inch pita breads, cut into small triangles

1. Preheat the oven to 450°. Wrap the garlic in a double thickness of foil and place in a medium baking dish with the eggplant. Bake for about 30 minutes, or until the eggplant is soft. Let cool for about 15 minutes; do not unwrap the garlic.

2. Working over a bowl to catch the cooked pulp, trim the eggplant stem and peel off the skin. Discard any pieces of browned pulp.

3. Separate the garlic head into cloves. Cut off the end of each clove and squeeze the soft garlic into a food processor. Add the eggplant and salt and process until smooth. Add the chopped parsley and lemon juice and pulse until incorporated. Add the olive oil and pulse 2 or 3 more times. Transfer to a bowl, garnish with the parsley sprig and serve with the pita triangles.

One Serving: Calories 244 kcal, Protein 8 gm, Carbohydrate 45 gm, Cholesterol 0, Total Fat 4.4 gm, Saturated Fat .6 gm

—*Diana Sturgis*

CARROT AND CHESTNUT SOUP

The chestnuts give this soup a rich, creamy consistency.

8 First-Course Servings

½ pound fresh chestnuts or ¾ cup canned unsweetened chestnut puree (6 ounces)
½ cup coarsely chopped onion
1½ pounds carrots, sliced crosswise ½ inch thick
1 celery rib, thinly sliced crosswise
1 tablespoon finely chopped fresh ginger
6 cups Vegetable Stock (p .224)
Salt and freshly ground pepper
Chopped fresh chives

1. If using fresh chestnuts, preheat the oven to 400°. Cut an "X" on the flat side of each chestnut. Roast them on a small baking sheet for 15 minutes. Let cool, then peel.

2. In a large saucepan, simmer the onion with ¼ cup of water, stirring, until softened, 7 to 8 minutes.

3. Set aside 1½ cups of the carrots. Add the remaining carrots, celery, ginger, Vegetable Stock and chestnuts to the saucepan. Simmer over moderate heat until the carrots are tender, about 25 minutes.

4. Meanwhile, steam the reserved carrots until tender, about 10 minutes.

5. In a blender, puree the soup in 2 batches until smooth. Transfer to a warm soup tureen, add the cooked carrots and season with salt and pepper. Garnish with chives and serve.

One Serving: Calories 137 kcal, Protein 3 gm, Carbohydrate 30 gm, Cholesterol 0, Total Fat 1 gm, Saturated Fat .2 gm

—*Sally Sampson*

BORSCHT WITH GREENS AND CHICKPEAS

6 Servings

4 medium beets with greens (about 1⅓ pounds)
1 tablespoon extra-virgin olive oil
1 medium onion, cut into ¼-inch dice
1 medium carrot, cut into ¼-inch dice
1 large tomato—peeled, seeded and coarsely chopped
2 cups Light Vegetable Stock (recipe follows) or canned low-sodium chicken broth
Coarse sea salt
1 cup cooked dried or drained canned chickpeas, rinsed
2 tablespoons dry sherry
2 tablespoons fresh lemon juice
Chopped fresh dill, for garnish

1. Cut off the beet greens, leaving about 1 inch of the stems attached. Rinse and coarsely chop the greens. In a large saucepan, cover the beets with cold water and bring to a boil. Cover and simmer over moderately low heat until tender, 50 to 60 minutes. Drain, reserving the liquid; there should be at least 1 quart. Let the beets cool, then peel them with your fingers. Cut into ¼-inch dice.

2. Heat the oil in a large nonreactive saucepan. Add the onion and sauté over moderately high heat until translucent, 2 to 3 minutes. Add the carrot and sauté for 1 minute. Stir in the tomato, Light Vegetable Stock and ½ teaspoon sea salt and bring to a boil. Cover and simmer over moderately low heat for 15 minutes.

3. Add the beet greens and cook, stirring, until the vegetables are tender, about 15 minutes.

4. Add 1 quart of the reserved beet liquid and the chickpeas, diced beets, sherry, lemon juice and ½ teaspoon sea salt to the saucepan and simmer for 5 minutes. Serve in soup bowls, sprinkled with chopped dill.

One Serving: Calories 157 kcal, Protein 6 gm, Carbohydrate 25 gm, Cholesterol 0, Total Fat 4 gm, Saturated Fat .6 gm

—Annemarie Colbin

LIGHT VEGETABLE STOCK

This flavorful stock can be used in almost any recipe calling for light chicken stock or in place of water in many soups and stews.

Makes About 2 Quarts

*2½ cups coarsely chopped celery
   leaves and trimmings*
1½ cups asparagus trimmings
8 mushroom stems
*½ cup carrot trimmings or 1 medium
   carrot, coarsely chopped*
1 medium onion, coarsely chopped
*1 medium leek, green part only,
   coarsely chopped*
3 fresh thyme sprigs
3 flat-leaf parsley sprigs

ITALIAN SOUP SUPPER
Serves 4

*Carrot and Chestnut Soup
   (at left)*
Asparagus Risotto (p. 237)
*Watercress and Radicchio Salad
   (p. 229)*

Cocoa Brownies (p. 239)
Caffè Latte

---

1 bay leaf
8 black peppercorns

Place all the ingredients in a large stockpot. Add 3 quarts of water and bring to a boil. Simmer over moderate heat until the liquid is reduced by one-third, about 45 minutes. Strain the stock. *(The stock can be refrigerated for up to 3 days or frozen for up to 2 months.)*

One Cup: Calories 12 kcal, Protein 1 gm, Carbohydrate 3 gm, Cholesterol 0, Total Fat .1 gm, Saturated Fat 0

—Annemarie Colbin

MINESTRONE

You can sprinkle each serving of soup with one tablespoon of grated Asiago cheese, which will add 22 calories and 2 grams of fat to the dish.

6 Main-Course Servings

*½ cup dried white beans, such as
   Great Northern, rinsed and picked
   over*
*1 large Spanish onion (13 ounces), cut
   into ¼-inch dice*
1 celery rib, cut into ⅓-inch dice
*1 large baking potato (8 ounces),
   peeled and cut into ⅓-inch dice*
*1 medium parsnip (4 ounces), cut into
   ⅓-inch dice*
2 garlic cloves, finely chopped
*1 zucchini (7 ounces), quartered
   lengthwise and sliced crosswise ¼
   inch thick*
*1 yellow squash (7 ounces), quartered
   lengthwise and sliced crosswise ¼
   inch thick*
*4 sun-dried tomatoes (not packed in
   oil), finely chopped (¼ cup)*
2 bay leaves
1 tablespoon basil
1 teaspoon marjoram

*One 28-ounce can Italian peeled
   tomatoes, chopped, with their juice*
8 cups Vegetable Stock (recipe follows)
½ cup orzo
Salt
¼ cup chopped flat-leaf parsley

1. In a medium saucepan, simmer the beans in 2 quarts of water over moderate heat until tender, about 1 hour. Drain, rinse and drain again.

2. In a large nonreactive saucepan, combine the onion, celery, potato, parsnip, garlic and ½ cup water and bring to a boil. Cook over moderate heat, stirring, until the onions are translucent, about 7 minutes. Stir in the zucchini, yellow squash, sun-dried tomatoes, bay leaves, basil and marjoram and cook for 10 minutes.

3. Add the tomatoes and Vegetable Stock and bring to a boil. Cover partially and simmer over moderately low heat, stirring occasionally, for 1½ hours. Stir in the white beans. *(The recipe can be prepared to this point up to 2 days ahead and refrigerated.)*

4. Bring the soup to a boil and add the orzo. Season with salt. Cook, stirring, over moderate heat until the orzo is tender, about 10 minutes. Discard the bay leaves and stir in the parsley.

One Serving: Calories 246 kcal, Protein 11 gm, Carbohydrate 52 gm, Cholesterol 0, Total Fat 1 gm, Saturated Fat .2 gm

—Sally Sampson

VEGETABLE STOCK

Makes About 4 Quarts

*4 pounds leeks (about 6), sliced
    crosswise ½ inch thick*
2 pounds carrots, coarsely chopped
6 celery ribs, sliced
1 cup parsley sprigs
12 medium garlic cloves, peeled
2 large bay leaves
1 tablespoon salt
2 teaspoons whole black peppercorns

Place all the ingredients in a stockpot. Add 6 quarts of water and bring to a boil. Cover partially and simmer over moderately low heat for 1 hour. Strain the stock. *(The stock can be frozen for up to 3 months.)*

One Cup: Calories 22 kcal, Protein .6 gm, Carbohydrate 5 gm, Cholesterol 0, Total Fat .1 gm, Saturated Fat 0

—*Sally Sampson*

FIVE-LILY CHOWDER

8 First-Course Servings

*5 cups chicken stock or canned
    low-sodium broth*
2 teaspoons olive oil
2 pounds onions, finely chopped
3 medium shallots, thinly sliced
3 medium leeks, white part only, sliced
½ cup dry white wine
1 large bay leaf
*2 teaspoons minced fresh thyme or
    1 teaspoon dried*
*2 teaspoons minced fresh oregano or
    1 teaspoon dried*

1 medium celery rib, finely diced
2 tablespoons dry sherry
*2 tablespoons finely minced fresh
    chives*
1 teaspoon salt
½ teaspoon freshly ground pepper
1 teaspoon finely chopped garlic
2 teaspoons minced flat-leaf parsley
2 teaspoons finely grated lemon zest

1. Pour the chicken stock into a container and freeze until the fat congeals on the surface, about 20 minutes. Remove the fat with a spoon and discard. Set the stock aside.

2. Meanwhile, in a large nonreactive saucepan, heat the oil over moderately high heat until hot. Add the onions, shallots and half of the leeks. Cook, stirring often, until soft and golden, about 18 minutes.

3. In a food processor, puree half of the onion mixture until relatively smooth. Return the puree to the saucepan and stir in the reserved chicken stock, wine, bay leaf and dried thyme and oregano (if using fresh, add in the next step). Bring to a boil over moderately high heat, then reduce the heat to moderate and simmer for 10 minutes.

4. Stir in the celery, sherry, fresh thyme and oregano, if using, and the remaining leeks. Simmer for 2 minutes. Do not overcook; the celery and leeks should remain crisp. Remove and discard the bay leaf.

5. Stir the chives into the chowder and season with the salt and pepper. Ladle the soup into 8 cups. In a small bowl, stir together the garlic, parsley and lemon zest and add a pinch to each serving of soup.

One Serving: Calories 103 kcal, Protein 3 gm, Carbohydrate 15 gm, Cholesterol 0, Total Fat 2 gm, Saturated Fat .4 gm

—*John Ash & Sid Goldstein*

OYSTER MUSHROOM SOUP WITH SCALLOPS

Scallops frequently have a small, tough but flavorful membrane attached to the side. Pull them off and use them to flavor the broth.

4 First-Course Servings

*4 ounces large sea scallops, sliced
    horizontally ⅓ inch thick*
*4 ounces oyster mushrooms, stems
    trimmed, mushrooms halved if large*
3 tablespoons light brown miso*
2 scallions, thinly sliced crosswise
**Available at Asian markets and
    health food stores*

1. In a medium saucepan, combine the scallop side muscles and mushroom stems with 4 cups of water. Boil over high heat for 2 minutes. Pour the broth through a colander or coarse strainer and then return it to the saucepan. Discard the solids.

2. Bring the broth to a simmer over moderate heat. Whisk in the miso paste until completely dissolved. Add the sliced scallops and the mushrooms and simmer until the sea scallops are just opaque, about 1 minute. Remove from the heat and stir in the scallions.

One Serving: Calories 61 kcal, Protein 7 gm, Carbohydrate 6 gm, Cholesterol 9 mg, Total Fat 9 gm, Saturated Fat .1 gm

—*Marcia Kiesel*

*Spiced Red Wine Fruit Soup
with Candied Orange (p. 217).*

**Above, Vanilla Ice Cream with Coffee Granita and Candied Orange (p. 214).
Left, Red Wine-Raspberry Sherbet (p. 214).**

SMOKY BLACK BEAN
AND VEGETABLE SOUP

This soup gets better as it sits, so make it at least one day ahead.

4 Main-Course Servings

1 large Spanish onion (13 ounces), coarsely chopped

2 celery ribs, halved lengthwise and thinly sliced

2 carrots (4 ounces), cut into ⅓-inch dice

4 garlic cloves, finely chopped

2 canned chipotle chiles in adobo—rinsed, seeded and chopped (1 tablespoon)

2 bay leaves

2 teaspoons cumin

2 teaspoons basil

1 teaspoon chili powder

1 teaspoon oregano

Three 16-ounce cans black beans, rinsed

One 28-ounce can Italian peeled tomatoes, chopped, with their juice

8 cups Vegetable Stock (p. 224)

Salt

½ cup plain nonfat yogurt

Lime or orange wedges

Chopped fresh coriander (cilantro)

1. In a large casserole, cook the onion, celery, carrots, garlic and ½ cup of water over moderate heat until the vegetables soften, about 12 minutes. Stir in the chiles, bay leaves, cumin, basil, chili powder and oregano and cook for 3 minutes.

2. Stir in the black beans, tomatoes and Vegetable Stock and bring to a boil. Cover partially and simmer over moderately low heat, stirring occasionally, for 2 hours.

Pan-Roasted Peaches and Blackberries with Ginger and Caramel Ice Cream (p. 218).

3. Discard the bay leaves. Puree 3 cups of the soup in a food processor or blender until smooth. Stir the puree back into the soup. Season with salt and serve hot with the yogurt, lime wedges and fresh coriander.

One Serving: Calories 363 kcal, Protein 20 gm, Carbohydrate 69 gm, Cholesterol .6 mg, Total Fat 3 gm, Saturated Fat .3 gm

—Sally Sampson

CURRIED
CAULIFLOWER AND
LEEK SOUP

8 Servings

Two 10-ounce cans low-sodium chicken broth

3 large leeks, white and tender green only, thinly sliced crosswise

2 teaspoons olive oil

1 medium baking potato (½ pound), peeled and coarsely chopped

1 tablespoon plus 2 teaspoons curry powder

6 packed cups cauliflower florets (from a 2-pound cauliflower)

2 imported bay leaves

2 teaspoons sea salt

¾ teaspoon freshly ground pepper

½ cup plain nonfat yogurt

1. Freeze the chicken broth until the fat congeals on the surface, about 20 minutes. Discard the fat.

2. In a large saucepan, cook the leeks in the oil over moderately low heat, stirring occasionally, until partially wilted, about 7 minutes. Add the potato and 1 tablespoon of the curry powder and stir for 1 minute. Add the cauliflower, degreased broth, 2½ cups of water and the bay leaves. Bring to a boil over high heat. Reduce the heat,

cover and simmer until the vegetables are very soft, about 30 minutes.

3. Meanwhile, in a small skillet, toast the remaining 2 teaspoons curry powder over moderate heat, shaking the pan, for 2 minutes.

4. Discard the bay leaves from the vegetables. Working in batches, puree the vegetables and all but 1 cup of the cooking liquid in a blender. Boil the remaining 1 cup cooking liquid until reduced to about 3 tablespoons, then add it to the soup in the blender. Season with sea salt and pepper. Top each serving with 1 tablespoon of the nonfat yogurt and a pinch of toasted curry powder.

One Serving: Calories 100 kcal, Protein 4 gm, Carbohydrate 18 gm, Cholesterol .3 mg, Total Fat 2 gm, Saturated Fat .3 gm

—Diana Sturgis

WATERCRESS AND
RADICCHIO SALAD

6 Servings

1 cup Light Vegetable Stock (p. 223) or ⅓ cup canned low-sodium chicken broth

2 tablespoons sesame seeds

1 large head of radicchio (7 ounces)

2 medium bunches of watercress (½ pound), large stems removed

¼ cup (packed) flat-leaf parsley leaves

1 tablespoon fresh lemon juice

1 tablespoon apple cider vinegar

Coarse sea salt

1. If using Light Vegetable Stock,

boil it until reduced to ⅓ cup. Toast the sesame seeds in a small skillet over low heat, shaking the pan occasionally, until lightly browned, 2 to 3 minutes. Let cool.

2. Core the radicchio and remove 6 whole leaves. Thinly slice the remaining radicchio and toss in a large bowl with the watercress.

3. In a food processor or blender, puree the reduced vegetable stock, toasted sesame seeds, parsley, lemon juice, cider vinegar, and ¼ teaspoon sea salt until smooth. Add half of the dressing to the salad and toss.

4. Place a whole radicchio leaf on each salad plate. Mound the tossed salad on the leaf and drizzle the remaining dressing on top.

One Serving: Calories 30 kcal, Protein 2 gm, Carbohydrate 3 gm, Cholesterol 0, Total Fat 1.7 gm, Saturated Fat .2 gm

—Annemarie Colbin

ORANGE, RADISH AND CUCUMBER SALAD

If you're making this salad ahead of time, omit the two tablespoons of orange juice added just before serving.

4 Servings

3 large navel oranges
1 small bunch of radishes, sliced ⅛ inch thick (1 cup)
½ of a large European cucumber, sliced ⅛ inch thick (1 cup)
1 tablespoon finely chopped fresh mint
1 teaspoon extra-virgin olive oil
Salt and freshly ground pepper

1. Using a small sharp knife, peel the oranges, removing all the bitter white pith. Working over a serving bowl, cut in between the membranes to release the sections. Add the radishes, cucumber and mint and toss. *(The salad can be prepared to this point and refrigerated for up to 2 hours.)*

2. Squeeze 2 tablespoons of juice from the orange membranes into the salad. Add the oil and toss. Season with salt and pepper and serve chilled or at room temperature.

One Serving: Calories 85 kcal, Protein 2 gm, Carbohydrate 19 gm, Cholesterol 0, Total Fat 1.5 gm, Saturated Fat .2 gm

—Michele Scicolone

ASPARAGUS-PEPPER SALAD WITH GINGER DRESSING

4 Servings

6 small scallions, green part only, minced (½ cup)
2 tablespoons minced fresh ginger
2 tablespoons rice vinegar
1 tablespoon dark Japanese sesame oil
1 garlic clove, minced
1½ pounds thick asparagus, peeled and sliced diagonally ¼ inch thick
1 medium red bell pepper, cut into 2-by-¼-inch strips
1 medium yellow bell pepper, cut into 2-by-¼-inch strips
Salt and freshly ground black pepper

1. In a small bowl, combine the scallions, ginger, rice vinegar, sesame oil and garlic.

2. In a large pot of boiling salted water, cook the asparagus until crisp-tender, about 1 minute. Drain, refresh under cold running water and pat dry with paper towels.

3. In a large bowl, mix the asparagus with the red and yellow bell peppers. Toss with the ginger dressing, season with salt and pepper and serve.

One Serving: Calories 93 kcal, Protein 5 gm, Carbohydrate 13 gm, Cholesterol 0, Total Fat 4 gm, Saturated Fat .6 gm

—Janet Hazen

JICAMA-ORANGE SALAD WITH JALAPENO DRESSING

4 Servings

2 large jalapeño peppers
1 small red onion, cut into thin wedges
3 medium navel oranges (6 ounces each)
3 tablespoons minced fresh coriander (cilantro)
1 tablespoon olive oil
Salt
¼ teaspoon cumin
Freshly ground black pepper
1 small bunch of watercress, large stems removed
½ of a small jicama (about ¾ pound), peeled and cut into ¼-inch-thick sticks

1. Roast the jalapeños under a broiler or on a sturdy wire rack set over a gas flame, turning frequently, until blackened all over. Place the peppers in a sturdy paper bag and let steam for 15 minutes.

2. Soak the onion wedges in ice water for 15 minutes. Drain thoroughly and transfer to a medium bowl.

3. Using a small sharp knife, peel the oranges, removing all the bitter white pith. Working over a small bowl to catch the juices, cut in between the membranes to release the sections. Add the sections to the onion wedges. Squeeze the membranes into the small bowl; you should have about 3 table-spoons of juice.

4. Under gently running water, peel the jalapeños. Remove the stems and seeds and finely mince the jalapeño peppers. Add them to the orange juice with the coriander, oil, ½ teaspoon salt, the cumin and ⅛ teaspoon black pepper; mix well. *(The salad can be prepared to this point up to 4 hours ahead. Set the salad and dressing aside separately.)*

5. Arrange the watercress on individual plates. Add the jicama sticks to the onion wedges and oranges. Whisk the dressing and toss with the salad. Season with salt and pepper and mound the salad on the watercress.

One Serving: Calories 124 kcal, Protein 3 gm, Carbohydrate 22 gm, Cholesterol 0, Total Fat 4 gm, Saturated Fat .5 gm

—Janet Hazen

GRILLED MUSHROOM SALAD

4 Servings

1 large red bell pepper
½ pound plum tomatoes—peeled, seeded and chopped
1 garlic clove, minced
1½ tablespoons fresh orange juice
1 teaspoon fresh lemon juice
1½ teaspoons sherry vinegar
1 teaspoon soy sauce
1 tablespoon chopped fresh spearmint or basil
12 ounces shiitake mushrooms, stemmed
1¼ teaspoons olive oil
Salt and freshly ground black pepper

1 bunch of arugula, leaves torn into bite-size pieces
¼ of a head of Boston lettuce, leaves torn into bite-size pieces

1. Roast the red bell pepper directly over a gas flame or under the broiler as close to the heat as possible, turning frequently, until charred all over. Transfer the pepper to a paper bag and set aside to steam for about 5 minutes. Using a small sharp knife, scrape off the blackened skin; remove the core, seeds and ribs. Rinse the pepper under water if you like, pat dry and cut into thin slices.

2. In a food processor, puree the tomatoes with the garlic. Pour the puree into a small bowl. Stir in the orange juice, lemon juice, sherry vinegar, soy sauce and spearmint.

3. Preheat the broiler. Thread the mushrooms on four 10-inch bamboo skewers by piercing through the center of each mushroom cap at an angle. The mushrooms should be tightly fanned out on the skewers, like roof tiles. Put the skewers on a baking sheet and brush them all over with the oil. Season the mushrooms with salt and pepper. Broil the mushrooms gill-side down, rotating the pan as necessary, for about 3 minutes, until tender and toasty brown on top; keep warm.

4. In a large bowl, toss the arugula and Boston lettuce with the tomato dressing, thoroughly coating each leaf. Mound the salad on 4 large plates. Scatter the roasted pepper strips over the salads and lean a mushroom skewer against the greens. Alternatively, remove the mushrooms from the skewers and scatter them over the salads.

One Serving: Calories 68 kcal, Protein 4 gm, Carbohydrate 11 gm, Cholesterol 0 mg, Total Fat 2 gm, Saturated Fat .3 gm

—Marcia Kiesel

NEW POTATO AND WAX BEAN SALAD

4 Servings

½ pound yellow wax beans or green beans, cut diagonally into 1-inch pieces
½ pound small red potatoes, quartered
1 tablespoon plus 1 teaspoon white wine vinegar or Champagne vinegar
1½ teaspoons Dijon mustard
1 tablespoon mild olive oil
1 small garlic clove, minced
1 teaspoon minced fresh thyme
1 teaspoon minced fresh rosemary
Salt and freshly ground pepper
2 medium bunches of arugula, large stems removed

1. Cook the beans in a medium saucepan of boiling salted water until crisp-tender, about 3 minutes. Using a slotted spoon, transfer the beans to a colander and refresh under cold running water. Pat dry with paper towels, then transfer to a medium bowl.

2. Cook the potatoes in the same boiling water until fork-tender, about 10 minutes. Drain well, let cool and add to the beans.

3. In a small bowl, whisk together the vinegar and mustard until thoroughly blended. Slowly whisk in the oil. Stir in the garlic, thyme, rosemary, a pinch of salt and ¼ teaspoon pepper. *(The salad can be prepared to this point up to 4 hours ahead. Set the salad and dressing aside separately.)*

4. Arrange the arugula on individual plates. Whisk the dressing and toss

gently with the beans and potatoes; season with salt and pepper. Mound the salad on the arugula.

One Serving: Calories 98 kcal, Protein 3 gm, Carbohydrate 15 gm, Cholesterol 0, Total Fat 4 gm, Saturated Fat .5 gm

—Janet Hazen

VEGETABLE PASTA SALAD

4 Main-Course Servings

2 teaspoons extra-virgin olive oil
2 red onions (1 pound)—loose skin discarded but root ends left intact, cut lengthwise into eighths
4 medium plum tomatoes (1 pound), halved lengthwise
2 large red bell peppers (1 pound)
2 large yellow bell peppers (1 pound)
4 large garlic cloves, unpeeled
½ cup finely shredded fresh basil
1 teaspoon minced fresh oregano
1 teaspoon minced fresh thyme
1 teaspoon freshly ground black pepper
Salt
¾ pound penne
½ cup flat-leaf parsley leaves
1 ounce Parmesan cheese, thinly shaved

1. Preheat the oven to 450°. Drizzle 1 teaspoon of the oil in a large roasting pan. Scatter the onions in the pan, rubbing them in the oil to coat thoroughly. Add the tomatoes, red and yellow peppers and garlic and rub with the remaining oil. Bake in the lower third of

the oven for about 40 minutes, or until the vegetables are slightly charred and soft. Set aside to cool.

2. Working over a strainer set over a medium saucepan, remove the cores, ribs and seeds from the peppers. Peel off the charred skin. Cut the peppers into 1-by-½-inch strips and place them in a large bowl.

3. Working over the same strainer, squeeze the seeds and cores from the tomatoes, peel off the skin and add the pulp to the peppers. Boil the accumulated juices until reduced to ¼ cup, 3 to 5 minutes.

4. Cut off the root ends from the onions and discard the skin. Add the onions to the peppers. Squeeze the garlic from its skin into the vegetables.

5. Add the basil, oregano, thyme and black pepper and toss. *(The recipe can be prepared to this point up to 4 hours ahead. Cover and store the vegetables and reduced juices separately.)*

6. Bring a large pot of salted water to a boil. Add the penne and cook, stirring, until al dente. Drain and transfer to a large bowl. Add the reduced vegetable juices and toss.

A MEDITERRANEAN MENU

Serves 4

Eggplant and Garlic Dip
(p. 222)

—

Vegetable Pasta Salad (at left)

—

Fresh Strawberries and Melon
—Diana Sturgis

7. Stir 1 teaspoon of salt into the vegetables and toss with the pasta. Toss in the parsley and Parmesan and serve.

One Serving: Calories 497 kcal, Protein 18 gm, Carbohydrate 95 gm, Cholesterol 4.8 mg, Total Fat 6.5 gm, Saturated Fat 1.8 gm

—Diana Sturgis

LENTIL SALAD WITH FRISEE, PEARS AND LEEKS

Because lentils quickly absorb liquid while they sit, dress the salad just before serving.

4 Main-Course Servings

2 medium leeks, white and pale green parts only—sliced crosswise ⅛ inch thick (1¾ cups)
1 teaspoon mild olive oil
½ teaspoon salt
1½ ounces smoked ham, trimmed of fat and cut into 1-inch pieces
6 large fresh basil leaves
1 serrano or jalapeño chile, halved and seeded
2 tablespoons plus 2 teaspoons balsamic vinegar
1 tablespoon extra-virgin olive oil or French walnut oil
1 teaspoon sugar
6 ounces frisée, young chicory or arugula, torn into bite-size pieces
1 Belgian endive, halved and sliced lengthwise into ¼-inch strips
3 medium Comice pears (6 to 7 ounces each)—peeled, quartered, cored and sliced crosswise ⅛ inch thick
Basic Cooked Lentils (p. 234)
Freshly ground black pepper

1. Preheat the oven to 450°. In a medium bowl, toss the leeks with the mild olive oil to coat completely. Season with ¼ teaspoon of the salt. Scatter the leeks in a heavy baking sheet or large ovenproof skillet and bake for 12 to 15 minutes, tossing 2 or 3 times with a metal spatula, until golden brown and crisp. Set aside to cool.

2. In a small nonreactive saucepan, combine the ham, basil, chile and 1 cup of water and bring to a boil over moderate heat. Reduce the heat to low and simmer until the water has reduced to about ½ cup, about 20 minutes.

3. Using a slotted spoon, remove the ham, basil and serrano chile and discard. Stir in the balsamic vinegar, extra-virgin olive oil and sugar, increase the heat to moderate and bring to a boil, stirring until the sugar is thoroughly dissolved; remove the dressing from the heat.

4. In a medium bowl, gently toss together the frisée, Belgian endive and pears. Place the cooked lentils in another bowl. Spoon half of the dressing into each bowl and toss to coat thoroughly. Season both mixtures with the remaining ¼ teaspoon salt and black pepper to taste.

5. Arrange the frisée, endive and pears on 4 dinner plates. Mound the lentils on the greens. Scatter the leeks on top and serve immediately.

One Serving: Calories 346 kcal, Protein 20 gm, Carbohydrate 57 gm, Cholesterol 5 mg, Total Fat 7 gm, Saturated Fat 1 gm

—*Sally Schneider*

PASTA AND LENTILS WITH WALNUT CREAM

Since imported French walnut oil is made with roasted nuts and has a more intense flavor than domestic walnut oil, you need to use very little. This dish tastes best served warm or at room temperature.

❦ An ideal foil for the mild, creamy texture of this rich-tasting dish is a substantial young red with bite and depth. Good choices would be Gigondas, such as 1989 Domaine Les Goubert "Cuvée Florence" from the Rhône, and Merlot, such as 1988 Columbia Crest Barrel Select from Washington State.

4 Servings

½ of a serrano or jalapeño chile
½ pound small pasta shells (2 cups)
2 cups Basic Cooked Lentils (p. 234) and ½ cup of their cooking liquid
1 teaspoon balsamic vinegar
¾ cup buttermilk
¼ cup light sour cream
1½ tablespoons French walnut oil
⅛ teaspoon salt
¼ teaspoon freshly ground black pepper
2 ounces thinly sliced lean prosciutto, cut into ½-inch-wide strips
1 tablespoon minced chives
1 tablespoon finely chopped flat-leaf parsley

1. Put the chile in a large saucepan of water and bring to a boil. Add the pasta and cook until al dente. Drain; discard the chile.

2. Meanwhile, in a medium nonreactive saucepan, stir the lentils with their cooking liquid. Cover and cook over low heat, stirring frequently, until the lentils are hot. Stir in the balsamic vinegar.

3. In a large bowl, whisk the buttermilk, sour cream, walnut oil, salt and black pepper to taste.

4. Add the pasta, lentils and prosciutto to the cream sauce and toss to coat. Transfer to a serving platter and sprinkle the chives and parsley on top.

One Serving: Calories 453 kcal, Protein 23 gm, Carbohydrate 68 gm, Cholesterol 16 mg, Total Fat 10 gm, Saturated Fat 2.5 gm

—*Sally Schneider*

LENTILS WITH FRAGRANT RICE

In combination, the lentils and this lovely scented rice make a complete protein and a meal unto themselves. Red lentils—milder than green or brown—are best with the rice.

4 Main-Course Servings

1 tablespoon vegetable oil
½ teaspoon cumin seeds
1 medium onion, chopped (¾ cup)
4 garlic cloves, finely chopped
½ teaspoon minced serrano or jalapeño chile
¼ teaspoon saffron threads, crushed (optional)
1 cup basmati rice
1⅛ teaspoons garam masala*
1½ tablespoons grated fresh ginger
¾ cup canned low-sodium chicken broth
½ teaspoon salt
Basic Cooked Lentils (recipe follows), preferably red lentils, and ½ cup of their cooking liquid
1 teaspoon balsamic vinegar

½ cup chopped fresh coriander
   (cilantro)
¾ cup plain low-fat yogurt
*Available at Indian markets

1. In a heavy medium saucepan, heat the oil over moderate heat. Add the cumin seeds and cook until fragrant, 1 to 2 minutes. Add the onion and cook, stirring frequently, until translucent and beginning to brown, about 5 minutes.

2. Stir in the garlic, chile and saffron and cook for 1 minute. Stir in the rice and garam masala until the rice is completely coated with the spices and oil. Stir in the ginger and cook for 30 seconds.

3. Add the broth, salt and 1 cup of water and bring to a boil over high heat. Reduce the heat to low, cover and cook for 17 minutes. Set aside, covered, for 5 minutes.

4. In a heavy, medium nonreactive saucepan, stir the lentils and their cooking liquid. Cover and cook over moderate heat, stirring, until the lentils are hot, about 8 minutes. Add the balsamic vinegar and ¼ cup of the coriander and toss.

5. Spoon the rice and lentils into 4 shallow bowls, mixing them together slightly. Pass the yogurt and the remaining coriander separately.

One Serving: Calories 449 kcal, Protein 23 gm, Carbohydrate 78 gm, Cholesterol 3 mg, Total Fat 5 gm, Saturated Fat 1 gm

—Sally Schneider

BASIC COOKED LENTILS

Lentils cooked by this method can be used in recipes from salads to casseroles. Save the flavorful cooking water to stir into the lentils when reheating, as in Lentils with Fragrant Rice (p. 233).

Makes About 3 Cups

½ pound green, brown or red lentils
   (1¼ cups plus 1 tablespoon)
1 small onion, stuck with 2 whole
   cloves
2 garlic cloves, unpeeled, lightly
   smashed
½ serrano or jalapeño chile, seeded
   and deribbed
Bouquet garni made with 5 flat-leaf
   parsley sprigs, 3 to 4 thyme sprigs
   (or ½ teaspoon dried thyme) and
   1 bay leaf tied in cheesecloth
¼ teaspoon salt

1. In a medium saucepan, cover the lentils with 2 inches of cold water. Discard any lentils that float to the surface; then drain in a colander and rinse.

2. Return the lentils to the saucepan. Add the onion, garlic, serrano chile and bouquet garni. Stir in 4 cups of cold water and bring to a boil over moderate heat. Reduce the heat to moderately low and simmer the lentils until they are tender but still hold their shape, about 8 minutes for red lentils and 20 minutes for brown or green. Stir in the salt halfway through the cooking.

3. Drain the lentils, reserving the cooking liquid for reheating. Remove and discard the onion, serrano chile, garlic and bouquet garni. Transfer the lentils to a bowl and set aside to cool, tossing occasionally.

One Serving: Calories 198 kcal, Protein 16 gm, Carbohydrate 34 gm, Cholesterol 0 , Total Fat .6 gm, Saturated Fat .1 gm

—Sally Schneider

BROCCOLI RABE WITH ORECCHIETTE

4 Servings

½ pound orecchiette
1½ tablespoons extra-virgin olive oil
6 garlic cloves, thinly sliced
1 large red bell pepper, cut into ⅓-inch
   dice
½ teaspoon crushed red pepper
½ teaspoon salt
1 to 1¼ pounds broccoli rabe, trimmed
   and cut into 1-inch lengths

1. In a large pot of boiling salted water, cook the orecchiette, stirring occasionally, until al dente; this can take as long as 30 minutes for some imported brands. Drain, transfer to a serving bowl and keep warm.

2. In a large heavy skillet, heat the olive oil. Add the garlic, bell pepper and crushed red pepper and cook over moderate heat, stirring, until the garlic is tender but not browned, 10 to 12 minutes. Stir in the salt.

3. In a saucepan of boiling water, cook the broccoli rabe until tender, 3 to 5 minutes. Drain well. Stir it into the garlic mixture and reheat briefly if necessary. Season with additional salt if desired. Stir the vegetables into the pasta and serve at once.

One Serving: Calories 316 kcal, Protein 12 gm, Carbohydrate 55 gm, Cholesterol 0, Total Fat 7 gm, Saturated Fat .9 gm

—Diana Sturgis

PAN BAGNA

4 Servings

2 medium red bell peppers or one
   7-ounce jar of roasted red peppers,
   drained
1 loaf of crusty French or Italian bread
   (12 ounces)
1 tablespoon olive oil
1 tablespoon red wine vinegar
¼ teaspoon freshly ground black
   pepper
1 garlic clove, halved
1 large tomato, thinly sliced
½ cup thinly sliced red onion
One 6½-ounce can of water-packed
   tuna, drained
One 2-ounce can of flat anchovy fillets,
   drained and patted dry
6 large fresh basil leaves

1. If using fresh bell peppers, roast, peel and slice them. Slice off the upper third of the loaf of bread. Pull out and discard the soft crumb from the top half.

2. In a small bowl, combine the oil, vinegar and black pepper. Rub the cut sides of the bread with the garlic and drizzle with the dressing.

3. On the bottom half of the loaf, layer the tomato and onion slices, tuna, roasted peppers, anchovies and basil. Press the top half of the bread over the filling.

4. Wrap the loaf tightly in plastic wrap, then in foil. Weigh the sandwich down with a cutting board and let stand at room temperature for 1 to 2 hours to blend the flavors. Cut the sandwich into quarters and serve.

One Serving: Calories 383 kcal, Protein 24 gm, Carbohydrate 54 gm, Cholesterol 26 mg, Total Fat 7.4 gm, Saturated Fat 1.3 gm

—Michele Scicolone

SOBA NOODLES WITH GRILLED TUNA AND SOY GINGER SAUCE

8 Servings

1 cup chicken stock or canned
   low-sodium broth
1 tablespoon olive oil
Eight 4-ounce tuna steaks (about
   ½ inch thick)
Salt and freshly ground black pepper
3 tablespoons minced garlic
2½-inch piece of fresh ginger, peeled
   and minced
1 cup rice vinegar
⅔ cup reduced-sodium soy sauce
1 tablespoon plus 1 teaspoon finely
   grated lemon zest
1 teaspoon minced serrano chile or
   ½ teaspoon crushed red pepper
1 teaspoon sugar
6 scallions, trimmed and thinly sliced
   on the diagonal
1 pound dried soba or rice noodles, or
   linguine
¼ cup minced fresh chives
1 tablespoon minced fresh mint plus
   whole sprigs, for garnish

SUMMER SANDWICH MENU
Serves 4

Pan Bagna (at left)
*Orange, Radish and Cucumber
   Salad (p. 230)*
🍷 *Pinot Grigio*
—
*Chocolate-Cherry Biscotti
   (p. 239)*
Iced Espresso
—Michele Scicolone

1. Pour the chicken stock into a container and freeze until the fat congeals on the surface, about 20 minutes. Remove the fat with a spoon and discard.

2. Light a grill or preheat the broiler. Rub 1 teaspoon of the olive oil over the tuna steaks and season lightly with salt and pepper. Set aside.

3. In a small nonreactive saucepan, heat the remaining 2 teaspoons oil over moderately high heat. Add the garlic and ginger and cook, stirring briefly until just beginning to color, about 1 minute. Stir in the stock, vinegar, soy sauce and 1 teaspoon of the lemon zest. Add the chile and sugar and bring to a boil. Remove from the heat, stir in the scallions and keep warm.

4. Bring a large pot of salted water to a boil over high heat. Grill or broil the tuna steaks for about 5 minutes, turning once, until charred outside and still pink in the center. Transfer to a plate and cover to keep warm.

5. Cook the noodles in the boiling water until tender. Drain and toss with half the soy sauce mixture.

6. Mound the noodles on 8 warm plates. Place the tuna steaks on the noodles and spoon the remaining sauce over the fish.

7. In a small bowl, toss the remaining 1 tablespoon lemon zest with the chives and minced mint and sprinkle over each serving. Garnish with the mint sprigs and serve immediately.

One Serving: Calories 406 kcal, Protein 37 gm, Carbohydrate 49 gm, Cholesterol 43 mg, Total Fat 8 gm, Saturated Fat 2 gm

—John Ash & Sid Goldstein

GRILLED CHICKEN BREASTS WITH ONION MARMALADE

Pounding the chicken breasts produces a uniform thickness that facilitates even cooking.

4 Servings

3 tablespoons Dijon mustard
1½ teaspoons fresh lemon juice
1 teaspoon Worcestershire sauce
1 teaspoon minced garlic
½ teaspoon freshly ground pepper
4 skinless, boneless chicken breast
   halves (about 5 ounces each)
8 medium scallions, trimmed
Caramelized Red Onion Marmalade
   (at right)

1. Light a grill or preheat the broiler. In a medium nonreactive bowl, whisk together the mustard, lemon juice, Worcestershire sauce, garlic and pepper.

2. Place the chicken breasts between sheets of wax paper and pound lightly to a uniform thickness. Add the breast halves one at a time to the mustard mixture and turn to coat well on both sides.

3. Grill or broil the chicken, turning once and brushing occasionally with the mustard mixture, just until firm and opaque throughout, about 4 minutes per side. Meanwhile, grill or broil the scallions, turning once, until slightly charred all over, about 4 minutes.

4. Arrange the chicken breasts and grilled scallions on individual plates. Serve with 3 tablespoons of the Caramelized Red Onion Marmalade.

One Serving: Calories 184 kcal, Protein 29 gm, Carbohydrate 12 gm, Cholesterol 68 mg, Total Fat 2 gm, Saturated Fat .4 gm

—Laurie Burrows Grad

CARAMELIZED RED ONION MARMALADE

This onion marmalade is delicious with grilled chicken or other grilled or roasted meats or vegetables.

Makes About 2 Cups

2 large red onions (about 1¼ pounds),
   thinly sliced
3 tablespoons brown sugar
¾ cup dry red wine
3 tablespoons balsamic vinegar
Salt and freshly ground pepper

1. In a large, heavy, nonreactive saucepan, combine the red onions and brown sugar and cook over moderate heat, stirring often, until the onions begin to caramelize and turn golden, 20 to 25 minutes.

2. Stir in the wine and vinegar, increase the heat to moderately high and bring to a boil. Reduce the heat to moderately low and cook, stirring often, until most of the liquid has evaporated, about 15 minutes. Season to taste with salt and pepper and set aside to cool. *(The onion marmalade can be made up to 3 weeks ahead; cover and refrigerate.)* Serve at room temperature.

One Tablespoon: Calories 11 kcal, Protein .2 gm, Carbohydrate 3 gm, Cholesterol 0, Total Fat 0, Saturated Fat 0

—Laurie Burrows Grad

CHICKEN ON THE GRILL

Serves 4

Grilled Chicken Breasts (above)

Caramelized Red Onion Marmalade (above)

Quinoa and Vegetable Pilaf (p. 238)

Salade de Pêches (p. 238)

—Laurie Burrows Grad

THREE CABBAGES WITH CARAWAY

Use small, tender kale leaves. If kale or red cabbage is not available, substitute an equal amount of green cabbage.

6 Servings

1 tablespoon extra-virgin olive oil
1 cup finely chopped red onion
2 cups (packed) thinly sliced red
   cabbage
4 cups (packed) thinly sliced kale,
   leaves and stalks
4 cups (packed) thinly sliced green
   cabbage
1 teaspoon caraway seeds
Salt and freshly ground pepper

1. In a large heavy saucepan, combine the olive oil and red onion. Top with the red cabbage, kale and green cabbage. (If you cannot fit the green cabbage in your pan, cover and cook the red cabbage and kale for 5 minutes to wilt the kale slightly, then press it down and add the remaining cabbage.) Cover the saucepan tightly and cook over moderately low heat for 15 minutes to wilt the cabbages.

2. Add the caraway seeds and stir well. Cover and continue cooking until the cabbages are tender and the onion begins to caramelize, about 12 minutes. Season with salt and pepper and serve.

One Serving: *Calories 74 kcal, Protein 3 gm, Carbohydrate 12 gm, Cholesterol 0, Total Fat 3 gm, Saturated Fat .4 gm*

—Diana Sturgis

ASPARAGUS RISOTTO

6 Servings

Light Vegetable Stock (p. 223)
¼ teaspoon saffron threads
2 tablespoons extra-virgin olive oil
3 medium shallots, minced
2 garlic cloves, minced
2 cups short-grain brown rice (14 ounces)
Coarse sea salt
1 pound thin asparagus, trimmed and cut into ¾-inch pieces
1 tablespoon apple cider vinegar
1 tablespoon dry sherry (optional)
Freshly ground pepper

1. Warm the stock in a large saucepan. Transfer ¼ cup to a small bowl, add the saffron threads and set aside to steep. Keep the remaining stock warm over low heat.

2. Heat the oil in a large nonreactive saucepan. Add the shallots and garlic and cook over moderate heat, stirring, until softened, about 4 minutes. Add the rice and stir until coated with oil. Stir in about 1½ cups of the stock, enough to cover the rice, and simmer, stirring, until the stock is absorbed. Continue adding about ½ cup stock every 5 to 7 minutes, stirring occasionally, until it is absorbed before adding more.

3. After cooking the risotto for 30 minutes, add the saffron liquid and 1 teaspoon sea salt and cook, stirring, for 15 minutes, continuing to add about ½ cup stock every 5 to 7 minutes. Add the asparagus and stir until the rice is cooked but not mushy, about 10 min-

utes. Add more liquid if necessary so that the risotto has a creamy consistency; you may have up to 1 cup of stock leftover. Stir in the vinegar and sherry and cook for 2 minutes. Season with sea salt and pepper.

One Serving: *Calories 327 kcal, Protein 9 gm, Carbohydrate 59 gm, Cholesterol 0, Total Fat 6.8 gm, Saturated Fat 1.1 gm*

—Annemarie Colbin

MUSHROOM AND CHESTNUT RISOTTO

4 Servings

½ pound white mushrooms, including stems
4 ounces fresh morel, chanterelle, shiitake or cremini mushrooms, caps sliced and stems reserved for stock
1 tablespoon sliced dried mushrooms (any type)
8 whole fresh chestnuts
2 tablespoons coarsely chopped flat-leaf parsley
3 garlic cloves, minced separately
1 teaspoon olive oil
1 medium onion, finely chopped
½ cup arborio rice (3½ ounces)
¼ cup dry red wine
2 fresh thyme sprigs or ½ teaspoon dried
2½ tablespoons freshly grated Parmesan cheese
Salt and freshly ground pepper

1. Make the mushroom stock: In a medium saucepan, boil the white mushrooms and any wild mushroom stems in 5 cups of water over high heat for 20 minutes. Strain over a bowl and discard the solids.

2. Add the dried mushrooms to the hot stock and set aside to steep for at least 20 minutes.

3. Meanwhile, cook the chestnuts. Make a small incision on 1 side of each chestnut and place in a small saucepan. Cover with water and simmer over moderate heat until tender when pierced with a knife, about 20 minutes. Drain and peel the chestnuts while still hot. Break the chestnuts in large pieces and cover with plastic wrap.

4. In a small bowl, mix the parsley and 1 of the minced garlic cloves.

5. Carefully pour the mushroom stock and the reconstituted dried mushrooms back into the saucepan, stopping when you reach any grit. Bring the stock to a simmer over low heat; maintain at a simmer.

6. In a medium nonreactive saucepan, combine the oil, onion and the remaining 2 minced garlic cloves. Cover and cook over low heat, stirring often, until wilted, about 4 minutes. Add the rice and cook, stirring, for about 1 minute. Increase the heat to moderately high, add the red wine and cook, stirring, until the wine has evaporated, about 1 minute.

7. Stir in the thyme and about 1 cup of the hot mushroom stock, enough to just cover the rice. Stir constantly until just absorbed. Continue adding the stock, 1 cup at a time, stirring, until it is absorbed, 12 to 14 minutes. The rice should be tender but still firm to the bite with a slightly thickened sauce surrounding it. During the last 5 minutes or so of cooking, stir in the sliced fresh morels.

8. Remove from the heat and stir in

the chestnut pieces, parsley-garlic mixture and Parmesan cheese. Season with salt and pepper.

One Serving: Calories 215 kcal, Protein 6 gm, Carbohydrate 38 gm, Cholesterol 3 mg, Total Fat 3 gm, Saturated Fat 1 gm

—*Marcia Kiesel*

QUINOA AND VEGETABLE PILAF

This easy side dish also makes a satisfying light lunch. Any leftovers? Just add a little vinaigrette and you have a quinoa salad.

6 Servings

1 cup quinoa, rinsed and drained (see Note)
1¾ cups canned low-sodium chicken broth, degreased
2 teaspoons olive oil
¼ cup finely diced red bell pepper
¼ cup finely diced yellow bell pepper
2 leeks, white part only, finely chopped
2 medium carrots, finely diced
1 large celery rib, finely diced
1 teaspoon minced garlic
1 tablespoon freshly grated Parmesan cheese
Salt and freshly ground black pepper
¼ cup chopped flat-leaf parsley

1. In a medium saucepan, combine the quinoa and chicken broth and bring to a boil over moderately high heat. Reduce the heat to moderately low, cover and simmer until the quinoa is very tender and all the liquid has been absorbed, about 15 minutes.

2. Meanwhile, in a medium skillet, heat the oil over moderately high heat. Add the red and yellow bell peppers, leeks, carrots and celery and cook, stirring occasionally, until just softened, 6 to 7 minutes. Stir in the garlic and cook for 1 minute longer. Remove from the heat and keep warm while the quinoa cooks. Stir the warm vegetables into the quinoa. *(The recipe can be made to this point up to 1 day ahead; cover and refrigerate. Reheat over moderately low heat before proceeding.)*

3. Stir in the Parmesan cheese and season to taste with salt and black pepper. Serve hot, sprinkled with parsley.

NOTE: Most varieties of quinoa have a naturally occurring bitter-tasting coating. Although this coating is removed during processing, there may be a small amount of bitter residue left on the grains. It can be removed simply by rinsing under cold running water before cooking.

One Serving: Calories 144 kcal, Protein 5 gm, Carbohydrate 23 gm, Cholesterol .8 mg, Total Fat 4 gm, Saturated Fat .7 gm

—*Laurie Burrows Grad*

SALADE DE PECHES

4 Servings

4 peaches
2 tablespoons fresh orange juice
1 tablespoon fresh lemon juice
One 8-ounce container of vanilla nonfat yogurt
Mint sprigs, for garnish

1. Drop the peaches in a pot of boiling water. Boil for 1 minute, drain, then refresh under cold water. Peel the peaches, pit and thinly slice.

2. In a nonreactive bowl, toss the peaches with the orange and lemon juices. Refrigerate for 1 hour.

3. Transfer the peaches to dessert bowls or goblets, dollop ¼ cup yogurt on each serving, garnish with mint sprigs and serve at once.

One Serving: Calories 86 kcal, Protein 1 gm, Carbohydrate 16 gm, Cholesterol 0, Total Fat .1 gm, Saturated Fat 0

—*Laurie Burrows Grad*

FRESH PEARS, KIWIS AND ORANGES WITH ROSEMARY SYRUP

8 Servings

¾ cup sugar
¾ cup dry white wine
3 tablespoons balsamic vinegar
¼ cup fresh rosemary leaves plus whole sprigs, for garnish
1 large or 2 small bay leaves
½ teaspoon whole black peppercorns
4 pears (2 pounds)—halved, cored and cut into wedges
2 kiwis, peeled and sliced crosswise
4 large navel oranges, peeled and sliced crosswise

1. In a small nonreactive saucepan, combine the sugar, wine, balsamic vinegar, rosemary leaves, bay leaves, peppercorns and ⅓ cup of water. Bring to a boil over moderately high heat. Reduce the heat to moderately low and simmer gently for 10 minutes. Strain the syrup and let cool to room temperature, then refrigerate in a covered jar. *(The rosemary syrup can be made up to 1 week ahead.)*

2. Arrange the pears, kiwis and oranges on a large platter. Drizzle the rosemary syrup over the fruit and garnish with the rosemary sprigs.

One Serving: Calories 210 kcal, Protein 2 gm, Carbohydrate 50 gm, Cholesterol 0, Total Fat .8 gm, Saturated Fat .02 gm

—*John Ash & Sid Goldstein*

PINEAPPLE-KIWI COMPOTE

This makes a delicious dessert served with vanilla nonfat frozen yogurt.

Makes About 4 Cups

1 large ripe pineapple (3 pounds)— peeled, cored and cut into 1-inch pieces
3 tablespoons pure maple syrup
2 kiwis, peeled and cut into 1-inch pieces
1 teaspoon pure vanilla extract

1. In a large nonreactive skillet, mix the pineapple pieces with the maple syrup. Cover and cook over low heat until the pineapple is almost tender, about 8 minutes. Raise the heat to high and boil uncovered until the juices are slightly thickened, about 3 minutes. Spoon the pineapple and juices into a medium nonreactive bowl and let cool to room temperature. *(The compote can be prepared to this point up to 3 days ahead and refrigerated. Return to room temperature before proceeding.)*

2. Just before serving, stir the kiwis and vanilla into the pineapple.

One Serving: Calories 140 kcal, Protein 1 gm, Carbohydrate 35 gm, Cholesterol 0, Total Fat 1 gm, Saturated Fat .04 gm

—*Marcia Kiesel*

COCOA BROWNIES

Makes 48 Brownies

4 large eggs, at room temperature
2 cups sugar
1 cup canned unsweetened pumpkin puree
1 tablespoon pure vanilla extract
1 tablespoon vegetable oil
1¼ cups unsweetened cocoa powder, preferably Dutch process
1 cup all-purpose flour

1. Preheat the oven to 350°. Lightly coat a 9-by-13-by-2-inch metal baking pan with vegetable cooking spray.

2. In a large bowl, using an electric mixer, beat the eggs and sugar on high speed until thick and pale. Beat in the pumpkin, vanilla and oil.

3. Sift the cocoa and flour over the mixture and lightly fold in until just combined.

4. Spread the batter in the prepared pan and bake for 25 minutes, or until the brownies feel set when lightly pressed in the middle. Let cool on a rack, then cut into 48 squares. *(The brownies can be made up to 2 days ahead and kept in an airtight container, or they can be frozen.)*

One Brownie: Calories 59 kcal, Protein 1 gm, Carbohydrate 12 gm, Cholesterol 18 mg, Total Fat 1 gm, Saturated Fat .4 gm

—*Diana Sturgis*

CHOCOLATE-CHERRY BISCOTTI

Makes About 3 Dozen

1⅓ cups all-purpose flour
½ cup unsweetened cocoa powder
1 teaspoon baking powder
½ teaspoon salt
2 large eggs
1 cup sugar
1 teaspoon pure vanilla extract
1 cup dried sour cherries*
*Available at specialty food shops

1. Preheat the oven to 350°. Line a large cookie sheet with foil and lightly coat it with vegetable cooking spray.

2. In a medium bowl, sift together the flour, cocoa, baking powder and salt. In a large bowl, using an electric mixer, beat the eggs, sugar and vanilla until very pale and thick, about 3 minutes. Stir in the dry ingredients, then the cherries; the dough will be stiff.

3. Divide the dough in half. With damp hands, shape each half into a smooth, 12-inch log on the prepared cookie sheet. Bake for about 30 minutes, or until the logs spring back when lightly touched in the center.

4. Carefully transfer the logs to a cutting board. Using a serrated knife and a gentle sawing motion, slice the logs crosswise ¾ inch thick. Stand the biscotti on a baking sheet ½ inch apart. Bake for about 10 minutes, or until crisp. Transfer to a wire rack to cool. *(The biscotti can be kept in an airtight container for up to 1 week.)*

One Cookie: Calories 60 kcal, Protein 1 gm, Carbohydrate 13 gm, Cholesterol 13 mg, Total Fat .7 gm, Saturated Fat .3 gm

—Michele Scicolone

GINGERBREAD LOAF

Makes Sixteen ½-Inch Slices

1 cup (packed) dark brown sugar
½ cup unsulphured molasses
2 tablespoons unsalted butter
1 large egg
½ cup skim milk
2½ cups all-purpose flour
1 tablespoon ground ginger
1 teaspoon baking soda
⅓ cup coarsely chopped candied ginger (2 ounces)

1. Preheat the oven to 325°. Lightly coat a 9-by-4½-by-2-inch loaf pan with vegetable cooking spray. Line the bottom of the pan with a piece of parchment or wax paper.

2. In a medium saucepan, combine the brown sugar, molasses and butter. Cook over moderate heat, stirring occasionally, until the butter has melted, 2 to 3 minutes.

3. In a small bowl, beat the egg with the milk.

4. In a large bowl, sift together the flour, ground ginger and baking soda. Stir in the brown sugar mixture and the milk until smooth. Stir in the candied ginger.

5. Scrape the batter into the prepared pan and bake in the lower third of the oven for about 1 hour and 20 minutes, or until a cake tester inserted in the center comes out clean. Transfer to a wire rack to cool for 10 minutes.

6. Run a thin knife around the sides of the gingerbread. Turn the loaf out on a rack, then turn it right-side up and let cool to room temperature. *(The gingerbread can be prepared up to 1 day ahead and kept tightly covered at room temperature.)*

One Slice: Calories 181 kcal, Protein 3 gm, Carbohydrate 39 gm, Cholesterol 17 mg, Total Fat 2 gm, Saturated Fat 1 gm

—Diana Sturgis

RASPBERRY JELLY ROLL

This cake is best the day it's made.

12 Servings

½ cup granulated sugar
2 large eggs
2 egg whites
1 tablespoon pure vanilla extract
1 cup all-purpose flour
⅔ cup seedless raspberry jam
1½ tablespoons confectioners' sugar

1. Preheat the oven to 425°. Coat a 13-by-9-by-½ inch jelly-roll pan with vegetable cooking spray and line it with a sheet of parchment or wax paper. Spray the paper too.

2. In a large heatproof bowl, combine the granulated sugar, whole eggs and egg whites. Set the bowl over a medium saucepan with 1 inch of simmering water. Using an electric mixer, beat the eggs at high speed until tripled in volume, about 5 minutes. Beat in the vanilla.

3. Sift the flour over the egg mixture and lightly fold it in until just combined; do not overmix. Pour the batter into the prepared pan, spreading it into the corners. Bake for about 6 minutes, or until golden.

4. Meanwhile, in a small bowl, stir the jam until smooth. Spread a 15-inch sheet of parchment or wax paper on a work surface and evenly sift 1 tablespoon of the confectioners' sugar over it.

5. As soon as the cake is done, turn it out onto the sugar-covered parchment sheet. Peel off the baking paper. Working quickly, trim a scant ¼ inch from each side of the cake. Cut a lengthwise slit three-quarters of the way through the cake ½ inch in from the long edge nearest to you (this will facilitate rolling the cake into a neat, tight log). Spread the jam evenly over the cake. Hold the parchment paper in both hands and, starting from the side with the slit, push with your knuckles to roll up the cake. Wrap the parchment around the cake and let stand for 30 minutes, seam-side down.

6. Remove the parchment from the cake and sift the remaining ½ tablespoon confectioners' sugar on top.

One Serving: Calories 148 kcal, Protein 3 gm, Carbohydrate 32 gm, Cholesterol 35 mg, Total Fat 1 gm, Saturated Fat .3 gm

—Diana Sturgis

SAUCES,
PRESERVES &
CONDIMENTS

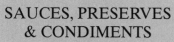
BALSAMIC VINAIGRETTE

Makes About 1 Cup

⅓ cup balsamic vinegar
⅔ cup extra-virgin olive oil
1 tablespoon fresh lime juice
Salt and freshly ground white pepper

Pour the vinegar into a small bowl. Whisk in the olive oil in a thin stream. Whisk in the lime juice and season to taste with salt and pepper.

—*Michael McCarty*

HERB AND SHALLOT VINAIGRETTE

Lemon thyme and lemon verbena contribute subtle lemony hints, but if you can't find them, use one teaspoon of regular thyme plus one-half teaspoon freshly grated lemon zest.

Makes About 1 Cup

¼ cup Champagne vinegar or white wine vinegar
2 large shallots, finely chopped
3 tablespoons finely chopped fresh chervil or flat-leaf parsley
1 tablespoon finely chopped fresh marjoram
1 tablespoon minced fresh chives
½ teaspoon minced fresh lemon thyme
2 lemon verbena leaves, minced
¾ cup extra-virgin olive oil
¾ teaspoon salt
⅛ teaspoon freshly ground pepper

In a medium bowl, whisk the vinegar with the shallots, chervil, marjoram, chives, lemon thyme and verbena. Let stand for 10 minutes. Whisk in the olive oil in a thin stream. Season with the salt and pepper. Stir well before using.

—*Deborah Madison*

MUSTARD-ANCHOVY VINAIGRETTE

Makes About ⅓ Cup

1 tablespoon anchovy paste
1 medium garlic clove, finely minced, then mashed to a paste
2 teaspoons grainy mustard
3 tablespoons red wine vinegar
¼ cup mild olive oil
2 teaspoons capers, rinsed
¼ teaspoon salt
¼ teaspoon freshly ground pepper

In a medium bowl, whisk the anchovy paste with the garlic, mustard and vinegar. Gradually whisk in the olive oil until emulsified. Stir in the capers, salt and pepper.

—*Susan Shapiro Jaslove*

MINT PESTO

Makes About 1¼ Cups

2½ (packed) cups fresh mint leaves
1 cup (packed) fresh basil leaves
½ cup (packed) flat-leaf parsley leaves
1 cup walnuts (3½ ounces)
8 garlic cloves, coarsely chopped
1 cup olive oil
Salt and freshly ground pepper

In a food processor, combine the mint, basil, parsley, walnuts and garlic. Process to a coarse puree. With the ma-chine on, pour in the olive oil in a thin stream. Scrape the pesto into a bowl and season with salt and pepper. Press a piece of plastic wrap directly on the surface of the pesto and keep at room temperature for use that day or refrigerate for up to 2 days.

—*Mary Novak*

BASIC PESTO

Use fresh basil; the dried herb lacks aroma. Frozen basil leaves won't work well either; they turn black and lose most of their volatile oils.

Makes About 1 Cup

2 cups (loosely packed) basil leaves
3 garlic cloves
½ teaspoon salt
½ teaspoon freshly ground pepper
¾ cup extra-virgin olive oil

In a food processor or blender, combine the basil, garlic, salt and pepper. Pulse the machine to chop the leaves. With the machine on, gradually add the oil in a slow stream until blended.

—*Carol Cutler*

BASIL OIL

Makes About ⅓ Cup

¼ cup olive oil
½ cup fresh basil leaves
Salt and freshly ground pepper

Blend the olive oil with the basil leaves in a blender until smooth. Season with salt and pepper to taste. Strain the oil through several layers of cheesecloth into a small bowl. Cover and refrigerate for up to 1 month.

—*Daniel Boulud*

FISH SAUCE WITH HOT CHILES

This sauce is extremely hot when it is first made, but over the course of a few weeks it mellows considerably. We always keep a jar in our refrigerator, and when it gets low we simply top it off with more fish sauce and chiles.

Makes About 1 Cup

2 tablespoons minced bird chiles with seeds (12 to 15)
1 cup fish sauce

Put the chiles in a glass jar and pour in the fish sauce. Serve in individual condiment bowls.

—*Jeffrey Alford & Naomi Duguid*

VINEGAR-CHILE SAUCE

Makes About ½ Cup

½ cup rice vinegar
½ teaspoon sugar
1 banana chile

Pour the vinegar into a bowl, add the sugar and stir until dissolved. Cut the stem off the chile and halve it lengthwise. Remove and discard the seeds and membranes. Thinly slice the chile crosswise and add to the vinegar. Serve in individual small bowls.

—*Jeffrey Alford & Naomi Duguid*

CREAMY WINE SAUCE

Makes About 2 Cups

2⅔ cups chicken stock or canned low-sodium broth
6 tablespoons unsalted butter
2 tablespoons minced shallots
1 cup dry Chenin Blanc
¼ cup plus 2 tablespoons all-purpose flour
½ cup heavy cream
½ teaspoon salt
Pinch of freshly grated nutmeg

1. In a small saucepan, heat 2 cups of the chicken stock; keep warm.

2. In a medium nonreactive saucepan, melt the butter. Add the shallots and cook over moderate heat, stirring, just until golden, about 5 minutes. Raise the heat to high, add the wine and simmer until reduced by half, about 10 minutes.

3. Whisk the flour into the remaining ⅔ cup chicken stock until smooth, then whisk the mixture into the saucepan. Cook over moderately low heat, stirring occasionally, for 10 minutes.

4. Add 1½ cups of the hot chicken stock and bring just to a boil. Add the cream and cook, stirring, until heated through. Add more stock until the sauce is the desired consistency. Strain through a fine sieve, season with the salt and nutmeg and serve warm.

—*Molly Chappellet*

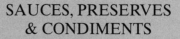
TOMATO COULIS

Makes About 4 Cups

1 tablespoon olive oil
¼ cup finely chopped onion
3 garlic cloves, finely chopped
1 bay leaf
1 fresh thyme sprig
3 pounds tomatoes, cut into 1-inch chunks, drained
One 35-ounce can Italian peeled tomatoes, well drained
1 celery rib, cut into thirds
Pinch of sugar
Salt and freshly ground pepper

1. In a large nonreactive saucepan, warm the olive oil over moderate heat. Add the onion, garlic, bay leaf and thyme and cook, stirring occasionally, until soft and translucent, 5 to 7 minutes.

2. Add the fresh and canned tomatoes, celery and sugar. Season with salt and pepper. Mix well, bring to a boil, and reduce the heat to low. Cover and cook for 40 minutes.

3. Remove from the heat and discard the bay leaf, thyme and celery. Pass the sauce through a food mill and season to taste with salt and pepper. *(The coulis can be made up to 1 month ahead. Let cool, cover and freeze. Reheat before serving.)*

—*Daniel Boulud*

TOMATO SAUCE

Tomato sauce is as distinctive as a fingerprint and just as revealing. This very simple, direct sauce relies on three basic ingredients—tomatoes, olive oil and plenty of garlic.

Makes About 10½ Cups

Four 28-ounce cans plus one 14-ounce can of Italian peeled tomatoes, preferably from the San Marzano region
3 tablespoons extra-virgin olive oil
¼ cup plus 2 tablespoons chopped garlic (about 15 cloves)
1½ tablespoons coarse (kosher) salt
1¼ teaspoons coarsely ground pepper
6 tablespoons chopped fresh basil

1. Pour the tomatoes and their liquid into a large bowl. Crush the tomatoes by hand until you can't feel any large pieces and the texture is like velvet; discard any skins and stems.

2. In a large, heavy, nonreactive saucepan, warm the olive oil over low heat. Increase the heat to moderate, add the garlic and stir until golden. Stir in 2 cups of the crushed tomatoes. When the mixture begins to bubble, stir in 2 more cups of tomatoes. Bring to a boil and continue in this fashion until all the tomatoes have been added and the sauce is boiling.

3. Reduce the heat to low and simmer the sauce for 1½ hours, stirring occasionally. Stir in the salt and pepper and continue to simmer until reduced to 10½ cups, about 1½ hours longer. *(The sauce can be prepared to this point up to 4 days ahead. Let cool, then cover and refrigerate. Rewarm before continuing.)*

4. Stir in the basil and simmer the sauce for an additional 15 minutes before using.

—*Francine Maroukian*

NONNA'S RAGU

Of all the tomato sauces I've ever tasted, this one, from my grandmother, is my favorite. Well-browned meats are cooked with the tomatoes to flavor the sauce. This recipe makes an ample amount; any leftover sauce can be frozen.

Makes About 2 Quarts

¼ cup extra-virgin olive oil
⅓ pound piece of beef, such as eye of the round
⅓ pound piece of pork
1 whole chicken leg, separated into thigh and drumstick
1 small onion, thinly sliced
Three 35-ounce cans Italian peeled tomatoes
¼ teaspoon salt
½ teaspoon freshly ground pepper

1. In a large nonreactive saucepan, heat the oil over moderately high heat. Pat the meats and chicken dry and brown them on all sides in the oil, turning as necessary, about 10 minutes. Stir in the onion and cook, stirring often, until translucent, 2 to 3 minutes.

2. Pass the tomatoes and their liquid through a food mill set over the saucepan. (Alternatively, puree the tomatoes and their liquid in a blender or food processor, then press the tomatoes through a strainer, leaving behind only the seeds.) Stir in the salt and pepper and bring to a boil over moderately high heat. Continue to cook the sauce briskly for 15 minutes, then reduce the heat to low and cover partially. Simmer for 2 to 2½ hours, stirring occasionally, until the sauce is reduced to 2 quarts. Remove the meats. Discard the chicken, but save the beef and pork for another use. *(The sauce can be frozen for up to 2 months.)*

—*Nancy Verde Barr*

PLUM-YUM SAUCE

Molly Chappellet developed this sauce to use the tart Japanese plums from her garden, but any type of plum works well. The amount of sugar you'll need depends on the sweetness of the plums.

Makes About 2 Cups

2 pounds plums (about 7), pitted and cut into eighths
½ cup sugar, or to taste
1 teaspoon fresh lemon juice

In a medium nonreactive saucepan, mix the plums, sugar, lemon juice and ¼ cup of water and bring to a boil. Simmer over moderately high heat until the plums are soft, about 15 minutes. Pass the mixture through a food mill set over a large bowl. Serve warm. *(The sauce can be refrigerated for up to 2 days. Reheat before serving.)*

—*Molly Chappellet*

RASPBERRY SAUCE

Makes About 1½ Cups

Two 12-ounce bags frozen unsweetened raspberries or 2⅔ cups fresh
⅔ cup sugar

In a medium nonreactive saucepan, bring the raspberries and sugar to a boil. Simmer over moderately high heat for 10 minutes. Let cool slightly. Strain the sauce through a fine sieve and serve warm or at room temperature. *(The sauce can be refrigerated for up to 2 days. Let return to room temperature or reheat before serving.)*

—*Molly Chappellet*

CARAMEL SAUCE

Makes About 2 Cups

1 cup heavy cream
1 cup dark brown sugar
⅓ cup granulated sugar
¼ cup pure maple syrup
¼ cup light corn syrup

In a heavy medium saucepan, stir together all the ingredients until thoroughly combined. Cook over high heat until the mixture reaches 210° on a candy thermometer. Set aside to cool for 20 minutes. *(The sauce can be made up to 3 days ahead; transfer to an airtight container and refrigerate. Reheat over warm water or in a microwave oven.)*

—*Stephan Pyles*

CARAMELIZED DRIED APRICOTS

Makes 8

Ice water
8 plump dried apricot halves
½ cup sugar

1. Fill a bowl with ice water. Carefully insert a skewer in the center of the underside of each apricot.

2. In a small heavy saucepan, combine the sugar and ¼ cup of water and stir until the sugar is completely moistened. Cover and bring to a simmer over moderate heat without stirring. Uncover and wash down the sides of the pan with a wet pastry brush. Cover and cook until the sugar is completely dissolved, about 2 minutes. Uncover and cook until the syrup turns a pale amber, about 12 minutes. Shake the pan gently, wash down the sides with the wet pastry brush and cook until the syrup darkens to a medium amber, 2 to 3 minutes longer. Immediately plunge the bottom of the saucepan into the bowl of ice water for 2 seconds to stop the caramel from cooking further.

3. Tilting the saucepan to facilitate dipping, dip the skewered apricots one by one into the hot caramel, then prop them up on the edge of a pan or bowl to cool.

4. When the caramel has hardened, snip off any caramel drips or "tails" with a pair of scissors. *(The apricots will keep in an airtight container for up to 3 days.)*

—*Alice Medrich*

WINTER FRUIT AND NUT CONSERVE

Makes About 4 Cups

2 tablespoons lightly salted butter
2 Granny Smith apples, peeled and cut into small dice
2 winter pears, such as Comice, peeled and cut into small dice
12 fresh kumquats, quartered
1 cup pecans, black walnuts or wild nuts, such as hickory nuts or beechnuts
8 fresh or dried dates, pitted and cut into small dice
½ cup dried currants, dried wild blueberries or huckleberries
½ cup dried cranberries
2 tablespoons light brown sugar
2 tablespoons fresh lemon juice
¼ cup cider vinegar
Pinch of allspice
Pinch of cumin
Pinch of freshly grated nutmeg

1. In a large nonreactive saucepan, cook the butter over moderate heat until light brown. Add the apples, pears, kumquats and nuts and cook, stirring, until the apples are tender, 5 to 7 minutes. Stir in the dates, currants and dried cranberries and cook until heated through, 1 to 2 minutes.

2. Stir in the brown sugar, lemon juice, vinegar, allspice, cumin and nutmeg and cook for 2 minutes longer. Transfer the conserve to a bowl and let cool completely. *(The conserve can be prepared up to 5 days ahead and refrigerated.)* Serve at room temperature.

—*Larry Forgione*

SWEET AND CHUNKY APPLE BUTTER

Makes About 2 Quarts

*4 pounds Granny Smith apples—
peeled, cored and cut into ½-inch
pieces*
*4 pounds McIntosh apples—peeled,
cored and cut into 1-inch pieces*
2 cups unsweetened apple juice
4 cups sugar
¼ cup fresh lemon juice

1. In a large enameled cast-iron casserole, bring the apples and apple juice to a boil. Simmer over moderate heat, skimming occasionally, until the mixture is reduced by half, about 20 minutes.

2. Stir in the sugar and lemon juice and continue simmering until the apple butter is thick and dotted with tender chunks, about 25 minutes longer. Let the apple butter cool.

3. Ladle the apple butter into two 1-quart sterilized Mason jars. Cover and refrigerate for up to 2 weeks.

—*Sarabeth Levine*

OVERNIGHT SQUASH AND RED ONION PICKLES

After a couple of days, the color of the pickles darkens, but the pickles will still be tasty for up to two weeks.

Makes About 4 Cups

2½ cups apple cider vinegar
1½ tablespoons sugar
1½ teaspoons salt
2 medium garlic cloves, thinly sliced
*1 tablespoon mixed whole black, green
and red peppercorns*
1 teaspoon black mustard seeds
½ teaspoon turmeric
1 bay leaf
*1 pound small, yellow pattypan squash,
sliced crosswise ⅛ inch thick*
2 medium red onions, thinly sliced
1 quart boiling water

1. In a large bowl, whisk 3 cups of cold water with the cider vinegar, sugar and salt. Stir in the garlic, peppercorns, mustard seeds, turmeric and bay leaf.

2. Place the squash and onions in a large colander set in the sink and slowly pour the boiling water over them.

3. Place the squash and onions in 1 or more glass jars, pour in the pickling liquid, cover tightly and refrigerate overnight or for up to 2 weeks.

—*Deborah Madison*

BLACK BEAN SALSA

The dried chile called for here is pure ground red chile, not commercial chili powder, which is actually a spice blend. If you don't have it or can't find it, the salsa will be fine without it.

Makes About 5 Cups

*One 15-ounce can black beans, drained
and lightly rinsed*
*1½ cups cooked fresh corn kernels
(from 3 ears)*
*2 medium tomatoes, cut into ¼-inch
dice*
1 red bell pepper, cut into ¼-inch dice
*1 green bell pepper, cut into ¼-inch
dice*
½ cup finely diced red onion
*1 to 2 fresh green serrano or jalapeño
peppers, thinly sliced, seeds and all*
⅓ cup fresh lime juice
⅓ cup extra-virgin olive oil
*⅓ cup chopped fresh coriander
(cilantro)*
1 teaspoon salt
½ teaspoon cumin
*½ teaspoon pure ground red chiles or
a pinch of cayenne pepper*

Combine all the ingredients in a large bowl. Mix well. Set aside to let the flavors blend until ready to serve. *(The salsa can be made up to 1 day ahead; cover and refrigerate. Bring to room temperature before serving.)*

—*Nancy Harmon Jenkins*

JALAPENO-CILANTRO LIME SALSA

Makes About ½ Cup

1 jalapeño pepper
1 tablespoon chopped fresh coriander
  (cilantro)
½ cup extra-virgin olive oil
Salt and freshly ground white pepper
Juice of 1 lime

1. Roast the jalapeño directly over a gas flame or under the broiler as close to the heat as possible, turning, until charred all over. Let cool, then peel and discard the stem, core and seeds. Finely chop the jalapeño and place in a small bowl.

2. Add the coriander and olive oil and season to taste with salt and pepper. Just before serving, stir in the lime juice. (The lime will turn the coriander brown if added any earlier.) Use immediately.

—*Michael McCarty*

BLACK-EYED PEA RELISH

Makes About 3 Cups

1 cup dried black-eyed peas
1 small sweet potato, peeled and cut
  into ½-inch dice
Salt
¼ cup extra-virgin olive oil
4 medium Vidalia or other sweet
  onions, minced
¼ cup minced red bell pepper
¼ cup minced flat-leaf parsley
2 tablespoons minced fresh basil

2 tablespoons minced chives
2 tablespoons raspberry vinegar
Freshly cracked black pepper

1. In a bowl, cover the black-eyed peas with warm water and let soak for 1 hour. Drain, rinse carefully to remove any dirt and drain again.

2. Place the black-eyed peas in a saucepan and add enough water to cover by 1 inch. Add the sweet potato and a dash of salt and bring to a boil over high heat. Reduce the heat to low and simmer gently until the peas and potatoes are tender, 15 to 20 minutes. Drain and set aside.

3. In a large skillet, heat the oil over moderate heat. Add the onions and cook, stirring, until translucent, about 7 minutes. Set aside to cool.

4. Stir in the red bell pepper, parsley, basil, chives, vinegar, peas and potatoes. Season with black pepper. Serve at room temperature.

—*Elizabeth Terry*

GINGER-GARLIC CHUTNEY

This zesty, uncooked chutney is fast and easy to make.

Makes About 1 Cup

1 Greening or other tart apple (about
  ½ pound)—peeled, cored and
  chopped
½ cup raisins
⅓ cup chopped peeled fresh ginger
  (from a 2-ounce piece)
3 large garlic cloves, peeled and
  chopped
2½ tablespoons fresh lemon juice
½ teaspoon salt

Chopped fresh coriander (cilantro) or
flat-leaf parsley, for garnish

In a food processor, combine the apple, raisins, ginger, garlic, lemon juice and salt until finely chopped. Transfer to a small bowl and sprinkle with the coriander just before serving.

—*Diana Sturgis*

INDEX

A

All-american apple turnovers, 195
Almonds, roasted, with red chile, 20
Angel food cake, chocolate, with mocha frosting, 176
Appalachian dressing, 83
APPETIZERS. *See also First courses*
  asparagus cheese puffs, 28
  black bean salsa, 246
  bombay chicken wings, 28
  bruschetta rossa, 22
  california tea sandwiches, 25
  cheese swizzles, 23
  crostini, 22
  crunchy chicken salad sandwiches, 24
  eggplant and garlic dip, 222
  eggplant dip with country bread, 21
  fontina and tomato squares, 23
  herbed shallots in phyllo, 25
  lemon cheese with lovage, 21
  olives with cumin, 20
  pecorino and fresh mint canapés, 24
  phyllo purses with black beans and pepper-jack cheese, 25
  potato nests with crème fraîche and caviar, 27
  prosciutto and papaya with lime-tequila splash, 29
  rice paper rolls with shrimp and vegetables, 27
  roast beef and goat cheese triangles, 25
  roasted almonds with red chile, 20
  sheer shrimp dumplings with coriander-mint dipping sauce, 26
  smoked chicken mousse canapés, 23
  spicy orange pecans, 20
  tapenade, 21
  watercress and cream cheese swirls, 24
APPLES
  all-american apple turnovers, 195
  apple frangipane turnovers, 195
  apple-almond custard tart, 200
  apple-raisin spice cake with caramel sauce and pecan ice cream, 172
  baked apples with apple jelly and ginger, 219
  buttery apple tart, 199
  celery root and apple puree, 103
  pear and apple salad with gruyère and toasted pecans, 125
  quick apple cake, 171
  quince and apple puree, 113
  sweet and chunky apple butter, 246
  tarte tatin with cinnamon ice cream, 196
Apricots, caramelized dried, 245
ARTICHOKES
  artichoke and potato stew with mint, 45
  Michele's stuffed artichokes, 100
ASPARAGUS
  asparagus cheese puffs, 28
  asparagus risotto, 237
  asparagus salad mimosa, 120
  asparagus with tarragon lemon sauce, 28
  asparagus, goat cheese and prosciutto strudel, 29
  asparagus, leek and new potato chowder, 43
  asparagus-pepper salad with ginger dressing, 230
  grilled asparagus, 100

B

Baba, rum, 181
BANANAS
  black bottom banana tart, 201
  orange, lemon and banana sherbet, 213
  roasted banana ice cream, 213

BARLEY
  barley and millet pilaf with wild mushrooms, 159
  barley salad with roasted corn and peppers, 133
BASIL
  basic pesto, 242
  basil oil, 242
BEANS, DRIED OR CANNED. *See also Lentils*
  smoky black bean and vegetable soup, 229
  white bean, fennel and sausage soup, 52
  white beans and herbs with red onion topping, 101
Beans, green, with balsamic-glazed onions, 100
BEEF
  beef and potato enchiladas, 87
  fillet of beef salad with blue cheese dressing and sesame seeds, 142
  pot-roasted beef brisket with ancho chile sauce, 86
BEETS
  borscht with greens and chickpeas, 222
  oven-roasted beets with wilted greens, 101
BELGIAN ENDIVE
  endive and carrot salad, 120
BISCOTTI
  cashew-coffee biscotti, 190
  chocolate-cherry biscotti, 239
Biscuits, whipping-cream, 164
Black bass with port wine, 54
BLACK BEANS
  black bean salsa, 246
  smoky black bean and vegetable soup, 229
Black bottom banana tart, 201
Black trumpet mushrooms, lobster with fava bean puree and, 61
Black-eyed pea relish, 247
Blanquette of veal vallée d'auge, 87

BLUE CHEESE
  pears with dried cherries and stilton,
    217
BLUEBERRIES
  blueberry turnovers, 192
  fresh blueberry tart, 199
  orange-blueberry salad with arugula
    and tarragon, 124
Bombay chicken wings, 28
Borscht with greens and chickpeas, 222
BREAD. *See also Biscuits; Muffins;*
    Toasts
  buttermilk dinner rolls, 165
  country bread rolls, 165
  italian breadsticks, 164
  lemon-poppy seed biscuit sticks, 162
  rosemary-potato focaccia loaves,
    166
  Sarabeth's english muffins, 163
  spiced cranberry rolls, 166
Bread-and-tomato soup, 42
BREAKFAST/BRUNCH
  cornmeal waffles, 162
  pecan sticky buns, 167
  whole wheat berry pancakes, 162
Brioche dough, food processor, 55
BROCCOLI
  broccoli with spicy sesame oil, 102
  broccoli, orange and roasted pepper
    salad, 120
  brown-butter broccoli with
    caramelized carrots, 102
Broccoli rabe with orecchiette, 234
Brown betty, pear, 219
BROWNIES
  cappuccino brownies, 182
  chocolate brownies, 182
  cocoa brownies, 239
Bruschetta rossa, 22
Brussels sprouts with malted cream,
  102
BULGUR
  bulgur salad with oranges, fennel
    and olives, 126
  green lentils and bulgur with fresh
    herbs, 160
  tabbouleh, 127
Burgers, turkey, with herbed lemon
  mayonnaise, 80
BUTTERCREAM
  chocolate-coffee buttercream, 178
  easy meringue buttercream, 177
  raspberry buttercream, 177
  spirited buttercream, 178
Buttermilk spoonbread, 164

C

CABBAGE
  braised cabbage with apples and
    toasted coriander, 103
  three cabbages with caraway, 236
Caffè latte cheesecake, 170
CAKES. *See also Cheesecake*
  apple-raisin spice cake with caramel
    sauce and pecan ice cream, 172
  buttery nut cake, 174
  chocolate angel food cake with
    mocha frosting, 176
  chocolate apricot torte, 180
  chocolate-walnut ganache torte, 180
  classic chocolate cake, 176
  classic white cake, 177
  coconut-pecan cake, 173
  gingerbread loaf, 240
  hazelnut torte with maple
    buttercream frosting, 178
  lemon mousse cake, 179
  lightning cake, 174
  mexican chocolate cake, 175
  Mrs. McGregor's carrot cake, 171
  polenta cake, 172
  quick apple cake, 171
  raspberry jelly roll, 240
  rum baba, 181
CANTALOUPE
  melon and mango salad with mint
    and parsley, 126
Cappuccino brownies, 182
CARAMEL
  caramel sauce, 245
  caramelized dried apricots, 245
  caramelized red onion marmalade,
    236
Carlos' rack of lamb, 97
Carnival lasagna, neapolitan, 157
CARROTS
  brown-butter broccoli with
    caramelized carrots, 102
  carrot and chestnut soup, 222
  crisp root-vegetable cakes, 115
  endive and carrot salad, 120
  Mrs. McGregor's carrot cake, 171

Cashew-coffee biscotti, 190
Cauliflower and leek soup, curried,
  229
CAVIAR
  corn waffles with smoked salmon
    and osetra caviar, 38
  mixed field greens with potato
    surprise and caviar, 119
  potato nests with crème fraîche and
    caviar, 27
CELERY ROOT
  celery root and apple puree, 103
  puree of celery root with leeks and
    scallions, 103
CHEESE
  artichoke and goat cheese spread, 22
  cheese swizzles, 23
  lemon cheese with lovage, 21
  new england cheddar cheese soup,
    45
  pecorino and fresh mint canapés, 24
  ricotta, prosciutto and basil spread,
    22
  sheep's milk cheese and lemon
    fritters with honey, 220
  spicy grilled radicchio with
    bocconcini, 30
CHEESECAKE
  caffè latte cheesecake, 170
  cranberry swirl cheesecake, 170
CHERRIES
  peach, plum and cherry salad with
    cucumber ribbons, 125
  pears with dried cherries and stilton,
    217
  pineapple and dried sour cherry
    turnovers, 192
CHESTNUTS
  carrot and chestnut soup, 222
  mushroom and chestnut risotto, 237
CHICKEN. *See also Game hens;*
    Poussins
  bombay chicken wings, 28
  broiled ginger-hoisin chicken thighs,
    68
  chicken and goat cheese salad with
    jalapeño-cilantro lime salsa, 140
  chicken and three-mushroom
    casserole, 75
  chicken with raisins and black
    pepper, 73
  chinese chicken soup with rice, 49
  family-style chicken fricassee, 67

fried chicken with peppery pan gravy, 73

grilled chicken breasts with onion marmalade, 236

grilled chicken salad with frizzled tortillas, 139

minced chicken salad with fresh herbs, 139

poached chicken breasts with herb and shallot vinaigrette, 66

poulet basquaise, 67

red chicken curry, 74

sautéed chicken breasts with fresh sage, 66

sautéed chicken breasts with mustard sauce, 66

tuscan chicken and artichoke soup, 49

Chinese chicken soup with rice, 49

Chinese lacquered duck with coffee mandarin glaze, 82

CHOCOLATE

black bottom banana tart, 201

chocolate angel food cake with mocha frosting, 176

chocolate apricot torte, 180

chocolate brownies, 182

chocolate custards, 211

chocolate ganache, 178

chocolate ice cream, 212

chocolate-coffee buttercream, 178

chocolate-walnut ganache torte, 180

classic chocolate cake, 176

mexican chocolate cake, 175

mocha-chocolate float, 215

CHOWDER

asparagus, leek and new potato chowder, 43

five-lily chowder, 224

Chutney, ginger-garlic, 247

Cinnamon ice cream, 212

Clam, garlic-, pizza with thyme, 60

Claremont Diner coconut cream pie, 197

COCONUT

Claremont Diner coconut cream pie, 197

coconut shrimp with lemon grass vinaigrette, 138

coconut-pecan cake, 173

CONDIMENTS

black-eyed pea relish, 247

caramelized red onion marmalade, 236

fish sauce with hot chiles, 243

ginger-garlic chutney, 247

jalapeño-cilantro lime salsa, 247

vinegar-chile sauce, 243

Conserve, winter fruit and nut, 245

COOKIES AND SMALL CAKES. See also Brownies

almond meringues, 204

butter sprinkle cookies, 190

cashew-coffee biscotti, 190

chocolate cookie dough, 189

chocolate-cherry biscotti, 239

deep-south pecan cookies, 183

ginger cookie dough, 189

lemon shortbread, 189

mexican tea clouds, 184

peanut crisps, 182

pecan caramel triangles, 183

pine nut-brown sugar shortbread, 184

polenta cookies, 184

raspberry trolls, 190

CORN. See also Hominy

barley salad with roasted corn and peppers, 133

corn soup with roasted peppers and crab, 48

creamy polenta with corn, 104

Corn bread muffins, pecan, 163

CORNISH HENS. See Game hens

CORNMEAL

buttermilk spoonbread, 164

cornmeal waffles, 162

creamy polenta with corn, 104

pecan corn bread muffins, 163

polenta cake, 172

polenta cookies, 184

Cottage pie, turkey, 80

COUSCOUS

couscous timbales with asparagus and corn, 160

curried couscous salad, 134

CRAB. See also Soft-shell crab

corn soup with roasted peppers and crab, 48

CRANBERRIES

cranberry swirl cheesecake, 170

pear and cranberry turnovers with black pepper, 194

spiced cranberry rolls, 166

Cream, whipped, 178

Crostini, 22

CRUST. See Pastry, pie

Cucumber salad with rice wine vinegar, 119

CUSTARD

chocolate custards, 211

sweet potato custard with a brown sugar crust, 211

D-E

Deep-south pecan cookies, 183

DESSERTS. See also Cakes; Cookies and small cakes; Ice Cream; Pies and tarts, sweet

baked apples with apple jelly and ginger, 219

baked pears with ginger, 220

baked pumpkin and buttermilk pudding, 210

chocolate custards, 211

figs in snow, 216

fresh pears, kiwis and oranges with rosemary syrup, 238

frozen peach soufflé with fresh peaches and plum wine nectar, 209

gingersnap-plum ice cream sandwiches, 214

harvest fruit parfait, 219

mocha-chocolate float, 215

orange trifle, 204

pan-roasted peaches and blackberries with ginger and caramel ice cream, 218

peach frappé, 218

peaches with honey zabaglione, 216

pear brown betty, 219

pears with dried cherries and stilton, 217

pineapple-kiwi compote, 239

salade de pêches, 238

sheep's milk cheese and lemon fritters with honey, 220

spiced red wine fruit soup with candied orange, 217

strawberry salad with lemon-pepper petals, 215

sweet potato custard with a brown sugar crust, 211

DIPS
    eggplant and garlic dip, 222
    eggplant dip with country bread, 21
    tapenade, 21
DRESSING, POULTRY. *See Stuffing*
DRESSING, SALAD. *See Salad*
    dressing
DUCK
    chinese lacquered duck with coffee
        mandarin glaze, 82
    wok-seared duck salad, 141
Dumplings, sheer shrimp, with
    coriander-mint dipping sauce, 26
EGGPLANT
    eggplant and garlic dip, 222
    eggplant dip with country bread, 21
EGGS
    swiss chard omelet, 114
Enchiladas, beef and potato, 87
English muffins, Sarabeth's, 163

F

Family-style chicken fricassee, 67
FENNEL
    fennel gratin, 104
    leek and potato gratin, 104
    winter squash gratin, 108
FETTUCCINE
    fettuccine with basil and almonds,
        146
    pesto fettuccine with chicken and
        vegetables, 147
Figs in snow, 216
FIRST COURSES. *See also Appetizers;*
    Salads; Soups
    asparagus salad mimosa, 120
    asparagus with tarragon lemon
        sauce, 28
    asparagus, goat cheese and
        prosciutto strudel, 29
    corn waffles with smoked salmon
        and osetra caviar, 38
    creamed oysters and mushrooms, 31
    crisp pan-fried sweetbreads with
        balsamic vinegar sauce, 40
    french onion tart, 31
    grilled garlic-studded portobello
        mushrooms with tomato salad and
        herb oil, 122

mixed field greens with potato
    surprise and caviar, 119
roasted quail with marinated
    tomatoes, eggplant and tomatillo
    sauce, 39
roasted vegetable and goat cheese
    terrine, 30
sautéed soft-shell crabs with
    hazelnuts, 32
scallops with zucchini and thyme, 37
seared salmon with sweet corn,
    shiitakes and spinach, 38
shrimp in kataifi with purple relish,
    37
skewered bread and wild mushrooms
    with pungent herbs, 105
spicy grilled radicchio with
    bocconcini, 30
spicy squid salad, 39
tomato salad with sea scallops, maui
    onions, piccolo basil and olive oil
    dressing, 137
warm mozzarella salad with sun-
    dried tomato vinaigrette, 123
Fish sauce with hot chiles, 243
FISH/SHELLFISH. *See also specific*
    types
    black bass with port wine, 54
    braised snapper with sake and soy
        sauce, 57
    broiled salmon with mustard cream
        sauce, 56
    cornmeal-toasted red snapper, 57
    garlic-clam pizza with thyme, 60
    grilled lime-glazed seafood kebabs,
        60
    Julia Child's fish en croûte, 54
    lobster and coconut milk soup with
        ginger, lemon grass and a garden
        of vegetables, 47
    lobster fricassee with artichokes, 62
    lobster with fava bean puree and
        black trumpet mushrooms, 61
    marinated filet mignon of tuna, 59
    neo-classic seafood salad, 136
    poached salmon fillets with two
        vinaigrettes, 56
    provençale seafood soup, 46
    sautéed monkfish and portobello
        mushrooms on a bed of mesclun,
        55
    scallops with pesto cream sauce, 63
    seared fresh tuna niçoise, 59

seared scallops with citrus-ginger
    vinaigrette, 62
seared sea scallop salad with citrus
    vinaigrette, 137
shrimp in hot and sour broth, 63
spicy squid salad, 39
spicy tomato-mussel soup, 48
thai seafood salad, 136
tuna, swordfish or sturgeon
    alabardero, 57
Five-lily chowder, 224
Focaccia loaves, rosemary-potato, 166
Food processor brioche dough, 55
Frappé, peach, 218
French onion tart, 31
Fresh ham, roast, with garlic gravy, 93
FRICASSEE
    family-style chicken fricassee, 67
    lobster fricassee with artichokes,
        62
Fritters, sheep's milk cheese and lemon,
    with honey, 220
FROSTING
    chocolate ganache, 178
    chocolate-coffee buttercream, 178
    easy meringue buttercream, 177
    orange frosting, 171
    raspberry buttercream, 177
    spirited buttercream, 178
    sugar glaze, 196
FRUIT. *See also Fruit salads*
    baked apples with apple jelly and
        ginger, 219
    baked pears with ginger, 220
    figs in snow, 216
    fresh pears, kiwis and oranges with
        rosemary syrup, 238
    harvest fruit parfait, 219
    peaches with honey zabaglione, 216
    pears with dried cherries and stilton,
        217
    pineapple-kiwi compote, 239
    salade de pêches, 238
    strawberry salad with lemon-pepper
        petals, 215
FRUIT SALADS
    grapefruit-kiwi salad with poppy
        seeds and chicory, 124
    Jamie's fruit salad, 124
    melon and mango salad with mint
        and parsley, 126
    mixed red berries in red wine syrup
        with radicchio, 125

orange-blueberry salad with arugula and tarragon, 124

peach, plum and cherry salad with cucumber ribbons, 125

pear and apple salad with gruyère and toasted pecans, 125

pineapple and jicama salad with red grapes and basil, 126

strawberry salad with lemon-pepper petals, 215

G

GAME
mustard barbecued quail with vidalia onion and black-eyed pea relish, 83

roast quail with tarragon, 84

roasted quail with marinated tomatoes, eggplant and tomatillo sauce, 39

roasted rock cornish hens, 77

rock cornish hens with rosemary and garlic, 76

GAME HENS
roasted rock cornish hens, 77

rock cornish hens with rosemary and garlic, 76

GANACHE
chocolate ganache, 178

chocolate-walnut ganache torte, 180

Garlic soup, cream of, 44

Gazpacho sevillano, 42

Gingerbread loaf, 240

Gingersnap-plum ice cream sandwiches, 214

GOAT CHEESE
artichoke and goat cheese spread, 22

asparagus, goat cheese and prosciutto strudel, 29

chicken and goat cheese salad with jalapeño-cilantro lime salsa, 140

roasted vegetable and goat cheese terrine, 30

Goose, roast, with plum glaze, 82

GRAINS. See also Rice; Wild rice
barley and millet pilaf with wild mushrooms, 159

barley salad with roasted corn and peppers, 133

bulgur salad with oranges, fennel and olives, 126

couscous timbales with asparagus and corn, 160

curried couscous salad, 134

green lentils and bulgur with fresh herbs, 160

moroccan millet salad, 133

quinoa "tabbouleh," 134

quinoa and vegetable pilaf, 238

tabbouleh, 127

whole wheat berry pancakes, 162

wild rice salad, 128

wild rice salad with green beans, mushrooms and tarragon, 128

Grande salade aux côtes d'agneau, 143

Granita, coffee, and candied orange, vanilla ice cream with, 214

Grapefruit-kiwi salad with poppy seeds and chicory, 124

GRAPES
pineapple and jicama salad with red grapes and basil, 126

GREENS
oven-roasted beets with wilted greens, 101

pan-wilted winter greens with fresh ginger, 114

sautéed swiss chard with tomatoes, 113

swiss chard omelet, 114

H-I

HAM. See also Fresh ham
country ham baked in cider, 95

Harvest fruit parfait, 219

Hash, turkey and sweet potato, 79

Hazelnut torte with maple buttercream frosting, 178

Herb ravioli with basil oil and tomato coulis, 147

Herb salad with watercress dressing, 118

Hominy and bell pepper sauté, 104

HONEYDEW MELON
melon and mango salad with mint and parsley, 126

ICE CREAM
chocolate ice cream, 212

cinnamon ice cream, 212

gingersnap-plum ice cream sandwiches, 214

mocha-chocolate float, 215

pecan ice cream, 212

plum ice cream, 213

roasted banana ice cream, 213

vanilla ice cream with coffee granita and candied orange, 214

J-K

Jamaican golden split pea soup, 43

Jamie's fruit salad, 124

JASMINE RICE
jasmine rice salad with asparagus and walnuts, 127

plain jasmine rice, 158

JERUSALEM ARTICHOKES
crisp root-vegetable cakes, 115

JICAMA
jicama-orange salad with jalapeño dressing, 230

pineapple and jicama salad with red grapes and basil, 126

Julia Child's fish en croûte, 54

KALE
pan-wilted winter greens with fresh ginger, 114

Kataifi, shrimp in, with purple relish, 37

KIWI FRUIT
fresh pears, kiwis and oranges with rosemary syrup, 238

grapefruit-kiwi salad with poppy seeds and chicory, 124

pineapple-kiwi compote, 239

L

LAMB
Carlos' rack of lamb, 97

grande salade aux côtes d'agneau, 143

grilled baby lamb chops with warm insalata tricolore, 96

grilled marinated leg of lamb, 97

roast rack of lamb with shiitake
    mushrooms, 98
Leek and potato gratin, 104
LENTILS
    basic cooked lentils, 234
    cornmeal waffles, 162
    green lentils and bulgur with fresh
        herbs, 160
    lentil salad with frisée, pears and
        leeks, 232
    lentils with fragrant rice, 233
    oxtail and lentil soup, 51
    pasta and lentils with walnut cream,
        233
Lightning cake, 174
Little devils, 76
LOBSTER
    lobster and coconut milk soup with
        ginger, lemon grass and a garden
        of vegetables, 47
    lobster coleslaw with basil, tarragon
        and chives, 138
    lobster fricassee with artichokes, 62
    lobster with fava bean puree and
        black trumpet mushrooms, 61
LOW-CALORIE COOKING
    asparagus risotto, 237
    asparagus-pepper salad with ginger
        dressing, 230
    basic cooked lentils, 234
    borscht with greens and chickpeas,
        222
    broccoli rabe with orecchiette, 234
    caramelized red onion marmalade,
        236
    carrot and chestnut soup, 222
    chocolate-cherry biscotti, 239
    cocoa brownies, 239
    curried cauliflower and leek soup,
        229
    eggplant and garlic dip, 222
    five-lily chowder, 224
    fresh pears, kiwis and oranges with
        rosemary syrup, 238
    gingerbread loaf, 240
    grilled chicken breasts with onion
        marmalade, 236
    grilled mushroom salad, 231
    jicama-orange salad with jalapeño
        dressing, 230
    lentil salad with frisée, pears and
        leeks, 232
    lentils with fragrant rice, 233

light vegetable stock, 223
    minestrone, 223
    mushroom and chestnut risotto, 237
    new potato and wax bean salad, 231
    orange, radish and cucumber salad,
        230
    oyster mushroom soup with scallops,
        224
    pan bagna, 235
    pasta and lentils with walnut cream,
        233
    pineapple-kiwi compote, 239
    quinoa and vegetable pilaf, 238
    raspberry jelly roll, 240
    salade de pêches, 238
    smoky black bean and vegetable
        soup, 229
    soba noodles with grilled tuna and
        soy ginger sauce, 235
    three cabbages with caraway, 236
    vegetable pasta salad, 232
    vegetable stock, 224
    watercress and radicchio salad, 229

M

Mango and melon salad with mint and
    parsley, 126
Marmalade, caramelized red onion,
    236
MEAT. See specific types
Melon and mango salad with mint and
    parsley, 126
MERINGUE
    almond meringues, 204
    easy meringue buttercream, 177
    figs in snow, 216
    safe meringue, 210
Mexican chocolate cake, 175
Mexican tea clouds, 184
Michele's stuffed artichokes, 100
Milanese vegetable soup, 44
MILLET
    barley and millet pilaf with wild
        mushrooms, 159
    moroccan millet salad, 133
Minestrone, 223
Mint pesto, 242
Monkfish and portobello mushrooms,
    sautéed, on a bed of mesclun, 55

Moroccan millet salad, 133
MOUSSE, SWEET
    lemon mousse, 209
    lemon mousse cake, 179
MOZZARELLA
    spicy grilled radicchio with
        bocconcini, 30
    warm mozzarella salad with sun-
        dried tomato vinaigrette, 123
Mrs. McGregor's carrot cake, 171
Muffins, pecan corn bread, 163
MUSHROOMS. See also Wild
    mushrooms
    chicken and three-mushroom
        casserole, 75
    creamed oysters and mushrooms, 31
    grilled garlic-studded portobello
        mushrooms with tomato salad and
        herb oil, 122
    grilled mushroom salad, 231
    mushroom and chestnut risotto, 237
    mushroom soup with cabbage rolls,
        51
    oyster mushroom soup with scallops,
        224
    skewered bread and wild mushrooms
        with pungent herbs, 105
    three mushroom soup, 46
MUSSELS
    spicy tomato-mussel soup, 48

N-O

Neapolitan carnival lasagna, 157
Neapolitan pizza, 105
Nectar, plum wine, 209
Neo-classic seafood salad, 136
New england cheddar cheese soup, 45
Nonna's ragú, 244
NOODLES. See also Pasta
    fresh thai rice noodles with meat and
        greens, 148
    soba noodles with grilled tuna and
        soy ginger sauce, 235
NUTS. See also specific types
    roasted almonds with red chile, 20
    spicy orange pecans, 20
Oil, basil, 242
OLIVES
    olives with cumin, 20

orzo with green and black olives, 146
Omelet, swiss chard, 114
ONIONS
  caramelized red onion marmalade,
    236
  french onion tart, 31
  green beans with balsamic-glazed
    onions, 100
  roasted onions with red peppers and
    garlic croutons, 106
  roasted potatoes, parsnips and
    onions, 107
ORANGES/ORANGE JUICE
  fresh pears, kiwis and oranges with
    rosemary syrup, 238
  orange, lemon and banana sherbet,
    213
  orange-blueberry salad with arugula
    and tarragon, 124
ORZO
  orzo with dill, 146
  orzo with green and black olives,
    146
Oxtail and lentil soup, 51
Oyster mushroom soup with scallops,
  224
Oysters, creamed, and mushrooms, 31

P

Pan bagna, 235
Pan-roasted blackberries, peaches and,
  with ginger and caramel ice
  cream, 218
Pancakes, whole wheat berry, 162
Papaya, prosciutto and, with lime-
  tequila splash, 29
PARSNIPS
  crisp root-vegetable cakes, 115
  roasted parsnips with orange zest,
    107
  roasted potatoes, parsnips and
    onions, 107
PASTA. See also Noodles
  asparagus, shrimp and penne with
    saffron sauce, 153
  baked penne rigate with eggplant,
    155
  baked penne with roasted
    vegetables, 154

baked penne with zucchini, 156
baked shells with fresh spinach and
  pancetta, 155
baked spaghetti with artichokes and
  peas, 153
baked ziti with sausage and peppers,
  155
broccoli rabe with orecchiette, 234
fettuccine with basil and almonds,
  146
fresh pasta with arugula, tomatoes
  and shaved parmesan, 146
herb ravioli with basil oil and tomato
  coulis, 147
neapolitan carnival lasagna,
  157
orzo with dill, 146
orzo with green and black olives, 146
pasta and lentils with walnut cream,
  233
pennette with mushrooms and
  cream, 153
pesto fettuccine with chicken and
  vegetables, 147
vegetable pasta salad, 232
PASTRY, PIE
  basic prebaked pie shell, 197
  cream cheese dough, 196
  prebaked tart shell, 199
  sweet tart shell, 201
PEACHES
  frozen peach soufflé with fresh
    peaches and plum wine nectar,
    209
  pan-roasted peaches and
    blackberries with ginger and
    caramel ice cream, 218
  peach frappé, 218
  peach, plum and cherry salad with
    cucumber ribbons, 125
  peaches with honey zabaglione, 216
  salade de pêches, 238
Peanut crisps, 182
PEARS
  baked pears with ginger, 220
  fresh pears, kiwis and oranges with
    rosemary syrup, 238
  pear and apple salad with gruyère
    and toasted pecans, 125
  pear and cranberry turnovers with
    black pepper, 194
  pear and custard tart, 198
  pear brown betty, 219

pears with dried cherries and stilton,
  217
PECANS
  deep-south pecan cookies, 183
  pecan caramel triangles, 183
  pecan corn bread muffins, 163
  pecan ice cream, 212
  pecan sticky buns, 167
  spicy orange pecans, 20
PENNE
  asparagus, shrimp and penne with
    saffron sauce, 153
  baked penne rigate with eggplant,
    155
  baked penne with roasted
    vegetables, 154
  baked penne with zucchini, 156
Pennette with mushrooms and cream,
  153
PEPPERS, BELL
  broccoli, orange and roasted pepper
    salad, 120
  fall vegetable spiedini, 116
  gratin of tomatoes and grilled
    peppers with roasted polenta, 115
  hominy and bell pepper sauté, 104
  roasted onions with red peppers and
    garlic croutons, 106
  tomato and red pepper soup, 42
PESTO
  basic pesto, 242
  mint pesto, 242
  pesto fettuccine with chicken and
    vegetables, 147
PHYLLO
  herbed shallots in phyllo, 25
  phyllo purses with black beans and
    pepper-jack cheese, 25
Pickles, overnight squash and red
  onion, 246
PIE CRUST/DOUGH. See Pastry, pie
PIES AND TARTS, SAVORY. See
    also Pizza
  french onion tart, 31
  turkey cottage pie, 80
PIES AND TARTS, SWEET. See also
    Turnovers
  almond-raspberry tart, 198
  apple-almond custard tart, 200
  black bottom banana tart, 201
  buttery apple tart, 199
  Claremont Diner coconut cream pie,
    197

fresh blueberry tart, 199
pear and custard tart, 198
tarte tatin with cinnamon ice cream, 196
three-cheese tart with lemon curd and berries, 202
Pine nut-brown sugar shortbread, 184
PINEAPPLE
pineapple and dried sour cherry turnovers, 192
pineapple and jicama salad with red grapes and basil, 126
pineapple-kiwi compote, 239
PIZZA
garlic-clam pizza with thyme, 60
neapolitan pizza, 105
Plum wine nectar, 209
PLUMS
ginger-plum turnovers, 192
peach, plum and cherry salad with cucumber ribbons, 125
plum ice cream, 213
plum-yum sauce, 244
POLENTA
creamy polenta with corn, 104
gratin of tomatoes and grilled peppers with roasted polenta, 115
PORK. See also Fresh ham
braised pork loin with prunes and cream sauce, 93
pork barbecue on a bun, 95
pork medallions with balsamic vinegar and sage, 94
roasted pork loin with garlic, 88
rosemary pork roast, 94
PORTOBELLO MUSHROOMS
sautéed monkfish and portobello mushrooms on a bed of mesclun, 55
grilled garlic-studded portobello mushrooms with tomato salad and herb oil, 122
Pot-roasted beef brisket with ancho chile sauce, 86
POTATOES
artichoke and potato stew with mint, 45
crisp root-vegetable cakes, 115
leek and potato gratin, 104
new potato and wax bean salad, 231
oven-toasted potato chips, 107
parslied red potatoes, 107

potato nests with crème fraîche and caviar, 27
roasted potatoes, parsnips and onions, 107
Poulet basquaise, 67
POUSSINS
little devils, 76
PRESERVES
sweet and chunky apple butter, 246
winter fruit and nut conserve, 245
Prosciutto and papaya with lime-tequila splash, 29
Provençale seafood soup, 46
PUDDING, SWEET
baked pumpkin and buttermilk pudding, 210
chocolate custards, 211
sweet potato custard with a brown sugar crust, 211
PUMPKIN
baked pumpkin and buttermilk pudding, 210
candied pumpkin with rum-plumped cranberries, 108

Q-R

QUAIL
mustard barbecued quail with vidalia onion and black-eyed pea relish, 83
roast quail with tarragon, 84
roasted quail with marinated tomatoes, eggplant and tomatillo sauce, 39
Quince and apple puree, 113
QUINOA
quinoa "tabbouleh," 134
quinoa and vegetable pilaf, 238
Radicchio, spicy grilled, with bocconcini, 30
Ragú, nonna's, 244
RASPBERRIES
almond-raspberry tart, 198
mixed red berries in red wine syrup with radicchio, 125
raspberry sauce, 245
raspberry trolls, 190
red wine-raspberry sherbet, 214

Ravioli, herb, with basil oil and tomato coulis, 147
RED SNAPPER
braised snapper with sake and soy sauce, 57
cornmeal-toasted red snapper, 57
Red wine fruit soup, spiced, with candied orange, 217
Red wine-raspberry sherbet, 214
Relish, black-eyed pea, 247
RICE. See also Wild rice
asparagus risotto, 237
jasmine rice salad with asparagus and walnuts, 127
lemon risotto, 158
lentils with fragrant rice, 233
mushroom and chestnut risotto, 237
plain jasmine rice, 158
rice pilaf with bay leaf, 158
risotto cakes, 159
sticky rice, 158
vegetable fried rice, 157
Rice noodles, fresh thai, with meat and greens, 148
Rice paper rolls with shrimp and vegetables, 27
RISOTTO
asparagus risotto, 237
lemon risotto, 158
mushroom and chestnut risotto, 237
risotto cakes, 159
ROLLS
buttermilk dinner rolls, 165
country bread rolls, 165
spiced cranberry rolls, 166
Root-vegetable cakes, crisp, 115
Rum baba, 181

S

Safe meringue, 210
SALAD DRESSING
balsamic vinaigrette, 242
herb and shallot vinaigrette, 242
mustard-anchovy vinaigrette, 242
SALADS, MAIN-COURSE
chicken and goat cheese salad with jalapeño-cilantro lime salsa, 140
coconut shrimp with lemon grass vinaigrette, 138

composed turkey salad with cranberry vinaigrette, 141
fillet of beef salad with blue cheese dressing and sesame seeds, 142
grande salade aux côtes d'agneau, 143
grilled chicken salad with frizzled tortillas, 139
lentil salad with frisée, pears and leeks, 232
lobster coleslaw with basil, tarragon and chives, 138
minced chicken salad with fresh herbs, 139
neo-classic seafood salad, 136
salade niçoise, 134
seared sea scallop salad with citrus vinaigrette, 137
shrimp in kataifi with purple relish, 37
spicy squid salad, 39
thai seafood salad, 136
tomato salad with sea scallops, maui onions, piccolo basil and olive oil dressing, 137
vegetable pasta salad, 232
wok-seared duck salad, 141
SALADS, SIDE-DISH
asparagus salad mimosa, 120
asparagus-pepper salad with ginger dressing, 230
barley salad with roasted corn and peppers, 133
broccoli, orange and roasted pepper salad, 120
bulgur salad with oranges, fennel and olives, 126
cucumber salad with rice wine vinegar, 119
curried couscous salad, 134
endive and carrot salad, 120
garden lettuces with light vinaigrette, 118
grapefruit-kiwi salad with poppy seeds and chicory, 124
grilled mushroom salad, 231
herb salad with watercress dressing, 118
Jamie's fruit salad, 124
jasmine rice salad with asparagus and walnuts, 127
jicama-orange salad with jalapeño dressing, 230

melon and mango salad with mint and parsley, 126
mixed field greens with potato surprise and caviar, 119
mixed red berries in red wine syrup with radicchio, 125
moroccan millet salad, 133
new potato and wax bean salad, 231
orange, radish and cucumber salad, 230
orange-blueberry salad with arugula and tarragon, 124
peach, plum and cherry salad with cucumber ribbons, 125
pear and apple salad with gruyère and toasted pecans, 125
pineapple and jicama salad with red grapes and basil, 126
quinoa "tabbouleh," 134
red leaf lettuce and chicory salad, 118
salad of summer vegetables, 122
shredded lettuce and radish salad, 118
spinach salad with chèvre and roasted shallots, 121
summer vegetable salad with herb and shallot vinaigrette, 121
tabbouleh, 127
tossed salad with radish sprouts and parsley, 119
vegetable salad with arugula, 123
watercress and radicchio salad, 229
wild rice salad, 128
wild rice salad with green beans, mushrooms and tarragon, 128
winter greens salad with warm sherry vinaigrette, 120
SALMON
broiled salmon with mustard cream sauce, 56
poached salmon fillets with two vinaigrettes, 56
seared salmon with sweet corn, shiitakes and spinach, 38
SALSA. See also Chutney; Relish
black bean salsa, 246
jalapeño-cilantro lime salsa, 247
SANDWICHES
california tea sandwiches, 25
crunchy chicken salad sandwiches, 24
pan bagna, 235
pork barbecue on a bun, 95

roast beef and goat cheese triangles, 25
turkey sandwiches on corn bread with curry-apple mayonnaise, 81
watercress and cream cheese swirls, 24
Sarabeth's english muffins, 163
SAUCES, SAVORY. See also Salad dressing; Salsa
creamy wine sauce, 243
nonna's ragú, 244
tomato concassée, 141
tomato coulis, 243
tomato sauce, 244
SAUCES, SWEET
caramel sauce, 245
plum-yum sauce, 244
raspberry sauce, 245
SCALLOPS
oyster mushroom soup with scallops, 224
scallops with pesto cream sauce, 63
scallops with zucchini and thyme, 37
seared scallops with citrus-ginger vinaigrette, 62
seared sea scallop salad with citrus vinaigrette, 137
tomato salad with sea scallops, maui onions, piccolo basil and olive oil dressing, 137
Schnitzel, turkey, 80
SEAFOOD. See Fish/shellfish and specific types
Shallots, herbed, in phyllo, 25
Sheep's milk cheese and lemon fritters with honey, 220
SHERBET
orange, lemon and banana sherbet, 213
red wine-raspberry sherbet, 214
SHIITAKES
grilled mushroom salad, 231
roast rack of lamb with shiitake mushrooms, 98
skewered bread and wild mushrooms with pungent herbs, 105
SHORTBREAD
lemon shortbread, 189
pine nut-brown sugar shortbread, 184
SHRIMP
coconut shrimp with lemon grass vinaigrette, 138

sheer shrimp dumplings with
coriander-mint dipping sauce, 26

shrimp in hot and sour broth, 63

Smoked salmon and osetra caviar, corn
waffles with, 38

Soba noodles with grilled tuna and soy
ginger sauce, 235

Soft-shell crabs, sautéed, with
hazelnuts, 32

Soufflé, frozen peach, with fresh
peaches and plum wine nectar, 209

SOUPS

asparagus, leek and new potato
chowder, 43

borscht with greens and chickpeas,
222

bread-and-tomato soup, 42

carrot and chestnut soup, 222

chinese chicken soup with rice, 49

corn soup with roasted peppers and
crab, 48

cream of garlic soup, 44

curried cauliflower and leek soup,
229

five-lily chowder, 224

gazpacho sevillano, 42

jamaican golden split pea soup, 43

lobster and coconut milk soup with
ginger, lemon grass and a garden
of vegetables, 47

milanese vegetable soup, 44

minestrone, 223

mushroom soup with cabbage rolls,
51

new england cheddar cheese soup,
45

oxtail and lentil soup, 51

oyster mushroom soup with scallops,
224

provençale seafood soup, 46

smoky black bean and vegetable
soup, 229

spiced red wine fruit soup with
candied orange, 217

spicy tomato-mussel soup, 48

three mushroom soup, 46

tomato and red pepper soup, 42

turkey-paprika soup with spaetzle,
50

tuscan chicken and artichoke soup,
49

white bean, fennel and sausage soup,
52

Spaghetti, baked, with artichokes and
peas, 153

Spiedini, fall vegetable, 116

SPINACH

pan-wilted winter greens with fresh
ginger, 114

spinach salad with chèvre and
roasted shallots, 121

Split pea soup, jamaican golden, 43

Spoonbread, buttermilk, 164

SPREADS

artichoke and goat cheese spread, 22

lemon cheese with lovage, 21

ricotta, prosciutto and basil spread,
22

SQUASH. *See also Pumpkin*

fall vegetable spiedini, 116

overnight squash and red onion
pickles, 246

summer squash sauté with dill and
tomatoes, 108

winter squash gratin, 108

Squid, spicy, salad, 39

STEWS

artichoke and potato stew with mint,
45

blanquette of veal vallée d'auge, 87

family-style chicken fricassee, 67

lobster fricassee with artichokes, 62

red chicken curry, 74

Sticky buns, pecan, 167

Sticky rice, 158

STOCK

chicken stock, 44

lamb stock, 98

light chicken or turkey broth, 43

light vegetable stock, 223

rich chicken stock, 46

turkey stock, 51

vegetable stock, 224

STRAWBERRIES

mixed red berries in red wine syrup
with radicchio, 125

strawberry salad with lemon-pepper
petals, 215

Strudel, asparagus, goat cheese and
prosciutto, 29

STUFFING

appalachian dressing, 83

Sturgeon alabardero, 57

SWEET POTATOES

sweet potatoes with toasted
almonds, 113

turkey and sweet potato hash, 79

Sweetbreads, crisp pan-fried, with
balsamic vinegar sauce, 40

SWISS CHARD

oven-roasted beets with wilted
greens, 101

pan-wilted winter greens with fresh
ginger, 114

sautéed swiss chard with tomatoes,
113

swiss chard omelet, 114

Swordfish alabardero, 57

T

TABBOULEH

quinoa "tabbouleh," 134

tabbouleh, 127

Tapenade, 21

Tarte tatin with cinnamon ice cream,
196

TARTS. *See Pies and tarts*

Terrine, roasted vegetable and goat
cheese, 30

THAI CUISINE

fish sauce with hot chiles, 243

fresh thai rice noodles with meat and
greens, 148

fried tofu with holy basil, 116

red chicken curry, 74

thai seafood salad, 136

TOASTS

bruschetta rossa, 22

crostini, 22

Tofu, fried, with holy basil, 116

TOMATOES

baked tomatoes with crunchy
crumbs, 114

bread-and-tomato soup, 42

gazpacho sevillano, 42

gratin of tomatoes and grilled
peppers with roasted polenta, 115

tomato and red pepper soup, 42

tomato concassée, 141

TORTES

chocolate apricot torte, 180

chocolate-walnut ganache torte, 180

hazelnut torte with maple
buttercream frosting, 178

Trifle, orange, 204

TUNA
marinated filet mignon of tuna, 59
pan bagna, 235
salade niçoise, 134
seared fresh tuna niçoise, 59
soba noodles with grilled tuna and
soy ginger sauce, 235
tuna alabardero, 57
TURKEY
composed turkey salad with
cranberry vinaigrette, 141
roast thanksgiving turkey with wild
rice stuffing, 77
sage-roasted rolled turkey, 78
turkey and sweet potato hash, 79
turkey burgers with herbed lemon
mayonnaise, 80
turkey cottage pie, 80
turkey sandwiches on corn bread
with curry-apple mayonnaise,
81
turkey schnitzel, 80
turkey-paprika soup with spaetzle,
50
Turnips, sautéed, 115
TURNOVERS
all-american apple turnovers, 195
apple frangipane turnovers, 195
blueberry turnovers, 192
dried fruit turnovers, 193
ginger-plum turnovers, 192
lemon curd turnovers, 193
pear and cranberry turnovers with
black pepper, 194
pineapple and dried sour cherry
turnovers, 192
Tuscan chicken and artichoke soup, 49

V

VEAL
blanquette of veal vallée d'auge, 87
veal and eggplant rolls, 88
VEGETABLE MAIN COURSES
artichoke and potato stew with mint,
45
fried tofu with holy basil, 116
neapolitan pizza, 105
swiss chard omelet, 114
VEGETABLES. *See also specific types*

asparagus with tarragon lemon
sauce, 28
baked tomatoes with crunchy
crumbs, 114
braised cabbage with apples and
toasted coriander, 103
broccoli with spicy sesame oil, 102
brown-butter broccoli with
caramelized carrots, 102
brussels sprouts with malted cream,
102
candied pumpkin with rum-plumped
cranberries, 108
celery root and apple puree, 103
creamy polenta with corn, 104
crisp root-vegetable cakes, 115
fall vegetable spiedini, 116
fennel gratin, 104
gratin of tomatoes and grilled
peppers with roasted polenta,
115
green beans with balsamic-glazed
onions, 100
grilled asparagus, 100
hominy and bell pepper sauté, 104
leek and potato gratin, 104
Michele's stuffed artichokes, 100
oven-roasted beets with wilted
greens, 101
oven-toasted potato chips, 107
pan-wilted winter greens with fresh
ginger, 114
parslied red potatoes, 107
puree of celery root with leeks and
scallions, 103
quince and apple puree, 113
roasted onions with red peppers and
garlic croutons, 106
roasted parsnips with orange zest,
107
roasted potatoes, parsnips and
onions, 107
salad of summer vegetables, 122
sautéed swiss chard with tomatoes,
113
sautéed turnips, 115
skewered bread and wild
mushrooms with pungent herbs,
105
summer squash sauté with dill and
tomatoes, 108
summer vegetable salad with herb
and shallot vinaigrette, 121

sweet potatoes with toasted
almonds, 113
three cabbages with caraway, 236
vegetable salad with arugula, 123
white beans and herbs with red
onion topping, 101
winter squash gratin, 108
VIETNAMESE CUISINE
coconut shrimp with lemon grass
vinaigrette, 138
VINAIGRETTE
balsamic vinaigrette, 242
herb and shallot vinaigrette, 242
mustard-anchovy vinaigrette, 242
Vinegar-chile sauce, 243

W-Z

WAFFLES
corn waffles with smoked salmon
and osetra caviar, 38
cornmeal waffles, 162
Whipping-cream biscuits, 164
WHITE BEANS
white bean, fennel and sausage soup,
52
white beans and herbs with red
onion topping, 101
WILD MUSHROOMS
barley and millet pilaf with wild
mushrooms, 159
grilled mushroom salad, 231
mushroom and chestnut risotto, 237
oyster mushroom soup with scallops,
224
skewered bread and wild
mushrooms with pungent herbs,
105
three mushroom soup, 46
WILD RICE
wild rice salad, 128
wild rice salad with green beans,
mushrooms and tarragon, 128
Wok-seared duck salad, 141
Zabaglione, honey, peaches with, 216

CONTRIBUTORS

Jeffrey Alford and Naomi Duguid are the authors of *Tastes of Travel* (Dharma) and an upcoming book titled *Flatbreads and Flavors* (Morrow).

Ann Chantal Altman is a food writer and cooking teacher.

John Ash and Sid Goldstein are chefs, teachers (Valley Oaks Cooking School, Fetzer Vineyards) and the authors of *American Game Cooking* (Addison-Wesley).

Nancy Verde Barr is a food writer, cooking teacher and the author of *We Called It Macaroni* (Knopf).

Daniel Boulud is chef/owner of Restaurant Daniel in New York City and the author of *Cooking with Daniel Boulud* (Random House).

Bob Chambers is a New York-based chef and food stylist.

Molly Chappellet is vice president of Chappellet Vineyard in St. Helena, California, and the author of *A Vineyard Garden* (Viking Studio Press).

Michael Chiarello is chef/owner of Tra Vigne in St. Helena, California.

Julia Child is the country's foremost television cooking teacher and the doyenne of French cooking in America.

Annemarie Colbin is the founder of The Natural Gourmet Cookery School & Institute for Food and Health in New York City and the author of several books on natural cooking and healing.

Francis Ford Coppola is a film director and producer.

Mark Cox is the executive chef at Tony's in Houston.

Peggy Cullen is a baker, candy maker and food writer.

Carol Cutler is a syndicated columnist, restaurant critic and the author of eight cookbooks.

Jamie Davies is co-owner of Schramsberg Vineyards in Calistoga, California.

Binh Duong is a chef and the co-author, with Marcia Kiesel, of *Simple Art of Vietnamese Cooking* (Simon & Schuster).

Odette Fada is executive chef at Rex in Los Angeles.

Jeannette Ferrary and Louise Fiszer are food writers and co-authors of *Sweet Onions and Sour Cherries, Season to Taste, California-American Cookbook* (all from Simon & Schuster) and the forthcoming *A Good Day for Soup* (Chronicle Books).

Ted Fondulas is chef/owner of Hemingway's in Killington, Vermont.

Larry Forgione is chef/owner of An American Place in New York City.

Camille Glenn is a cooking teacher (Camille Glenn's School of Gourmet Cooking in Louisville), food journalist and the author of *The Heritage of Southern Cooking* (Workman).

Jean-Pierre Goyenvalle is chef/owner of Le Lion d'Or in Washington, D.C.

Laurie Burrows Grad is the host of a television cooking show called "Laurie Cooks Light and Easy."

Vincent Guerithault is chef/owner of Vincent Guerithault on Camelback in Phoenix.

Martin Hamann is *chef de restaurant* at the Fountain Restaurant in Philadelphia.

Janet Hazen is a food writer, cooking teacher, restaurant critic and the author of a number of cookbooks, including *Hot, Hotter, Hottest* and *Janet's Juice Book* (both Chronicle Books), as well as the upcoming *Pears* (HarperCollins), *Turn It Up* and *International Chicken Soup Book* (both Chronicle Books).

Virginia Ibarra is a home cook in St. Helena, California.

Lila Jaeger is co-proprietor of Rutherford Hill Winery in Rutherford, California.

Susan Shapiro Jaslove is a food writer and recipe developer.

Nancy Harmon Jenkins is the author of two forthcoming books from Bantam: *The Mediterranean Kitchen* and *Cornucopia: America's Ethnic Food Heritage*.

Evan Jones is the author of *Epicurean Delight: The Life & Times of James Beard* and *The World of Cheese* (both Knopf).

Gerry Klaskala is an Atlanta-based chef currently working on opening a new restaurant in Atlanta.

Christopher Kump is chef at Cafe Beaujolais in Mendocino, California, and the author of the forthcoming *Evening Food from Cafe Beaujolais* (Ten Speed Press).

Viana La Place is a cooking teacher and the author of several cookbooks, including the recent *Verdura* and the upcoming *Panini, Bruschetta, Crostini* and *Flora* (all from Morrow).

Sarabeth Levine is the owner of Sarabeth's Kitchen in New York City.

Emily Luchetti is the executive pastry chef at Stars in San Francisco and the author of *Stars Desserts* (HarperCollins).

Stephanie Lyness is a food writer and cooking teacher.

Deborah Madison is a cooking teacher, chef and the author of *The Savory Way, The Greens Cookbook* and the upcoming *The Joy of Vegetarian Cooking* (all from Bantam).

Nick Malgieri is a pastry chef, cooking teacher and the

author of *Great Italian Desserts* (Little, Brown) and *Nick Malgieri's Perfect Pastry* (Macmillan).

Francine Maroukian is a food columnist and caterer.

Lydie Marshall is a cooking teacher and the author of *A Passion for Potatoes* and the upcoming *A Passion for My Provence* (both HarperCollins).

Michael McCarty is chef/owner of Michael's in Santa Monica and the author of *Michael's Cookbook* (Macmillan).

Elin McCoy and **John Frederick Walker** are contributing wines and spirits editors for *Food & Wine* and the authors of *Thinking About Wine* (Simon & Schuster).

Danny Meyer is the owner of Union Square Cafe in New York City. He is currently co-writing, with Michael Romano, a cookbook entitled *Union Square Cafe's Cookbook* (HarperCollins).

Mark Militello is chef/owner of Mark's Place in Miami.

Leslie Newman is the author of *Feasts* (HarperCollins) and is currently working on a cookbook called *The Family Table*.

Mary Novak is the owner of Spottswoode Vineyard & Winery in St. Helena, California.

Patrick O'Connell is chef/owner of The Inn at Little Washington in Washington, Virginia.

Charles Palmer is chef/owner of Aureole in New York City.

Carl and **Grace Parisi** are New York food writers and chefs.

Jacques Pépin is a cooking teacher and the author of numerous cookbooks, the most recent of which are *Today's Gourmet* and *Today's Gourmet II* (KQED, Inc.).

Odessa Piper is chef/owner of L'Etoile in Madison, Wisconsin.

Stephan Pyles is chef/owner of Star Canyon in Dallas and the author of *The New Texas Cuisine* (Doubleday).

Francesco Ricchi is chef and co-owner, with Christianne Russo Ricchi, of i RICCHI in Washington, D.C.

Michel Richard is chef/owner of Citrus in Los Angeles.

Eric Ripert is executive chef at Le Bernardin in New York.

Annie Roberts is resident chef at Robert Mondavi Winery in Oakville, California.

Michael Romano is chef of Union Square Cafe and co-author, with Danny Meyer, of a cookbook entitled *Union Square Cafe's Cookbook* (HarperCollins).

David Rosengarten is a cooking teacher, food writer, wine columnist and the author of the forthcoming *Crashing the Borders* (Crown Harmony).

Sally Sampson is a cooking teacher, food writer and the author of *Recipes from the Night Kitchen* (Fireside/Simon & Schuster) and a forthcoming low-fat cookbook from Doubleday.

Richard Sax is the co-author of *Eat at Joe's* (Clarkson Potter) and *The Way We Eat Today* (Van Nostrand Reinhold) and an upcoming book on old-fashioned desserts.

Sally Schneider is a cooking teacher, food stylist and the

author of *The Art of Low-Calorie Cooking* (Stewart, Tabori & Chang) and *The New Way to Cook* (Morrow).

Michele Scicolone is a food and travel writer and the author of *The Antipasto Table, La Dolce Vita* (both from Morrow) and a forthcoming book on Italian regional cooking.

Lindsey Shere is a partner in the Downtown Bakery and Creamery in Healdsburg, California, a chef and the author of *Chez Panisse Desserts* (Random House).

Elizabeth Terry is chef/owner of Elizabeth on 37th in Savannah and the author of the forthcoming *The Elizabeth on 37th Cookbook*.

Barbara Tropp is chef/owner of China Moon Cafe in San Francisco and the author of *The Modern Art of Chinese Cooking* (Morrow) and *The China Moon Cookbook* (Workman) and the upcoming *The China Diet*.

Patricia Wells is a journalist and the author of a number of food books, including most recently *Patricia Wells' Trattoria* (Morrow) and an upcoming book tentatively titled *Patricia Wells' French Country*.

Martin Woesle is *chef de cuisine* at Mille Fleurs in Rancho Santa Fe, California.

Andrew Ziobro is a chef and corporate dining director in New York City.

We would also like to thank the test kitchen (Diana Sturgis, director; Marcia Kiesel, associate director; Tracey Seaman, tester-developer) and the following restaurants and individuals for their contributions to *Food & Wine* and to this book: **Christian Albin; Auberge de l'Ill**, Illhaeusern, France; **Kevin Graham; Hubert Keller; Alice Medrich; La Palazzetta**, Todi, Italy; **Le Tre Vaselle**, Torgiano, Italy; **Les Alisiers**, Lapoutroie, France; **Alfred Portale; Ristorante Apollinare**, Spoleto, Italy; **Theo Schoennegger; Guenter Seeger; Gabino Sotelino; Don Yamauchi; Sherry Yard.**

PHOTO CREDITS
Cover: Jerry Simpson. **Page 33:** Jerry Simpson. **Page 34:** Mark Thomas. **Page 35:** Peter Ardito. **Page 36:** Ellen Silverman. **Page 69:** Kip Brundage. **Pages 70-71:** Elizabeth Watt. **Page 71:** Mark Thomas. **Page 72:** Ellen Silverman. **Page 89:** Jerry Simpson. **Pages 90-92:** Mark Thomas. **Page 109:** David Bishop. **Page 110:** Jerry Simpson. **Pages 110-111:** Grey Crawford. **Page 112:** David Bishop. **Pages 130-132:** Jerry Simpson. **Page 149:** Jerry Simpson. **Pages 150-151:** Cynthia Brown. **Pages 151-152:** David Bishop. **Page 185:** Robert Jacobs. **Page 186 top:** Jerry Simpson. **Page 186 bottom:** Susan Goldman. **Page 187:** Mark Thomas. **Page 188:** Elizabeth Watt. **Page 205:** Robert Jacobs. **Pages 206-207:** Jerry Simpson. **Page 208:** Kip Brundage. **Page 225:** Elizabeth Watt. **Pages 226-227:** Mark Thomas. **Page 228:** Tom Eckerle.